PRIVILEGE AND PUNISHMENT

# Privilege and Punishment

## HOW RACE AND CLASS MATTER IN CRIMINAL COURT

*Matthew Clair*

PRINCETON UNIVERSITY PRESS

PRINCETON & OXFORD

Published by Princeton University Press
41 William Street, Princeton, New Jersey 08540
6 Oxford Street, Woodstock, Oxfordshire OX20 1TR
press.princeton.edu

ISBN 978-0-691-19433-2
ISBN (e-book) 978-0-691-20587-8

British Library Cataloging-in-Publication Data is available

Editorial: Meagan Levinson and Jacqueline Delaney
Production Editorial: Brigitte Pelner
Production: Erin Suydam
Publicity: Kate Hensley (US) and Kathryn Stevens (UK)
Copyeditor: Melanie Mallon

Jacket Images and Background: Shutterstock

This book has been composed in Miller

Printed on acid-free paper ∞

Printed in the United States of America

10 9 8 7 6 5 4 3 2 1

For Mom and Dad

*The time has come, God knows, for us to examine ourselves, but we can only do this if we are willing to free ourselves of the myth of America and try to find out what is really happening here. Every society is really governed by hidden laws, by unspoken but profound assumptions on the part of the people, and ours is no exception. It is up to the American writer to find out what these laws and assumptions are.*

—JAMES BALDWIN, "THE DISCOVERY OF WHAT IT MEANS TO BE AN AMERICAN"

# CONTENTS

# TABLES

JUST OVER 60 PERCENT of adults in the United States know a family member who has been to jail.[1] For black people, that number is closer to 80 percent. I suppose I should not have been surprised, then, when I stumbled on one of my own relatives standing at the front of a courtroom, handcuffed after a night in jail.

It happened several summers ago. I was with a colleague in Chicago for a sociology conference. We were both graduate students at Harvard at the time and were presenting a paper on how trial court judges think about racial disparities in the criminal legal system. Did they think racial disparities were a problem? If so, did they take any steps to reduce them? These were important questions, and we were eager to share some of our answers with other sociologists. After presenting, we took a break from the conference to observe court proceedings in a Cook County, Illinois, courthouse. It had become a habit of ours to explore courthouses in different cities, and we were especially curious to catch a glimpse of judicial behavior in Cook County—a court system larger and far more notorious in its treatment of criminal defendants than the courthouses we had studied in the Northeast.

We chose a random courthouse in the area, went through its metal detectors, and walked its halls. We peeked our heads into various courtrooms. Though the halls were eerily quiet, a few of the rooms were packed: the galleries full of seemingly poor black and Latino people, waiting to be called in front of discerning judges. We chose one of the quieter rooms, took our seats in the gallery, waited for a few minutes, and then I saw him. He looked oddly familiar. A husky twenty-something black man, he was brought into the room by a court officer. The court clerk announced his name for the court record; he had the same last name as I had (a fairly uncommon one). I knew that very moment that I was somehow related to him. As I watched him more closely, I was struck by how much his face looked like mine and my brother's—oval, with a button nose and small ears. I was stunned.

Hours later at lunch, I called my dad to tell him the man's name. After checking with one of my aunts on my dad's side, we learned that he was a first cousin. I am not sure I ever saw, much less heard of, that cousin until his day in court. You see, my father grew up in Woodlawn, a low-income black neighborhood in Chicago. In his teens, he earned a scholarship to a boarding school in New England. When he left the South Side of Chicago for high school, he left behind seven siblings, none of whom ever left the neighborhood. Those siblings did not go off to college, much less medical school. And they did not marry another physician and raise two boys in a faraway state.

My aunts and uncles have worked, lived, laughed, loved, and—far too often—struggled to make ends meet in the same socioeconomically marginalized, but increasingly gentrifying, neighborhood in Chicago where they were raised. When I was a child growing up in the suburbs of Nashville, we would make occasional trips back to Chicago to visit dad's side of the family. My brother and I would devour savory food and play video games with a few cousins we had come to know. My parents would sit in modest kitchens or on back porches and get the updates—about that one relative who was recovering from gunshot wounds endured during a drive-by shooting or another who was sitting in jail for carrying a dime bag of marijuana. Over the years, our visits were fewer and fewer, the updates more and more sparse.

After the conference that summer, I returned to Cambridge, Massachusetts, and googled my cousin. The first search result was not a LinkedIn page or even a Facebook profile. Instead, it was his mugshot. He grimaced for the camera. I imagined how all the complexity of his life—his hopes, his love for his girlfriend and children—could be papered over by this administrative photograph. It was the image of him that would be available to the police, the prosecutor, the judge, and even his defense attorney. This image would follow him in his every interaction with the court and into his daily life. Even though I knew next to nothing about this cousin, I saw myself in him—even in his mugshot. I understood that were it not for my dad's good fortune, I easily could have been in his position: a black boy growing up in poverty, attending schools underfunded by the government, and worrying about the gun violence that had taken a few members of our family far too young. Sadly, I never got to know my cousin for precisely that reason. He, like one of our uncles before him, died from gunshot wounds. He passed not long after his court appearance, and before I took the time to meet him, meet his family, and learn his story. I regret never reaching out to him directly.

This book is largely motivated by my cousin's experience—and my brief and insufficient encounter with it and with him. The shock of witnessing him in court that summer was at once unbelievable and perfectly predictable, given what we know about the scale of mass criminalization in the United States today. Despite our shared family history, our lives were worlds apart. This contrast frustrated me and tugged at my sociological imagination.[2] I wondered: What if I had been arrested and faced the same charge he faced? The exercise was not purely theoretical—I drank alcohol when I was in my late teens and used marijuana in a state where it had yet to be decriminalized. When I was in college, I knew of a couple students a few years above me who had been arrested in a dorm room for drug possession. What had happened to them? How had they dealt with their court cases? Had their relative privileges as elite college students protected them from punishment in ways unavailable to people like my cousin?

I decided to study the experiences of criminal defendants, people who are facing a criminal charge in court but have yet to be convicted of a crime. Defendants are a surprisingly diverse group of people whom scholars know surprisingly little about. Scholars often talk to people about their arrest experiences or about their experiences of incarceration but less so about what happens between arrest and incarceration: the experiences of being processed in court. I decided to examine whether and how defendants carried the racial and class privileges and burdens embedded in American society with them to court. I never got a chance to speak to my cousin about his encounter in court that day and during the length of his criminal case, but I figured I could at least speak to others who had been through similar experiences. In many ways, the study that this book is based on was my chance to listen to, analyze, and unmask stories of state punishment like his.

I chose to conduct my study in the Boston area. In Boston, unlike in Chicago, the court system is often thought to be progressive. State judges are thought to be liberal (most were appointed by Democratic governors), public defenders are well funded compared to other states, city prosecutors are said to be fair minded, if not progressive, in their charging and bargaining decisions (in 2018, while I was conducting research, Rachael Rollins was elected district attorney of Suffolk County on a reformist platform), and the state has a relatively low rate of incarceration. At the same time, racial disparities in policing, court processing, and incarceration are stark. Studying Boston would provide a revealing look at how inequalities and injustices might be produced in one of our more lenient court systems.

What came of my research surprised me. In graduate school, I had read book after book about racial and class inequality and the ways privileged people maintained their advantages in institutions by being assertive and demanding of accommodations, whereas working-class and poor people were portrayed as deferential. But my research on defendants in court did not perfectly align with our typical scholarly perspectives. Instead, I found that the working class and poor, especially racial minorities, often sought to learn their legal rights, contest their defense lawyer's expertise, and advocate for themselves in court. Meanwhile, the middle-class people I got to know found themselves in trusting relationships with lawyers and thus were more likely to defer to their lawyers and the court. Privileged people were rewarded for their deference, whereas the disadvantaged were punished for their resistance and demands for justice. These dynamics arose from differences in the relationships that defendants were able to create with their defense attorneys—relationships profoundly shaped by the advantages and disadvantages defendants have in their everyday lives.

I owe a debt of gratitude to the men and women who shared their experiences with me. They were patient with me and generous with their time and knowledge, even amid dealing with the loss of friends to heroin overdoses, the loss of their families to burned social ties, and at times, the loss of their liberty to the state. I will never forget watching in court as one of the people in the study rose up from the bench next to me, traversed the bar (which separates the gallery of the courtroom from the lawyers' tables and the judge's bench), pleaded guilty to drug distribution charges, and calmly allowed two court officers to handcuff him and take him off to prison. He was one of the first, but certainly not the last, people I watched plead guilty after being so adamant about fighting the charges against him.

Many of the defendants I met expressed to me their hope in the value of this study. They hoped that my collection of their stories would provide those in power with the resolve to craft effective solutions. While they recognized, just as I do, that their individual lives likely would not change for the better, they hoped that the lives of people like them would change in the future. I hope they are right.

PRIVILEGE AND PUNISHMENT

# Introduction

DREW, A WORKING-CLASS black man in his early thirties, is no stranger to the legal system.[1] When we met in fall 2018, he told me that he had been arrested numerous times in Mattapan and Dorchester, two predominantly black and low-income neighborhoods in Boston, Massachusetts. When he was in his twenties, he had served several years in state prison for gun possession. Months before I met him that fall, Drew had been arrested on another gun possession charge. He had been stopped by the police for rolling through a stop sign. He sped off when the police asked to search his vehicle. After a short chase, he was apprehended, along with an unlicensed firearm. This time, he was desperate not to return to prison. Over the years, speaking with friends in his neighborhood and in prison, Drew had gained much knowledge about his legal rights and the potential court process ahead of him. He wanted to use this knowledge at trial to beat his current case. But, as he would soon come to find, his own legal knowledge would not be of much use in the criminal courts—in fact, his efforts to exercise his legal rights would often backfire.

The day he was arraigned on the new gun charge, Drew remembered growing frustrated. His lawyer at the time, a white male public defender with nearly a decade of experience, did not seem to be listening to him. The prosecutor relayed the allegations of the traffic stop and short chase as she asked the judge to set a several-thousand-dollar bail. She argued that the judge should be aware that Drew was currently facing another gun charge that had yet to be resolved. But this claim was inaccurate: Drew's unresolved case involved possession of an illegal knife, not a gun. Drew grew livid, fearing this mischaracterization would provide the judge an excuse to set a higher bail amount. He urged his lawyer to correct the prosecutor's misstatement. But his lawyer did not have a chance to do so before the judge ruled. Although the judge ultimately set bail at an amount he could afford, Drew was angry. His lawyer seemed indifferent to him and his case.

Drew knew of another lawyer whom he trusted more—another white male public defender named Tom who was already representing him on his knife case (which, it turns out, would be dismissed later that same day). Drew asked Tom to represent him on the gun charge. Tom had a "reputation" for fighting for his clients, Drew later told me. Tom agreed to represent him on the gun case. Over the next few months, they worked well together. During one of their meetings at the public defender's office, I watched as they spent an hour and a half discussing Drew's new job, the details of his arrest, his allegations of police corruption, and what possible motions—procedural requests to the judge to rule on certain matters that pertain to the case, such as whether to permit certain forms of evidence at trial—they could file. Drew listened, and at times he spoke excitedly, gesticulating with his tattooed arms when talking about the unfairness of the police. It was Drew who had suggested they pursue a motion to dismiss the charges on the grounds that the police did not provide sufficient evidence to the grand jury. He also wanted to expose the officers' corruption through another motion, in which they would present evidence that the officers who arrested him exhibit a pattern of racial bias in their traffic stops. But Tom would never get to argue this motion, because their relationship would "hit a bit of a rocky patch," as Tom put it.

Over the next several months, Drew and Tom experienced multiple moments of tension and disagreement before their relationship ultimately ended. In one meeting, Tom suggested that Drew take a plea deal. Tom explained that the prosecutor would drop one of the charges (which contained a mandatory minimum sentence of several years in prison) in exchange for his guilty plea on the gun charge. If he took the deal, he would likely serve far less time in prison than if he were convicted at trial. But Drew had always been insistent on taking the case to trial. He did not want to hear about a possible plea. "He started to really push back," Tom recalled. At one point in the meeting, Drew told Tom that he felt their relationship was on the skids and that he needed a new lawyer. A week later, Drew texted Tom, hoping to reconcile. They agreed to continue working together and to focus on winning their pretrial motions.

But during one of the motion hearings, things fell apart for good. One of the police officers did not show up to the hearing; the judge asked Tom and the prosecutor to approach the bench and discuss why the officer was not present and how they would like to proceed. Drew wondered aloud why their conversation needed to be held privately at the judge's bench. The judge ignored his comment, and Tom whispered to Drew that he would share what they discussed. But Drew, with his jaw clenched and his hands in his pockets, blurted out: "This is my life we're talking about here." The judge told him to take his hands out of his pockets. Drew did not budge. Tom pleaded for him to comply. "I heard him," Drew said and slowly removed his hands. After this incident, Tom decided to stop serving as Drew's lawyer. Tom later explained:

> I can't manage him, and I can't litigate his case effectively if at every moment I fear there's an outburst that'll intrude upon my litigation. . . . He's threatened it at trial. He would stand up on the witness stand himself and tell the jury his own thoughts about how fucked up these officers were. And I said, "You realize that may not be possible because there are rules that govern trial." And he said, "I don't care."

At Drew's next court date, the court assigned his third lawyer. According to Tom, the lawyer on duty that day was "passive" and "not very competent." Drew's case "could drag on indefinitely," Tom suspected.

Drew's experience with his defense attorney is common among the poor people and working-class people of color I met over several years of research on the Boston-area court system. Like Drew, many disadvantaged people feel that they cannot trust their defense attorneys. They often attempt to work around their lawyers. Using the legal knowledge and skills they have cultivated in their communities, in jail or in prison, and in their all-too-frequent encounters with the law, they seek to advocate for themselves. But defense attorneys—caught between the expectations and power of prosecutors and judges, on the one hand, and the hopes of their clients, on the other—often ignore, silence, or even coerce defendants who attempt to do so. Lawyers' efforts to control their clients are often well intentioned: passionate defense attorneys view their jobs as reducing their client's legal costs, costs that can result from the exercise of certain legal rights. But for many defendants, such control far too often feels like punishment, and more is at stake than formal legal outcomes. Thus, disadvantaged people are stuck in a bind: they feel they cannot trust their lawyers to help them, and when they try to help themselves, they face negative consequences. The stories of people like Drew reveal how important the attorney-client relationship can be for disadvantaged criminal defendants in court.

Meanwhile, privileged people's experiences with their lawyers and the court are quite different. Their attorney-client relationships are just as central to their experiences, but for the better. Take, for instance, the experience of Arnold, a middle-class black man in his twenties. In another courthouse, situated in a mostly white town west of Boston, Arnold was facing his own gun possession charge. He had been driving home to Boston from a vacation in New York when he and a couple friends were pulled over by a state trooper. The trooper alleged that the car had been stolen, providing probable cause to search the vehicle. After a search, the trooper found an unlicensed gun in the trunk. Arnold was shocked. He had borrowed the car from a friend and did not know about the gun, as he would later explain to me. Indeed, Arnold's fingerprints were never found on the weapon. At the time of his arrest, Arnold had been working as a freelance writer while training for a career as a professional basketball player—a dream since college. With the help of his basketball agent and his family, he was able to pay thousands of dollars to hire a private lawyer rather than rely on the public defender the state had initially appointed him.

Arnold got along quite well with his private attorney, a young-looking but serious white man named Brett. Like Arnold, Brett had also played college basketball. This shared experience was a huge comfort for Arnold. "He actually had a previous understanding of who I was as an individual and athlete. He was a former athlete himself," Arnold reflected. This background mattered because it helped to contextualize his trip to New York and his affiliation with his friends in the car, who happened to have criminal records:

> I knew he could understand the dynamics, which would not necessarily be understood. Because most people wouldn't understand why I would be going to New York with no money in my pocket with a couple of people who were basically convicted felons on paper, you know? But he knew I had suffered an injury and was going through a period where I was leaving one situation and entering another stage—this transition period [from being a] college athlete.

Their shared experiences made Arnold "confident of what he [Brett] was doing" as a lawyer. As part of his legal practice, Brett also worked as a bar advocate, meaning that in addition to his work as a private lawyer he also served as a court-appointed lawyer for indigent clients. Bar advocates in Massachusetts are often conflated with public defenders among people who do not pay for their services; one main difference, however, is that public defenders are salaried state employees, whereas bar advocates are contracted hourly by the state. To many poor defendants, they are all "public pretenders" anyway. For Arnold, paying for Brett's services put him at ease regardless of his simultaneous work as a bar advocate. "In hiring him and paying him a huge lump of money, there is a certain level of trust there," Arnold told me.

Arnold and Brett met regularly over the course of his case; their meetings were productive and agreeable. It was Arnold's first time in court for a crime that held the possibility of jail time. He was worried. He did not know much about the law, his legal rights, or how best to choose among various legal options, but Brett helped to fill his gaps in understanding. "He's broken things down even further than most people have," Arnold said. Together, they worked through possible motions. One motion sought to prove there was no reasonable suspicion for the stop. During the motion hearing, Arnold watched as Brett caught "the police officer lying" (in Arnold's words) about one element of the stop. He was impressed and hopeful. Although the judge denied the motion, Arnold continued to have faith in Brett, insisting that if they could not make the case go away through motions, then he wanted to go to trial. He understood the risk of jail time but was adamant about his innocence. Brett agreed. Brett felt, as he later told me, that the only reason Arnold and his friends were stopped was "because they were black." When the prosecutor offered a plea deal, Brett rejected it on Arnold's behalf. They both felt the case was winnable in front of a jury.

On the morning of his trial, Arnold was sitting nervously next to his mother in the courthouse's front hallway. She was dressed in a dark gray pant suit and wore her hair in a 'fro. Arnold was wearing a navy blazer, a tie, fitted khakis, and brown loafers. As the three of us waited for Brett to arrive, a middle-aged white man started a conversation with Arnold. "What are you here for today? Jury duty?" he asked. Arnold politely shook his head and tried to change the subject. Brett arrived just in time, and we huddled in his direction. Brett had just learned that the judge in the trial session that day was a former defense attorney; he wondered aloud whether Arnold would like to do a bench trial instead of a jury trial. Arnold thought for a second, then looked to Brett and asked, "What do you think I should do?" Brett explained the benefits of a bench trial. In a bench trial, the judge, rather than a jury, would rule on his guilt. Brett suggested that taking a chance with this former defense-attorney judge was less risky than taking a chance with what appeared to be an all-white jury pool. Without hesitation, Arnold said, "Okay, let's do it. I trust you."

Later that day, Arnold's case would be called twice before the judge—once for Arnold to state that he would like a bench trial and another time for the trial to begin. During the trial, Arnold sat quietly upright at the defense table as Brett made opening arguments, cross-examined the trooper, and made closing arguments. After the prosecutor made her closing arguments, the judge was ready to rule. He quickly found Arnold not guilty, stating that even though the trooper had probable cause to stop the car, there was not enough evidence that Arnold possessed the firearm. Arnold exhaled in relief. From the back of the courtroom, near where I was seated, I heard his mother whisper, "Thank you, judge. God bless you."

Arnold's experiences with his lawyer and in court contrast sharply with Drew's. Although both men faced gun possession charges and both men were desperate to avoid legal punishment, their attorney-client relationships unfolded in divergent ways. Their social positions in American society brought different life experiences and access to different kinds of resources. Commonly, scholars and ordinary people conflate the experiences of people of color, especially when it comes to the criminal legal system.[2] Although both Drew and Arnold felt they experienced racism in their encounters with the law, particularly in their experiences of policing, Arnold was able to leverage class-based resources and experiences unavailable to Drew. Ironically, Arnold's relative lack of knowledge about the law and willingness to defer to his lawyer afforded him relative ease in his court experience. By contrast, Drew's knowledge of his legal rights and various legal procedures often backfired, fostering mistrust of his lawyer and, ultimately, resulting in difficulties navigating the courts. These differences are rooted in the intersections of their classed and racialized experiences in American society and in interactions with their lawyers and other legal officials. Of course, other details about their cases differed, such as their actual innocence and their prior criminal histories. These differences are important elements that are also rooted in inequalities and that undoubtedly shaped their divergent trajectories through court. And yet, the differing quality of their attorney-client relationships was also a key component of how those trajectories unfolded.

This book examines how race and class inequalities in society are embedded in and reproduced through the attorney-client relationship, a defendant's most important relationship in court. I draw on interviews and courthouse observations among criminal defendants from various walks of life and among various kinds of legal officials (including lawyers, judges, police officers, and probation officers) living and practicing in the Boston, Massachusetts, area. By analyzing their experiences, this book develops a detailed understanding of the way privilege and inequality work in court interactions. Much of what we know about the interactional dynamics of privilege in American society comes from research on mainstream everyday institutions, such as schools, workplaces, and doctor's offices. We know that when middle-class people interact with these institutions, they tend to be assertive and demanding.[3] They exhibit entitlement when asking for accommodations to the rules, such as exemptions from homework in school, and are unafraid to ask for more resources, such as medical attention.[4] Meanwhile, the working class and poor, scholars argue, tend to defer to institutional authorities and rarely make demands for accommodations or extra resources. This typical understanding of privilege and inequality in institutional interactions, however, cannot fully account for Drew and Arnold's divergent experiences with their lawyers and the court.

The criminal courts are now an all-too common institution in people's lives; and yet, privilege works differently here. In the courts, it is the disadvantaged who are demanding and seeking accommodations through their attempts to advocate for themselves in court and exercise their legal rights, whereas the privileged defer to their lawyers and the court's authority and have little knowledge about criminal law. Inequality exists in both the content of these attorney-client relationships and in their implications. Race and social class inequalities are *constituted* in the numerous tiny moments between lawyers and their clients.[5] In other words, the different experiences privileged and disadvantaged people have, and the meanings they make from them, are themselves markers of inequality. Whereas the privileged tend to experience attorney-client relationships like Arnold and Brett's, the disadvantaged tend to experience relationships like Drew and Tom's. Not only are these relationships markers of inequality, but they also have implications for inequality. The attorney-client relationship *reproduces* race and class inequalities.[6] For the disadvantaged, a relationship with a lawyer often results in coercion, silencing, and punishment. For the privileged, a relationship with a lawyer often results in leniency, ease of navigation, and even some rewards. Therefore, race and class disparities in legal outcomes likely emerge, in part, from the taken-for-granted and hidden rules of the courts, which discriminate between defendants based on how they interact with their lawyers and present themselves in front of judges.

I define disadvantaged people as those who live in neighborhoods with high levels of punitive police surveillance and who have routine (and often negative) experiences with the legal system, limited social ties with empowered people, and limited access to financial resources. Privileged people, by contrast, are those who have access to empowered social ties and financial resources and who rarely have negative encounters with police or other legal officials.[7] These dimensions of privilege and disadvantage vary along traditional axes of racial (e.g., black/Latino/ white) and socioeconomic (e.g., middle-class/working-class/poor) stratification among the people in this study. Much like other sociologists, I define middle class as having a four-year college degree and stable employment; working class as having stable employment but less than a college degree; and poor as lacking both a degree and employment.[8] In the pages that follow, I share the experiences of sixty-three defendants— some who are disadvantaged people of color struggling to make ends meet, and others who are white and/or middle class, from aspiring basketball players to nurses to investment consultants, who have fallen on hard times and wound up facing a criminal charge. As we will see, middle-class people of all racial backgrounds (like Arnold) and white working-class people in this study tend to fall into the privileged category with respect to attorney-client relationships, whereas working-class people of color (like Drew) and the poor of all racial backgrounds tend to fall into the disadvantaged category.

Throughout the book, I adopt a situational approach, paying careful attention to the intersections of race and class inequality as felt in interactive moments among the people I met and as enacted by the hidden rules of the court.[9] Privilege and disadvantage are better understood as characteristics of the situations in which people often find themselves rather than as fixed characteristics of individuals.[10] One characteristic of inequality that this book does not fully examine is gender. Men in the United States, especially poor black and Latino men, are more likely to face various forms of punishment—from policing to incarceration—than women. And yet, when compared to others, our country punishes women more harshly than other countries punish their average citizens, of all genders.[11] Indeed, as part of my research, I met eleven women defendants whose experiences I have included and analyzed alongside those of the fifty-two men defendants in the study. Although I do not find systematic differences between men and women, a different study with greater gender diversity might uncover important, and even counterintuitive, realities about gendered interactions between lawyers and their clients.[12] The focus of this book, however, is on race and class inequality—enduring features of inequality in the criminal legal system.

This book is about *injustice* as much as it is about inequality. Over the past forty years, the number of people arrested, processed in court, and incarcerated has skyrocketed. This increase in punitive legal control has disproportionately impacted poor and marginalized communities of color. The experiences of Drew, Arnold, and the other people in this book take place in a uniquely punitive moment in American history. This moment, as it is experienced in our courts, raises fundamental questions about fairness and justice. As we will see throughout the book, legal representation alone does not ensure justice. The disadvantaged, who are afforded court-appointed attorneys by law, nevertheless find themselves in attorney-client relationships that are fraught, commonly resulting in unfavorable legal outcomes and almost always leaving defendants feeling unheard and resentful. The mere fact of being represented by a lawyer, for the disadvantaged, is not a means to equitable outcomes. For the privileged, however, a trusting relationship with an effective lawyer is often accompanied by a reduction in one's sentence or—far less often, but still possible—a not guilty verdict. The inequality between the two groups is unfair and could be remedied, but all is not well for the privileged either. A positive attorney-client relationship cannot make up for the stigma, lost resources, and stress that comes with court processing. Among almost all the defendants I met, the court process rarely contributed positively to their rehabilitation, willingness to admit fault for their crimes, or efforts at repairing the harm they caused their victims. The injustice of the courts, I have come to realize, extends well beyond the inequalities disadvantaged defendants face.

## The Courts in an Era of Mass Criminalization

Countless books, articles, and essays have been written about "mass incarceration." The term speaks to the sheer size—unmatched both in American history and anywhere else in the world—of our incarcerated population.[13] Beginning as early as the 1960s, the US federal government and state governments shifted from investing in social services to investing in punitive programs and policies meant to control the poor and other stigmatized groups, particularly young black men. Jail and prison were increasingly seen as the best-available tools for dealing with social problems and harms such as drug use, civil disorder, poverty, and various forms of violence, which appeared to be increasing during that period. Incarceration rates began rising in the late 1970s and peaked in 2008, but more than a decade later, the United States continues to have the highest incarceration rate in the world. In 2016, 450 of every 100,000 residents in the country were incarcerated in state or federal prisons; in 1978, that number was 131.[14] Although incarceration rates have slightly declined in the past decade, the number of people incarcerated in prison, jail, and other detention facilities today totals more than two million.[15]

This present era of punitiveness extends far beyond the prison. Beyond incarceration, other forms of punitive legal control have similarly expanded over the past forty years. State and federal governments have invested more and more resources in policing, pretrial detainment, probation, and parole.[16] Meanwhile, local jurisdictions have used criminal fines and fees to raise revenue.[17] In 2015, nearly 4.7 million adults were on probation or parole, which are forms of legal control that often require people to abide by certain conditions—such as drug testing or GPS monitoring— to remain in their communities rather than be incarcerated.[18] In the same year, nearly a million people over the age of sixteen had been arrested in the past twelve months, and 53.5 million experienced some form of contact with the police.[19] Instead of mass incarceration, then, we can speak of *mass criminalization*, or the use of an array of punitive legal techniques and institutions—from policing to court-manded probation and parole to incarceration—that have affected a broad swath of Americans. Lawyer and social activist Deborah Small contrasts the term "mass criminalization" to the term "mass incarceration," noting how the former is a broader term that "includes the expansion of law enforcement and the surveillance state to a broad range of activities and settings."[20]

Mass criminalization emerged from a confluence of social and political shifts in the mid to late twentieth century. Partly motivated by a rise in crime rates in the 1960s, the government shifted from social welfare provision to punishment.[21] Federal and state governments stopped investing in social initiatives, such as job programs, housing, and neighborhood revitalization, and started investing in punitive programs, such as police militarization, prison expansion, and the imposition of fines and fees meant to manage "dispossessed and dishonored populations."[22] Young urban black men, portrayed as uniquely deviant and violent, were used as props by multiple presidents and numerous congresspeople to motivate public support for political campaigns, perhaps most infamously the war on drugs.[23] "Between 1982 and 2001, the United States increased its public expenditures for police, criminal courts, and corrections by 364% (from $36 to $167 billion, or 165% in constant dollars of 2000) and added nearly 1 million justice staff," writes sociologist Loïc Wacquant.[24] Despite a dramatic decline in crime rates beginning in the mid-1990s, this instinct toward punishment has largely remained in place into the twenty-first century.[25]

Poor communities of color have been disproportionately and negatively impacted by mass criminalization.[26] Arrest and incarceration rates are higher among blacks and Latinos compared to whites and among those with lower levels of education compared to their better-educated peers.[27] At the same time, mass criminalization has been felt across demographic groups. Legal control has expanded so much that people who have had contact with the criminal legal system come from all walks of life. Over the past several decades, members of more privileged demographic groups—even if they are not the intended targets of punitive governmental policies—have been pulled into the system in increasing numbers. For instance, the rate of incarceration has slightly increased among highly educated men. About 5 percent of black men with some college education born in the 1940s experienced incarceration by their mid-thirties, compared to over 6 percent of similarly educated black men born three decades later.[28] Among white men, these numbers tripled—from 0.4 percent to 1.2 percent. The percentages of black and white men with some college education who have been incarcerated seem small, but they represent hundreds of thousands of people. Moreover, the geographic location of criminalization has expanded from urban, mostly black areas to whiter suburban and rural areas.[29] Criminalization appears to be expanding its demographic reach.

This dual reality—the disproportionate criminalization of poor people of color alongside increased criminalization of more privileged groups—also manifests, not surprisingly, in the courts. Numerous studies show that the courts tend to magnify race and class disparities at arrest, translating them into more pronounced disparities at incarceration.[30] Black people, Latinos, and the unemployed receive harsher court outcomes than similarly situated white people and employed people who happen to be brought into court.[31] From the prosecutor's decision to charge a person for a crime to the judge's decision to sentence someone to probation or prison, disadvantaged defendants often fare worse. The data vary by court jurisdiction and crime type, but they nevertheless paint a consistent and overarching portrait of inequality in the courts that cannot be fully explained by differences in legal factors, such as the nature of the offense committed or the defendant's criminal record.[32]

These big-picture statistics are damning enough, but my concern in this book is different. I offer another vantage point—a look at how race and class inequalities in the criminal courts are experienced on the ground. Doing so requires an analysis of everyday experiences, not just an analysis of macrolevel trends. It requires moving from the quantitative and abstracted toward the qualitative and lived. It requires asking not just how many white people, black people, or poor people are represented in the nation's police stations, courts, and prisons in any given year but also how these different groups of people experience the criminal legal system when they are up against it. It requires assessing how the advantages and disadvantages of occupying particular race or class categories in everyday life spill over into the way people experience being sorted by the criminal legal system.

We know an increasing amount about the courts as an organization and how court officials (that is, judges, prosecutors, probation officers, and defense attorneys) make decisions; but we know far less about the other side of the equation—the experiences of defendants. When a person is arrested and charged with a crime, they become designated, by law, as a defendant who is legally presumed innocent until they are convicted. Popular and scholarly accounts of the courts portray defendants as passive consumers of legal sanctions, constrained by powerful forces beyond their control. Courts are oft imagined as processing institutions—simple machines, spitting out convictions with little care for the particular circumstances or factual guilt of the defendant.[33] Even when cases receive individualized attention, the process is thought to move quickly for most defendants and to provide little room for negotiation. At best, only the most privileged defendants can afford lawyers who exercise every legal avenue on their behalf, heroically litigating motions and prompting days-long trials. Meanwhile, most defendants have their cases adjudicated through plea deals or dismissals, which are thought to involve little, if any, participation from defendants. There is a reason these narratives are taken for granted—there is much truth in them. And yet, while common narratives speak to certain realities of our nation's courts, they are incomplete.

This book offers a corrective to this literature by describing the many ways defendants exert agency during the court process in the face of various constraints and opportunities.[34] Shifting attention toward the defendant as an undertheorized actor, I examine defendants' experiences of the court process through the lens of their most important relationship in court: the attorney-client relationship. My argument departs from how most academics have come to understand and study the criminal courts, precisely because of my attention to defendants' interpretations of, and interactions with, their lawyers. Just as schools cannot be understood only from the perspective of teachers or workplaces only from the perspective of employers, courts cannot be understood only from the perspective of court officials. Scholarship on workplaces, schools, and other institutions is growing more comprehensive, affording us a better understanding of the complexities of all kinds of relationships, and revealing how the exploitation between an employer and employee, for instance, is complex, often produced through interaction and rooted in fundamental power asymmetries. By peering into the attorney-client relationship, we can see the many ways defendants strategize, resist, and even consent with respect to the power of officials and the hidden rules of the court process. Consequently, this book paints a more complete portrait of injustice as it manifests inside, and reverberates outside, the courtroom.

One of the earliest detailed ethnographies of the courts was sociologist Abraham Blumberg's 1967 book *Criminal Justice*. Before its publication, many scholars and journalists assumed that criminal courts involved vigorous trials and passionate disagreements between prosecutors and defense attorneys. Blumberg dispelled that myth and gave us the bleak vision of the courts that still prevails a half century later. He argued that most defense attorneys and prosecutors engaged in "justice by negotiation," whereby they relied on plea deals to quickly dispose of court cases. He characterized the courts as engaging in "assembly line" justice: overwhelmed court officials facing heavy caseloads disposed of cases quickly and with little attention to the unique features of a case or a defendant.[35] A gloomy portrait of rampant plea deals and the conviction of innocent defendants replaced the more dramatic (and desirable) narrative of defense attorneys zealously defending their clients at trial. Blumberg's findings also critiqued the then-common assumption that defendants could fight their cases if they had the right resources at hand. He argued that resources related to a defendant's class status—such as money or social esteem—had little influence on a defendant's legal outcomes. According to Blumberg, the processing bureaucracy did not differentiate between the rich and the poor.[36] And yet, racial and class disparities have remained a durable feature of the courts—a feature for which Blumberg's many important insights could not account.

In the 1960s and 1970s, the US Supreme Court expanded due process rights for criminal defendants across the country—rights that seemed destined to slow down the court process, provide greater leverage to defendants, and ensure the criminal law's fair application across social groups. These newly enshrined procedural rights included the right to a defense attorney, the right to remain silent, and the right to know about exculpatory evidence held by the prosecution.[37] In 1963, in *Gideon v. Wainwright*, one of the most celebrated rulings expanding the right to an attorney, Justice Hugo Black wrote:

> From the very beginning, our state and national constitutions and laws have laid great emphasis on procedural and substantive safeguards designed to assure fair trials before impartial tribunals in which every defendant stands equal before the law. This noble ideal cannot be realized if the poor man charged with crime has to face his accusers without a lawyer to assist him.[38]

Justice Black's opinion suggested that extending the right to counsel would help to ensure "equal[ity] before the law" for poor defendants. Over time, the right to counsel has been extended to numerous stages of the criminal process, including police interrogations, arraignment, pretrial hearings, probation revocation hearings (in some states), and the plea colloquy.[39]

Despite these constitutional guarantees, researchers kept documenting more of the same: high plea rates, a lack of adversarialism, and coercion by defense attorneys. For instance, James Eisenstein and Herbert Jacob studied felony courts in Baltimore, Chicago, and Detroit in the early 1970s. They found that public defenders felt pressure to control their clients, given their high caseloads and limited time (state funding for the defender's office was based on the efficiency by which defenders disposed of their clients' cases).[40] Yet, in contrast to Blumberg's description of the court as an assembly line, Eisenstein and Jacob argued that defendants' cases—at least felony cases—did receive some individualized attention from officials seeking to determine whether they were truly guilty or innocent. Studying a lower court in New Haven in the 1970s, political scientist Malcolm Feeley also observed overworked defense attorneys and a preponderance of plea deals. He offered his own critiques of Blumberg and other scholars, arguing that high plea rates in courts do not necessarily suggest a lack of adversarialism. He showed that even plea deals involve sparring between defense attorneys and prosecutors. For instance, defense attorneys appeared to use motions and off-the-record negotiations to uncover the facts of the case and convince prosecutors and judges to be more lenient toward their clients.[41] Although he focused on the role of court officials in shaping these negotiations, he suggested that defendants might also play a role in influencing the process. He wrote: "The interests of the accused can also shape the outcome of a case. Many defendants are intense, and willing to do whatever is necessary to avoid conviction or minimize their sentence."[42]

A handful of interview-based studies conducted among defendants in the 1970s revealed pervasive frustration with lawyers (especially the new wave of indigent defense attorneys and public defenders, who emerged as a result of the recent Supreme Court rulings). Frustration, mistrust, and skepticism was especially common among defendants from disadvantaged backgrounds—the very people who were supposed to have benefited most from the Supreme Court's expansion of the right to counsel.[43] A study published in 1971 reflected this sentiment in its title: "Did You Have a Lawyer When You Went to Court? No, I Had a Public Defender."[44] Often, indigent defendants reported feeling that their attorneys pressured them to take plea deals against their best interests.[45] Meanwhile, defendants who retained private attorneys reported higher levels of trust in their lawyers and a greater belief in their lawyers' legal competence.[46] More recent research has found that involvement is a key factor: when a defendant felt that their lawyer (whether court appointed or privately retained) allowed them to participate in their own legal defense, they were more likely to trust that lawyer.[47]

Since the late 1970s, the criminal courts have experienced even higher caseloads and more apparent racial and class disparities. Although racial disparities in incarceration, for instance, have been a feature of the criminal legal system since the beginning of the twentieth century, such disparities peaked in the 1990s nationwide and persist today.[48] These disparities also manifest in bloated courtroom caseloads and police arrest records, which vary from jurisdiction to jurisdiction. In New York City, for instance, broken windows policing in the 1990s—a proactive form of policing that focuses on policing disorder and low-level offenses rather than reacting only to serious offenses—resulted in a sharp rise in misdemeanor arrests, with racial disparities reaching their peak in 2007.[49] In Massachusetts, marijuana possession arrests in the first decade of the twenty-first century peaked in 2007 and sharply declined after decriminalization in 2009. Despite these reforms, racial disparities increased from 2001 to 2010. In 2001, black people across the state were 2.2 times more likely than white people to be arrested for marijuana possession and 3.9 times more likely in 2010.[50] In Suffolk County alone, where Boston is located, blacks were 4.8 times more likely than whites to be arrested for marijuana possession in 2010.

Recent qualitative and mixed-methods research on the court has begun to unpack these inequalities. In sociologist Nicole Gonzalez Van Cleve's 2016 study of the court system in Cook County, Illinois, she reveals how race is embedded in punishment.[51] She argues that prosecutors, judges, and even defense attorneys rely on racist moral labels to determine which defendants to punish and which to treat leniently. Defense attorneys— worried about their "street cred" among prosecutors and judges, which is necessary to obtain favorable plea deals for certain clients—participate in the court's racist culture by mocking their clients, treating them as burdens, and devoting time only to those deemed worthy of their advocacy. Sociologist Issa Kohler-Hausmann, in her 2018 study of misdemeanor courts in New York City, examines how today's courts responded to the rise in low-level arrests, a defining feature of the period of mass criminalization.[52] From 1980 to 2010, the annual number of people arrested in the city for a misdemeanor nearly quadrupled. Faced with this bevy of new arrestees, but constrained by the same resources, court officials responded by sorting, testing, and monitoring defendants rather than adjudicating their guilt or innocence. The likelihood of being convicted of a misdemeanor decreased over the period, but an abundance of adjacent tools were refined and regularly employed by officials. These tools—creating misdemeanor arrest records, requiring frequent court appearances, issuing restraining orders, and requiring enrollment in drug abuse programs— only deepened the courts' investment in social control rather than justice, further entrenching existing inequalities.

While this research tradition has contributed to our understandings of the logics, tools, and actions of court officials and how they contribute to the function of the courts, scholars have far less understanding of how defendants and their interactions with lawyers play a role in the system. Interactions with lawyers are important features of the system that, this book argues, has profound implications for people's court experiences. To be sure, Feeley, Van Cleve, Kohler-Hausmann and others have hinted at defendants' agency in courtrooms.[53] And a handful of interview-based studies have provided important insights into defendants' attitudes about their lawyers.[54] But these studies, many of which were conducted in the 1970s, do not tell us how defendants think and interact today, in a time when they have greater access to legal resources and rights.[55] Moreover, studies drawing only on interview data do not afford sufficient insight into the complex dynamics of attorney-client interactions. We have yet to observe and unpack the small, yet important, moments of attorney-client interactions in private and in open court settings. What theoretical tools might we need to understand more fully the making of privilege and inequality in the attorney-client relationship?

## The Perils of the Attorney-Client Relationship

To understand how inequalities are constituted and reproduced between lawyers and their clients, we must examine the *relationships* between the two, rather than the attitudes or behaviors of one or another. I draw on cultural sociological theory and relational theory—two related sociological approaches that have been used by scholars to analyze the human relationships at the heart of a wide variety of other institutions.

Each defendant, as they make their way through the legal process, is faced with several consequential choices. Legal scholars studying the rights of defendants regularly note the myriad choices defendants are theoretically afforded. For instance, they must choose (or refuse) legal counsel, have privileged conversations with their attorneys, consider their lawyer's proposed pretrial strategy, choose to take their case to trial or plead guilty, decide to take the witness stand, and consent to sentencing alternatives.[56] These decisions involve immense uncertainty and risk; each choice opens or forecloses further choices and uncertainties that have important implications in defendants' lives. And these decisions take place in an asymmetrical relationship (no matter how wealthy the defendant is), whereby lawyers often have more power to control the terms of interaction.[57] We can think of the choices of each defendant as being as constrained as they are consequential; thus, it is important to understand how they make their decisions, at what cost, and with what effect.

A defendant's choices and ways of engaging with the court are relational, meaning they unfold with respect to other social actors who have their own motivations, power, and constraints. Nothing in a courtroom happens in isolation. And the process is enacted by people. Despite popular portrayals of the criminal courts as processing machines, defendants do not stand before an inanimate system known as the "court" that mechanically dispenses one punishment after another. Rather, the court is a collection of humans—a judge, a prosecutor, a defense attorney, a probation officer, a court officer, and a court clerk—before whom the defendant must stand.[58] With their own professional and personal motivations, worries, and blind spots, these officials make decisions in relation to, and in expectation of, one another.[59] Outside the courtroom, each of these court officials belongs to broader organizations, such as the prosecutor's office or the defender's office, to which they must report. These organizations, in turn, have organizational policies that constrain the on-the-ground decision making of each official. These policies are themselves enacted in a relational way through directives from those in charge (e.g., a district attorney or a chief counsel) to their subordinates (e.g., assistant district attorneys and staff public defenders). Those in charge of these organizations are themselves constrained by legal policies created by their respective legislative bodies (bodies also made up of humans who have relationships to constituents, donors, and the like), and then upheld by appellate judges.[60]

The attorney-client relationship, in particular, is unrivaled in its significance for a defendant. It is the only relationship that legally protects every single interaction. Conversations between lawyers and defendants are privileged, meaning the lawyer is bound not to share any confidential information the defendant shares with them, save for statements about plans to commit future crimes. Indeed, in Boston, public defenders send letters to their clients warning them that they should speak only to their lawyers—not even their friends or family—about their case.[61] No relationship is more fraught, despite, and precisely because of, its seeming import in the minds of defendants. Of course, defendants also have relationships with other court actors. They regularly appear in front of judges, who assess them and may speak directly to them. If they are on probation, they may have regular check-ins with probation officers, who report back to the court. They may even have informal relationships with court officers, who are law enforcement officers in courthouses and who can come to know repeat defendants by name. Yet, these other relationships are almost always mediated through their relationship with their lawyers.

Understanding how these relationships work is key to understanding race and class inequalities in the courts. Most scholarship on race and class inequality in court focuses on either defendants' individual attributes in isolation or court officials' individual attributes in isolation. Research in this vein has importantly documented, for instance, racism and classism—sometimes subtle, sometimes explicit—among lawyers, judges, and probation officers throughout the country.[62] Journalistic accounts, citizen-generated social media posts, governmental investigations, and appellate decisions have also uncovered officials' racism and classism.[63] Other research has shown how the attitudes of defendants, such as whether they ascribe to a "code of the street" mentality, and their material resources, such as access to private lawyers, can be associated with differences in sentencing outcomes.[64] Still other work simply documents the existence of unequal outcomes at various stages of criminal processing, from arrest and the bail decision to charge reductions and conviction to incarceration and sentence length. All this work provides important lenses into inequality. But these accounts do not provide *thorough descriptions* of how inequalities are constituted in everyday moments, nor do they provide *thorough explanations* of how inequalities are reproduced as attributes unfold, are challenged, and change in social interaction with others.[65]

When I first began research for this book, I was focused on individual attributes rather than relational processes, much like other researchers. I thought I would focus on defendants' perspectives and attitudes only. But I soon realized that their accounts were fully interpretable only in reference to their interactions with other people—their lawyers, mostly, but also the judges who sentenced them, the prosecutors who negotiated with their lawyers, and their family and friends. They were not moving through the courts with their own unchanging perspectives; instead, they seemed to be both acting on and reacting to other people. Their actions emerged in anticipation of, and through their interpretations of, the actions of others—a fundamental insight about social behavior long theorized among interactionist scholars in sociology.[66] As I continued to gather more interviews and ethnographic observations, I refocused my analysis on the contingent and unfolding nature of attorney-client interactions. Some of these dynamics have been considered by scholars studying civil court contexts, such as divorce law and employment law, but not by those studying criminal court, where questions of state power and the loss of liberty are of great concern.[67] In many ways, more is at stake for clients in attorney-client relationships on the criminal side. I slowly came to see more fully what was at stake from various vantage points. I saw how tensions and concessions emerged as lawyers and clients from different backgrounds and social positions and with different things to lose came (and were often compelled) to interact with one another.[68] I also began to understand how court officials saw defendants as indicative of a particular social category, rather than as individuals, and made assumptions accordingly.

Let us return, for a moment, to the examples of Drew and Arnold. Understanding their experiences as relational (that is, in relation to their lawyers) provides deeper insight into their unequal court experiences than simply viewing their behaviors in isolation. Drew's relationship with his lawyer Tom can be understood as a *relationship of withdrawal*. The two of them experienced multiple moments of mistrust and tension that pulled them further from their mutually recognized goal of assisting Drew in altogether avoiding, or at least minimizing, legal punishment. Their mounting tensions can be understood as a dynamic I refer to as *withdrawal as resistance*. For Drew, his own legal ideas and strategies—his cultivated legal expertise—directly conflicted with those of his lawyer, not to mention the norms of the court. Multiple moments of conflict drove the relationship apart. At times, their disagreements related to the very definition of the goal of the court process, or what was at stake. For Drew, the goal was not just acquittal but also recognition of the bias of the police in arresting him in the first place. Resistance happens behind closed doors and in open court sessions. Other disadvantaged defendants, as I discuss in chapter 2, often experience another form of withdrawal—what I call *withdrawal as resignation*. Resignation arises less from a conflict between attorneys and their clients and more so from a defendant's exhaustion from striving to survive under oppressive conditions within and outside the legal system. Missed meetings and missed court dates, which frustrate lawyers and leave them unaware of crucial information about their clients' lives and legal preferences, are rarely intentional acts of resistance. Rather, they occur when defendants are dealing with more pressing matters, which can be a laundry list of anything from drug addiction to housing troubles to mental illness.

Withdrawal, in both its forms, often—though not always—has negative consequences. More common among poor defendants and working-class defendants of color, withdrawal is itself a marker of disadvantage. The racism and classism poor people experience in their neighborhoods, communities, and prior interactions with legal officials provide them with countless reasons to distrust the system and mistrust their current lawyers.[69] Their resultant withdrawal from lawyers throughout their relationships constitutes what it means to be a disadvantaged person in the courts. Moreover, withdrawal reproduces disadvantage. Sometimes, minor forms of resistance can force a lawyer to pay better attention to their client's needs or even raise a lawyer's awareness of procedural possibilities; yet, withdrawal more often has negative implications for court experiences. When disadvantaged defendants withdraw into resistance or resignation, they are often ignored, silenced, or coerced, whether by their own lawyers or by judges. Withdrawal is mutual: when clients withdraw from their lawyers, lawyers, in turn, often withdraw from their clients.

Meanwhile, privileged people experience quite different interactions with their lawyers. In contrast to relationships of withdrawal, attorney-client relationships like that of Arnold and Brett are more common among middle-class people of all racial groups and white working-class people. Arnold and Brett's relationship can be understood as a *relationship of delegation*. They experienced multiple moments of trust and engagement that pulled them closer to each other and toward their mutually recognized goal of assisting Arnold in avoiding, or at least minimizing, legal punishment. Whereas withdrawal entails mistrust and resistance or resignation, delegation entails trust and consensus in interaction, and it unfolds in one common way. Lacking prior experience with the legal system and benefiting from a relative lack of experiences of racism and classism in their neighborhoods and communities, privileged defendants are more likely to engage with their lawyer's professional expertise, defer to their lawyer's advice behind closed doors, and defer to judges and other officials in open court sessions. They are often on the same page about the defendant's ultimate goals, often because, unlike the disadvantaged who seek redress from police bias and other injustices, privileged people rarely want more than to avoid a harsh sentence. Some privileged defendants, like Arnold, may perceive racism or unfairness from police, but they often do not view these experiences as systemic or as necessarily indicative of an untrustworthy *court* system. Even when they do view the broader legal system as unjust or corrupt, they view their encounter with the law as rare and unexpected rather than routine and oppressive.

Relational theory in sociology provides theoretical insight into how and why attorney-client relationships are unequal. For relational theorists, social relationships—as documented in all aspects of our lives—themselves *constitute inequality*. In sociologist Charles Tilly's book *Durable Inequality*, he argues that differences in material and symbolic goods, such as wealth, education, respect, and deference, often exist along categorical lines.[70] Paired categories of social groups—men/women, black/white, the middle class/the poor—are defined, in many ways, in relation to their differential access to resources. Whiteness, when understood as a marker of privileged status or of greater access to material resources, takes on its most vital meaning in relation to blackness (or another nonwhite racial category).[71] Similarly, the working class has meaning only in relation to the middle class (or another class category). Sociologist Pierre Bourdieu famously theorized that the cultural styles and tastes of the middle and upper classes (e.g., taste in opera or fine art) are valued precisely because they are characteristic of the privileged class and therefore serve as a form of dominant cultural capital that can accrue resources, material and symbolic.[72] Such tastes become a marker of what it means to be privileged; the lack of such tastes, in turn, becomes a marker of what it means to be disadvantaged. In thinking about inequality among defendants, then, I argue that delegation in attorney-client relationships (and the trust in lawyers and lack of experience with the law that it entails) constitutes what it means to be a privileged defendant. Withdrawal in attorney-client relationships (and the mistrust of lawyers and cultivation of legal knowledge and skills that it entails) constitutes what it means to be a disadvantaged defendant.

Unequal relationships also *reproduce inequality*. The withdrawn relationships of disadvantaged defendants, as well as the delegating relationships of privileged defendants, likely reproduce disparities in their court outcomes. Relational theorists and cultural sociologists have, for some time, been interested in understanding how interactions between people reproduce macrolevel patterns of inequality.[73] Relational theorists in particular have insisted that sociologists, when interrogating the causes of inequalities in organizations and institutions, should move away from studying static variables as the unit of analysis (e.g., students or teachers independently) and toward studying dynamic relationships as the unit of analysis (e.g., student-teacher interactions). As sociologist Donald Tomaskovic-Devey writes, "Inequalities are . . . *not* lodged in people, races, or genders but in the relationships between people and between status categories. . . . It is the relations between people and positions that generate the power, status, and selves that appear to be traits of individuals and jobs."[74] Or as sociologist Mustafa Emirbayer puts it: "Unfolding transactions, and not preconstituted attributes, are thus what most effectively explain equality and inequality."[75] Meanwhile, cultural sociologists have often, though not always, remained content to study groups in isolation, more so than they have ventured into studying groups in relation, as they search for the processes undergirding inequality. In part, the dominant use of interview data has made it difficult to analytically see interactions unfold. Still, even when studying groups as static categories, cultural sociologists' claims are ultimately about how cultural clashes between groups shape inequality.[76]

Both relational and cultural sociological theories have illuminated how relational inequalities between groups are reproduced within mainstream institutional spaces, such as workplaces and schools. While the rules and practices of such organizations often appear standardized and neutral, symbolic power imbalances are often at play and can result in material inequalities. Institutional gatekeepers and organizational policies have been shown to value the social, cultural, and economic resources of the privileged and devalue the resources (or lack thereof) of the disadvantaged; they distribute their institutional resources accordingly, which only furthers inequality. For instance, sociologist Annette Lareau has been influential in examining how cultural knowledge and skills matter in navigating institutions.[77] Her work shows how elementary school teachers' rules and expectations about homework assignments, honors class placements, and proper parent-school engagement systematically disadvantage working-class and poor parents and children.[78] Whereas middle-class parents in her study displayed entitlement by intervening on behalf of their children, questioning teachers, and seeking accommodations when their children struggled with class work, working-class and poor parents often deferred to teachers' professional expertise and maintained distance from the school. Both groups valued education and wanted to see their children succeed; yet, she argues, the expectations of the school devalued the knowledges, approaches, and resources of working-class and poor parents.

Numerous studies have followed in this tradition, examining similar power dynamics—sometimes informal but very constraining—within secondary schools, universities, workplaces, and even health-care institutions. Scholars have documented how cultural resources (e.g., knowledge of cultural objects, educational credentials, or organizational procedures) and cultural styles (e.g., skills, habits, dispositions, or ways of speaking) play a crucial role in who successfully navigates these spaces, and who does not.[79] While this research literature is large and diverse, a central finding is that middle-class people tend to interact in ways that are individualistic, entitled, and demanding, whereas working-class and poor people tend to lead with deference.[80] These differences have implications for people's trajectories. Demanding and entitled styles have been shown to accrue valued resources—everything from better health care to more attention in classrooms. Thus, the privileged rely not only on money or social ties to hoard resources and maintain their advantages but also on styles of interaction that are either valued by gatekeepers (such as doctors, employers, and teachers) or that force these gatekeepers to provide them with more resources than their peers.[81] Sociologists Kathryne Young and Katie R. Billings have recently called for a "Bourdieusian construction of legal consciousness" that examines how "individuals in different power positions [within the legal field] understand and interact with the law."[82] Such an analysis, in the study of criminal legal institutions, would require using cultural concepts (like cultural capital, resources, and styles) along-side relational epistemologies (like relational ethnography). Drawing on relational theory and cultural sociology, this book moves research on the criminal courts in that direction.

In many ways, *Privilege and Punishment* complements core conclusions of cultural sociological literature, but it offers two novel contributions. First, the book shows that the divergent interactional styles typically associated with the middle class, on the one hand, and the working class and poor, on the other, are not perfectly transposable across institutional spaces. Given our existing understanding of class cultures in mainstream spaces such as schools and workplaces, it would be easy to assume that defendants who are skeptical of their lawyers' expertise and make demands of their lawyers and the court would be rewarded, and that those who defer to their lawyers' influence and the court's authority would receive harsher sanctions. But the opposite is the case. Instead, withdrawal, resistance, and assertiveness (characteristic of the disadvantaged in court) are punished. Meanwhile, delegation and deference (characteristic of the privileged in court) are rewarded. This difference has much to do with the different rules, expectations, and structural constraints that more mainstream institutions hold in comparison to punitive institutions. Where schools and workplaces might value initiative, thoughtfulness, and creativity, the courts value compliance, silence, and admitting fault, as we will see in the pages to come. Other institutions similar to, and increasingly entwined with, the courts—such as welfare agencies and sober houses— may operate in the same way. Sociologist Jennifer Reich's study of parents engaging with child protective services documents how a middle-class black woman with various forms of resources ultimately lost her children to the state because she did not exhibit deference toward the police, physicians, and case workers handling her child's case.[83] As punitive logics and tools of criminalization continue to expand and morph across institutional spaces and demographic groups in American society, it becomes ever more necessary to understand how privilege in relational interactions works in these spaces.

Second, this book demonstrates the added value of moving away from a study of culture as group or individual centered to a study of culture as embedded in relationships and dynamic interactions.[84] Much research in cultural sociology, as noted earlier, continues to center analysis on individuals and groups rather than interactions. A focus on relationships better explains why people's behaviors are not always consistent over their lives. For instance, Arnold's relationship with his lawyer Brett was a typical example of delegation; yet, months earlier, he had been assigned a different lawyer by the court. His relationship with that public defender was characterized by withdrawal. He did not trust this public defender and felt that he needed to try to cultivate knowledge about the law himself. Ultimately, he was able to secure financial resources to hire Brett with the help of his family and his basketball agent. Arnold thus went from experiencing withdrawal to experiencing delegation in the same court case. His experience shows how behaviors are not rooted in innate features of individuals or groups but rather in access to resources such as money or social ties that matter in interaction. Such access varies by situational context as well as relational context. By analyzing Arnold as a person in relation to other people (his assigned public defender and his hired private lawyer) rather than as an individual with supposedly one coherent cultural perspective on life, I could more clearly see how Arnold's seemingly irreconcilable perspectives on lawyers emerged from two very different relationships influenced by the immediate resources available to him at particular times and in particular situations. Thus, attention to culture as it emerges from relationships also reveals how many features of class and race inequality can be rooted in situational advantages or disadvantages, rather than long-lasting, inflexible dispositions.[85]

## The Study

This book is based on interviews and ethnographic observations collected in the Boston, Massachusetts, area between fall 2015 and winter 2019. Here, I provide a brief overview of the study's design and relevant background information about the Boston court system. For curious readers, more details about gaining access to research sites, conducting interviews, observing court, and analyzing data can be found in the book's appendix. There, I also reflect on how my social position as a middle-class black man without a criminal record influenced the study. My identity—along with my experience witnessing my cousin in court, described in the preface— not only motivated the study but may have played a role in how defendants and lawyers interacted with me and accounted for my brief presence in their lives. The researcher-respondent relationship has its own dynamics and uncertainties.

To understand attorney-client relationships, I interviewed and observed criminal defendants and court officials in the Boston area. I interviewed defendants in cafes, on street corners, and in food courts— neutral places, where they might feel comfortable sharing their court experiences. Conversations and interviews with legal officials took place in courthouse hallways, in offices, or in the back of a police car. The sixty-three defendants in this study were intentionally selected to be from a diverse range of race and class backgrounds.[86] But they all shared one thing in common: they had dealt with at least one criminal court case in either Boston or Cambridge, a medium-sized city just north of Boston across the Charles River.[87] Most reported experiences with drug- or alcohol-related court cases.[88] Many of these people had also been charged in other cities and towns in Massachusetts and even in other states.[89] Nearly all names of defendants, lawyers, judges, and other officials are pseudonyms, save for the rare instances when a person asked that I use their real name.

Eleven courthouses serve Boston and Cambridge.[90] Nine are municipal-level district courts (eight of which are often referred to as the Boston Municipal Courts [BMC]). These district courts handle misdemeanors and low-level felonies that can result in up to 2.5 years in jail. Two of the eleven are county-level superior courts; they handle more serious cases that can result in lengthy prison sentences. I visited all eleven courthouses during the study period, but the bulk of my time was spent in three district courts in Boston and in the Suffolk County Superior Court.[91]

Between fall 2015 and summer 2017, I spent more than one hundred hours in these courthouses—visiting them for sustained periods, alongside conducting scores of in-depth interviews with defendants. Over the course of one month in fall 2018, I embedded in a public defender's office as an unpaid intern. Over the month, I spent thirty hours per week closely shadowing three public defenders—Selena (a Latina woman), Sybil (a black woman), and Tom (a white man)—as they went about their daily work in their offices and in court. I conducted additional interviews with a handful of defendants during the month.

Some differences between Boston courthouses likely shape defendants' formal court outcomes, even if they do not bear on fundamental features of the attorney-client relationship. One difference is the "going rate" of charges. The going rate refers to the common sentence applied to specific charges and facts relating to a crime. For instance, in most Boston courthouses, a first-offense operating under the influence charge (OUI) is typically sentenced to a continuance without a finding (CWOF)—a sentence that results in a finding of no guilt on the condition that the defendant successfully completes a period of probation.[92] While a CWOF is a common sentence for many first-time misdemeanors, the typical probation conditions attached to the CWOF—for example, drug treatment courses, payment of fees, urine screenings—vary by courthouse and by judge.[93] The policies of district attorney (DA) offices can play a large role in determining going rates between courts. The Suffolk County DA has authority over filing criminal complaints in Boston courts, whereas the Middlesex County DA has authority in Cambridge. Each DA's office and their line prosecutors, or assistant district attorneys (ADAs), negotiate with defense attorneys during bail and plea negotiations.[94] These negotiations contribute, in part, to a defendant's ultimate sentence, as numerous scholars have argued. This book shows how negotiations between court officials are themselves influenced by attorney-client interactions.

Boston provides an analytically useful setting for studying inequalities in the attorney-client relationship. Boston is racially and socioeconomically diverse—and unequal, especially as measured by the disproportionate arresting, charging, conviction, and incarceration of racial minorities. Black and Hispanic people are overrepresented in both district and superior courts in Boston relative to their share of the general population.[95] Statewide, racial minorities are overrepresented in conviction rates and incarceration rates.[96] These inequalities follow from a sordid history of racism in Boston and in its criminal justice agencies. Beginning in the

1980s, the Boston Police Department (BPD), like others across the nation, engaged in broken windows policing in predominantly black neighborhoods. Tactics included arrests for minor offenses, such as drinking in public or loitering, and an increased focus on certain neighborhoods and individuals who were deemed likely to commit more-serious crimes.[97] These tactics make it likelier to be stopped by the police in working-class and low-income communities of color like Roxbury, Dorchester, and Mattapan, neighborhoods where people like Drew live. Recent studies have found these police stop rates to be racially discriminatory and illegitimate.[98] Differences in the incarceration rate between blacks and whites in Massachusetts has also been shown to be not fully explained by differences in criminal involvement (as measured by arrest) and therefore is partly due to racial discrimination in court processing.[99]

Boston is also a revealing site of study because, despite these inequalities, the Boston-area court system is arguably one of the more lenient systems in the United States. Over the period of mass criminalization, Massachusetts' overall incarceration rate has been consistently low compared to that of other states. In addition, other indicators suggest that the Boston courts are less punitive than other systems. For instance, the indigent defense system is known to be accommodating. Courts use relatively generous criteria to determine whether a defendant can receive a court-appointed lawyer free of charge.[100] Moreover, the right to a lawyer attaches as early as arraignment and applies during probation hearings, which is not the case in many states. The Committee for Public Counsel Services (CPCS), which oversees the indigent defense system, is well resourced.[101] CPCS trains both bar advocates and staff public defenders, who are among the most respected public defenders in the nation.[102] Consequently, where this study finds fault in the way the Boston courts operate, one could assume that things are likely to be worse in other parts of the country. Journalistic accounts of court systems in places like New Orleans, Louisiana, and Ferguson, Missouri, suggest that a systematic study of attorney-client relationships in these other systems would not only confirm but magnify this book's core insights. Withdrawal in interactions with lawyers would likely be more common and result in worse consequences in systems where lawyers are comparatively more burdened and courts less willing to encourage defendants to use their lay legal expertise and assert their legal rights. Readers should understand the evidence presented here as a look at the inequalities that even one of the most ideal versions of our courts reproduces.

## Book Overview

The following pages tell the stories of ordinary people from various walks of life as they navigate the criminal courts alongside their lawyers.

Chapter 1 explains the different paths that lead to the same outcome: becoming a defendant. These paths are guided by race and class differences, but they are initiated by a common reality: nearly every defendant, privileged or disadvantaged, experienced some form of alienation from school, family, neighbors, peers, or broader society in adolescence. Criminalized behaviors, such as drug use and dealing, emerged amid alienation. Among the privileged, such behaviors were more likely to be described as acts of pleasure and diversion, whereas among the disadvantaged, these same behaviors were more likely to be linked to racial and economic structural constraints. Regardless, at some point in life, everyone in the study was caught by the police. But the privileged were more likely to report relying on social and cultural resources embedded in their neighborhoods, their class positions, or their racial identities (or all three) to negotiate their way out of police encounters or even avoid them altogether. The disadvantaged, not surprisingly, were not. These unequal pathways to the courts have important implications for the attorney-client relationship. The disadvantaged are predisposed to distrust the legal system and mistrust their lawyers, thanks to repeated negative experiences with the law in their communities, lack of social ties with empowered authorities, and lack of financial resources to choose their lawyers.

Chapter 2 shows how disadvantaged defendants often experience withdrawal in their relationships with lawyers. For some, like Drew, mistrust of their lawyers contributes to withdrawal as resistance. They resist their lawyers' expertise and strive to cultivate their own legal knowledge and skills. I show how defendants cultivate legal expertise in jail, in their communities, and through observation of court proceedings. They often contest their lawyers' legal recommendations behind closed doors and sometimes even in open court, so frustrated by the legal system's lack of attention to their needs. Sometimes cultivated expertise constrains defendants' legal options, making the choice of seemingly harsh legal punishments (such as incarceration) preferable to seemingly lenient punishments (such as probation). For other disadvantaged defendants, withdrawal operates differently. In interactions with their lawyers, their withdrawal manifests as resignation to the legal process. These defendants appear to care little about their legal choices and often ghost their lawyers by cancelling meetings or even skipping court dates. Mistrust of lawyers plays a part here, but poor defendants' concerns about forms of adversity they face outside the courts—everything from poverty and police surveillance to drug addiction and mental illness—play an even greater role.

For privileged defendants, the situation is the opposite: their relative lack of experience with the law, greater access to social ties with empowered authorities, and ability to hire lawyers of their choosing all foster trust in their defense attorneys. Chapter 3 shows how these elements of trust foster delegation of authority. Privileged defendants recognize their inexperience with the law, seek to engage with their lawyers about their legal goals and possible strategies for attaining them, and ultimately defer to their lawyers' professional assessments. Deference operates not only behind closed doors but also in open court, where privileged defendants remain silent and deferential to their lawyers and other court officials. They rarely have reason to be frustrated by their treatment in court, where they feel they are largely treated with respect. Still, they experience uncertainty, fear, and worry about their formal legal outcomes, much as their disadvantaged peers do.

Turning our attention to the perceptions of defense attorneys, chapter 4 considers how lawyers—constrained by the norms, expectations, and power of judges and prosecutors—behave in their interactions with defendants, and how the pattern of their responses functions as a covert form of race and class discrimination. Defense attorneys must navigate relationships with other court officials, not just their clients. Although many of them are passionate about defending clients they often believe have been unjustly treated by the law and broader society, defense attorneys understand effective representation to mean the mitigation of their clients' legal sentences, not necessarily the pursuit of justice. For different reasons, lawyers and judges alike ignore, silence, and coerce defendants who withdraw into resistance and resignation. Meanwhile, court officials reward defendants who delegate authority to their lawyers, offering them future legal services and opportunities for rehabilitation and other alternatives. Given race and class patterns in defendants' likelihood of withdrawal or delegation, court officials' tendencies to punish withdrawal and reward delegation operate as legitimated and taken-for-granted forms of race and class discrimination.

The conclusion considers the importance of the book's arguments for scholars, policymakers, lawyers, and ordinary people who care about race and class injustices and how they are embedded in our country's criminal courts. An important lesson of this book is that effective legal representation alone is not justice. A defense lawyer's presence and passion are neither indications of justice nor are they certain means to achieving a just legal outcome. Poor defendants, wealthy defendants, victims, and broader society rarely find justice from the way we currently process social problems (such as drug use) and social harms (such as assault and murder) in our court system. Alongside suggesting practicable reforms to the attorney-client relationship that might ensure relatively better legal outcomes for some defendants, I imagine possibilities for fundamentally transforming the attorney-client relationship, courthouse cultures, and the place of the courthouse in the management of social harm. Such transformation requires us to commit to rectifying race and class injustices that precede, and extend beyond, the courthouse doors.

# CHAPTER ONE

# Different Paths to the Same Courts

TIM AND I MET at a local grocer in Cambridge. After we found a table and sat down to begin the interview, I studied his face as he quietly filled out the survey I provided to everyone in the study before I started the tape recorder. He is black, in his early forties, and has a weary appearance. His wrinkled forehead and small chin combine to make him seem at once older and younger. Next to his chair that day, he had carefully placed a raggedy suitcase and an overflowing messenger bag. I would learn that these items were his only possessions. He carried his belongings everywhere he went because he did not feel comfortable leaving them at the shelter where he had been staying for the past several weeks. "I don't like staying with a whole bunch of people because there's a whole bunch of guys and everybody has a story to tell. Sometimes I don't want to be around that drama," he reflected once we had started the interview. Nowadays, Tim tries to keep to himself. He has been arrested eight times in his life, and many of his arrests arose from "drama" he has had with other people on the streets.

Tim's life has been marked by multiple forms of disadvantage, all of which combined to make his involvement with the criminal legal system seem inevitable. He grew up in the 1980s in public housing in Roxbury, a majority-black neighborhood in Boston. In his childhood, his mother was an inconsistent presence; his aunt raised him, providing him a home in a cramped apartment shared with several cousins and with just enough food and clothing between them. Growing up in Roxbury in the eighties meant that he regularly witnessed drug dealing in both his neighborhood and at school. "Everyone sold dope," he told me. The police were ever present; they seemed eager to harass the "kids in the projects." "Man . . . the police used to stop everybody," Tim remembered. Police harassment followed them elsewhere, too. Tim's first time being stopped and searched was when he was shopping at Downtown Crossing, a bustling outdoor mall in the center of Boston, with a group of other young black boys, the summer of his thirteenth birthday. "We'd just be chilling because we got a little money from our summer jobs, and [they] come and pat us down."

In his teens, Tim and his friends started experimenting with marijuana and alcohol. After high school, and after moving out of his aunt's apartment, he moved to Atlanta, Georgia, looking for work and eager to start a new life. But within a few months, he began selling cocaine to make ends meet. He quickly found himself homeless and spending nights at the airport, where he and others sought shelter. Just after he turned nineteen, he was arrested and jailed for trespassing. When he got out, all his belongings were gone. With no family or friends to support him, he started selling drugs to survive. Sometime in the next several years, he was arrested for cocaine possession and spent eighteen months detained in jail awaiting trial. "It was a big zoo," he remembers of the county jail in Georgia. After serving time, he moved back to Boston, where he has spent about a decade revolving between the streets and jail. His life has been shaped by avoiding, and far too often enduring, punishment from various components of the criminal legal system.

When we think about the typical criminal defendant in the United States—whether we are a researcher, a journalist, or an activist—we often imagine someone like Tim. A childhood of poverty and instability, the descent from drug use to drug dealing, the persistent presence of the police—all these features are terribly common among people involved in the criminal legal system. But portrayals of people like Tim do not tell the full story of our criminal legal system's reach. In fact, portrayals in scholarship and the media that focus exclusively on the disadvantaged often obscure just how unequal the criminal legal system really is. To fully comprehend the system's inequality, we must contrast the experiences of people like Tim with the experiences of the privileged.

Ryan is a white man in his early thirties who grew up in a middle-class family just outside Boston. He has walked the path into the court system typically taken by privileged people. The two of us met at a food court in Boston on a warm summer morning. He was wearing khaki shorts and an untucked polo shirt. He shook my hand graciously before we sat down. Unlike Tim, but like a third of the people I interviewed, Ryan was raised in a well-to-do two-parent household.[1] His parents are both college educated. To this day, his mother works as a paralegal, and his father works as a health insurance agent. No one in Ryan's family ever expected he would be arrested. But so far, he has been arrested three times in his life—twice for driving under the influence and once for shoplifting—crimes that stem from his addiction to alcohol and other drugs.

Despite his middle-class upbringing, Ryan has struggled with addiction since adolescence. His middle school and high school were both resource rich, the kind of quality suburban public education that many poor parents dream about for their kids. Ryan was an average student, did not find academics enjoyable, and did not establish meaningful relationships with his teachers. But he loved sports. He played on the soccer and golf teams in the fall and the basketball team in the winter. High school also brought peer pressure and the excitement of experimenting with drugs. In his teens, he started drinking, smoking marijuana, and using benzodiazepines (a class of antianxiety drugs). His parents did not know about the drug use, but they were well aware of his underage drinking. Even though his parents both struggled with their own alcoholism, as Ryan explained, "they weren't aware that it could be genetic or anything." They thought his drinking was just harmless teenage fun. And neither Ryan's parents nor his friends were concerned about getting in trouble with the law. One time, he and some friends were pulled over by a police officer with "four open beers" in the car but "got by on the skin of our teeth"; the officer was an acquaintance of one of his friends' parents, and he let them off with a warning.

It was not until college that Ryan's drinking created bigger problems. In the dorms, drinking became routine. "It was Thursday, Friday, Saturday, Sunday during the day," Ryan remembered. One weekend he was driving drunk near campus. An officer pulled him over. "I was scared shitless," Ryan told me. The officer was courteous but still arrested him. He spent the night in jail, got bailed out by his girlfriend the next day, and was charged with OUI in court that Monday. Terrified and confused, he called his father. "I wasn't brought up that way, and I'd never seen myself in that situation." Ryan's father contacted a friend who was a detective. The detective put him in touch with a reputable lawyer, who just happened to be the son of the county's DA. The lawyer negotiated a standard plea deal but with light terms—a CWOF with six months of administrative probation, meaning no conditions were attached to his probation time. After making it six months without another arrest, his probation would be over and the whole court experience behind him. He graduated college and got a job in investment consulting. Because his charge resulted in a CWOF, he was able to apply for jobs without reporting the OUI.[2]

For a while, he lived a typical middle-class life. But in his mid-twenties, his alcoholism got worse. His addiction was abetted by the "wining and dining" of corporate culture. And then he started drinking alone: "I wasn't out at bars. I wasn't hanging out with friends. I was by myself, isolated." He was arrested on another OUI charge. Later, he would be hospitalized and induced into a coma for problems with his pancreas. His girlfriend left him. He lost touch with most of his friends from high school and college. He moved back in with his parents and worked toward recovery, including stints in a revolving door of residential addiction programs, financed by his parents. "My parents have helped me out with anything I needed in between," he said. When we first met that summer morning, Ryan was living in a halfway house in Jamaica Plain, a racially diverse and mixed-income neighborhood in Boston, and dealing with a shoplifting case. He had recently been arrested after attempting to steal a vaporizer from a store while high. This was his third arrest. He was nervous about the court case. But he was almost certain he would get off with a light punishment—a small fine, he guessed, or perhaps another CWOF with six months of administrative probation. His past experiences with the law suggested he had little to worry about. Later in the book, we will see he was right not to worry about this most recent case.

At first blush, it may seem odd to focus our attention on a privileged person in the criminal legal system. We tend to imagine our country's jails and courthouses to be filled almost exclusively with poor people, especially those of color. To be sure, people with middle-class resources who live in predominantly white communities are substantially less likely to become defendants, even if they struggle with the same problems (and resort to the same crimes) as the poor. Problems such as social alienation, depression, and drug use, as we will see in this chapter, are simply treated differently in privileged communities than they are in poor communities. But then, even when privileged people do happen to be arrested, their legal involvement looks different—and even *means* something different—from that of disadvantaged people, given their privilege in broader society. Thus, the "privileged defendant" is something of an oxymoron, an intentional one that is meant to illuminate how the privileges some people benefit from in everyday life can soften their experiences with the criminal legal system in numerous ways.

As Ryan's story reveals, being both privileged and a criminal defendant means that certain criminalized behaviors—such as underage drinking and drug use—are often constructed as pleasurable diversions. When caught, the police often give privileged suspects the benefit of the doubt or grant second chances until they can no longer justify them. Arrest, or other forms of legal involvement, are an unexpected shock in the world of the privileged. Tim's story reveals the near opposite. Being both disadvantaged and a criminal defendant means that crime often feels like a necessary, even an inevitable part of life, given the fundamental constraints of poverty and racial marginalization. Arrest and other forms of legal surveillance are routine. When stopped by police, the police rarely accept explanations and often represent a threat to one's freedom and physical safety; police who are supposed to protect and serve are instead a palpable reminder of racism and classism. Ultimately, these negative experiences with the legal system and police sow seeds of distrust among the disadvantaged.

This chapter examines how people from different walks of life end up in the same situation: being a criminal defendant. I argue that privileged people walk a strikingly different path to court than disadvantaged people, even when they engage in similar behaviors. These different paths, and the different ways their behaviors are treated by police and other legal officials, contribute to divergent perceptions of the criminal legal system and, eventually, of their defense attorneys. Becoming a privileged criminal defendant carries very different meanings, and involves a very different set of experiences, than becoming a disadvantaged defendant. These divergent meanings and experiences ultimately color the attorney-client relationship. While the meanings they attach to crime and their experiences with lawyers diverge greatly, one thing is common across race and class lines: the sense of alienation—whether from family, teachers, and peers or from neighbors, the law, and broader American society—that appears to sustain and justify the problems and harms that draw the attention of legal officials.

## Alienation in Adolescence

No matter their background, nearly all the defendants I met described an adolescence marked by social alienation. Scholars have long defined alienation—and related concepts such as anomie—in various ways.[3] I define social alienation as a personal feeling of separation or rupture from the expectations and norms of institutions and broader society. A person can feel separate from the expectations of their family or school (two institutions) or from society's seeming valorization of attending college or purchasing a new home (two dominant norms). This separation can emerge from distaste for such expectations and norms or from strain—the feeling that one cannot meet society's expectations about how to be a well-behaved child, a smart student, or, as one grows older, a productive employee.[4] Structural differences in the quality of people's schools, neighborhoods, and experiences of discrimination in the labor market contribute to strain, often to the detriment of poor people of color.[5] Moreover, alienation can exist in relation to the law as an institution. Cynicism about the effectiveness of the law in marginalized communities can make it difficult to rely on the police in moments of trouble.[6] Rather than rely on police or other legal tools provided by the state, gang involvement and other criminalized activities may better ensure one's safety. Such legal cynicism does not exist to nearly the same extent in privileged communities, given differing structural realities of policing.[7] But privileged people in this study do experience strain and separation from other institutions, often emerging from or manifesting as abuse in the home, parents' and teachers' inattention, and unmanaged mental illnesses.

Feelings of alienation alongside structural constraints contribute to the problems and harms commonly faced by the people in this study. These problems and harms are criminalized by the law, explaining eventual arrest. Some in the study felt alienated at home, where they feared abusive family members or were ignored by inattentive parents. Others felt alienated at school, where their learning difficulties meant teachers excluded them, or where their boredom was supplanted by the diversions of peers doing reckless things. Still others experienced alienation from peers, neighbors, and the expectations society suggested for their futures. Given these feelings, people reported engaging in illicit activity of one kind or another, often to cope. Just about everyone had committed a crime by the time they were eighteen, with drug use, drug dealing, and larceny the most common. Many struggle with substance use disorders still today. Eighty-five percent of the defendants I interviewed reported current struggles with substance abuse, commonly alcoholism and opioid addiction.[8] Nearly as common are struggles with mental health. More than 60 percent of the people in the study responded "yes" to at least one survey question indicating possible depression at the time of the interview.[9] Other mental health conditions described in interviews include attention-deficit hyperactivity disorder, bipolar disorder, and schizophrenia.

When it comes to sources of alienation, physical and verbal abuse from parents and guardians was commonly mentioned no matter their race or class. Christopher, a heavy-set white man in his late thirties, spent most of his adolescence with his aunt and uncle in South Boston, a majority-white and largely working-class neighborhood. His aunt, a college-educated nurse, and his uncle, who worked in the piping trades, provided him a nurturing middle-class home and paid his tuition for Catholic school. Before moving in with his aunt and uncle, Christopher had spent the first twelve years of his life with his biological parents in a town on the North Shore, a coastal region of Massachusetts north of Boston. His father verbally abused him and physically abused his mother. One evening, everything changed for him:

> My father hit my mother, and she ended up going down a flight of stairs. Broke her arm. Got a fractured skull, you know, it was really, really bad, you know what I mean? And my uncle came over and basically told my father to stay away from her and made arrangements for me to live with my aunt. And that was the end of that.

Christopher was ambivalent about living with his aunt and uncle. On the one hand, he loved them and appreciated that they "functioned like a real family." They ate dinner together regularly and talked about current events. On the other hand, he "felt hurt" and "abandoned by my mother." He never found a place where he truly felt at home, fostering feelings of alienation.

Beyond witnessing physical abuse, some of the people I talked to directly experienced it. Mary, a Latina woman in her early twenties, grew up in East Boston, a mostly Latino and working-class community. She has always had an ambivalent relationship with her father. He is a complicated man: a man who is fun to be around and who used to coach her soccer team, but also a man who suffers from alcoholism and has been abusive toward her, her mother, and her siblings for as long as she can remember. In middle school, her father's abuse was so routine that it did not seem wrong until she mentioned it to a classmate:

> So, he was always binge drinking, and when he binge drinks he gets angry. He gets violent with everybody. . . . I remember the first time I told somebody about it was in middle school. I was just talking to my best friend, and it slipped out that "Oh, my dad beat me the other day." And she's like: "What?!" And I'm just like, "Yeah." I thought it was normal: "Oh this is so daily to me," it's like, "whatever."

Just after high school graduation, Mary moved in with her boyfriend after a particularly violent episode with her father. "Me and my father got into an altercation, and it was really bad that I was actually hospitalized," she said. "I had a ruptured eardrum and had a concussion." Living with her boyfriend was, at times, difficult. At one point, she was living in her car—on the outs with her boyfriend and unwilling to go back to her parents' home. Despite this volatility, she was able to maintain her job as a patient services coordinator at a Boston-area hospital, until she was arrested the following year for drug possession and larceny.

For some, especially the working class and poor, household abuse drew the attention of state authorities, typically child protective services (CPS)—resulting in a state-enforced alienation from the family.[10] Though the stated intentions of such services were good, the result was often further complications at home. Kareem, a skinny black man with light brown eyes, remembered the impact of child services in his life. Kareem spent his early childhood in Dorchester, a predominantly black and economically heterogenous neighborhood. Kareem's mother was an administrator for an insurance company, and his father was a firefighter. Neither of his parents graduated from college, and both struggled with alcoholism, which was accompanied by verbal and physical abuse. When he was twelve, they divorced, and Kareem and his sister moved in with their father, in "the projects" of Roxbury. Their mother had started dating a man who was using and selling drugs. CPS would regularly check up on the house when the siblings were visiting their mother. At one point, Kareem and his sister were not allowed at their mother's place unsupervised. His sister, he recalled, was placed in foster care because she wanted to stay with their mother rather than their father: "My sister ended up not following the rules because she was not supposed to go to my mother's house 'cause it had to be supervised with her . . . and, um, she ended up going to foster care for that. But that was on her, because she knew better." Kareem's forthright description hinted at the depths of the difficulty: "That was kind of a bumpy road. That was a stressful period."

One person in the study, because of parental abuse and neglect, spent much of her adolescence revolving between the streets and different foster care placements. Donna, a white woman in her mid-forties whose face is now weathered in red blisters, has spent much of her life homeless. She was born in Brockton, a city just south of Boston. She was one of three children in a single-parent household. Each child had a different, absent father. And, as Donna remembers, her mother was largely absent as well: "Well, she was never really a mother. I cooked for her, I used to dress her, bathe her. She's nuts. She tried drowning me when I was two in boiling [water]—[chuckles] I can laugh about it now, but to this day, it's like walking on eggshells with her." Donna's mother "gave [her] up" to foster care just before she turned thirteen. Donna did not stay long. She ran away and lived on the streets of Boston for weeks at a time. She was first arrested when she was fourteen and caught smoking marijuana in Boston Common with a group of older teenagers with whom she had started living. She remembered how she changed her appearance to fit in with the other kids: "I tried to look older than what I was, putting makeup on, a wig on."

Home was not alienating for all. For some, home provided safety, especially from trauma and harm at school or in their neighborhoods, which were their more immediate sources of alienation. Joseph was a black boy growing up in Roxbury; home was his haven. Now a fifty-year-old man with a handsome square face and dark complexion, Joseph recalled what it was like to be raised in a middle-class home in a low-income neighborhood. His mother, a college-educated receptionist at a large company, doted on him and instilled a work ethic in him by making him do chores: "walking my dog and taking out the trash." His stepfather, a construction worker, bonded with him over various hobbies: "He introduced me to bowling, you know what I mean, more of that camp thing, horseback riding, and stuff like that." But growing up in Roxbury in the 1970s meant that he was likely exposed to a greater incidence of violence and delinquency than in the average Boston neighborhood.[11] The kids he knew in the neighborhood would break into buildings, drink alcohol, and smoke marijuana—and he would join them. "The streets were more appealing, more exciting" than school and afterschool programs. Unlike most of his neighborhood friends, he attended a racially diverse Catholic school just outside Roxbury that his parents paid for him to attend. He told me: "I went to a private school but a lot of my friends they went to public schools, so that's where that peer pressure came in" to start "cutting school."

Many of the people I spoke with recounted a troublesome relationship with school. Some felt that school was boring and therefore sought out excitement among peers, pushing against the edges of the law (like Joseph); others experienced more serious problems within school, from feeling belittled to stigmatized, from experiencing exclusion to violence, whether from teachers or from classmates. Ninety percent of the people I interviewed completed high school, and a considerable minority went on to complete a four-year bachelor's degree or more.[12] The people in the study are, on average, slightly less educated than the general population.[13] By design, however, the study contains a fairly high number of college-educated people who have nevertheless been arrested at some point in their lives. That variety of education is an important reminder of how the criminal legal system touches many facets of American society. Amid this variation in how much education the people I spoke with received, one thing remained constant: alienation. Not surprisingly, for all those people who dropped out of high school (or never made it as far as high school), as well as for those people who never dreamed of going to college, or dropped out, some element of alienation contributed to bringing their education to an end. Even if they were able to make their way through school, most experienced alienation there. For those who completed their studies, doing so often required immense efforts to cope with boredom, detention, suspensions, misunderstandings, poor grades, and the lure and threat of classmates up to no good.

Some people were diagnosed with learning disabilities in school, coinciding with stigmatizing experiences from their diagnoses. Teachers were viewed as ineffective at accommodating their needs. Mark, a talkative black man in his fifties who has lost several teeth to his heroin addiction, was diagnosed with a learning disability in eighth grade. "I was that guy. I was in a little school next to the big school. I was that guy riding the little bus after the big bus," he told me. I asked him if he had any fond memories of school—from teachers or peers—and he abruptly said "No" to each of my probing questions. For Scott, a white man in his fifties who "barely" graduated from high school, his learning disabilities and mental illness diagnoses affected his schooling experience so deeply that he went through high school without ever finishing a book. The only book he ever read in full was *The Big Book*, a basic text used by individuals in Alcoholics Anonymous (AA). As he put it, "I learned how to read at AA."

Teachers were often remembered as cold and unapproachable, even for those who did not struggle with a learning disability.[14] For instance, Paul, a forty-something white man who grew up in a small mostly white town north of Worcester, felt that his teachers were unsupportive. Even though he readily admits to having been a "bully" in school, he told me that school felt oppressive because his teachers were too strict:

> [Teachers] treated everybody like nothing. There was none of this laughing in class or the teacher making jokes. It was like . . . sit like this, hands together, head up. If you put your head down it was a smack on the table. And you had to sit like this, look forward, and pay attention. It was like prison. It sucked.

Paul was still enrolled in high school when he was arrested for assault and battery at eighteen. His teachers were unforgiving. Rather than seeking to understand the circumstances around his arrest, they viewed his arrest as predictable—the result of his poor character. And his treatment from teachers in juvenile detention was even worse. Paul reflected: "Well, they [the teachers at his high school] kind of knew I was sort of a punk so they [said], 'It was about time you got caught.' And of course, the ten days I was in [detention], I had to go to school in juvie hall, and those teachers were assholes." Paul's story reveals how initial feelings of alienation and small acts of misbehavior can become exacerbated once a person is labeled and dismissed by authority figures in their lives.

As opposed to the commonly negative opinion of teachers, classmates were boxed into two categories: either as a source of annoyance or as a source of diversion. For some, it was difficult to fit in among peers, thereby providing another source of alienation. Stephen Douglas, a white man in his late thirties who refers to himself using two first names, remembered how much he disdained his high school classmates. He transitioned to a new school after moving from Mission Hill, a neighborhood in Boston, to Framingham, a city just west of Boston. He told me, "I thought it [the school] was the sticks. I hated it." Compared to his former school in Mission Hill, his new school was full of a bunch of "suburban kids" who "all acted like they were all ghetto and badass. And I just wanted to knock them out." Much of his anger was about fitting in. At his old school, he "was popular. I had all these friends, and I was like the class clown." Ultimately, he was able to convince his parents—a college-educated administrative assistant at a pharmaceutical lab and a high-school-educated pipe fitter—to send him to a technical high school. Even though he felt more socially integrated, he had a hard time adjusting to the potential opportunities of a technical education. He focused his studies on graphic arts but regrets that he did not learn a trade, such as plumbing. He told me that the students who studied plumbing "got their plumbing licenses as soon as they got out. They had a head start on everything." For Stephen Douglas, he felt apart from both his peers and the expectations of the job market.

For others, peers were remembered as exciting—a diversion from school's dullness. Among these individuals, school provided an enjoyable environment for engaging with other kids even when it did not provide an educational, or physically safe, space. For example, a small number of people, all of whom grew up in low-income neighborhoods, recalled how peer violence in schools was a daily—and sometimes enjoyable—reality. Royale, a black man who entered adolescence in Brooklyn, New York, in the early 1990s, told me: "The kids ran the schools! . . . Students were beating up teachers, slapping teachers, throwing chairs at teachers." Royale engaged in this violence from an early age, noting that "I've been getting into trouble since the first grade. Fighting and not wanting to do the work and fooling around." By high school, he "used to carry a gun" to

school. Police were often called to his school; their presence both epito-
mized the school's violence and also furthered his early feelings of distrust,
not just toward police but toward teachers and other authority figures,
too.[15] These feelings of distrust were also exacerbated by the conditions
of his neighborhood.[16] "I grew up in a very dangerous neighborhood," he
said. "A lot of crime, a lot of shootings, a lot of murders, robberies. . . . A
lot of police harassment."

It was not just other adolescents who encouraged illegal behavior; a
few respondents recalled these cues coming from teachers or neighbors,
either explicitly or by example. Justice told me that when he was thirteen
years old, one of his teachers, a white man, supplied him with marijuana
to sell in his neighborhood. A black man now in his sixties, Justice grew up
in public housing in Roxbury and attended school right across the street
from his family's apartment. He remembered how important and cool he
felt when his teacher approached him and his friend:

> I sold weed for a teacher. . . . A couple of us that was in his class. We
> thought he was the coolest thing, you know. And he wore nice shoes
> and things. He was sharp, you know. All of that. We thought he was
> cool. When he liked us, we liked him. He pulled us aside one day and
> said, "I want to give y'all some work."

Being recognized was validating. An impressionable kid who, like most
children, wanted to please the authority figures in his life, he was more
than willing to sell marijuana as a meaningful part of his relationship with
his teacher. Ironically, Justice's experience of validation—rather than of
alienation—with his teacher drew him into illegal activity. Like others,
however, Justice experienced alienation in other domains, especially at
home where his "parents were so busy trying to put food on the table, they
really couldn't pay a whole lot of attention to what we were doing as kids
out in the streets." He told me his dad was distant: "I have absolutely no
recollection of ever hearing my dad say, 'Son, I love you.'" Justice's fall into
selling drugs, then, was as much a way of avoiding feelings of alienation as
it was a search for affirmation.

## The Meaning of Crime

Whether well off or impoverished, whether a college graduate or a high
school dropout, whether raised in the suburbs or on the streets, everyone in the study felt alienated from institutions or the norms of broader
society growing up. By necessity, we all strive to deal with the strains and

difficulties we feel in our lives, in one way or another. Some of these ways are positive; others present problems. For the people I spoke to, breaking the law—whether intentionally or not—was one way to cope. Some drank underage, others smoked weed, others stole, others sold drugs.

But there was one vivid dividing line that separated some crimes from others: what those crimes *meant*. If you are black and poor, breaking the law simply means something different than if you are white and wealthy. The privileged and the disadvantaged both experienced adolescent troubles, but the meanings they attached to their behaviors differed. Similar illicit behaviors were differently understood along race and class lines. For those growing up in middle-class homes and mostly white communities, drinking, using drugs, and selling drugs were more often remembered as fun and exciting. For those growing up in working-class and poor homes, especially in predominantly black neighborhoods, these activities were more likely to be remembered as necessary—the result of economic or racial constraint. Disadvantaged people justified these delinquent behaviors as necessary given the realities of financially constrained parents and relatives, uncertain job prospects, and a racially oppressive society.[17] Advantaged people justified delinquent behaviors as teenage fun. Although drug use, drug dealing, and even theft were justified in these divergent terms, other crimes—such as assault and domestic violence later in life—were less often described in relation to the pleasure versus constraint dichotomy.

When I first started interviewing people, I was surprised at how readily defendants would describe their past crimes to me. Eventually, I realized that they felt a need to talk with me in part because they needed to explain their story—they desired, to some degree, to make sense of their crimes. When disadvantaged people described their adolescent behaviors as necessary in interviews with me, they were providing me an account of their past actions. All of us, in one way or another, try to justify, or rationalize, what we have done in our lives. Those justifications, of course, are inevitably biased; our accounting of the past is not necessarily an accurate, or complete, rendering of the causes of our past behaviors. Nevertheless, these accounts are important to examine because they provide insight into how people make sense of their pasts; for better or worse, the way we see our past shapes our present and our future. We use the meanings we have made from the past to justify our future actions, both to others and to ourselves.[18] These justifications allowed many of the people I met to continue to engage in illegal behaviors in the present day despite the many problems those crimes caused.[19] Among the disadvantaged, justifications of constraint and necessity are particularly noteworthy because of their contrast with those of the privileged. Therefore, while these justifications cannot be shown to cause illegal behaviors, either in the past or in the present, they reveal how similar acts can have very different meanings for people in different social positions.

Drug dealing was routinely described as necessary among the poor, given economic constraints. Gregory, a black Latino man who grew up "in the projects" in Roxbury, told me: "There wasn't no work. . . . It wasn't easy, you know, selling, you know, weed or drugs or heroin. And that's work." Royale, a black man described earlier, recounted how he started to steal, and then to sell, drugs, both to get the clothing he desired and to help his mother. Theft became an option as he realized his mother's limited ability to provide for his material wants. And as he grew older, he felt pressure to contribute financially to the household:

> ROYALE: So growing up as a young person in an impoverished neigh-
> borhood, you know, the things they like—nice sneakers and nice
> clothes and nice book bags and . . . now I understand where I
> come from, but at the time I was thinking that way because I liked
> nice stuff.
>
> MATT: Did you steal stuff ever? Or was your mom able to buy stuff?
>
> ROYALE: Yes! My mom spoiled me, so she always bought me what I
> wanted. I don't know how she got it. Now that I'm an adult—well,
> as I got older, I began to say, "You know something. I'm not going
> to take it from her anymore. I'm going to get it myself." But that's
> when the life of crime began. I didn't want to put that pressure on
> her anymore.
>
> MATT: Oh, okay. At what age?
>
> ROYALE: By the time I was . . . fourteen . . . fourteen, I started decid-
> ing that I can't afford to be making her buy me these nice things
> because she can't really afford it. I began to grasp the concept
> and understand that she can't afford that. Look at the bills she's
> paying—she can't even handle that. And I love her. I have to earn
> for me to take that burden off of her.

Economic constraint, in part, justified Royale's criminal behaviors. But the lure of drug dealing was undeniable as well: "I was infatuated with the street life at a very early age, you know? I was really attracted to it." Necessity and desire, as Royale's experience shows, can operate in tandem.

Some black men also described antiblack racism as a justification for illegal behavior. Justice told me how growing up in Boston in the 1960s meant that he felt myriad forms of prejudice and discrimination: taunting, threats to his physical safety, and white resistance to integration in schools and neighborhoods.[20] The border of his Roxbury neighborhood, on the edge of the predominantly white South End and South Boston neighborhoods, was a hotbed of antiblack racism. "As a black kid, you're not making it out of there safe," he told me about South Boston. He was adamant that this racism justified robbing white-owned stores and breaking into homes in white neighborhoods. He explained:

> Now, recognizing that all these white people don't like us and hate us and things of that nature. So now, it becomes an issue of revenge almost. You go into these white-owned stores and think, "You all owe us. Take anything we want. This is ours. You're wrong anyway. You enslaved us. You did this, you did that."

Justice framed theft as a rational, almost necessary, response to racism. Indeed, much of the racism Justice witnessed was characterized as economically exploitative rather than simply based in distaste or antipathy. His decisions to steal from white-owned stores were therefore rooted in a sense of economic fairness: "They're selling their goods to us. They're taking all our money. They're not giving any back."

Charlie, a white man who grew up in the 1960s and 1970s in Dorchester, a predominantly black neighborhood also on the edge of South Boston, also viewed antiblack racism as a justification for his delinquency. For Charlie, who grew up with black friends and is married to a black woman, his experiences with racism have been vicarious. Still, he described getting into fights to defend his black peers and his right to be friends with them:

> My goal in life was to be dead before the age of sixteen, and it was going to be in protection of someone else. My neighborhood was going through racial transformation and busing and everything, and I got involved in so many fights because I was the "N. lover." I was this, I was that. I went to a Catholic school where the kids from the Irish areas were sent by their families so they wouldn't have to go to school with black folks. Where I lived, my best friend was black. I mean, that was my whole neighborhood. So, I took beatings on a routine basis, and so I decided eventually I was going to die because of this, and I had no fear of it.

For Charlie, being a white boy in a black space also drew the suspicion of the police.[21] Charlie recalled one particular incident when the police were called to a local bar serving mostly black patrons. After breaking up a fight, the police asked him to leave the bar. One officer explained: "You know why we kicked you out? We never see white people up here."

For those who struggled with substance abuse in their adolescence and were poor or strapped for cash, drug selling and theft were framed as ways to maintain their expensive habit. As drug use became a physical need for their bodies to function, they sought to acquire drugs by any means. Owen, a white man raised by a single mother who suffered from her own addiction, told me that he personally started using at a young age. He had his first drink of alcohol at nine, smoked marijuana at fifteen, and by eighteen regularly used cocaine and pills. By twenty, he was addicted to heroin. Always looking for money to feed his addiction and without a regular job, he began stealing laptops and other small electronics. His most recent arrest, for stealing a laptop, was simply to "sell it for drugs." Similarly, Michael, a white man who grew up poor and is addicted to heroin, described his cycle of theft, arrest, and drug use: "Do the thirty days [in jail], and then I stay out of trouble for a few years. And then I get arrested, get mixed up with the drugs, keep getting arrested for shoplifting. I got a lot of shoplifting; it's just money to support my habit."

Some people framed drug use itself as a necessary way to cope with social alienation. This was a less common justification for drug use, which was often described as pleasurable—at least at first. (In the pages below, we will see that many people, especially the privileged, first experimented with drugs in a pleasurable way with their peers or family members.) But some disadvantaged people described drug use as a way to escape their lives rather than find pleasure. For instance, Nicholas, a white man who grew up in a working-class household, experienced instability at home. Living with his mother, her new husband, and younger half-siblings, he felt "lost" and that he did not belong. "I just felt like not a part of the family," he told me. When he was twelve, his parents decided he would move in with his biological father. At the time, his mother had started seeing someone else (a different man from his stepfather). He felt "blindsided" by the move, describing it as a "traumatic experience" because "I was so close with my mother" but "butted heads" with his biological father. By sixteen, he suffered from depression and an eating disorder. His first time drinking and smoking marijuana were framed as attempts to cope with depression. "I don't know if the first time I drank I used alcohol to sort of escape from that," he said. "But, I do know that when I started drinking I instantly fell in love with it." Later in his early adulthood when he moved to Florida to attend community college, his drug use developed more fully into a pleasurable act: "I got into club drugs—I got into a lot down there. I did a lot of things, a lot of crazy shit."

More commonly, people I spoke with framed drug use as arising from the necessity of coping with physical pain. This justification was more common among white people in the study across class lines. For instance, Amanda, a white woman raised by two college-educated parents (one an engineer and the other a project administrator at a pharmaceutical company), developed an addiction when she was injured on the swim team in high school. "That's when I had my first painkiller," she said. By the time she enrolled in college, she was taking prescribed and unprescribed painkillers regularly: "My addiction had progressed, you know, all these years. Painkiller to like, like Percocet and Vicodin to Oxycontin. So, I did that for a few years, then to Suboxone. Tried to get off Suboxone. Went to kratom, which is still legal to buy."

Like Amanda, Kevin also turned to illegal painkillers after an injury. A white working-class man from Kentucky who moved to Boston as part of his work in the carpet-selling industry, Kevin injured his back on the job. A doctor prescribed him Percocet. But when his prescription ran out and he was low on cash, he tried heroin—a much cheaper alternative. Kevin said:

> I was running out of medication. Couldn't get it here; doctor wouldn't prescribe them here. You know, it was Percocet. And somebody gave me heroin. Of course, I didn't know it was heroin. They said, "Here, just sniff this." So, I did. I threw up, threw my guts up. And . . . just continued doing it. You know I would do it, stop, leave, go do a job, come back. You know, I always came back to it. And then, it got to where I was looking for it.

While some privileged people explained their drug use as a response to physical disability and pain, it was far more common for the privileged to account for their illegal behaviors—especially drug use—as a pursuit of pleasure.[22] Seeking diversions from school or inattentive parents, many were lured in by the excitement of harmless, infrequent transgressions that eventually morphed into more-serious, recurrent addictions and other illegal activities.[23] Partying—whether with friends or even family—was a common backdrop for experimenting with drugs, especially among white middle- and working-class people. Jason, a tall white man with dark brown hair, recalled his pleasurable relationship with alcohol and drugs. Jason's mom was a clinical psychologist, and his dad was a business manager who co-owned several nightclubs with his sister. Jason spent weekends in these nightclubs with his father. His first drink was at thirteen during one of his older sister's keg parties at their house, where they stored the alcohol they sold at the club:

> It was my sister's keg party. She used to throw keg parties, and we had booze because my family owned nightclubs. And we had boxes of booze like this, and I remember the first time my sister got drunk, and they were drinking bottles of Absolut Vodka in my aunt's basement from the club that was stored in the basement. Lots of parties.

Others similarly recounted drinking or using other substances during family gatherings and parties. Kema, a white woman who grew up middle class in California, said her father actively supported her underage drinking. An engineer who drank a six pack of beer a day after work, Kema's father laughed about her alcohol consumption, viewing it as harmless. "I think my parents put it [alcohol] in the bottle, seriously. Seriously. . . . My father would find empty bottles of alcohol in my car, and it was a joke. He would say 'I have to get you this [alcohol] because you like it,'" Kema recalled.

Outside the home and among peers, drinking and drug use were also described as pleasurable. J. M., a white man who grew up amid considerable material wealth (his father was an engineer and business manager who held an MBA from a prestigious university) in Milton, a suburb south of Boston, started drinking heavily with friends in his early teens. When he moved to New York to attend college part time, he was well into the party scene:

> So I moved to New York, and we got an apartment on 75th and Broadway. And I started getting little jobs and started going to school at night. And my dad got me a car. And then I moved to Brooklyn and got a job. I was sort of able to support myself. Took me five years, but I finished college. And I loved being in New York because there was a lot of chaos and insanity and going to clubs. You know, this was in the eighties, and it was unbelievable. I loved it.

J. M. recalled that his alcoholism resulted in several minor car accidents. But his parents enabled his destructive behaviors, sending him money to buy new cars: "I'd be drunk and not take care of the car and just smash it up, and he [his father] would send me ten or fifteen grand to buy me a new car."

Selling drugs was sometimes recounted with a sense of pleasure and excitement among the privileged. For Amanda, mentioned earlier, selling marijuana in college was wrapped up in the new joys of young adulthood: living on her own and beginning a serious romantic relationship. Her freshman year of college, she fell for a boy on the swim team, who also happened to be running an involved drug operation, selling marijuana to other students. Amanda moved in with him and started selling too, driving with him to Vermont to pick up "fairly large quantities of marijuana" to bring back to campus. I asked Amanda if she ever thought they would get caught by the police. She told me that the possibility was never really on their minds:

> I don't know if it was just young stupidity, but we both had that "it can't happen to us" mentality. Um . . . we thought and felt we were being careful. Everything seemed to be working, so I didn't think that we could get caught. I don't know why. I mean, we knew to drive a little over the speed limit—not speeding—[and to] get the car checked out before each trip, you know? I feel like some precautions were made . . . but not really any serious thought on what would happen if we did [get caught], or [that it] is a real threat that we could get caught. It was only when we were arrested, charged, and convicted that things fell apart.

Amanda did not sell drugs out of economic necessity, as did Tim, Gregory, and Royale. Rather, she sold because she enjoyed using the drug and found it to be a meaningful aspect of her relationship with her boyfriend. After her first arrest for selling drugs, she remembered thinking: "I was stupid and young and felt I was in love for the first time. And my partner had been tragically ripped from me by the, you know, the legal system, and our stupid decisions."

Although pleasure was a more common account among privileged people, some disadvantaged people also described delinquency as pleasurable, especially when it occurred among peers.[24] Royale and Joseph revealed that pleasure and constraint can coexist in people's justifications. For Royale, a black man who grew up poor in Brooklyn, "fighting" and "fooling around" in school was a pleasurable diversion amid a violent and unsafe learning environment. "I was infatuated with the street life at a very early age, you know. I was really attracted to it," Royale said. For Joseph, a black man from Roxbury, it was outside school and among peers where he felt the "appeal" of "the streets." After his first arrest, he felt proud. He was "one of the cool guys. And I felt good because, man, you went to jail. Like, my chest is gloating a little bit. Like, you accomplished something." Still, both men simultaneously felt constrained by hard economic realities. Moreover, growing up in poor communities sometimes brought trouble by accident, given peer associations. Joseph recounted being stopped and frisked by the police one day while he was playing street hockey with his friends. Only one of his friends had marijuana on him, but all the boys were arrested. Just as the meaning of crime is racialized and classed, so too is the policing of crime, often to the detriment of black people, Latinos, and the poor.

## The Policing of Crime

Although everyone in this study was caught at some point in life for allegedly violating a criminal law, the privileged described to me very different encounters with police over the course of their lives compared with the disadvantaged. And the differences in those encounters have important ramifications—from the likelihood of arrest, to a person's opinions of the police and the criminal legal system, to their likelihood of committing further crimes. Tim, the disadvantaged black man who opened this chapter, has been arrested eight times in his life—almost triple the three arrests of Ryan, the privileged white man at the beginning of this chapter. This pattern is reflected across the people I interviewed: if you are disadvantaged, you have been arrested more times than your privileged peers.[25] But more remarkable than these numbers, which might not be representative and likely come as little surprise, is the *quality* of these police experiences and what people learned from them. What Tim has experienced from police and learned from his encounters is different from what Ryan has experienced and learned.

Here I explore how these varied encounters with police are understood by the people in the study—understandings that have implications for what it ultimately means to be a privileged defendant or a disadvantaged one. People's accounts of their experiences avoiding and negotiating police interactions reveal that it is far more difficult and far less distressing to be arrested as a privileged person than it is to be arrested as a disadvantaged person. Whereas the privileged people I spoke to recount ease in avoiding police officers, and instances of being given the benefit of the doubt or provided second chances when they are stopped, the disadvantaged recount constant police surveillance—both of themselves and their communities—as well as perceptions of police being racist and classist. Consequently, when disadvantaged people in this study become criminal defendants, they are less likely to view court officials as trustworthy or legitimate.[26] The dynamics of police encounters, therefore, set the stage for understanding both the profound mistrust disadvantaged defendants bring to their attorney-client relationships, as well as the surprising willingness by the privileged to trust their lawyers.

Nearly all the people I spoke with described their efforts to avoid police, sometimes with glee and sometimes with terror. In interviews, I asked people, "Have you ever been stopped by the police for doing something illegal but ended up not being arrested?" This question elicited vivid tales of not just striving to negotiate with police, but also striving to avoid police altogether. Avoiding the police is necessary to avoid other forms of contact with the criminal legal system—from arrest to court processing, from the revocation of your probation to incarceration. Successful avoidance was more commonly reported among the middle class (especially the white middle class) in the study, whereas poor whites and people of color across class backgrounds often reported difficulties. These accounts align with what we know about the concentration of police activity in poor communities of color in Boston as well as the poor's lack of access to private space.[27]

Private space was often mentioned as important for avoiding the police. The home, or lack thereof, was especially salient. For instance, Kareem, a black man who works part time at a clinic but has recently been staying in a homeless shelter, described the importance of doing drugs privately. At the time of our interview, marijuana possession in small amounts had been decriminalized in Massachusetts.[28] Regardless, Kareem did not trust police to go easy on users. He told me that many officers have an "old school attitude," and that regardless of the law, he does not "need the hassle" of them asking him questions. Since living in the shelter, it has been hard for him to smoke because you have to do it "off the premises and, you know, you need to be low key." In the past, he used to smoke at his uncle's house, where he felt completely safe:

> I'll go to a secluded area, or I'll go to an area where I know [there's someone] who doesn't mind [me] smoking as long as it's on the back porch or it's in the basement or something . . . like my uncle's house, for instance. When the kids are asleep or they're not home, I can smoke in his house; he doesn't mind.

As in Kareem's experience with homeless shelters, others who had stayed in shelters described the difficulty of using drugs in public. Some found that the risk of being removed from a shelter for using drugs on the premises was lower than the risk of being caught by police doing drugs on the street. Keith, a black man addicted to heroin who has cycled in and out of shelters and low-income housing since he lost his job as a cook, told me:

"I'm safe at all times. I'll be in the shelter. I will not be out here [on the streets] doing drugs."

When engaging in illegal activity in public, people described attempting to avoid police by choosing specific, familiar neighborhoods or street corners that they perceived to be safe from surveillance. When buying or selling drugs, many recounted how a lack of familiarity with the place made them vulnerable to being caught. For instance, Troy, a white man in his midtwenties with a boyish face, recounted how unfamiliar he was with the alley where he was arrested for drug possession. A former marine without a job, Troy became addicted to heroin while serving in Afghanistan and has spent most of his time back in the United States seeking and using dope. He told me that a year prior to our interview, he had driven to an alleyway to meet a heroin dealer. After the exchange, the dealer had returned to his apartment through a side door, leaving Troy alone. As he walked out of the alley, he was caught: "I walked back down an alleyway, and the cops immediately surrounded me, all plainclothes with badges around the neck and stuff like, and they came up on me. They came up on me so quick—they had already been watching me. They had been watching for a while, and I didn't even know."

For those who sold drugs, engaging in deals in public also presented a risk. Many caught selling in public believed they had been done in by confidential informants. To mitigate risk, some described shifting the responsibility of selling in public to trusted "runners"—friends, family, or "employees" who would not snitch on them if caught. For instance, William, a husky black man who currently works for an addiction recovery organization, told me that after his first arrest in his late twenties for selling cocaine, he felt pressure to unload his cocaine supply before he was incarcerated. He had "almost a little more than an ounce of cocaine in [his parents'] basement." To sell it, he enlisted his girlfriend: "So I had to let her in on the deal to let her know what's going on and I had to give her such and such, you know, just having to sneak."

People without homes, or who regularly hang out on the street, recounted how they were bothered by police, even when they were not doing anything illegal. Over time, police officers would come to recognize them by name and engage them. Michael, a skinny white man with a shaved head, recounted constant police surveillance—and even harassment. "I was running away from the cops all the time," he told me of his high school experiences. His first arrest was at fifteen for violating a restraining order to stay away from a girl he was dating. Having spent most of his adult life in and out of homeless shelters and addiction recovery organizations, he has become known to police in Boston, Somerville, and Cambridge. He is most worried about the Cambridge Police Department (CPD). Several CPD officers "have seen me or recognize or, you know, and then they'll be like 'Oh, I remember him. Oh, yeah, Michael,' and then they run my name and make sure I don't have any warrants." Michael now finds it nearly impossible to avoid being stopped by police when going about his daily round. He complained to me that many police officers feel that they can stop a person for any reason, such as "acting suspicious. How the hell do you act suspicious?!" Michael concludes: "To them, we're all guilty. We're all guilty of something to them."[29]

Black people, regardless of their class background, commonly reported being bothered by police for simply going about their day, especially in their adolescence.[30] They had an especially difficult time avoiding police when in public, even if they had never been arrested. Jimmy, a twenty-something black man with a well-trimmed beard, provides a typical example. The son of two college-educated parents, Jimmy grew up in a racially mixed and middle-income neighborhood in Cambridge. He recalled few police in his neighborhood growing up: "Not where I grew up. . . . The closer you lived to City Hall, the less police presence." At the same time, he and his friends regularly drew the attention of police as they made their way through different parts of Cambridge, for school or to visit friends' homes. He told me:

> JIMMY: It was just random. Like . . .'cause when me and my friends
> used to walk home from school, that's when you have the police
> following us, [asking us], "Oh, what are you guys doing?" Or,
> "Where are you guys headed?" Like, watching what we do. That's
> what they were mainly doing.
> MATT: And so, they'd stop you and talk to you?
> JIMMY: Yeah. Like, "What are you guys doing?" It was mostly when
> I used to hang out in different neighborhoods. . . . I was just hang-
> ing out with my friends after school, but as soon as I go over there,
> I see more police presence than where I live. . . . "Stop hanging
> around here. You guys can't stand here. You guys have to move.
> You guys are too loud. This lady keeps calling us. Everybody has
> to leave now. It's curfew." That's what it was.

Such seemingly minor but constant forms of police surveillance could easily transition into arrest. Routine contact with police means that disadvantaged people, when they are engaged in illegal behaviors, are more likely to be caught. Even when this surveillance does not result in arrest, it nevertheless routinizes and normalizes police questioning among disadvantaged people and communities.[31]

By definition, everyone in the study has been arrested, which means that at some point (or for most of them, at multiple points), they were unable to avoid the police. When avoidance fails, the next option is negotiation. A person's ability to negotiate with a police officer depends, fundamentally, on the officer's willingness to give them the benefit of the doubt or offer them a second chance. Such police discretion is applied unequally. Conversation after conversation revealed to me how certain encounters allow for more room to negotiate than others, and how social ties with police and cultural markers of respectability are important determinants of what happens next. Not surprisingly, these resources are often available to white middle-class and working-class people but far less available to the poor and people of color.

Negotiation with police is more likely to be successful during routine stops than more-constrained encounters. Terry stops, commonly known as "stop and frisks," occur frequently in Boston, especially in black and Latino neighborhoods.[32] Such stops occur, by law, when police have reasonable suspicion that a person is committing a crime. Often, though not always, Terry stops include questioning, searching, and even detaining the stopped individual. When encountering the police through a Terry stop on the street or a traffic stop following an officer's reasonable suspicion, stopped individuals have some room for negotiation because an arrest requires probable cause—a higher standard than reasonable suspicion alone. There is a chance that the stopped person will be let go after being questioned or detained, especially if no weapon or other illegal item is found on them. Some encounters with police, however, meet the standard of probable cause almost immediately; the most common examples are when police are executing a bench warrant, or conducting a search warrant, or arriving at the scene of a crime as it is unfolding after a 911 call. These kinds of police encounters are more constrained, affording people far less room for negotiation, even for the privileged. Such encounters are more likely to end in an arrest.

For instance, Amanda has several markers of privilege, including her whiteness and her middle-class upbringing; nevertheless, when police came to her home with a warrant, there was little room for negotiation. One of her and her boyfriend's marijuana customers ended up snitching on them, after he had been caught in possession by police. To get his charges dropped, he worked to build a case against Amanda and her boyfriend by coordinating an undercover buy. Weeks later, Amanda and her boyfriend heard a loud knock on their apartment door—it was the police. Amanda described what happened next in vivid detail:

> And they came in, pouring in! Like rifles up their chests, screaming—like, it was chaos, total chaos. I immediately knew what they were there for because like what the hell else could it be? Despite knowing why they were there, it was still like, just, I don't know. . . . It was really scary. I was, like, shaking . . . so they, um, they grabbed us, sat us down. They put—we weren't cuffed at all yet while they were doing their search. They had the search warrant, um . . . and had the, you know, one or two officers standing with each of us and then maybe half a dozen going through the rooms searching, tearing the cushions, as I said, emptying the trash, emptying cereal boxes out. Like, they searched everything.

Terrified, she and her boyfriend answered the officers' questions after they tore through their house. "I didn't know anything of my rights," she recalled. "I just knew maybe the more I cooperate with them, the easier it's going to be for me at the end." They were both arrested and charged for possession and distribution.

Aside from instances like Amanda's when police arrive at their homes with a warrant, most people in the study experienced police encounters that allowed some room for negotiation. Some privileged people reported that officers seemed to give them the benefit of the doubt, without any negotiation; others said they had to more strategically negotiate with officers to convince them to let them exit the encounter with their liberty intact. Middle-class people and white working-class people in the study were more likely to describe successfully presenting themselves as morally worthy and respectable or successfully relying on their friendships or family ties with police officers.

White people often recounted instances when police turned a blind eye to their illegal behavior, with little effort on their part. Ken, a working-class white man, described how he would often drink underage and be stopped, but not arrested, by police: "They'd catch us, but then they'd give us a break. Like, we'd pour out beer. Like, I had a cop in Philadelphia once, you know, smashed some cocaine on the ground and said, 'Get the hell out of here.'" Such benevolent treatment from police was particularly common among white people in working-class occupations. For instance, Jane, a college-educated white woman who works as an emergency medical technician (EMT), described how she nearly escaped being arrested for an OUI, despite being clearly intoxicated. The officers recognized that she was an EMT because of the boots she was wearing and the information on her

ID. After "calling in to their supervisors," they begrudgingly informed her that they had to arrest her. "I think they were going above and beyond just to make sure it was completely necessary [to arrest me]," she explained. At the police station, they were "particularly nice"—allowing her to delay taking the Breathalyzer test so that her reading would be lower. Jane attributed this leniency to the officers' respect for EMTs: "They were being friends rather than cops it seemed like. . . . Maybe they understood [my situation]. I know a lot of cops drink, and EMTs drink." Her boots were a shared cultural marker that signaled, with little effort on her part, that Jane was a worthy individual.

Others more actively tried to present themselves as worthy of the benefit of the doubt or a second chance when interacting with police. Among those who successfully avoided an arrest, being respectful, cooperative, and likable were often mentioned as key. Wolf, a working-class white man in his late thirties, described one encounter on Cape Cod in his twenties. He and a couple friends were smoking marijuana in a car in the middle of a cemetery. At the time, he was working at a local pizza shop, which he knew was regularly frequented by police officers when they were on their shifts. He said, "I didn't even say [to the officer] where I lived. I just said I work at the pizza shop." Wolf believes that his respectful style, and his knowledge of the meaning of the pizza shop to many of the officers in town, helped him and his friends avoid arrest. After checking their IDs, the officer said, "I don't ever want to see you guys come back here again, all right?" and let them go without a citation. Wolf recalls:

> I'm like, "No problem. Thank you very much!" I'm just thinking that [mentioning the shop] had to have done it. It had to have helped, you know? Or maybe it was the fact that we weren't assholes about it. We denied it [even though it] was blatantly obvious. And it was just weed. [The officer probably thought:] "Well, it's not crack, you know. They're not beating somebody up."

The power of these cultural presentations is confirmed by police officers I interviewed.[33] On a ride along with two officers, I learned how they differentiate between civilians they should arrest and those they should not. Their decision making is based, in part, on their views of whether the individual is a morally worthy member of society. For instance, one of the officers explained that he sometimes must decide whether he should arrest a person or send them a summons in the mail to appear in court. He bases his choice on whether the person appears worthy of leniency. He told me, "If they are a person with a car, with a baby seat in the back of the car, and they're on their way home to their wife after going out to get milk, it's not worth it for that person. Especially if they don't have a long record of traffic violations and citations." He described how these middle-class cultural markers factor into his choice to arrest or issue a summons. Another police officer told me that his perception of a person's compliance and respect is part of his decision to arrest or let a person go—a common finding in studies of police officers' attitudes toward civilians.[34] He said, "If the person is compliant, respectful, polite, and well mannered, we won't ruin this kid's life." Recent social psychological research has shown that police officers are less likely to view African Americans and Latinos as exhibiting respect, even if they are behaving the same as whites.[35]

I additionally found evidence that *dis*respect appears to be racialized, to the benefit of some white people.[36] A small number of white people in the study described encounters in which they were able to avoid arrest despite being disrespectful. Paul, a white man in his forties with missing front teeth and gray hair, grew up the son of a college-educated police chief in a town north of Worcester, Massachusetts. An army veteran, Paul moved to Boston a few years ago in search of construction jobs. He regularly drives between Boston and Worcester to visit family. On one of these trips, he and his sister were stopped by state troopers just outside Boston for speeding. "He [the trooper] was giving my sister a hard time," Paul told me. So, Paul started yelling at him, telling him that he should learn how to be respectful:

> "Hey buddy, why don't you take a ride to Boston and see how real cops are? They treat you like you're human. They don't treat you like you're some backward piece of shit like you do, asshole." And he goes, "Well, I can arrest you for that." [And I say]: "Well, no you can't. Freedom of speech." . . . He just looked at me. "Do you want to arrest me? Arrest me!" Nothing he can do. It's called freedom of speech.

Paul and his sister received a $160 ticket, but they continued on their road trip. No blacks or Latinos in the study reported being able to get away with behavior like Paul's without being arrested.

Meanwhile, black people in the study sometimes reported experiencing racist suspicion from police even when they were respectful. For them, when avoidance and negotiation failed, their best hope was to prevent the situation from escalating.[37] Caleb, a young middle-class black man who suffers from chronic back pain, experienced police suspicion during a "well-being" check on his friend, ultimately resulting in Caleb's arrest. One afternoon, he learned that his friend was having a mental breakdown, so he rushed from Boston to her house about an hour outside the city to help calm her down. Just after he arrived, another friend called the police, concerned that their mutual friend was going to harm herself. When the police arrived, Caleb answered the door:

> There's a knock on the door. I go and open the door. . . . It's two cops. And they're like, "We're doing a well-being check." And immediately, I'm like: "She's not having a good time, and she's mentally unstable. She needs to go to a hospital, and she doesn't have her phone with her, so I can't call her dad, but I don't know where her phone is." And they're like, "All right. Put your hands up for a second." And immediately they start searching me. . . . "Do you have anything or any needles on you?" And I'm like, "I'm wearing a fucking suit. Do I have a needle in my pocket?" And I was just like, "No, I don't have anything illegal." . . . And then he goes and finds the CVS little pill container. "What's this? Bingo!" And he shows the partner, and the partner goes, "Yep, we got you!" "That's my prescription," I explained to them. "Listen, I have chronic back pain. I just went through surgery, and that's my prescription you have in your hand." And he's like, "All right, where's your prescription bottle?" And I'm like, "I can't carry nine pills with me everywhere I go." . . . They immediately put cuffs on me.

Caleb's experience shows how police can use a well-being check as a justification for reasonable suspicion to search a person. Caleb felt that the police refused to believe his insistence that his pills were prescribed to him in part because of their racism. He said, "Race was involved here. And I'm not a person who uses the race card at all. I grew up in Cambridge, you know. I've had it nice . . . but they just searched me from head to toe."

Social ties with police officers were mentioned as another invaluable resource among middle- and working-class white people. Living around and socializing with police officers aided them in negotiating out of encounters. Ryan, the middle-class white man who opened the chapter, recounted how he and some friends avoided being arrested in high school because the officer knew one of his friends' dad. Ryan described how the officer stopped them for reckless driving and saw several open containers of alcohol in the car. Still, the officer let the boys go with just a verbal warning:

> It was me, and one of my buddies. And he was driving, and I was in the passenger seat. And two more buddies in the back seat. They got a

thirty [case of beer] in between them, and I got one of them between my legs in front of me. Four open beers, and the guy pulls us over. He gets all of our IDs, and he's looking through them. He gets my buddy Kyle's ID. Kyle's dad is the [hockey] coach, and this guy [the officer] used to play hockey for the high school. . . . So, he looks at it and is like, "Are you so-and-so's son?" And then he's like, "Get the hell out of here." You know? There were a few times like that where we got by on the skin of our teeth.

Social ties can also help to mitigate future legal consequences, by providing information on strategies for negotiating police encounters or avoiding them altogether. Take the case of Stephen Douglas. Although his mother was college educated, and he attended a private Catholic school, he grew up in a mostly working-class community. His neighbors and relatives were construction workers, firefighters, and police officers. "I have two cousins who are cops," he told me. "I actually wanted to be a cop, but I got arrested my senior year, right before graduation." His relationships with his cousins have given him insight into police officers' discretion. Describing one of his OUI arrests, he reflected on how his cousin sometimes does not arrest people even when he knows they are driving under the influence:

> Cops. It's their discretion if they want to arrest you for DUI. He could have said, "Leave your car here and walk home." You know what I'm saying? My cousin is a cop in [city name], and he doesn't always arrest people for DUI. I know cops that don't. They don't always arrest people, unless of course you're shit-faced. You're shit-faced, then you shouldn't be driving. But if you have just had a couple of drinks—I don't know.

Stephen Douglas also told me that one of his cousins directly assisted him in avoiding police. His cousin alerted him to a confidential informant who was "ratting him out" to detectives working on a case in his department. Learning this information, Stephen Douglas told me he stopped selling heroin to this potential informant, fearing he might get busted. Such close ties to police are likely more common among people in similar socioeconomic and racial positions as most police officers—people who are white and working class.[38]

Choosing to serve as a confidential informant, as a negotiation tactic, can also prevent arrest. This negotiation tool depends not just on a police officer's perception of an alleged offender as someone with the skills to serve as an informant, but also on the civilian's willingness to "snitch." A couple detectives I spoke to described how confidential informants must be "reliable" and have a "basis of knowledge" with respect to a major drug distributor. When police provide the opportunity to serve as an informant, some people in the study reported agreeing to do so, but others reported refusing. For those who said they refused, they described how their morals prevented them from "snitching" or "ratting out" others.[39] Such beliefs were more often mentioned among working-class and poor people in the study. For instance, Justin, a white man who grew up in a working-class home in Somerville, told me that he refuses to serve as an informant. He expressed moral disapproval of being "a rat":

JUSTIN: "Hey, you want to make some money?" they ask. And you think, Hey, I can make some money, so of course! I need money, you know, who doesn't? Everybody needs money, right? So I've had them make the offer. A couple of times.

MATT: Why do you say no?

JUSTIN: Because I don't have it in me. It's not in my fabric. A lot of it is from my—you know, growing up with some of them. The day you're a rat, you know.

Others, like Don, a working-class black man raised in a middle-class home, described how they refuse to serve as informants because of the fear of retaliation. Don exclaimed: "It's dangerous, man!" "People [other offenders] find out," he said. Furthermore, when he was apprehended on drug charges, Don felt he had no reason to believe that police and prosecutors would drop the charges against him if he cooperated with them: "If I do something like this, these charges have to disappear; it's as simple as that. But they didn't want to do that."

In contrast to Justin and Don, Brianna, a working-class white woman who grew up in a middle-class home in Somerville, described how she has no qualms serving as a confidential informant. When officers arrived at her house with a search warrant and found drug paraphernalia, she recalled that an officer offered her a deal. She could avoid arrest if she would work with them to build a case against her supplier. She would have to make several staged transactions with the supplier. "The people I deal with know what they're getting themselves into anyway, so it's whatever," she told me, justifying her choice to be an informant to avoid being arrested and charged. Plus, the police "paid me $50 for each transaction," she said. Differing moral codes with respect to snitching could disadvantage some people in their efforts to negotiate with police. Moreover, police, not the people subject to their control, have the ultimate power to decide whether a person appears worthy enough to be offered the chance to serve as an informant.

## Conclusion

People take one of two general paths to becoming a criminal defendant—a path shielded by privilege or one besieged by disadvantage. To be sure, nearly everyone, no matter their race or class position, experienced social alienation in adolescence. Their widespread alienation is not a trivial matter. When we think about the injustices faced by those embroiled in the criminal legal system, we must take seriously the troubles faced by disadvantaged and privileged people alike. At the same time, this chapter shows that the troubles that emerge from people's social alienation in adolescence are seen and treated differently according to social status.

The structuring forces of race and class made all the difference in people's path to court involvement. The disadvantaged, like Tim, often framed their crimes as resulting from economic and social constraints. Drug use, drug dealing, and theft were viewed as a necessary means of survival by those who grew up poor, and by African Americans and Latinos who grew up in working-class homes. They recounted how experiences of homelessness, racist interactions in their neighborhoods and schools, and watching parents struggle to make ends meet contributed to pressures to sell drugs, rob convenience stores, or skip school. They more often recounted exposure to violence in school. The police were a constant presence in their neighborhoods and in the lives of their friends and loved ones. And when they reluctantly encountered the police, they found it difficult to negotiate their way out of arrest, given their inability to display the legitimated social or cultural resources valued by police officers, such as familial ties to police officers or being read by officers as respectful, cooperative, or agreeable. Many reported racism and classism from individual officers. Thus, alienation from the law and legal officials gradually grew alongside alienation from schools, family, and the labor market. Their experiences contributed to deep feelings of distrust of the criminal legal system, especially police, and mistrust and skepticism toward defense attorneys.

For privileged defendants, like Ryan, committing a crime more often emerged from pleasure rather than from constraint. Drug use and dealing were often described as enjoyable by white people who grew up in middle-class homes as well as several working-class white people in the study. Meanwhile, the police were not a punitive presence. When the police were mentioned in stories about their adolescence, they were often family members or the friends of parents. Avoiding police was easier, given the lack of punitive surveillance in their neighborhoods. When they were stopped by an officer, they often were able to fall back on social and cultural resources valued by police. They embodied respectability and were viewed as cooperative and agreeable, all markers of middle-class status. Some working-class whites also reported an advantage unavailable even to some middle-class people: close social ties to police officers. These ties afforded them second chances. Of course, these privileged people eventually found their way into the courts despite these second chances (after all, to be a part of this study, one must have been a criminal defendant). But their age of first arrest was later in life than that of disadvantaged people.[40] Moreover, many of the privileged recognized their relative advantages compared to the poor people of color they found themselves sitting next to in court and in jail. Their relatively privileged experiences contributed to a relative naïvete about the legal system and a greater willingness to trust legal officials, including defense attorneys.

This chapter contributes to enduring concerns in the social sciences about adolescence and delinquency. Scholars studying adolescence have shown the power of family and schooling in predicting later life outcomes. We know that everything from household income to physical health is influenced by the quality of a person's early education and the resources their families have.[41] Sociologists in particular have led the way in documenting how neighborhoods shape both the resources available to families and schools and the exposure to social and environmental harms, such as pollution or violence.[42] Because the quality of neighborhoods in this country—and the process by which people are sorted into them—is deeply unequal depending on your race and class, so too are the social, political, and economic resources available to the families, schools, and adolescents growing up in them.[43] In Boston, mostly white neighborhoods like the South End have more resources than mostly black neighborhoods like Mattapan.[44] It should come as no surprise, then, that the perils and possibilities of adolescent life look very different between these neighborhoods.

What is surprising, however, is that despite these differences, problems and crimes arise—and can even intensify—in pockets of affluence. Seemingly tranquil middle-class communities contain social problems that the media and scholars often ignore.[45] The reality of social problems and harms among adolescents in privileged communities and households should be taken more seriously. For more than a century, most scholarly attention has focused on problems in poor communities of color, where delinquency and violence are often depicted as ever present.[46] Much research has sought, and still seeks, to understand why the conditions of poverty, inequality, and racial marginalization might be criminogenic— and how different people take different paths with respect to crime over their lives.[47] Poor communities have been characterized as socially disorganized communities, and their residents have been characterized as both perpetrators and victims of disorder.[48] This research has produced important insights and has allowed for policy interventions meant to stem the very real threat of violence on certain blocks and street corners.[49] Yet, scholars have left largely uninterrogated the nature of criminal(izable) behavior that exists in privileged communities, at times unintentionally reinforcing harmful stereotypes about the urban poor by comparison. Recently, a handful of scholars have begun to examine drug dealing in white suburban communities and on college campuses.[50] This chapter contributes to this nascent work by comparing the adolescent narratives of privileged people and disadvantaged people in the same city in relation to drug use, drug dealing, and other crimes.[51] I show how neighborhood conditions, social ties, and presentations of worthiness and respectability structure both crime's meaning and the way it is policed.

As a result of their different paths to the same court system, people from privileged backgrounds learned to view criminalized behaviors as pleasurable and came to expect second chances from legal officials. The disadvantaged, meanwhile, learned to view criminalized behaviors as necessary and came to expect to be treated punitively. These everyday dynamics of American life—in which reality is experienced very differently depending on whether you are black or white, poor or wealthy—filter into the attorney-client relationship. As we will see in the rest of the book, the different paths taken influence the trust that the privileged and the disadvantaged are willing to place in their lawyers, as well as their broader orientations toward the law, legal knowledge, and court procedures. Their immediate experiences once inside court only reinforce these preexisting understandings, as the privileged experience ease of court navigation, and the disadvantaged experience frustration and resignation.

# CHAPTER TWO

# Disadvantage and Withdrawal

TONYA HAS OLIVE skin and dyed blond hair and has worked odd jobs "under the table" since she was fifteen, when she was employed for only a few days at a local convenience store. She is part white and part Native American. She has many of the markers of disadvantage—routine and negative encounters with police, few ties to empowered people, and little in the way of financial resources. When I first met her, in a food court in downtown Boston, she kept telling me about all the "public pretenders" who had represented her in court over the years. I asked her what she meant by the term. She responded: "Made and paid by the courts. [They] work for the courts. . . . They're all buddies with the district attorneys! They all go out drinking together after work." Such skepticism of lawyers came up again and again in my conversations with disadvantaged people but rarely in my interviews with the privileged, who less often rely on court-appointed lawyers. In the minds of the disadvantaged, defense attorneys—especially court-appointed ones—may technically be tasked with defending their clients, but in reality, they are only pretending to do so.

As we have seen, people in Massachusetts can be represented by three kinds of defense attorneys: privately retained lawyers, public defenders, and bar advocates. The latter two—public defenders and bar advocates—are known collectively as court-appointed lawyers. They are appointed by the court to represent indigent people who cannot afford to privately retain an attorney. The disadvantaged defendants in this study nearly always lumped all court-appointed lawyers together in the same category, despite public defenders' distinct training and regular access to resources such as social workers and investigators. The mistrust of all court-appointed lawyers was profound; the complaints, numerous. Some, like Tonya, felt that because they did not pay (or paid only a small amount) for the services of court-appointed lawyers, these attorneys could not be trusted to devote resources needed to advocate in their clients' best interests. A handful felt that court-appointed attorneys worked for the benefit of the government rather than their individual clients; keeping the legal bureaucracy running smoothly, it seemed, was a defense lawyer's primary goal, even in the face of abuse from police or prosecutors. Even more defendants were frustrated that their lawyers did not listen to their needs or understand their legal goals. Others, especially those who had been in the system for a long time, felt that their current lawyers could not be trusted because of their negative past experiences with the law, or stories they had heard from friends about lawyers who seemed uncaring, unprofessional, or just plain racist. For one reason or another—and often for several reasons in combination—about half of the disadvantaged defendants I interviewed reported that they did not feel their lawyers did enough to defend them, and even more expressed reservations, frustrations, and general mistrust. The bottom line was simple: court-appointed defense attorneys, as a group, could not be trusted to protect their interests or seek justice.

These various versions of mistrust all unfolded in one primary way: disadvantaged defendants withdrew from their lawyers. For a little under half of those who withdrew, withdrawal manifested as resistance.[1] These defendants were hesitant to accept their lawyers' legal expertise and instead worked to cultivate their own from their communities and through personal observations of court proceedings. From these sources, they learned about rights and court procedures that they should, by law, be afforded. Sometimes, they also learned that their personal goals—such as explaining the extenuating circumstances around their alleged wrongdoing or contesting corrupt police practices—were rarely validated as legitimate or possible legal outcomes. Immensely frustrated by the criminal legal system's lack of attention to their needs, they often contested their lawyer's recommendations in private meetings and sometimes in open court hearings. Their lay expertise also included knowledge about court-imposed sanctions, not just legal rights and procedures. Such experiential knowledge about court-imposed sanctions—such as awareness of the way police surveil their communities and target people on probation—sometimes constrained the legal options they perceived to be available to them, pushing them to make difficult, seemingly counterintuitive choices. In turn, lawyers sometimes withdrew from their most resistant clients, expressing frustration of their own or even spending less time on their cases. For the other half of defendants who withdrew, withdrawal manifested as resignation to the legal process. Mistrust of lawyers played a part here, but concerns about life's many other adversities played an even greater role.

A month after I first met Tonya, I went to court to watch her most recent hearing, a probation hearing related to a past drug case. Over the next couple hours that day and a month later during her final probation revocation hearing, I saw how many of her complaints about defense attorneys developed in small moments and unfolded to influence her case. Tonya's criticism of court-appointed lawyers as "public pretenders" was not just idle chatter. She enacted this criticism in her interactions with her lawyer, both in court and behind closed doors in their private meetings.

When we first met, Tonya had been arrested a few months earlier for violating the terms of her probation.[2] After spending a little more than a year in jail awaiting trial on a cocaine charge, she had been convicted and summarily released with time served but under probation supervision. Out on probation, she found herself in trouble multiple times—as she told me, first she had no place to stay on release from jail except a friend's house. The friend used cocaine and offered her some. She was arrested after failing a drug test. Her probation officer worked with her to find a sober house. She went for a few months but felt it "wasn't a good fit for me" because it involved too many therapy meetings and counseling sessions. Without her probation officer's approval, she sought out another sober house—a house that she was now finding to have its own problems. Now, she was facing a probation hearing to determine whether these various actions violated the terms of her probation. She was worried about the upcoming hearing. She willingly admitted that she "had a slip" but did not think she should be sent back to jail as a result.

Tonya had been down this road before. Growing up on public assistance in western Massachusetts, she dropped out of school in eighth grade and began using cocaine not long after. Now in her forties, she has been arrested twelve times in her life and has been on probation nearly as often. She has not had a steady job in years, even prior to her incarceration. Part of the reason, she told me, is that it has been hard to keep a job when so much of her time is spent either abiding by probation requirements or trying to avoid the police who cruise through her neighborhood. Currently, she is living in a women's sober house south of Dorchester in a largely working-class community; several times a week, she commutes to downtown Boston for various meetings with her probation officer and drug counseling and treatment groups.

The day of her first probation hearing, Tonya was annoyed. We were waiting in the hallway outside the courtroom. Her lawyer, a white female public defender named Mollie, was late. Mollie always seemed to be late. The court session had yet to start, but still, Tonya did not understand why she had to be on time, but Mollie did not. She went on to vent that Mollie "never has time to visit me during my probation meetings." Because her lawyer never seemed to be around to answer her questions or come with her to probation, Tonya decided to handle important aspects of her case on her own. Recently, she had been chatting with the women in her sober house about how she could get a letter from a psychologist who studies the brains of people with addictions; she planned to acquire the letter to show at her next court date. "He looks at how addicts' neurons work differently," she explained. This letter, she believed, would prove to the judge that she had a disease and thus could not be blamed for her recent cocaine relapse. Tonya also told me about a letter she acquired from an administrator at her sober house that shows she has been abiding by the house's rules over the past month. She stood up and began rifling through her large purse to find the letter. She pulled out a crumpled letter from the Department of Transitional Assistance, a welfare agency in Massachusetts. "Hmm, that's not it," she sighed. Just then, Mollie rounded the corner and greeted us.

The hearing that day was largely uneventful, and Tonya did not end up finding, much less using, the sober house letter she had mentioned to me. The judge informed her of the probation department's allegations, her rights during the next and final revocation hearing, and the potential consequences if she were to be found in violation of probation. Tonya was asked to return in a month for the final hearing and then excused. After leaving the courtroom, we moved to a small dimly lit room just between the exit from the courtroom and the main hallway.

There, Tonya and Mollie seemed to talk past each other. Mollie was concerned about Tonya abiding by her probation conditions between now and the final hearing. "More than anything, we don't want you locked up again," Mollie implored. But Tonya had her own concerns. Various nonlegal matters—some of which were a direct consequence of her probation conditions—seemed more pressing for her daily life. The sober house, where she was currently staying, was squalid. The house was overrun with mice. If she had to stay in the sober house, she wanted to know what could be done about the infestation. "Is there someone I can call?" she asked. Mollie sighed. She was not sure whom to call but emphasized that, above all else, Tonya must stay in the sober house because it was a probation mandate. After the meeting, outside the courthouse, Tonya rummaged through her purse and pulled out a cigarette. She lit it and sighed. She was frustrated by her attorney's insistence on "following the rules" no matter the cost to her personal life. And she did not quite understand her attorney's lack of knowledge about how to issue a complaint about her sober house. Tonya and Mollie's withdrawal from each other often meant that Tonya relied on her own instincts and knowledge of the legal system.

One month later, in her final probation hearing, the tensions between Tonya and Mollie bubbled to the surface in open court. Just before entering the courtroom, she told her attorney that she wanted a chance to tell the judge her version of events—to explain that she only used cocaine the first time she was let out because she was homeless, was almost raped, and had nowhere to sleep but her cocaine-using friend's house. She also wanted to explain that she left the sober house she was originally assigned to not because she broke any rules, as alleged by the sober house, but because of her dissatisfaction with the house's many requirements. Mollie cautioned against this strategy, telling Tonya the judge "doesn't want excuses"; he only cares about whether "you play by the rules [and] take responsibility." Tonya agreed that she would admit to violating probation and accept the probation department's recommendation that her probation be extended without prison time; but still, Tonya was eager to have the judge hear her side of the story. Part of her still believed that providing the context to her wrongdoing might mitigate the proposal to extend her probation time.

When they walked into the courtroom, Tonya had made up her mind to go with her gut. She would lay out her full story in front of the judge, no matter Mollie's reservations. The probation officer and Mollie presented their joint sentencing recommendation to the judge (an extension of probation, but no prison time). The judge asked Tonya if she had anything to say to the court before he ruled. Mollie turned toward Tonya, palms open, as if gesturing that she could speak if she wanted. Tonya took the opportunity. She began detailing the reasons for her relapse and criticizing the living conditions of her former and current sober houses, expressing her frustration that she would be sent to such facilities by the court. "The sober house is chaotic and instable—er, *un*stable," she explained. She continued: "It's a struggle staying sober. I'm not going to lie. I've been at this for thirty-some-odd years now. I don't think I have the brain cells left to get all of the info that they are trying to tell me in group every day." I could see from the back of the courtroom that the judge—sitting on the bench above her, eyebrows raised and lips pursed—was growing dubious. Tonya seemed to have sensed this shift in mood and quickly changed her tune: "I'm trying to learn and be responsible, Your Honor. And also, I want to apologize. . . . I'm doing the best I can."

After she sat down, the judge ruled. He ultimately followed probation's recommendation to reinstate her probation. She was mandated to remain on probation for two more years, at the least. But the judge left her with one final warning: "Undergirding all of this is you wanting to do things your way. I don't want to find out weeks from now that you violated again." His message was clear: the trouble was not the court's mandates but rather her unwillingness to abide by them.

This chapter shows how disadvantaged defendants like Tonya often mistrust their lawyers and, as a result, are more likely to withdraw into resistance or resignation. Both kinds of withdrawal call into question the dominant assumption among many scholars and journalists that criminal defendants, especially the poor, are passive actors in the criminal legal system. On the contrary, disadvantaged defendants are active and involved in ways scholars underestimate. They make concerted efforts to accrue knowledge about, and assert, their rights. The problem is, as we will see more clearly in chapter 4, that the particular way these defendants strive to be involved in the process is devalued by legal officials who silence, coerce, and punish them.

## Mistrust of Lawyers

Feelings of mistrust toward lawyers were common among disadvantaged defendants in the study. When I asked people about lawyers who had represented them, past or present, the phrases that I often heard included that a defense lawyer "doesn't even help you fight," "could have did a better job," is "working for the court, not me, " and "want[s] you to take a plea all the time." These feelings emerged even before I got to hear the details of defendants' lives and experiences in court: in the preinterview survey each person filled out, disadvantaged defendants were more likely than privileged defendants to report that they did not believe that their lawyer in their most recent case had done their best to defend them. In response to the survey statement "My lawyer did his/her best to defend me," black people and other people of color were slightly less likely than white people to agree, but class differences were even more striking.[3] No person in the study—white or black—who was currently middle class disagreed with that statement; but a majority of poor people did. To be sure, the survey question is not a direct measure of trust.[4] Yet, the race and class differences in their responses confirm the accounts that emerged, again and again, when these defendants told me their stories: the poorer you were, the more likely you were to be dissatisfied with your lawyer.

This prevailing attitude is, arguably, not surprising. After all, we know that poor people, and people of color, are more likely to be convicted of a crime and sentenced to prison. If a judge sentences you to prison, it would stand to reason that you would not be fully satisfied with the lawyer who was tasked with defending you.[5] Yet what I found was a far more complex and multiply reasoned rationale for this mistrust. Poor defendants, as well as working-class defendants of color, provided several reasons for their mistrust of their lawyers. What was initially most striking to me was that mistrust went far beyond dissatisfaction with their legal outcomes.[6] While some defendants certainly blamed previous lawyers for too much prison time or burdensome probation requirements, they also described more structural and a priori reasons for mistrusting lawyers, previous and current alike—reasons that had little to do with final adjudications and even went beyond issues with the specific case process itself. These reasons include skepticism about lawyers' incentives (given the structure of the indigent defense system and the pressures of high caseloads), cultural distance and a lack of common life experiences, and previous negative experiences with other legal officials.[7] Some of these reasons bear on the nature of defendants' interactions with their current lawyers—whether they felt the process of working with their lawyers was fair and respectful.[8] Other reasons bear on defendants' experiences in everyday life that give them reason to be distrusting of the system as a whole, no matter how the process of interaction unfolds with any particular lawyer.[9] Often, when disadvantaged defendants meet new lawyers for the first time, they show up already skeptical of the lawyer's willingness and ability to help.

The structure of the indigent defense system itself fosters mistrust. If you are middle class, you probably know someone who can refer you to a private lawyer. And you can perhaps even pay for that lawyer's services or can turn to friends or family for help. But if you are poor, you most likely do not have these options; instead, you have no alternative but to work with a lawyer assigned to you by the court. As described previously, two types of lawyers are assigned to indigent defendants in Boston: bar advocates and public defenders. Most disadvantaged defendants are likely to be represented by bar advocates, who represent about three-fourths of the indigent caseload.[10] Bar advocates and public defenders differ in some ways, but their clients rarely differentiate between them because the way they are assigned is the same. Both public defenders and bar advocates are typically assigned to clients at arraignment, when a defendant is formally charged. In any given arraignment session, there may be one public defender on duty among a few bar advocates, all of them sitting at the same table and wearing similar professional attire. Although bar advocates and public defenders are paid differently by the state, defendants pay the same fee—typically $150—to the court no matter who represents them. For the most economically disadvantaged, this fee is often reduced or waived.

Disadvantaged defendants regularly recounted mistrusting court-appointed lawyers as a group because they were perceived to be poorly compensated or underresourced. Royale, a working-class black man, expressed his belief that public defenders have no incentive to devote time to their clients' cases: "He's not getting paid enough, and half the time, the public defenders are working with the DA. So, they try to get you to take deals." Royale believes that court-appointed attorneys are not only poorly paid but also professionally compromised given their routine relationships with prosecutors—a point that Tonya, and numerous others, told me repeatedly. Robert, a working-class white man, similarly said: "Sometimes you get the feeling like a lot of these public defenders are friends with the DAs, you know. They don't want to fight them because they have to eat lunch together later in the day."

Moreover, disadvantaged defendants often believe that their court-appointed lawyers are burdened by too many cases. Their heavy caseload suggests they regularly make tradeoffs between clients. Thus, they cannot be trusted to devote the needed amount of time to any one client's case. Christopher, a white man who was raised in a middle-class home but has been jobless and has received Supplemental Security Income for years, told me:

> I mean, public defenders—I just don't think they have too much of a chance. I think it's a huge difference, a huge jump to hiring your own attorney. I think the results would be 100 percent different 100 percent of the time, you know? Um, I mean, I don't doubt she worked hard for me [but] she seemed flaky to me. I know public defenders have like huge caseloads and no time; you know, you're not the only person. I mean, a private attorney—if you get them—they're going to court for *you* that day. That's it. Public defenders could have like ten other people up there that they're doing cases with that day.

In the eyes of poor defendants, a heavy caseload creates perverse incentives: the best way for a lawyer to reduce their caseload is not to help their clients, but rather to coerce them to plea, or to refuse to make motions and other time-consuming legal procedures.[11]

Another frequently lamented component of the indigent defense system is the lack of choice in attorney assignment. After a person is arrested and charged with a crime, the first step in their court processing is to appear at arraignment. Here, the defendant stands before a judge who determines whether bail should be set and, if so, by how much. Before the arraignment hearing, nearly all disadvantaged defendants will have been assigned a lawyer by the court clerk. Typically, the lawyer will chat with their new client for a few minutes, discussing the details of the criminal charge, the police report, and any personal information the lawyer could use to make an argument for a more lenient bail decision, such as whether the client has a history of returning to court in the past and the client's financial circumstances. After the arraignment hearing, lawyers typically provide clients with information for how they should stay in touch. These brief first interactions set the stage for the rest of their relationship. Defendants assigned to court-appointed lawyers in this way often report feeling rushed and confused—and, importantly, bothered by their lack of choice in the lawyer they are assigned.

Caleb, the college-educated black man we met in chapter 1, was unemployed during his first court case due to a severe back injury and thus was assigned a court-appointed attorney at arraignment. He therefore experienced disadvantage for a moment, despite his middle-class status. Caleb described to me his ensuing frustration: "He gave me a card and was like, 'Call me.' And walked away. And I was like: 'That's it? I have a lot of things to tell you. Wait, wait.'" After several phone calls to his lawyer went unreturned, he went online:

CALEB: I did a little bit of research online and I was like, "You know what? I'm going to ask for a new lawyer."

MATT: I see. Were you nervous to ask for a new lawyer in front of the judge? What was your experience like asking for a new lawyer?

CALEB: It was like I had a written statement prepared, so that made it a lot easier because I didn't realize how on the spot I would be. I just thought I'd go to his office and be like "Hey, I'd like a new lawyer," but, um, I didn't realize how much of a big deal they make it. Um, so I, um, had a written statement, and I just read the written statement, and he was like, "Okay, that's fair."

MATT: So, you sort of—what was on your statement? Like, what was your justification?

CALEB: I said I didn't feel comfortable that this person had my interests at heart 100 percent. I'm not sure how many clients this person has but, um, you know, I don't feel completely comfortable that my, um, rights will be protected and my case will be treated the way I want it to be. And that's pretty much the gist. I don't know if I used those exact words, but that's pretty much the gist.

Caleb's efforts paid off. He was assigned a new lawyer, and they got along beautifully. The lawyer was "an old man" who was "so jolly and clearly loved what he did [for a living]." "He was happy to deal with me," Caleb remembered. Ultimately, his case was dismissed. But Caleb, a highly educated man whose concerns about his assigned lawyer were taken seriously by the judge, is the exception.

Most disadvantaged defendants who wanted to change their lawyers reported difficulty doing so. People described how judges would rarely allow them to be reassigned counsel. Kevin, a working-class white man, lamented being stuck with his lawyer: "I tried to fire him, and the judge wouldn't let me." Tonya, describing to me a court case several years ago, recalled the unique complexity of trying to obtain a different court-appointed lawyer while she was incarcerated while awaiting trial. One day when she was taken from jail to appear at one of her court hearings, she tried telling the judge she would like a new lawyer. "They were like, 'What is wrong with him? He's representing you perfectly fine.' And I was pissed, like: 'I don't feel he's doing the right job for me.'" After returning to jail, she tried writing letters to the judge:

> I would put letters into the court saying, "I want to change my lawyer." I would get nowhere. I wouldn't hear back, and then I'd be in the court-room, and I'd be like, "I don't feel I'm getting correct representation." [And the judge would say:] "Why haven't you sent anything in?" I said, "I've sent several papers. I have copies of them." "Well, do you have documentation that you mailed these out?" I said, "Well, if I knew I needed that, I would have gotten copies before I came here."

She ultimately gave up, realizing the judge would not budge. One court-appointed attorney told me that judges do not want defendants "shopping for new attorneys," and so they require "strong justifications" for reassigning counsel.

Cultural differences between disadvantaged defendants and their assigned lawyers also frustrate their relationships. In everyday interactions, people from different social backgrounds are less likely to develop trusting relationships than people from similar social backgrounds. The barriers to establishing cross-group trust have been demonstrated across various fields, through laboratory experiments, interviews, and survey data.[12] In particular, people of lower social status are more likely to find it difficult to trust people from a higher social status to assist them in accomplishing specific tasks.[13] The attorney-client relationship is inherently asymmetric, given that a lawyer has professional expertise and license to operate as an officer of the court, and their client—unless they are a lawyer themselves—does not. No matter the socioeconomic or racial status of the client, the lawyer inherently has more power in court. Beyond the inherent power asymmetry of any professional-client relationship, working-class, poor, and racially marginalized defendants have the added disadvantage of being less likely to share everyday cultural experiences with their defense attorneys, who are mostly white and middle class.[14] Sharing cultural experiences, tastes, or worldviews (defined as "cultural matching" among sociologists) tends to facilitate trust, whereas not sharing these qualities of one's social standing tends to be grounds for mistrust.[15]

Black working-class and poor defendants were especially likely to tell me of this difficulty in finding cultural commonality. Even when their lawyer was black, many felt they could not establish a connection. For instance, Tim, the poor black man whose life story opened chapter 1, was initially excited that a lawyer on one of his cases was a black woman. When he met her at arraignment, he had high hopes that she would listen to him and take his case seriously. But they ultimately failed to establish a trusting relationship. After a few meetings, Tim recalled that she was "stereotyping me . . . like I was some drug dealer," because "so many black kids come through there with criminal records." By contrast, "she was surprised that I had only, like, petty cases like trespassing." He was annoyed that she kept telling him how surprised she was that he had no major drug-related arrests on his Massachusetts record. Rather than sharing sympathies related to the drug war or police surveillance in black communities, this lawyer was, in his words, a "sellout"—"one of them type of [black people] who is like 'Yes, sir.' 'No, sir.'"

Other black defendants felt that white lawyers in general would not represent them well, given their presumed antiblack biases. Slicer, a black man with gray-green eyes and a strong Jamaican accent, works as a car mechanic and has been arrested twice for OUI. One of his lawyers was a white woman, and the other was a black man. Both were court-appointed attorneys who achieved similar outcomes for him—a CWOF with terms of probation. Nevertheless, Slicer described his white lawyer as a "white liar" who was "working for them"—the government. Meanwhile, his black lawyer was "looking out for a black brother in a certain way." He contrasted his experiences with each lawyer, concluding: "But when you're black and you have a white lawyer, you're tucked." Despite receiving very similar legal outcomes, the process of interaction with each lawyer profoundly defined Slicer's court experience. For defendants like Slicer, the attorney-client relationship itself can be an indication of justice (or its lack thereof).

When observing court, I noted moments when black defendants were overlooked or mistaken for another client—evidence, to some defendants, of a lawyer's racism. For instance, one morning I was sitting in a courtroom gallery next to four people—two black women and two black men. A white male lawyer turned from the front of the courtroom toward the gallery and whispered a woman's name, looking questioningly at the five of us seated in the gallery. One of the women raised her hand. The lawyer whispered, "Sorry, I had to do a double take to notice you. I wasn't sure if that was you!" The lawyer and the woman left the room to talk in the hall. When the woman returned minutes later, she—rolling her eyes— whispered to the other black woman in the gallery: "That was my racist fucking lawyer!" They both laughed. On another day in another courtroom, I watched as a black man's case was called during a pretrial hearing. The man approached the bar. An older white male bar advocate rolled up from the gallery and stood next to the black man, assuming the man was his client. After an awkward fifteen seconds or so, the judge looked up from his papers and said to the lawyer: "No, this isn't your client." Unfazed and unapologetic, the lawyer nodded and returned to his seat in the gallery as the court waited for the client's actual lawyer to arrive. I additionally observed four instances of what could be described as "subtle," or cultural, racism—when court-appointed attorneys made stereotypical comments about clients when chatting among themselves in courtrooms but off the court record.[16] The apparent absence of blatant racism in my observations should not be mistaken for a lack of it—my presence as a black man may have diminished the likelihood that I would witness such racism. What this book ultimately demonstrates, moreover, is that racial injustice today need not depend on blatant racism to thrive; rather, such injustice is perpetuated through the silencing and coercion of disadvantaged defendants.

Defendants' prior negative experiences and observations can, in turn, carry over into future relationships. Bad experiences with lawyers, judges, police, and other court officials often weighed on people. These experiences taught them to be skeptical of legal institutions, and thus prompted immediate mistrust of a newly assigned lawyer. Richard, a working-class black man who wore a New England Patriots T-shirt to our interview, described the legal system as "the New Jim Crow."[17] After spending years in prison, he came to realize the many ways the system exploited him and other black people. For instance, he articulated how paying to use phones in prison is exploitative: "I'm a slave to these people. . . . They have this new system which is generating money, which is slavery in disguise in my eyes. And now you expect me to pay them to call you and assist in the downfall of our people?" When I asked Richard about the first time he was arrested, when he was in his teens, he told me how he tried to work with his court-appointed lawyer. But nowadays, he has come to view that relationship, and indeed all relationships with court-appointed lawyers, as problematic. He said:

> The lawyer doesn't give a fuck, because they work hand-in-hand with the DA and the judge. So, they know exactly what the outcome of each case is going to be. At the end of the day, he's talking to them hand-in-hand, you know. These people, after they leave [court], they go sit and do lunch. They sit; they go to each other's family's houses. . . . It's pretty much he [the lawyer] doesn't give a fuck. If you pay them money, they give a fuck.

Among the people in this study, it was quite common for them to recount trusting their first lawyer the very first time they were arrested. But after repeated involvement with court, they slowly came to develop many reasons to distrust the legal system and to mistrust future lawyers.

The relationship between disadvantaged defendants and their lawyers is certainly an odd one—you are assigned a person you have never met before who is suddenly granted access to the most personal, and sometimes bleakest, parts of your world. And that person is, at the same time, responsible for shaping the next months, years, or even decades of your life. Though odd in many ways, the attorney-client relationship is quite similar to many other professional-client relationships, such as that between a doctor and patient or a teacher and student. These relationships often require trust if they are to function to the benefit of clients. The same is true here. Mistrust both indicates and sets the stage for tension between lawyers and defendants.

## Resistance

Given their mistrust, disadvantaged defendants often experience multiple moments of tension with their lawyers as they deal with their court case. When their lawyers seem unwilling or unable to help, they cultivate their own legal knowledge and skills and attempt to use them in court or to pressure their lawyers to make particular legal decisions. Defendants' small and large "everyday forms of resistance" are sometimes "hidden" from their lawyers but other times appear more explicit, such as when disagreements about legal strategy boil over into outbursts in court.[18] Some defendants even contest what should be considered a preferable legal outcome. For example, where a lawyer might assume their client would prefer a sentence of probation to a sentence of incarceration, some disadvantaged defendants prefer the opposite given the realities of police surveillance in their communities and the costs of being arrested while on probation. A choice of prison over probation makes sense if it means freedom sooner.

At root, resistance constitutes a struggle over legal expertise—over what legal rules and procedures should be employed during a criminal court case and who has the power to employ such tools. Legal expertise in the criminal legal system can be understood as a combination of knowledge about criminal law and procedures and the skills and relationships used to put such knowledge into action.[19] It is a cultural resource that court actors—from lawyers and judges to criminal defendants—can wield both during and between court proceedings to alter legal outcomes to their benefit. Although many disadvantaged defendants are surprisingly well informed about their rights and court procedures, as we will see, their legal knowledge is less precise and less legitimated than that of legal professionals. Theirs is a lay form of expertise. Defense attorneys, prosecutors, and judges, however, are professionals; they are licensed through bar associations and have access to specialized knowledge about case law and legal procedures acquired in law schools and honed in the daily practice of law. These court officials are also courtroom regulars; their repeated practice and presence expands their professional expertise and gives it value and legitimacy among their peers. By contrast, defendants cultivate their expertise through family, friends, and their own informal legal education in jail or in observation of court proceedings. They gain experiential knowledge of how legal sanctions operate in their personal lives and communities. Thus, defendants' expertise may not be legible to professionals, whose expertise is shaped by the professionalized norms of the law schools where they studied and the expectations of the courtrooms where they practice.

Nearly all defendants in this study recounted cultivating legal expertise to some extent, but poor defendants of all races and working-class defendants of color were more likely than their privileged peers to cultivate more specific kinds of knowledge about rights and procedures and to struggle with their lawyers. Defendants like Drew (from the book's introduction) and Tonya (from the beginning of this chapter) embody the typical attorney-client relationship characterized by withdrawal and resistance. They both disagreed with their lawyers' and the court's characterization of their alleged crimes and approaches to handling their cases. Amid their ongoing involvement with the criminal legal system, they also cultivated their own lay legal expertise, which they used to make sense of their legal rights and advocate for themselves. For instance, Drew expressed frustration with both of the lawyers initially assigned to his case. His first lawyer ignored his insistence that he correct the court record at arraignment and clarify that he had a concurrent knife possession case. Drew felt this fact would be important in reducing his bail amount, whereas his lawyer seemed unworried about correcting the record. Later, Drew and his second lawyer, Tom, could not agree about the legal strategy of pursuing several motions. Through his cultivated legal expertise, Drew had learned about, and insisted on pursuing, motions that Tom felt did not apply to his case. Their disagreement was intense at times, resulting in them ending on bad terms at one of their meetings and then, later in court during the motion hearing, Drew being unwilling to defer to the judge's norms.

In several moments, Tonya also withdrew from and resisted her lawyer, as she sought to put her own cultivated expertise to use. Her attempt to procure a letter from a psychologist (which she was ultimately unable to do) was one strategy her lawyer never affirmed would help. Nevertheless, she had spoken with the women in her sober house, and they had collectively understood that such a strategy could be useful for her case. During Tonya's final probation hearing, when the judge asked if she wanted to speak, she attempted to set the record straight on her own terms, providing justifications for violating probation, rather than heeding her lawyer's suggestion to simply admit fault. Tonya believed that doing so would provide the court a narrative that would excuse her drug use. But sensing her approach was not working, she ultimately followed her attorney's advice and was sentenced to a continued period of probation, with a stern warning from the judge.

Defendants described several ways they cultivated expertise. One way is by reading about the law. John Blaze, a working-class white man who could not make bail during one of his cases, told me that he read about the law while awaiting trial in jail: "I studied about my case. And I got all the paperwork. And I felt very confident about the case." Similarly, when I asked Gregory, a black Latino man who grew up poor, about his familiarity with legal procedures, he said, "I was studying it [in jail]. I kind of learned, and it was just reading and comprehending, you know?" He also described how jail and prison provided a community for cultivating legal expertise: "Just being around people like, you know, people, um, from jail, prison, like that . . . there were jailhouse lawyers." Prison—and sometimes jail—provides formal opportunities to read case law (that is, legal precedent about how criminal statutes and criminal procedures have been applied in real court cases, both in Massachusetts and federally). In Massachusetts, state prisons provide access to case law databases and other legal materials through their library services. According to the Massachusetts Department of Correction's regulations, access to these documents is provided to "every inmate."[20] Access to materials in prison—where those who have already been convicted of a crime are serving time (as opposed to jail, where many who are awaiting trial serve time)—provides already convicted people the opportunity to work on appealing their prior convictions. Often, they also strive to learn about the law in ways that will help them avoid future convictions. In our conversations, it was not uncommon for defendants to make analogies between their own cases and those they have read about in the past.

Ken, a working-class white man in his early fifties who works as a gym instructor, has cultivated legal expertise over the years, both through his own reading and by taking legal classes in prison. With tan skin, bulging muscles, and bright white teeth, Ken exuded a confident intensity during our interview. He was most animated when describing his lay expertise. While serving a stint in prison several years ago, he decided to take classes to avoid future problems. He told me:

> I took constitutional law. I like the law. You know, when you're incarcerated, you know, some guys do, and I think everybody should get to that law library and look at your case and learn about it. If you're going to commit a crime, you want to learn how not to be caught. It's like if you're going to be a mechanic: you need to study some car manuals, I'd imagine.

While incarcerated, Ken used his cultivated expertise to assist fellow incarcerated people. For instance, he described helping another incarcerated person file a motion to resolve a bail problem:

> KEN: I helped another kid get $100,000 back that his mother put up, um, and he violated, um . . . the conditions of his bail so . . . the city prosecutor's office was trying to, um, seize the bail money, and they did seize it. And I filed a motion, citing a language barrier because his mother does not speak one word of English. And

I cited *Ramos*, which is active law—an act of God—so in other words they have to. . . . There's a hurricane and I can't get to court so I forfeit my bail. This guy couldn't get to court because the dumbass got caught the night before court selling drugs, and he was in another courtroom that morning under a new charge. *Ramos* was word for word verbatim. That's gold. So we shepardized and cross-referenced, and you find the precedent or you create your own. You do it, and if you get in front of the right judge, they get shocked! If you word it properly and frame it correctly and support it? But they don't like to see first of all citing cases that are overturned. I mean—

MATT: Judges don't like to see—?

KEN: Yeah, you're wasting their time! They don't like to see anything pro se first of all. Okay? And . . . [For example, say that] [t]here's a PhD kid, and you earned your PhD, and you go into your field, and the last thing you want is some, some, um, you know, some self-taught guy who doesn't have the proper credentials, who knows just enough to kind of bullshit someone.

Ken's account reveals two important realities about why the cultivated expertise of defendants is devalued by court officials. First, that expertise may be imprecise or unclear to legal professionals. Ken's citation of *Ramos*, for example, may have been unintelligible to legal officials who establish their own routine references to certain cases.[21] In another interview, I asked a public defender who regularly practices in Boston whether she was aware of such a case; she was not. Her lack of awareness about *Ramos* suggests that even if *Ramos* is the name of an appellate case, it is not one that is regularly cited and thus might not seem useful in the eyes of the judge. Second, and as Ken acknowledged, judges rarely listen to defendants who attempt to use their expertise without the mediation of their lawyer. Ken said, "They don't like to see anything pro se," meaning judges, he believes, prefer defendants to make legal arguments through a lawyer rather than without representation. It was unclear from Ken's story whether his suggestion ultimately proved decisive in helping his fellow incarcerated person who violated his bail conditions.

Another way defendants cultivate expertise is through observation. In Boston courthouses, defendants can spend all or part of their day in court in hallways, in lockup, in a holding area in the courtroom, or in the gallery. Defendants who are not detained in lockup often sit in the gallery waiting for their cases to be called. Sometimes, family or friends are by their side. During recesses, people can be seen whispering with their families or watching as court officers make casual conversation with one another. They may overhear lawyers talk about everything from their clients' cases to the morning news. Other defendants may take a break to go smoke outside, grab a bite to eat, chat briefly with their lawyer, or sit idly in the hall. Over a muffled speaker, a court officer or clerk alerts everyone when they need to return to the courtroom gallery: "All parties with matters in the third session, please report to the session." For defendants held in the lockup area, most of their time is spent sitting and waiting among other detainees in rooms or cells out of view of the courtroom, sometimes in the courthouse basement. While some detainees may swap stories, many of them sit quietly, too scared to talk or too far gone under the influence of drugs to be aware of their surroundings. When they are taken into the courtroom, they sit on wooden benches in a holding area, often enclosed by glass. When their case is called, they stand near a circular opening in the glass that sits at about neck level. They crane their necks toward the opening, alternating between sticking their ears through the hole to listen to the proceedings and sticking their lips through the opening to whisper to their lawyer or answer a judge's question.

These places in the courthouse each present opportunities to observe and learn. Defendants learn from the arguments and strategies they see other defendants and lawyers use. They can glean some limited understanding of how the law appears to operate—on the ground, in real-world courtrooms, and in front of judges. When sitting in on an arraignment session in the gallery or in the holding area waiting for their case to be called, for example, a defendant who is at the end of the docket that day has the chance to watch the bail arguments of the five or ten or thirty cases before theirs. That defendant can gather information about what kinds of cases receive what kinds of bail amounts, as well as any pet peeves of the judge who is about to listen to their own case. Similarly, when in a pretrial hearing session, defendants can observe various kinds of motions in action, noting the case law cited and the strategies lawyers and other defendants employ when articulating their reasoning in front of judges. Of course, the details of cases often differ in ways that are evident to court officials but may not be apparent to defendants, contributing to a defendant's knowledge about rights, procedures, and arguments that exist but may be irrelevant, at least in the minds of lawyers, in the defendant's particular case.

Don, a working-class black man who ultimately developed a trusting working relationship with his lawyer in his most recent case, cultivated legal expertise through observation. Unlike most other working-class defendants of color and poor defendants, Don had social ties to the police (his mother-in-law was a police officer) and was married to a college-educated woman who provided emotional support and strategic advice during his court case. Although Don ultimately experienced privilege and delegation, his initial encounters with his lawyer exhibited markers of disadvantage. He was hesitant to trust his lawyer at first but came to develop a positive relationship with him after his mother-in-law suggested the man was trustworthy. Before that, he had spent much of his time trying to cultivate expertise related to his heroin possession and distribution case. His hope for a sentence of drug treatment was buoyed by his observations. He told me, "I've seen it over and over again, where certain people get it: treatment facilities." He learned that the lawyers of people sentenced to drug rehabilitation often noted to the court various forms of evidence about their clients' histories of drug abuse. Don thus decided he would "keep documentation" of his own current and past drug treatment and history of substance abuse and share this documentation with his lawyer.

Almost inevitably, defendants also draw on what they have learned from their own prior experiences in court. Those regularly involved in court come to garner knowledge from their past—both with particular types of legal charges and with particular court officials whom they regularly encounter. In interviews, defendants with numerous arrests often remembered judges by name. Judges, in turn, recognized certain defendants. So too did court officers and other officials. Owen, a poor white man who has struggled with drug addiction since childhood, estimated that he had been arrested about 200 times in his life; his current public defender, Selena, confirmed to me that he appeared to have more than 150 cases on his Massachusetts record—two of which she has represented him on in the same courthouse. When I accompanied Owen to court, a black court officer recognized him: "What's up, boss, how you doin'?" he asked Owen. Owen replied, "Good, good." They continued talking about Owen's struggles with sobriety. I later learned, in a closed-door meeting between Owen and Selena, that Owen had developed a strong opposition to being on probation and taking part in drug court over the years, given his prior experiences with the same probation officers and drug court judges. He was currently on probation for one of his cases, despite not wanting to be, and was worried. "If I mess up, I'm worried about P. O. Hernandez violating me," he told Selena. Royale, a working-class black man who has been arrested fifteen times in life, described how past experiences taught him how to deal with routine cases, such as driver's license suspension.

Royale's driver's license has been suspended numerous times, almost always as a result of his legal entanglements. Although some people might hire a lawyer to deal with a license suspension, Royale insisted that doing so is unnecessary, given all that he has learned from his prior cases. "For certain cases you don't need public defenders—you don't even need a paid lawyer," he explained. "For a suspended license, you know, all they want you to do is fix your license and pay the fine. You don't really need a paid lawyer for that."

Talking to family, friends, and other defendants is another way people, especially the working class and poor, cultivate expertise. Disadvantaged defendants regularly talk about their legal cases—during downtime in courthouses, in their neighborhoods and in community meetings, and as a part of their work with justice-involved organizations. They bring their family and friends to court. For instance, Jade, a working-class black woman and one of Sybil's clients, brought a friend along to one of her court hearings. Jade insisted that this friend would be a witness for her if she went to trial. Jade remarked, "She'll testify. So will my dad. I'll bring them all. They *will* be my witnesses if need be. Promise." In this sense, some family and friends can directly contribute by formally participating in a defendant's case. Among the disadvantaged, family and friends serve as sources of alternative knowledge about the law that can be used to contest a lawyer's expertise. Friends and family can share stories and insights about the law, especially if they have been in similar situations. Such conversations can contribute to mistrust and legal cynicism as much as they can assist in the cultivation of legal expertise. But among the privileged, family—who often lack experience with the law—are more likely to serve as intermediaries between defendants and their lawyers, as we will see in the next chapter.

Troy, a white man in his mid-twenties with a boyish face and a high school education, described how he learned about the law from conversations in his neighborhood. Troy spent his childhood skipping school and "hanging out with the wrong crowd." But he was not arrested until very recently, for drug possession, at the age of twenty-five—older than the average age of first arrest for the people I spoke with. In his late teens, he joined the army and spent his early twenties deployed in Afghanistan and Iraq. There, he developed an addiction to heroin, which flowed freely through his army base. When he returned to the United States, he had trouble finding a job. His first arrest occurred in a small town an hour outside Boston, where he had driven to score dope from a dealer. Even though he had never been arrested before, he already knew how not to incriminate himself when interrogated by the police:

> TROY: [The police] were trying to make deals with me. They're like, "Who did you get that from? If you tell us who you got that from, we'll let you go." And sometimes that's true, but most of the time that's bullshit, you know what I mean? They just tell you that so you'll tell them things. I'm like: you just caught me with dope; you're not letting me go. Give me a break. [chuckles] Get out of here with that, you know what I mean?
>
> MATT: So they were interrogating you after arrest, and you were in the jail cell? Did they bring you to an interrogation room, or . . . ?
>
> TROY: No. They came down to talk to me a couple of times like, "Do you want to help yourself out?" And I'm like, "No thanks. I don't want to incriminate myself, thank you very much." I was my [own] lawyer. [chuckles]
>
> MATT: I mean, this was your first time being arrested, right—how did you know to not speak?
>
> TROY: Because I've had friends who have been in the system for a long time. And like I said, I know a lot of cops. Plus, for me, for me it's just common sense. They're not on your side.

Troy explained to me that his legal knowledge was acquired through his social ties with friends "who have been in the system" as well as his ties with the "cops" he grew up around.

Organizers in Boston have established community spaces for sharing legal knowledge in low-income and mostly minority neighborhoods. During my time in Boston, I spoke to an organizer in a community space a few blocks down the street from one of the district courthouses I frequented during my observations. This community organization engaged in "participatory defense," a grassroots approach whereby people, based on their own prior experiences with the court, share advice with others in their community.[22] The organizer I spoke to described participatory defense as a way for friends and neighbors to protect one another from the criminal legal system. Once a week, they hold a formal meeting. The goal of the meeting is not only to share legal knowledge but also to help people with ongoing cases prepare questions to ask their lawyers and strategize about how to pressure them to take their concerns seriously. "We want to push lawyers to work harder and be more zealous," the organizer told me. But when I asked about lawyers' professional expertise, she noted: "Lawyers do have expertise, and I recognize that. So, you have to know not to push too hard for some things. Sometimes they don't make arguments because they are not legally viable." None of the people in this study mentioned either participatory defense or this specific community organization, but the existence of such spaces speaks to how knowledge sharing has been formalized for at least some defendants. Striking a balance between cultivating legal knowledge, on the one hand, and being sure not to "push too hard," on the other, was difficult to put into practice for the disadvantaged people I met. Without formal community support, they often cultivated isolated knowledge about rights and procedures that should work in theory but were rarely effective in practice. The routine collective support that comes from formal community spaces practicing participatory defense could assist marginalized defendants in striking a balance in their interactions with lawyers as well as sustain collective efforts to resist mass criminalization in poor communities of color, as I argue in the book's conclusion.

Incarceration in jail or prison can also provide a space for defendants to have conversations with others. "Jailhouse lawyers," or people like Ken who have read case law, sometimes share their cultivated expertise with other incarcerated people.[29] Jeffrey, a poor black man his forties, chuckled as he described jailhouse lawyers to me. Leaning forward in his gray hoodie, he sounded a note of caution: "A lot of times you don't listen to jailhouse lawyers" because "how can they help your case when they can't even get out? Right?" He laughed. But he told me that he still liked to "sit and listen" to them, and "that's how I started learning about cases." He told me that after he was convicted on a cocaine charge and sent to prison for the first time, he was angry and frustrated at his lawyer. In prison, he began to plan for his future and learn about the law by talking to others:

The lawyers told me they would get me off, and they never got me off. And ever since then, that's what I've been dealing with. Because I don't have money [for] paying lawyers. . . . It's very messed up the way they take a case, but they don't want . . . to represent you the way they're supposed to, and then when you ask for a new lawyer, you can't even get any lawyers. If you're going to jail because of all these charges and he's not representing you—I mean I know a lot of people who know about the law more than the other people and [than] their lawyers! Um . . . that's one thing about jail, especially [facility name redacted], they have a law library where you can look over your case. You can do a lot with that. You know, a lot of people have overturned their case by getting into the law library.

Jeffrey's time in prison contributed to greater mistrust of lawyers, after hearing about others' experiences, as well as a heightened faith in his and other inmates' expertise.

Privileged people, by contrast, are less likely to talk about the law with anyone but their defense attorneys and their close family members. Some are embarrassed by their legal entanglements, which they fear would shock members of their social circles. Stephen Douglas, for instance, grew up in a middle-class home in a quiet, largely working-class community in Framingham, a city half an hour west of Boston. Just before high school graduation, he was arrested and charged with breaking and entering (B&E) and larceny under $250. His arrest was published in the newspaper. His parents were aghast. "The things they [my parents] don't like the most is being in newspapers all the time," Stephen Douglas told me about his several arrests since. He remembers his parents' reaction to his first newspaper mention:

> I made the front page for that one. . . . I remember coming home from school and there was the *Middlesex News*—that's the news in Framingham—with a Post-It note saying, "Stevie, read this." And I peeled it off. . . . So, I pick it up, and it flops down, and on the bottom it says. "Stolen Goods Turn Up." And I was like, "Oh shit." [chuckles] And I'm a junior [Stephen Douglas Jr.], so it said [Stephen Douglas] of 1025 Maplewood Drive. They were pissed.

I asked Stephen Douglas what his parents did with their anger at him. "Nothing," he said. He continued: "They got a lawyer for me—somebody my mom worked with [at the pharmaceutical lab]." Although his parents did not wish to share news of their son's legal entanglements with anyone but their lawyer, Stephen Douglas would, as he grew older, come to talk about the law with others outside his family. Now in his thirties, jobless, and living in a halfway house, he regularly discusses his court and police involvement with childhood friends and acquaintances he meets in various addiction programs. "Everyone knows about it now," he reflected about his experiences with the law. Like other presently disadvantaged defendants, Stephen Douglas now finds that he is willing—and eager—to exchange legal knowledge and experiences.

The things defendants know—or think they know—invariably influence their legal preferences. Not only does legal expertise provide them with tools that they attempt to use to effectuate certain legal outcomes, but expertise also alters how defendants understand the implications of such outcomes. In other words, cultivated expertise provides a practical understanding of the real-life meaning of a criminal sanction. To them, the meaning of a sanction may be quite different from its meaning to a lawyer or other court official. Therefore, defendants' resistance can constitute a disagreement over what legal outcomes are preferable.

Disadvantaged defendants' expertise regarding the everyday realities of their social positions in their communities influences their understandings of legal punishments. Their understandings can diverge radically from the intentions of the politicians and legal officials who craft laws, policies, and everyday adjudicative decisions. The most apparent instance of these divergent perspectives comes in regard to the purpose of various sentencing options. This disjuncture is especially evident with respect to the logic behind graduated sentencing schemes, such as intermediate punishments. Criminologist Norval Morris and legal scholar Michael Tonry define intermediate punishments as sentences that fall in the gray area between administrative probation and incarceration, such as "intensive probation, substantial fines, community service orders, residential controls, [and] treatment orders."[24] Such sentences are commonly referred to as alternative sanctions because they are often offered as ostensibly less punitive alternatives to incarceration. Alternatives to incarceration have been increasingly used, especially in district and misdemeanor courts.[25] Although such intermediate punishments are often assumed to be less punitive than incarceration, some scholars have shown that sentencing preferences are subjective.[26] I find that what is considered a better or worse sentence is indeed subjective, and additionally depends on a defendant's neighborhood and community ties, as well as the resources they have access to that would enable their compliance with such alternatives to incarceration.

The legal preferences of the middle-class defendants I spoke with often did align with lawyers' and policymakers' assumptions about what constitutes a better or worse sentence; but the legal preferences of disadvantaged defendants (especially those living in highly surveilled communities) often did not. At least four working-class and poor black defendants explicitly mentioned preferring sentences of incarceration over sentences of probation. For instance, William, a black man who grew up working class and was on probation after his first conviction, told me, "probation is not for black people." He elaborated:

MATT: What was being on probation like?
WILLIAM: It's . . . probation is not . . . Probation is not for black people.
MATT: Hmm. What do you mean by that?

WILLIAM: You're treated differently on probation—African Americans are treated totally different on probation than white people are treated on probation, than anyone else is treated on probation. And that goes for Asians, Hispanics, you name it, whatever nationality is. My personal experience and other people I've talked to on probation [is that] probation is not to be dealt with by black people. That's why you see a lot of black guys doing the time instead of taking the probation.

Whereas William indicts probation for unfair treatment, others focused on the burdensome requirements of probation given the realities of their disadvantaged social ties and heavily policed neighborhoods. More than viewing probation as discriminatory, these individuals exhibit what sociologist Monica Bell has described as "legal estrangement."[27] These disadvantaged people distrust probation because it fails to account for the structural realities of everyday life in poor communities of color. For instance, Richard, a working-class black man on probation at the time of our interview, recounted to me the difficulties of abiding by probation requirements while maintaining everyday relationships with friends and families in his neighborhood. He said:

You have to watch out for anyone doing dumb shit. I can't deal with anybody who's fucking around. I just, I watch out for my surroundings too. You know I could end up getting into a fucking fight and that could lead to being in the wrong place at the wrong time, . . . plus, being a black male, I just understand that you get caught up in a lot of stuff even if you don't want, even if you don't want to be there. . . . Man, it's crazy, [one time] I was with this dude who was smoking, . . . and I stayed away from it, but, you know, I came back and I had a urine, and when I took the urine, the THC line was kind of slim, kind of light. . . . I don't smoke or nothing but damn secondhand smoke can make that shit light up like that, so I'm like, you know, I definitely can't play around with nothing, I can't even be in the vicinity, so.

For Richard, "being a black male"—with the possibilities of having to defend himself or get "caught up"—makes him uniquely susceptible to the surveillance of probation. He also recounted how he is unable to be around people who smoke marijuana, lest he have a contact high and incur a technical violation.

Some poor white defendants also articulated their own frustrations, noting the difficulties of maintaining employment while abiding by conditions. As described earlier, Owen reported a desire to avoid probation even if the alternative was incarceration. His lawyer, Selena, recounted a conversation with him: "He's the one that told me, 'I'm not a probation candidate. I'm not gonna do well on probation.' . . . He was like, 'I'll take up to a year, maybe 18 months [in jail].'" During my interview with Tonya, she articulated the many burdens of probation that she has experienced. She said that being on probation was "like being in jail"—drawing an equivalence between the two types of sentences:

MATT: How was being on probation basically like being in jail?

TONYA: It's harder.

MATT: Hmm. Tell me more about that.

TONYA: Um . . . You can't live a normal life. They put demands on you that are almost impossible. Um . . . programs, counseling, drug counseling, drug programs . . . urines, coming in and out of Braintree and Boston and paying for that. Paying for your trips, paying for your fees, paying um . . . Plus they want you to work. Scheduling all this stuff around your work?! There's nobody going to want to hire you for all that, you know, to schedule you around groups that probation mandates you to do.

The many conditions on Tonya's probation made it difficult to maintain a job, which was yet another condition of her probation. Tonya has had many interactions with probation over her life, and her many unsuccessful experiences with probation have indelibly shaped her negative perspective on it as an alternative—and theoretically less punitive—sanction.

Indeed, choosing incarceration over probation for these defendants was often explained via reference to prior frustrations with alternative sanctions; therefore, despite their expressed unwillingness to engage in probation programs, they still participated in them at some point in their lives. It was unclear from my conversations how often defendants make legal decisions on the basis of expertise about probation and other alternatives. Nevertheless, lawyers' accounts confirm that at least some of their clients choose prison over probation; this happens often enough that a handful of lawyers I spoke with acknowledged this preference and did not assume that probation was always preferable. For instance, a public defender described how he, unlike some of his colleagues, always asks his clients, "What's your goal after trial if you lose?" He does so because he recognizes that some of his clients prefer to serve time in jail or prison rather than serve time on probation: "Some people may want to say, 'Get me jail time. I don't want to be on probation for the next three years. I'd rather go to jail for four to five months,' you know?" For many of the disadvantaged, this lawyer's awareness and willingness to listen to his clients' needs is rare. Even when they sensed their lawyers were well intentioned and truly did care about them, many poor and working-class defendants felt the court process did not allow them to articulate their needs and felt that their lawyers often did not fully understand their preferences. Withdrawal into resistance, therefore, embodies both disagreement about legal strategies required to achieve agreed-on goals as well as disagreement about what the goals are.

## Resignation

Whereas about half of those who withdraw grow resistant, the other half withdraw for a different reason: because they have come to feel resigned to the criminal legal system. Resignation, which I define as a feeling of defeat in the face of the legal system and its inevitable punishments, was most common among people who were dealing with a criminal charge at the same time as they were dealing with other problems in their lives; often, those other problems were more pressing than the criminal charge. People were more likely to feel resigned in court cases experienced later in their lives. Poverty, mental illness, and/or the pain of managing substance use disorders were common kinds of hardships experienced by those who exhibited resignation. As one public defender told me, "Many clients are just mentally ill or just in the throes of their substance use disorder, and so they're like, 'Whatever. Let's just get a deal and try to resolve this as soon as possible.'" Managing everyday hardships proved to be more important to some defendants than managing the costs of criminal system involvement.

Unlike resistance, resignation is a far more straightforward kind of attorney-client interaction precisely because far less interaction—positive or negative—occurs. Although there were about as many instances of resignation among the people in this study as there were instances of resistance, resignation did not come as much of a surprise to me, given what scholars already believe about most disadvantaged defendants. Scholars often portray poor defendants as passive and unengaged. I documented similar passivity among those who withdrew into resignation. And yet, resignation, as we will see, still involves an important kind of agency: beyond the courtroom, defendants who are resigned are often working to manage far more complex and immediate dilemmas. Thus, it is a mistake for scholars to always read poor defendants' resignation as disinterest in their legal cases and court outcomes. Instead, they are often overwhelmed by the difficulties of their daily lives and therefore willing to accept the relatively less-problematic consequences levied by the courts.

Mary, the working-class Latina woman from chapter 1, described her feeling of resignation about her current charge—assault and battery (A&B) with a dangerous weapon. She told me she was ambivalent about her lawyer—mistrustful of him in some ways but trusting in others. When he was first appointed to her case at arraignment, she did not know what to make of him: "I don't know how I felt about him, because I felt like he looked very inexperienced. And he looked very, just looked like he was nervous." After their initial meeting, she thought she might try to hire a private lawyer because she did not "think he's good enough for this case. This is a serious case." But neither she nor her parents could afford to do so. Later, after a few quick phone calls and court hearings with her lawyer, she felt she might be able to trust him. When I met her, her initial impression had dulled into an acquiescent kind of trust—a sense that even though she had reservations about him, she had no other options:

MATT: Do you trust him now?

MARY: Um, I think now I do. Now I do. At first, I did not. Not at first because he didn't really seem confident, but now that I see him, and he's like, "Don't worry, I've got all the information I need. You're fine." So, I think I'm going to be okay. I'm putting my trust in him, you know, I'm putting my trust in him. It's not like Sandra [a lawyer in a previous case], where I was straight confident because I knew she got me. He's not like that, but I'm putting my trust in him because I want this to work out. So yeah. I'm trying to trust him.

Mary's ambivalence toward her lawyer was also articulated as indifference—toward her lawyer and toward the legal process itself. The legal process felt out of her control. So much, in her telling, seemed dependent on the emotions of court officials on the day you happen to be there. Watching other people's cases from the courtroom gallery, she concluded that a judge's emotions are essential to what happens to you, yet they were unpredictable and out of her control. "Like one day, the judges will be in a good mood, and everybody's kind of getting good results. But then I would notice that when they're cranky and not really in a good mood, you kind of don't get the best results."

Beyond her court case, Mary was preoccupied by many other problems in her life: her recent break-up with her boyfriend; her recent move back home with her abusive father and her enabling mother; and her failed attempts to find a meaningful job after a court case in 2014 that had upended what seemed to be a stable career in a hospital's customer service department. All these problems—plus this most recent case—contributed to her depression, anxiety, and alcohol abuse. She lamented, "After that case, I've been on and off jobs. It's been very hard; like, I kind of changed a lot honestly. I just hit rock bottom. I went through a really bad depression, and it completely changed who I was. I'm not the same person." Feeling depressed and not wanting "to leave the house," she started abusing alcohol: "This last year I started drinking a lot. Like, drinking every weekend and even the weekdays."

Mary's everyday troubles resulted in missed court dates and, when she did show up, indifference. After our interview, I followed Mary to a pretrial hearing for her A&B case. She and her lawyer had initially planned for a motion to dismiss evidence. But I watched as her lawyer told the judge he would no longer be pursuing the motion. Instead, he asked for a trial date. In a gray sweater and blue jeans, Mary stood silently next to her lawyer, her face expressionless, as the judge and clerk set a date. It was unclear if Mary knew what was happening; yet, defendants who were more active would have been incensed at, or at least visibly annoyed by, this last-minute change. As we will see in chapter 4, some who are resistant will debate with their lawyers in the middle of court proceedings. Once the date was set, Mary's lawyer thanked the judged and whispered something to Mary. Mary nodded, then left the courtroom; her lawyer stayed behind to deal with other clients.

Two months later, I returned to the same courthouse, on the day of Mary's trial. Mary did not show. Her lawyer explained to the judge that she had been arrested on a new charge (an OUI) being tried in another courthouse and was currently hospitalized in a public mental health and addiction hospital. It was unclear if she was hospitalized voluntarily or by court order:

> PROSECUTOR: Your Honor, the defendant is in the hospital. And the witnesses were just called off for today. This case involves a cross-complaint. The cross-complainant will be here on [date], and we can match them up for that date.
> JUDGE: We need to give this case another date.
> MARY'S DEFENSE ATTORNEY: How long?
> JUDGE: It won't be long. . . . No one stays at [hospital name] for long.

At the judge's remark, a handful of other lawyers in the room waiting for their cases to be called began to chuckle. The judge continued, smirking: "I'll waive her appearance today since she's in the hospital. Let's set another trial date." The officials' mocking laughter about Mary's hospitalization suggests how common it is for the defendants before them to suffer from addiction or mental illness—and to miss court as a result. As if by routine, the judge set a new court date for her trial, informing the prosecutor that the witnesses would have to come to court at least one more time. After a few months, Mary and I would lose contact, but I would come to learn that her A&B with a dangerous weapon case was ultimately dismissed—perhaps because the witnesses did not return to court or because her other legal troubles suddenly appeared more serious, in comparison, to the court. Although she avoided a formal legal punishment for the A&B, she now had an OUI charge to deal with, on top of her worsening mental health and addiction.

Resigned defendants often do not show up to court. Lawyers lose contact with them and feel helpless in locating them. When I followed Sybil to court one morning, she had four hearings scheduled for four defendants. She told me that she did not expect two of the defendants to show. She was right. One of the defendants was homeless, addicted to cocaine, and did not have a cell phone. She had been unable to contact him for weeks. The other defendant also struggled with addiction, was last known to be in a sober house, and had a record of routinely defaulting, meaning he rarely shows up to his court appointments and often has warrants for his arrest issued by judges. Sybil had found a way to contact this defendant through a cousin of his who was willing to share her phone number with Sybil. A few days before court, Sybil called the man's cousin, asking her to remind him of his court date. The cousin said she would "if she saw him." When both defendants' cases were called by the judge, Sybil tried to stall each time: "Good morning, Your Honor. Unfortunately, I have not yet seen my client today. But I believe he is on his way." Not all lawyers are willing to stall for their clients. A black woman in her late twenties with a twinkle in her eyes, Sybil deeply cares about her clients. But her compassion cannot make up for the basic requirement that her clients show up to court. Later in the morning, after both men were called a second and then a third time, the judge issued preliminary default warrants for their arrest. After a recess, the judge asked the clerk to inquire about the men's whereabouts. One of the men was in another courthouse, after having been picked up on another warrant. "Apparently, he defaulted [in a courthouse] downtown yesterday, where he was supposed to show up for another case," the judge explained aloud for all in the courtroom gallery to hear. "I'll issue a preliminary default," the judge concluded.

When defendants are resigned and do not show up to court or even to meetings with their lawyers, their absence means that their lawyers have little or no information about their preferences, or about how their lives may be affected by one legal choice or another. Such information is crucial in creating arguments against the defendant's criminal culpability and in seeking concessions from prosecutors and the court that are truly in the client's best interest. In the defender's office where I spent a month, lawyers often expressed frustration with such resignation. Clients regularly missed meetings—both in-person meetings and those over the phone. When their lawyers followed up to reschedule, some clients would provide seemingly legitimate excuses (like a last-minute shift change at work); others would just apologize and make plans to reschedule; still others would simply ignore lawyers' repeated attempts to reach out to them. My plan for the month I was in the office was to observe five pre-planned client meetings. Just one of these meetings actually materialized, and only after a rescheduling. Most meetings between attorneys and clients only happened on the day of court, either in a private room or in courthouse hallways. Between court dates, brief updates were commonly communicated through text message or voicemail.

Resigned defendants who do not clearly communicate with their lawyers may unknowingly consent to legal outcomes that have unforeseen consequences in their lives. Jaylan, a brown-skinned nineteen-year-old whose mother is from Cape Verde, appeared resigned and noncommunicative the day I met him. That morning, he was going to take a plea deal on a possession of ammunition charge. Jaylan's lawyer, Selena, told me that he would plead to a CWOF that day with one or two years of probation and various potential conditions, including the requirement that he complete his GED, get a job, and pay probation fees. Not addicted to drugs or alcohol, Jaylan was a surprising case of resignation. But, as we will see, his apparent feeling that his court case was relatively less important in his life than his interactions with his peers and his desperation to get from under the controlling grip of his mother likely explains much of his resignation with his lawyer and in court that day. He wanted his case to be over quickly. Moreover, Jaylan had already been involved with the law before; his juvenile record included charges for trespassing, armed robbery, and distribution of marijuana. It seemed (though he never expressly told me) that he was struggling with profound alienation at home and school, as I would later come to see in the way he interacted with his mother.

Jaylan's lawyer, Selena, is a twenty-something Latina woman with a warm smile and friendly presence. Although she is the youngest public defender I followed, she had accumulated experiences with a range of clients in her two or so years in the office. She is also well liked and admired by other court officials, who view her as kind and patient. Like Sybil, she too worries about her clients: "I'm anxious until the very last second, like, until they say 'dismissed.'" Her worry manifests physically. Some days in court, I would watch as Selena would anxiously bite her lip or play with the ring on her finger while waiting for her clients' cases to be called. It was clear to me that she had a big heart; the potential outcomes her clients faced weighed on her.

Selena even worried about clients like Jaylan, who themselves seemed wholly unbothered. Selena told me that when she first met Jaylan, at arraignment, he had no questions about his case and seemed to barely be paying attention. After his arraignment, he left the courtroom in a hurry. Selena had to rush out with him, basically begging for him to slow down so she could get his contact information: "I'm like, 'Hey, can I get a phone number?' I got a phone number real quick." Over the course of several months on this case, Selena would contact Jaylan to see if he wanted to have a meeting to discuss any concerns or strategies for his case. He declined. "In fact, we only really talked about the court dates," Selena said. "I was like, 'Hey, you wanna have a meeting?' He said, 'No, not really.' So we didn't." Instead, Selena worked on his case alone. She tried for a motion to suppress evidence, waiving his presence so that he did not have to show up to court unless he wanted to. He chose not to. She would later negotiate what she thought would be a less punitive plea deal, but with little input from Jaylan with respect to the kind of deal he would prefer. "He's just like, 'sounds good,'" Selena recalled.

The morning of his plea hearing, Jaylan was late. Selena tried calling him several times, only to be met with a voicemail message. His mother, however, was already in court. Her presence was not just as a supportive mother but also as the alleged witness to Jaylan's crime. His mother was the person who had found ammunition in his room; she had called the police to report it, resulting in his summons to court and ultimate possession of ammunition charge. Worried about her son, Jaylan's mother had shown up to all his hearings on time, sitting attentively in the gallery. It was unclear if she was willing to testify against Jaylan, but she was clearly concerned about his activities—and the impending sense that she might be losing her son to the streets. When Jaylan finally arrived that morning and said hi to Selena, his mother tried to approach them. Jaylan quickly shooed his mother away with his lanky arms. He still seemed annoyed with his mother for calling the police on him. Early on during Jaylan's case, Selena had sent an investigator to his home to inquire as to whether his mother would be testifying against him. The investigator reported that he was not sure, but she probably would not. Regardless of his mother's testimony, the police officer who came to the home would still be able to testify.

After Jaylan's arrival and dismissal of his mom, the three of us—me, Selena, and Jaylan—moved to a private room in the courthouse to discuss his plea. The room had a large window, providing a view of the hallway outside one of the courtrooms. I watched as Selena carefully explained the plea process to him, the rights he was giving up, the answers he would have to give to the judge, and the likely conditions of his probation. Throughout, he nodded, punctuating her explanations with barely audible "Mmhmms." His eyes often veered from the plea sheet to the people passing now and then outside the room. Before signing the plea sheet, Selena asked if he had any questions. He did not:

> SELENA: The prosecutor's recommendation will be a CWOF with two years of probation, and requiring you to be back in the GED program and pass your GED. I'm going to write, though, that the terms should be that you just be in the GED program rather than also requiring you to pass the program. . . . Another condition is that the prosecutor wants you to reenroll in the Youth Build program or start the Next Step program. Is that okay with you?
>
> JAYLAN: Mmhmm. Yeah.
>
> SELENA: As long as these conditions sound good to you.
>
> JAYLAN: Yes, all right.
>
> SELENA: If the judge adopts the two-year CWOF, are you sure you'll be okay with two full years of probation and these conditions?
>
> JAYLAN: Mmhmm. That's okay.

Selena then began to describe the tender of plea form, alerting him to the rights he was giving up by pleading guilty:

> SELENA: So, when the judge asks you these questions in court, your answer will be "yes," as long as we want to accept this plea deal.
>
> JAYLAN: Mmhmm.
>
> SELENA: Okay, then the judge will ask the prosecutor to go over the nature of the charge. They will describe the alleged facts of the case.
>
> JAYLAN: Mmhmm.
>
> SELENA: And also, there will be a probation fee of $65, but I'm going to try to waive it because you're not working.

JAYLAN: I'm going to start working soon!

SELENA. Okay, that's great. And if you ever can't pay the fee, you just need to talk to your probation officer, and the judge will work something out. . . . Do you have any questions?

JAYLAN: No, I'm all right. I'm straight.

Selena slid the plea sheet across the table for Jaylan to sign it. When they went before the judge, Selena was able to convince the judge to a CWOF with one year (instead of two) of probation and the requirement that Jaylan get a job. His probation fee was reduced to $25.

Jaylan's ultimate sentence was a light one, but it was also a sentence that could—if he were to be rearrested, fail to pay his fees, fail to get a job, or have his mother call the police on him again—result in prolonged contact with the system. Jaylan's resignation in the face of all this was surprising. It was unclear, from my observations of Jaylan's discussions with Selena, how aware he was of all the ways the conditions of his sentence could come back to haunt him. He did not seek information from Selena about the potential pitfalls of his conditions. Moreover, he never told Selena whether any of the conditions bothered him or whether he wanted to ask for alternatives. As I sat quietly in the room watching him consent to take the plea, it was difficult for me not to intervene, to insist that he carefully consider all the possible ramifications of these conditions. But, perhaps for Jaylan, such consequences were minor compared to the disadvantages he faced in his everyday life.

## Conclusion

Withdrawal as resistance occurs when a defendant does not trust their lawyer's legal expertise or, at least, their lawyer's willingness to use their expertise effectively on the defendant's behalf. Defendants in turn feel the need to cultivate and employ their own legal knowledge and skills—lay forms of legal expertise.[28] They cultivate their expertise in jail, in their communities, and through their own observations of other defendants' court proceedings. Such lay expertise sometimes contradicts the professional expertise of their lawyer, or at least calls it into question; the results are disagreements, tension, and at times, outbursts in open court.

Defendants' efforts to cultivate legal expertise reveal a paradoxical trust in legal knowledge and skills, even amid a mistrust of legal officials and institutions. Scholars studying legal cynicism have shown how disadvantaged people living in punitively policed neighborhoods are more likely to view legal authorities as illegitimate and ill equipped to deal with crime.[29] Scholars have largely focused on how such cynical attitudes, or frames, shape levels of violence and willingness to call the police. Political scientists have examined how negative experiences with, and cynicism about, the law decreases faith in political institutions.[30] My findings, by contrast, reveal how cynicism of legal officials can exist alongside faith in legal rights and procedures. Many poor defendants and working-class defendants of color are eager to learn about the particulars of the law and share that knowledge in their communities. Thus, in the uncertainty of court processing, they are often more willing to trust in their own expertise than that of their lawyers, who often appear unwilling to exercise certain rights and procedures. It is therefore a mistake to conflate skepticism of legal officials and institutions with skepticism of the law itself.[31] A surprising number of disadvantaged people in the study retained faith in the law (as a set of tools and resources they hoped to employ in their cases) while expressing distrust in legal officials (police, lawyers, judges) and systems (police departments, courts). In sociologists Kitty Calavita and Valerie Jenness's study of a prisoner grievance system, they find a similar paradox: they show how incarcerated people "expressed a profound faith in law and evidence" despite cynicism about the grievance process and its likely unfavorable outcomes.[32] The authors uncover an apparent conflict between the dominant ideology of rights consciousness in the contemporary United States and our present period of mass incarceration. Royale summarized this paradoxical perception among disadvantaged defendants. Even though he believed the system treats black people unfairly, he felt that "the laws are actually created to be beaten." Royale's enthusiasm was clear: "They created it [the law] so they could beat it. Not for us to beat it, but for them to beat it. [. . .] So, if you know your law, you can beat it."

A defendant's expertise extends beyond procedural knowledge about rights that could be used in court to experiential knowledge of how court-imposed sanctions might operate in their daily lives.[33] Their knowledge in this latter regard is often more comprehensive than that of legal officials, who have little, if any, experience abiding by probation requirements, serving out a jail sentence, or paying fines and fees.[34] Expertise about the everyday realities of certain sentencing options can constrain defendants' choices and contribute to preferences for seemingly harsher legal outcomes. For defendants living in highly surveilled, poor neighborhoods of color in Boston, the realities of police and court surveillance constrain their abilities to take advantage of less punitive sentencing alternatives.

The most common, and surprising, example is prison versus probation. Many of us might assume the latter preferable to the former. But again and again, poor people in the study insisted that I understand the difficulties of life on probation. They were hassled by police, feared rearrest on new charges, and were punished for violating the court-ordered conditions of probation (such as violating curfew orders or missing meetings with probation officers), even when they had not broken any laws. Consequently, some reported preferring sentences of incarceration over that of probation. Their withdrawal manifested as resistance to a lawyer's assumptions about their preferred legal goals.

Withdrawal as resignation occurs when defendants appear, to their lawyers and the court, to care little about the legal process. Resignation may arise, in part, from mistrust of lawyers and other legal authorities. But attorney-client relationships characterized by resignation are more likely to occur because defendants' criminal cases are of secondary concern in their lives. For some, the problems they face outside the courts—problems such as poverty, gang involvement, homelessness, drug addiction, or mental illness—are more pressing than their legal troubles. When a defendant is struggling to find a place to sleep every night, a charge for marijuana possession that requires their presence in court once a month becomes a distant concern. Consequently, this client does lots of things that frustrate their lawyer and hinders their legal journey: they miss court dates, or fail to return their lawyers' phone calls, or develop a history of noncompliance with the court's mandates. There is little tension in these kinds of attorney-client relationships, but withdrawal between lawyers and their clients manifests in their distance from one another, their lack of communication, and the lawyer's own growing resignation to their client's whereabouts and well-being.

My hope is that this chapter has dispelled the myth that poor criminal defendants are passive recipients of the court process. Researchers and journalists, often taking the perspective of lawyers and other officials whom they have studied, describe disadvantaged defendants as passive to the legal process and focus on the frustrations of lawyers who feel as if their clients are not engaging with them.[35] This characterization does not account for the agency that exists in both resistant and resigned attorney-client relationships. When defendants withdraw into resignation, they may seem passive in court and in interactions with their lawyers, but their agency abounds outside the courtroom. Because I spoke to people about their lives beyond the legal process, I was afforded a unique view into the many struggles that their lawyers and the court only rarely see. I learned that many defendants who do not appear to care about their court cases are, at the same time, actively fighting their landlords, working toward recovery, or dealing with other pressing matters.

Moreover, attorney-client relationships characterized by withdrawal as resistance provide even clearer evidence that the trope of the passive poor defendant is incomplete. Few studies of criminal courts document attorney-client relationships characterized by resistance (though resistance has been documented in attorney-client relationships in civil contexts).[36] Rather, studies often report public defenders' frustrations with clients who seem unengaged—clients whom lawyers say do not show up for meetings or fail to share important background information about their lives and their cases with them.[37] Public defenders, these studies argue, must struggle to invest poor clients in the importance of participating in the attorney-client relationship and the court process writ large. But among all the people I spoke with who were withdrawn from their attorney, their relationships were nearly as likely to be resistant as they were to be resigned. Such resistance often occurs beyond the purview of the court. Although some defendants defied their lawyers in open court, much of the resistance I observed occurred in closed-door meetings with lawyers or in defendants' reports of their interactions in their communities, where they talked to their family and friends about their court cases, sought legal advice, and shared disappointments.

This chapter's exploration of resignation and resistance, combined with the experiences we will see in the next two chapters, should modify our theoretical understandings of professional-client relationships, professional and lay expertise, and the power of the law to control its subjects. Sociologists of science, knowledge, and the professions have written much about professional and lay expertise.[38] Beyond the attorney-client relationship, numerous similar relationships involve a client seeking the expertise of a professional; doctor-patient and teacher-student relationships are the two that we likely encounter most often. In these relationships, the professional holds legitimated control over the expertise necessary to solve certain problems the client brings. Professionals must decide to advocate, or not, on behalf of their clients in the face of administrative authorities such as hospitals, health insurers, university administrators, and other higher-level bureaucrats.[39]

Half a century ago, sociologists Marie R. Haug and Marvin B. Sussman described how professional authority was increasingly being challenged by collective "revolts" of clients across myriad institutions—from elementary schools in low-income neighborhoods to hospitals serving long-term patients.[40] A few years later, Haug predicted that our increasing access to education and user-friendly technologies, which allowed individuals to acquire their own forms of expertise, would mean that clients would increasingly mistrust and contest the authority of the professional.[41] The abundant availability, and pervasiveness, of Google searches and WebMD today is the epitome of what Haug predicted decades before the internet became mainstream. Sociologists of expertise have sounded similar warnings, especially with respect to natural scientists and scientific expertise in our contemporary political moment of "alternative facts" and climate change denialism.[42] Ordinary people have more and more access to more and more competing ideas and forms of knowledge. We can do our own research rather than seek the expert advice of a professional. In the legal world, a handful of scholars have documented such changes in attorney-client relationships in civil litigation; lawyers who were once accustomed to professional dominance over their clients now find themselves negotiating how, when, and to what extent they allow their clients to determine legal strategy.[43]

The efforts of many disadvantaged defendants certainly confirm part of this narrative. Those who feel they cannot trust their lawyer often strive to acquire their own expertise and contest the authority of professionals; yet, within the criminal legal system, a defendant's ability to effectively use their own expertise is quite limited. When clients resist, there is rarely a collective revolution or mass upheaval of the oppressive elements of criminal law. Nor is there much tangible improvement in the legal fates of the individuals who are doing this resisting. Instead, the results are often quite the opposite: more often than not, when a disadvantaged defendant seeks to insert their legal expertise into the process, their legal journeys get bumpier. These defendants may gain a certain amount of dignity or autonomy by contesting the definition of their crimes, or by seeking to file their own motions, or by refusing alternative sanctions.[44] Yet at the same time, they also face negative responses from their lawyers and judges that deny their efforts, as we will see in chapter 4. These realities suggest that resistance in attorney-client interactions, ironically, contributes to what sociologists Patricia Ewick and Susan Silbey describe as the law's hegemony as "a durable and powerful structure in American society."[45] The cumulative portrait is sobering: legal officials continue to wield immense power over defendants. Defendants who follow the hidden rules of deference and silence and accept professional authority are rewarded; those who do not are punished.

# CHAPTER THREE

# Privilege and Delegation

BRIANNA MET ME outside a bakery on a breezy summer day. White and in her thirties, Brianna is talkative. As we sipped our coffees, she told me all about her childhood in Somerville, a city just beyond both Boston and Cambridge. There, she lived in a mostly white, middle- and working-class neighborhood. "It was like *Mister Rogers' Neighborhood*," she said, referring to the popular late twentieth-century television show. "[There] was like one long road with all these side roads. We had our own parks. All our kids in the neighborhood were Irish, Italian, and a couple Portuguese kids. Big families." She lived with her parents and five siblings on one of the side roads, a corner of the neighborhood where kids liked to hang out on their front porch. Brianna's mother, a four-year college graduate with a nursing degree, worked long shifts as a registered nurse at a local hospital, and her father, a high school graduate and army veteran, worked as a taxi driver. He was home when the kids got back from school and would cook dinner for the family. To this day, even after her mother's passing and her own ongoing struggle with addiction to drugs and alcohol, Brianna is close to her family. Her father, now retired, insists she stay at his place when she is between apartments and sober houses.

In the middle of our conversation about her family, Brianna's phone rang. "Oh my god, this is my lawyer," she blurted. "Oh—answer it," I said. I waited as she talked with her lawyer about her current court case, involving an OUI (of drugs) and a drug possession charge. That winter, Brianna had been driving at night when her cell phone slipped to the floor of the car. She reached to get it, and the car swerved and hit a snowbank. When the police arrived, they thought she was acting "funny." She engaged them in conversation, and ever the talkative person, she joked that she needed "her meds." That was a mistake, she quickly realized. The police asked to search her vehicle and found a couple types of benzodiazepine medications in her car.

Her lawyer, a thirty-something woman named Leya, was now calling to follow up on her case. Over the phone, Leya reminded Brianna to bring the prescriptions for the benzodiazepines during her next court hearing. If they could show the judge that she possessed the drugs legally, her possession charge would go away. Brianna had the prescription for one of the drugs but said it might be hard to get a prescription for the other (because, as she would later confess to her lawyer, she never had a prescription for it). She told her lawyer she would "see what I can do to get it." Leya was also calling to apologize: she would be out of town on vacation for the next couple weeks. "Would it be okay for me to ask the judge to push the court date back?" Leya asked. Brianna, who had no pretrial conditions attached to her case, said she did not mind. They agreed they would plan to return to court two months from now—plenty of time for her lawyer to enjoy vacation and for Brianna to find some way to get a prescription. As we returned to the interview, I asked Brianna whether she trusted Leya. "I do," she said without hesitation. "I can talk to her. . . . I'm 100 percent on board with her."

Brianna was lucky to have a lawyer she could trust and who was easy to talk to. Brianna was privileged. And that makes all the difference. Brianna was not financially wealthy. But she was not financially poor, either, and she was white. With a two-year nursing degree, she was also better educated than many people in this study and, certainly, than most defendants across the country. Nearly all the defendants I met who were like Brianna—that is, a middle-class person or a working-class white person— told me some variation of the same thing: they trusted their lawyers in the face of their inexperience with the law; they felt heard by their lawyers; they engaged with their lawyers about their legal goals; and, ultimately, they deferred to their lawyers' professional legal expertise.

Unlike the disadvantaged in this study, middle-class people of all racial backgrounds, as well as white working-class people, were more likely to hire private attorneys, often chosen with the help of family or friends. Some were even able to retain lawyers free of charge, given the nature of their social circles, which tended to include other privileged people who knew lawyers or were lawyers themselves. To be sure, there were some relatively privileged defendants who could not afford to hire private attorneys. Brianna, for instance, never even considered a private attorney. After hip surgery a couple years back, she started using drugs and alcohol again amid the postoperation pain and missed so many shifts at work that she lost her job as a nurse. She could not afford a private attorney and felt she did not need one. Similarly, some privileged people had been arrested just when they found themselves down and out—recently unemployed, living in sober houses, or strapped for cash. Consequently, they sometimes relied on court-appointed lawyers. Even so, they still reported feeling they could trust the same public defenders and bar advocates that the disadvantaged could not trust. Their privileged backgrounds had afforded them positive prior experiences with the police and enabled them to share cultural commonalities with most attorneys. Even though they experienced social alienation in their adolescence, their alienation often manifested in relation to family, school, or peers rather than in relation to the law. Legal officials looked the other way or offered second chances. Even when alienated from family, their family members often stepped up to help them deal with their cases. Family members, such as spouses and parents, were often financially secure and well educated.

Trust enabled privileged defendants and their lawyers to develop relationships characterized by delegation. Such relationships are created through multiple interactions, each of which further builds trust as clients and their lawyers grow closer. Both parties develop a consensus as to their legal goals and options. Delegation unfolds through three processes: recognition that you are inexperienced with the law and legal concepts; engagement with your lawyer (who is viewed as a professional with legal expertise); and deference to your lawyer's recommendations. Inexperience with the law is central. Often, privileged defendants who have had few (or no) prior arrests have little cultivated expertise of their own. They have rarely had to try to understand how the criminal law works. Rather than debating with their lawyers over what legal strategies should be employed, they allow their lawyers to use their professional legal expertise on their behalf. Moreover, because privileged defendants find that they are heard by their lawyers, they can engage with them and clarify their legal goals, and then accept their lawyers' judgment of the likelihood that their goals are achievable. When privileged defendants grow frustrated about their cases, such frustration tends to be directed at the court or the legal system rather than defense attorneys. Behind closed doors, their lawyers serve as a sympathetic ear, allowing defendants to maintain their composure in open court, where they remain silent and appear to defer to the court's rulings.

Brianna's case embodies the possibilities of privilege within the attorney-client relationship. Brianna's slide into drug and alcohol misuse began recreationally. "I started doing it [cocaine] when I was seventeen.

And I got really into it when I was twenty-one. . . . At seventeen, we were taking acid and smoking weed, we did coke, mushrooms. . . . I mean, we drank all the time." Despite her substance use, she completed nursing school. It was hard to maintain a job as a nurse and struggle with addiction. But she managed for nearly a decade, sometimes sober, sometimes not. "Nursing kind of came easy to me," and she figured "no one's going to know [when I'm using]. My nose ain't running." She was right. For years, her co-workers did not know about her addiction. But then, after her surgery, she could no longer hide the consequences of her addiction and was fired for too many days off work. In her youth, she was sometimes caught using, but she had received multiple second chances from police and the courts. One time, she and several friends were found drinking underage near some railroad tracks. "They didn't arrest me, and I got to walk." But after her recent surgery and relapse, her troubles escalated. She checked herself into a detox facility, then stabilization services, and now she lives in a sober house and is working as a cashier at a small convenience store. Brianna voluntarily checked herself into her current sober house, unlike many disadvantaged people who are ordered there by the court. Brianna has been arrested five times in her life, but all her cases (ranging from marijuana possession to an OUI) resulted in CWOFs with no probation conditions. She has been fortunate to get off so easily. As such, her past experiences with the law have been largely inconsequential, and she has no complaints about her previous lawyers.

Leya, her current lawyer, was no exception. "She's awesome and has swag," Brianna told me. Brianna was particularly enamored with Leya's manicured nails, designer rings, and gold earrings. "I love her confidence." When Brianna was first in court, waiting to be arraigned on the OUI and drug possession case, she sat in the gallery and watched other people's cases. She and Leya had never met, but she watched Leya passionately advocating for a man to be released without bail. The judge, after considering Leya's arguments, agreed. The client was released on his personal recognizance, meaning he did not have to put up any money for bail. Brianna was impressed. During a break in the court session, Brianna approached Leya with a smile. Leya noticed her staring and asked: "Hi. Are you okay?" Brianna said, "Yeah, I've got this OUI case, and I'd love to have you represent me." Leya was the public defender on duty in the arraignments session that day, so she could take on her case. She talked to the clerk to have Brianna's file added to her caseload.

From the beginning, Brianna and Leya seemed to have an easy time developing mutual trust; the result was Brianna's willingness to engage with and defer to Leya in key moments. Initially, Brianna wanted to plead guilty. Rather than drag the case out, she just wanted to move on. Leya disagreed, warning her of the potential consequences of pleading guilty, which included losing her driver's license. Brianna described their conversation: "I was kind of saying to her, 'Let me [plead guilty and] take the [one] year's probation, just because I'd rather take it now.' [But] she [Leya] was like, 'No, you don't want a guilty. You're going to lose your license for a year.' She's like: 'No, just keep going. I'm going to fight to the end for you.'" Brianna decided to follow Leya's advice. They agreed to take the OUI charge to trial. Both recounted to me, with enthusiasm, how the trial resulted in a not guilty decision. Leya showed the jury a recording of Brianna being booked at the police station. The recording showed her walking deliberately and calmly after her arrest, thereby suggesting she was not under the influence of drugs. When Leya cross-examined the arresting officer at trial, she was able to demonstrate to the jury that the officer's only evidence for believing Brianna was intoxicated was that she failed a field sobriety test. That test required Brianna to hop on one leg. But Brianna's recent hip surgery, Leya reasoned to the jury, made hopping on one leg difficult—so of course she failed the test. "They came back in seventeen minutes with a not guilty," Leya told me with a triumphant laugh. This quick and early victory cemented Brianna and Leya's trusting attorney-client relationship.

Two months after my initial interview with Brianna, I followed her to court as she and Leya worked to resolve her other charge—drug possession. We met Leya briefly in the courthouse hallway; she waved from across the hallway and mouthed that she would be back soon to catch up. She had several clients with cases that day and was running between courtrooms. As we waited in the hall, Brianna and I chatted about previous court cases, her boyfriend, and the "girls" in her sober house. Half an hour later, Leya passed by again, pausing briefly to give Brianna the rushed details: the plan today would be to lobby the case to see if the judge would agree to a CWOF rather than a guilty conviction. Leya was hopeful. But Leya explained to Brianna that the lobby conference would not include her. Instead, the conference would take place between Leya and the prosecutor in front of a judge. Brianna would not be able to be in the room to hear, or contribute to, the conversation. Leya asked if she would not mind staying in the hall. Brianna nodded, allowing her lawyer to advocate on her behalf.

When Leya returned from the lobby conference ten minutes later, we moved from the hallway to a private room. Leya's face was uncharacteristically reserved; she did not bear good news. Rather than sentencing Brianna to a CWOF, the judge was leaning toward sentencing her to a guilty conviction with probation conditions. "The judge thinks that you are at the end of the CWOF rope," Leya explained. Given the many CWOFs she had received in her life, her criminal record had now become too long, even for a "cute white girl," as Leya put it. Leya was blunt: "The only way we can avoid a guilty conviction here is if you are able to provide the prescriptions for both drugs." Brianna's eyes narrowed, and she shifted in her seat. She was agitated. She had provided a prescription for one of the drugs, she griped. "We need both," Leya said. Brianna sighed. "I'll never be able to get that," she said. She then asked whether a letter from her sober house might help. She showed it to Leya. Her friends in the sober house had suggested that Massachusetts courts are lenient on people with addictions; maybe it would be a good idea to show the letter to the judge, Brianna thought aloud. Leya disagreed. Such a letter would likely have the opposite effect, providing further evidence that she was probably lying about having a prescription for both drugs. Brianna understood and tucked the letter back into her purse.

A month later, Brianna, unable to procure the second prescription, pleaded guilty and was sentenced to serve six months of probation, which included mandatory drug treatment. She was not happy about the mandatory treatment. Yet, she still felt Leya had done everything she could. It was hard to imagine Tonya or Drew or many of the disadvantaged defendants I met having Brianna's sanguine reaction.

Brianna's faith in Leya was quickly rewarded. Brianna did not fully realize it at the time, but Leya had negotiated that Brianna be allowed to have a substance abuse evaluation as a part of her probation terms. Such an evaluation would determine whether Brianna really needed the mandatory treatment the judge added to her terms. The judge, unaware of her current residence in a sober house or her past struggles with addiction (since Brianna did not share her sober house letter), agreed to allow the evaluation. Soon after, a clinician determined that Brianna did not require drug treatment. After just a month, her probation was terminated early. Brianna texted me with glee: "Woohoo! Lol. I'm all done!"

This chapter reveals how the privileged, like Brianna, experience relationships of delegation with their lawyers. Although some disadvantaged people in this study experienced delegation in some of their attorney-client relationships (typically when they found themselves in situations of privilege), it is the privileged who almost universally experienced the benefits of delegation.[1] The privileged are those who have ties to family and friends with resources, stable employment, and few encounters with the police. Although the privileged experience alienation in their adolescence, they rarely feel alienated in interactions with police and other officials. When they find themselves in court, they are surprised. Lacking legal experience, they engage with their defense attorneys to learn what they can expect from the court process and to share their own goals. Trust solidifies the unfolding relationship, and they are willing to defer to their lawyer's expert advice. Privileged people often feel comforted by their lawyers, even if their formal legal outcomes are not exactly what they had hoped for. The experience of court processing is one of relative ease in comparison to the frustration and resignation experienced among the disadvantaged. Privilege in the courts is thus about much more than achieving favorable outcomes; it is also about the relatively weightless feel of the court experience itself, even if worry and uncertainty dominate early moments of the process.

## Trust in Lawyers

It will come as no surprise, by now, that the privileged were far more likely than the disadvantaged to report trusting their lawyers. When I asked about their lawyers (past and present), people who were economically privileged—and therefore able to hire their own private attorneys—were overwhelmingly trusting of these lawyers, even if their legal outcomes were not as expected.[2] Even among middle-class people who could not afford a private lawyer, their relatively benign (or absent) prior experiences with the law and their social connections to lawyers and other professionals fostered trust in lawyers' legal expertise. For some, they were able to acquire private lawyers for free or at a reduced rate through their families or friends. For the privileged who did not retain private lawyers, many (though not all) nevertheless trusted court-appointed lawyers, despite the stigma that such lawyers have among the disadvantaged. Court-appointed lawyers, for the privileged, could be viewed as effective, especially when defending *them*—privileged people who are worthy, in their own minds, of competent professional advice.

The reasons that privileged people trust their lawyers mirror the reasons that disadvantaged people mistrust them. Race and class create astonishingly divergent experiences with the law; in turn, a defendant's story about their lawyer will similarly vary a great deal depending on whether they are black or white, rich or poor. Among the disadvantaged, skepticism about lawyers often emerges from the structure of the indigent defense system, which they believe incentivizes the quick processing of cases. Thus, court-appointed lawyers, they believe, are unable to pay attention to the individualized needs of their clients. But among the privileged, hiring private lawyers outside the indigent defense system is common. Payment is believed by many to offer some certainty that a lawyer will devote time and resources to one's case.[3] Moreover, the cultural distance between a defendant and their lawyer and the lack of common life experiences reported among the disadvantaged are rarely reported among the privileged. On the contrary, the privileged describe finding cultural commonalities with their lawyers. Finally, the privileged often—though not always, especially when referencing the poor people sitting next to them in courtroom galleries—agreed that the legal system worked. At least, it worked for them. Their general lack of experience with the law and the lenience they have received in prior encounters with police and the courts only contributed to this belief. They also reported that lawyers treat them well—lawyers listen attentively to them and appear to take account of their individual needs.[4] Comments from Leya that Brianna is a "cute white girl" contrast with the feelings of mistreatment experienced by the black working-class and poor defendants in the last chapter.

People who have access to financial resources rarely rely on the indigent defense system. People who grew up in middle-class homes often told me about how, if their adolescent run-ins with the law got serious, their parents paid to hire lawyers. For instance, J. M., mentioned in chapter 1, is the son of wealthy parents. As a teenager, he was arrested for marijuana possession and various other minor offenses. But he barely remembers these arrests, given the large role his parents played in his legal defense. He told me, "My dad had some good lawyers, and he put a lot of effort into it. And I come from a small town, so he knew some people, and he was getting a lot of my cases either sealed or dismissed."

Multiple stories revealed that people who hire lawyers often do so not just because they want to but because they have no other option. Indeed, you have to qualify for a court-appointed lawyer. To qualify for indigency in Massachusetts, defendants must meet one of three criteria: they must receive public benefits; their after-tax income must not exceed 125 percent of the federal poverty line; or, court costs must be shown to deprive their dependents of "the necessities of life, including food, shelter, and clothing."[5] Indigency status is determined by the probation department prior to a defendant's arraignment, when probation officers briefly interview defendants to determine if they meet any of these criteria. Judges, considering probation's assessment (and almost always accepting their recommendation), make the final decision about whether a person will be provided a court-appointed lawyer. I witnessed more than a score of probation determinations of indigency during my time observing court-houses. They were very brief, taking no more than five minutes per per-son. Either probation officers would ask defendants questions about their financial status and record them on an intake form, or defendants would quietly fill out an intake form themselves. Rarely were defendants' claims about their level of income, recent unemployment, or receipt of public benefits verified in any systematic way.

Some people who are deemed indigent by the court may nevertheless have access to financial resources; someone close in their social network has money, even if they do not. Such people are afforded the chance to choose whether they will rely on their appointed counsel or opt out of the indigent defense system. Some in this position choose to hire private attorneys instead. But people tend to wait to do so only if they find that they mistrust their court-appointed lawyer. In Brianna's case, for instance, she never felt she needed to draw on her family's financial resources to hire private attorneys; she always seemed to get along with her public defenders. But Arnold, from the beginning of the book, did not feel the same. Arnold qualified as indigent in his gun possession case. He was working as a freelance writer at the time of his arraignment, which meant he reported a low income. He initially was optimistic about working with his court-appointed lawyer, but after a few interactions, he decided that he could not trust her. He recalled she was not effective in the courtroom: "[She] worked diligently to put together a case for me [but] she had a strong [Eastern European] accent and so I think they [other court offi-cials] couldn't understand her." He also sensed that she did not believe he was innocent. She told him to "have canteen money ready" for jail, "a red flag for me that she was willing to accept what the courts wanted to do, rather than forcefully impose her will on the situation on my behalf." Skeptical of her, he contacted his basketball agent, who found a private lawyer, Brett. Arnold's experience suggests that black middle-class defen-dants may have more reason to mistrust court-appointed lawyers than their white middle-class peers. We will see below how cultural common-alities and racial bias advantage white people—middle class and working class alike.

Others with money opt out of the indigent defense system immedi-ately, especially if they believe that private lawyers may provide better—or at least, more tailored—services. Sybil, one of the public defenders I shadowed, described how some of her clients choose to hire private attorneys immediately after arraignment. For instance, she told me about a college-educated Asian woman arrested for an OUI who was classified as indigent because she was in between college and her new job at the time of her arrest. When they met at arraignment, Sybil recalled that the woman was considering hiring a private attorney. Sybil said:

> She told me pretty soon that she wanted to get a private attorney. She asked what did I think about that—did I think it was worth it. And I responded to her, "I think, based on what you told me, [that] if you want to resolve this case the way you told me, then I think it would be a waste of money because I could do the exact same thing for you that a private attorney could. But it's totally up to you. Whatever you're most comfortable with." And eventually she told me that she got one. So I was just like, "Make sure he files an appearance. Otherwise, I'll still be your attorney on paper. And you can just show up with him on the next court date."

The woman later confirmed with Sybil that she did hire a private lawyer. Ironically, before becoming a public defender, Sybil had previously worked in a private attorney's office and handled mostly OUI cases just like this woman's. Given her experiences, Sybil could have easily assisted this client without the extra cost of a private attorney. Sybil reflected that people with access to family money and with few prior experiences in court are the most likely to hire private lawyers: "I would say with those clients, generally when their family has money, a lot of times it is their first time in court ever."

Choosing to hire a lawyer outside the indigent defense system can feel like a vital way of coping emotionally, and providing stability, during a fraught moment in one's life. Some defendants reported that choosing the right lawyer was an important first step in dealing with the emotional stress of a court case. For instance, Amanda, the white woman introduced in chapter 1 who grew up in a middle-class home, described the significance of choosing her lawyer after her first arrest. A college student at the time, she was arrested for drug possession with intent to distribute. She and her boyfriend were selling marijuana out of their apartment when an informant—a fellow college student—tipped off the police to them. She recounted how confused and lost she was in making sense of the legal system: "[I remember being] scared and not really, um, comprehending anything and then having my lawyer kind of have to, you know, put it in layman's terms to me when we met after [each] actual court process." Being able to choose a lawyer helped to calm her nerves, especially since she found her lawyer through an advocacy organization for the legalization of marijuana that she had interacted with online many times before. It was through this organization that she was able to identify a private attorney who shared "the same [political] principles."

The act of payment is also described as a symbolically important social exchange that facilitates trust. Payment represents a contractual agreement that is seemingly more certain than court appointment. For instance, Diego, a middle-class Latino man, described how paying for an attorney put him at ease. When he was in college, he was arrested for marijuana possession with a group of other students. He hired a private attorney by borrowing money from one of his codefendants, the son of a well-to-do professor. When I asked Diego if he recalled any moments when he disagreed with his lawyer or questioned his legal advice, he told me that he could not recount any such instances. He said:

> I was convinced that given that, you know, we had paid so much and this, um . . . um . . . I guess they were regarded as like the top in the practice that, like, I guess my hands—or, I was like in good hands. And also just not really knowing . . . what or how to approach that. Like what to ask—I guess I just always thought that like, you know, they were in good judgment and not really in need of pushback.

For Diego, paying for his attorney made him feel as if he was "in good hands." Moreover, he suggested that he had always assumed that attorneys, in general, had "good judgment."

Privileged people's ability to pay for private lawyers affords them far more choice in their attorneys than is available to disadvantaged defendants, who rarely report being able to choose between lawyers within the indigent defense system. And even if a judge allows them to be reappointed new counsel, they are unable to choose who their reappointed lawyer will be. Lawyers can sometimes identify clients they want to work with and ask the court to assign these clients to their caseload (as Leya did with Brianna). But for those relying on the indigent system, the choice ultimately rests in the hands of legal officials rather than defendants. For those with financial resources, choice rests in their hands. For them, the act of choosing an attorney is a self-directed process that provides them with a sense of control, much as Amanda described earlier. Moreover, choice operates as a form of insurance; defendants who hire private attorneys are able to exit the relationship at any time, take their money elsewhere, and hire a more trustworthy attorney.[6] Lawyers are thus faced with greater incentives to appease clients who are paying for their services.

Cultural commonalities were also described as important in fostering trust. Such commonalities were more common among privileged people, and for privileged people without financial resources to hire private lawyers, such commonalities often were the fundamental basis of their trusting relationships with their court-appointed lawyers. Those raised in middle-class homes regularly recounted familiarity in the professional spaces where they interacted with lawyers.[7] Jane, introduced in chapter 1, illustrates such familiarity. A white woman with blue eyes, blonde hair, and a carefree demeanor, Jane wore flip flops and a hoodie to our interview. Her father was a federal judge, and her mother was a secondary schoolteacher with a master's degree. From childhood, she had felt pressure to choose a high-paying professional career. To add to the pressure, her older sister had graduated from an Ivy League university and currently works at a marketing firm in New York. Ultimately, Jane chose to become an EMT because "I had no idea what I wanted to do. . . . I didn't want an office job because I can't stay still." Even though she could not stand the idea of an office job, she recalled feeling quite comfortable in office settings, given her adolescent socialization. When she was arrested in her early twenties, her mother helped her find a lawyer. Jane appreciated that her lawyer was "down to earth," like her, but also that he and his office appeared professional. She told me, "I trusted him because I trust my mom [and] she has, like, good friends in town that are, like, trustworthy as well. But I guess [I also trusted him] because his office was nice. He seemed like a down-to-earth guy, like he knew the law." For Jane, trust was fostered through a cultural familiarity with, and expectation of, a certain level of professionalism and legal knowledge.

Some working-class white people in the study also reported cultural similarities with white lawyers—a striking contrast to the discrimination and disrespect reported among black working-class and poor people in chapter 2. Recall that about 75 percent of public defenders in Boston are white; the percentage is likely higher among bar advocates and other private attorneys. Brianna talked to me not just about her current OUI and drug possession case but also about a couple of her past court cases. In one of her cases, she found a lawyer who was Irish, like her. She recalls that his Irish identity was meaningful. She originally had him represent her as a court-appointed bar advocate in one case, and then enjoyed working with him so much that she sought him out and retained him privately in a later case:

> BRIANNA: He was one I got as a court appointed, but then I went and got and paid him for the [later] drunk driving [case].
>
> MATT: Why did you decide to do that?
>
> BRIANNA: Because he was awesome. He was so like . . . Irish, like American Irish. And [he] kind of knew my standings in life [chuckles] like what I was like, you know what I mean? Oh, he was so cool to me. He's like "You again?" like kidding around.

Brianna found her lawyer "awesome" partly because of their shared Irish background.

Other working-class white people recounted how sharing experiences and tastes, not just racial or ethnic identity, with their lawyers facilitated trust. Wolf, a white man in his late thirties who wore a Red Sox hat to our interview, explained to me how he bonded with his lawyer over their interest in bicycles and their shared sense of humor. Months before his arrest, he was working at a bicycle shop when a man came in asking to purchase a unique kind of bike for his daughter before she went off to college. The shop was busy at the time, so Wolf told the man that it might be difficult to get that particular bike ready within the time he needed it. But the two men started chatting, and Wolf started to like the guy: "He's pretty cool, and he's not being a jackass [about how long the bike would take]." So, Wolf rearranged his schedule at the shop to try to have the bike ready at an earlier date. Later, when Wolf was charged with an OUI, he was initially appointed a lawyer by the court. As he was leaving the courthouse, he ran into the man from the bike shop again. Surprised, Wolf asked him: "What are you doing here?" It turned out the man was a defense lawyer. They started chatting again: "He was awesome. He was just sitting there telling me jokes." He offered to represent Wolf for a reduced fee. Wolf recalls him saying: "I can help you out because you helped my daughter out and you pushed that bike through. So, my normal fee is $2,500, and I'll do this for 500 bucks."

The privileged also reported that their lack of prior experiences, especially their lack of prior negative experiences, with the law meant that they had little choice but to trust their lawyers and their lawyers' legal knowledge. For many middle-class people arrested for the first time, their sudden involvement in the criminal legal system was a major shock. Ryan, the middle-class white man who opened chapter 1, is a typical example of how such naïvete about the legal system fosters trust in lawyers. He recounted that he was scared during his first arrest in his late teens:

> I was scared shitless, yeah. You know, I'm seeing them bring up all these, you know, weirdos and, you know, all these people walking around in handcuffs. And I'm afraid I'm going to be arrested [charged]. And you know, I was so naïve to the whole criminal justice [process] and how it works. You know, I never, I never thought I'd be in court that way, you know? I wasn't brought up that way, and I'd never seen myself in that situation. But there I was.

Given his inexperience and shock at his first significant experience with the law, Ryan appreciated his lawyer's greater experience and knowledge. Ryan said:

> Yeah, he was good. He was real matter of fact, and he was like, it was reassuring in the sense he seemed like it was a routine thing, he wasn't worried about it. While I was scared shitless. So, it was nice to have him be like "Don't worry" and "Everything is going to be fine." He'd done thousands of these before so, you know, again, I needed that because I didn't know what the hell I was doing.

It was reassuring that his lawyer had handled "thousands" of cases like his—a wealth of experience that far surpassed his own.

Jimmy, a black man whose parents are both college educated and raised him in a racially diverse middle-class neighborhood, also recounted naïvete in his initial encounters with the legal system. His inexperience facilitated trust in his lawyer as well. When he was sixteen, he was arrested in his neighborhood for stealing a bike with a baby seat attached to the back of it. Riding around the neighborhood as a teenager with a baby seat attached drew the attention of a couple of police officers. Jimmy's arraignment in court was confusing. "I didn't understand anything they were doing," he said. "I didn't know why the process was so long." Jimmy's lawyer was an important intermediary. His lawyer joked with him about his arrest ("He was like 'And you had a baby seat?!' He was cool. Yeah, he was cool."), making him feel comfortable about confiding in him. Not only did his lawyer's jokes enable Jimmy to trust him, but his and his parents' lack of experience with the courts necessitated it. Jimmy said that his parents felt that they should just "let him [the lawyer] do his job" and everything would be all right.

Trust in lawyers can change over one's life, as people accumulate more knowledge of, and negative encounters with, the law. Repeated negative

experiences contribute to mistrust of future lawyers, a key marker of growing disadvantage in one's life. Robert, a white man who grew up working
class in the suburbs of Worcester (a major city west of Boston), illustrates
how initial trust among those who were once privileged can erode over
time as they face downward mobility. When Robert was seventeen, he was
arrested for marijuana possession. This was his first arrest, and it was a
"culture shock." He described the shock of the police station: "I'm in there
with guys who are older than me and they're talking about, you know,
they'd been through it before so they're talking about what they do, you
know, so I'm kind of like culture shock almost, you know? Because as I
said I was just a kid playing football and selling weed, you know?" Given
his inexperience and fear, he was willing to trust his lawyer. He believed
that his lawyer had greater knowledge of the system and hoped that he
would use his professional relationships "in accordance with the DA" to
negotiate a favorable plea deal. He ultimately pleaded to four months of
jail time, which he felt "was not too bad, I guess, in my eyes." But over the
years, after later being arrested for larceny and then for armed robbery, he
has grown ever more skeptical of lawyers, particularly of their professional
relationships with prosecutors: "Sometimes, yeah, you get the feeling like
a lot of these public defenders are friends with the DAs, you know. They
don't want to fight them." As a result of his continued system involvement
as well as his growing skepticism, he has begun to cultivate legal expertise,
much like other disadvantaged people. At one point in our interview, I asked
Robert how he determined whether he was getting a "fair outcome." He told
me, "I've had twenty years dealing with the court and I just—I've dealt with
a lot of it. I've seen what people get, what they get on their cases, you know?
So I have a general idea." Robert's experience underscores the centrality of
inexperience in fostering trust, and experience in fostering the opposite.

## *Inexperience*

The foundations of trust are established prior to privileged people's first
interaction with their lawyers, further solidifying as they continue to work
with them. After their first encounter with the court at arraignment and
during their earlier meetings with their lawyers, the privileged come to
recognize just how inexperienced they are when it comes to the minutiae
of criminal procedures, and even the general processes of a court—where
to sit, where to stand when called, whether they can leave to use the rest-
room down the hall. Recognition of their inexperience is the first step in
attorney-client relationships characterized by delegation.

Inexperience is age related in addition to being racialized and classed. People in the study reported being least experienced when they were young, especially if they grew up middle class—sheltered by family and afforded second chances by legal officials. Privileged people were first arrested at a later age than disadvantaged people.[8] The median age of first arrest for middle-class people was nineteen, whereas the median age for the working class was sixteen and for the poor was seventeen. White people's median age of first arrest was eighteen; the median age was sixteen for black people. During these late teenage years, privileged people's relationships with lawyers were often mediated through their parents. Scholars have shown how active middle-class parents are in the schooling and extracurricular lives of their children; the same is true when their kids face legal trouble.[9] Many pay for lawyers, sit in on meetings, and make legal choices, with deference to the lawyers they have hired and therefore trust. Middle-class parents, to be sure, also have little experience with criminal law.

Recall that when Ryan was arrested in college, his father found and hired a lawyer for him. He told me with a chuckle about how he was "so naïve to the whole criminal justice [process] and how it works." Similarly, Joseph, a currently working-class black man who grew up in a middle-class home, also mentioned the important role his mother played during his first arrest. When he was arrested at sixteen for B&E, he was more worried about his mother's punishment than the legal system's: "'My mom's gonna kill me, man!' I'm not worrying about the cops." His work with his lawyer was mediated wholly through his mother. After his mother and his lawyer "worked something out," he was sentenced to probation, and his mother had to pay restitution. Kema, a college-educated white woman in her early fifties with frizzy blonde hair, told me about her first arrest in the 1980s in California. Leaning over a cup of coffee at the café where we met for our interview, she giggled as she recalled its complete weightlessness. A high school student at the time, she crashed her car into a picket fence on her way home from a party. She was inebriated. The cops arrived, and she was arrested for driving under the influence. Her father, a college-educated engineer, hired a neighbor to represent her. And as she recalls, the case simply disappeared. She told me, "I never went to court or anything." She recalled delegating control of her case to her lawyer and her father, both of whom "took care of everything [and] just took the reins." Kema did not face any formal legal consequences for her crime and, to this day, continues to be happily unaware of the details surrounding her lawyer's resolution of the case.

Parents and other close family members continue to play a central role in privileged people's interactions with lawyers into adulthood. During my time in various Boston courthouses, I noticed again and again how young, seemingly middle-class adults would often be accompanied by one or two worried parents. Disadvantaged people, by contrast, were either alone or accompanied by a family member who was present for moral support but rarely a dominant presence in the defendant's interaction with their lawyer. I found a persistent pattern in my interviews and observations: the involvement of a middle-class family member alongside inexperience with the legal process coalesce into a defendant's delegation.

One day in court with Sybil, one of the public defenders I shadowed, was particularly revealing. That day, Sybil was working with a working-class white man in his twenties named Connor. Connor had blue eyes, blond hair, and a slight frame. The first time Sybil and Connor met was when he was arraigned for an attempted B&E charge. Sybil recalled to me that Connor's father and aunt were present during his arraignment and that Connor seemed oddly distant toward her. At first, Sybil, a black woman, thought that maybe he was racist "because he definitely doesn't like me. He doesn't [seem to] like black people." As some time passed, and they were able to chat a bit more, she seemed more understanding of him. He also seemed to warm up to her. She came to think that maybe he had just been in a bad mood during arraignment, or maybe even high on something. Sybil told me:

> When I asked him about what happened during the incident [at arraignment], he told me, "I don't remember anything." . . . I kind of just took it as he probably doesn't want to talk to me. Maybe he doesn't trust me. But now I'm thinking maybe he was high on something, or drunk, I'm not sure. But I still think he's a weird kid.

Despite Connor's strangeness toward her, Sybil felt an obligation to him. In part, she felt responsible not just to Connor but also to his aunt and father. Connor's aunt was very involved in his case and respect-ful toward Sybil. Sybil told me that she asked the court to have Connor diverted rather than continue with the court process because he was in his twenties, did not have a prior criminal record, and the evidence that he actually intended to break into the building was weak (the alleged wit-ness refused to speak to police). If she successfully got his case diverted, he would be on probation for ninety days, after which his charge would be dismissed and his arraignment vacated from his record.

Connor arrived late to court that day. His case had been called twice before he arrived. Each time, Sybil told the judge: "I expect him today, but I haven't seen him yet. I did speak with him yesterday, and he said he would definitely be here." The judge issued a preliminary default, moving on to other cases. Sybil began calling Connor on his cell phone to check in on his whereabouts. Over the phone, he was exceedingly apologetic, telling Sybil that he was stuck in traffic on a bus. He arrived an hour and forty minutes late, dressed in slim-fitting pants and a jacket with a T-shirt underneath. He also wore a hat and sunglasses. Sybil met him outside and placed his cell phone in her purse. Cell phones are not allowed in many courthouses in Boston, unless you are a court official. Most defendants know this rule, and depending on the courthouse, they simply leave their phone at home or at a store across the street, where they pay the owner a small fee to keep it behind the counter. Connor seemed unaware of this court rule; Sybil was willing to hold his phone for him so that he did not have to deal with the hassle that so many defendants are used to dealing with. As he went through the metal detector, one of the court officers asked him to take off his hat and his sunglasses, warning him he could not wear his hat in the courtrooms. Only his second time in court, Connor was unaware of many of its basic routines.

Connor's aunt arrived in court just before his case was called a third time. A thin woman wearing fashionable slacks and a black sweater, she looked to be in her sixties and middle class. I thought that she looked like she might be a librarian, a schoolteacher, or a professor. She watched intently and quietly as Connor walked up to the bar and stood next to Sybil in front of the judge. Sybil made a motion for the diversion of his case:

SYBIL: Good morning, Your Honor. I filed a motion in this case last
    week for diversion. It was arraigned in [a month in the summer]
    and because of the congestion in the court and the frantic pace
    of what was happening at the time, I couldn't ask for diversion at
    that time. I'm asking now for his arraignment to be vacated. He
    has no warrants and no criminal record.
JUDGE: This is a felony, right?
SYBIL: No, this is an *attempted* B&E. Based on the statute, this charge
    is at most five years. Also, the witness did not provide any infor-
    mation to the police, so it's not the strongest case for the Com-
    monwealth. He was twenty-[something] at the time the crime was
    committed, and even though he's currently outside the age range
    for diversion, the statute allows for your discretion.
ADA: Just for the record, Your Honor, the defendant has no criminal
    record in any other state.

SYBIL: He's currently working as a cook, and he is working to fin-
ish his education. So, I ask that he be evaluated by the probation
department and considered for diversion.

ADA: I object, for the record.

JUDGE: I'm not sure about vacating the arraignment, and probation
would probably object to it if I did, but let's refer him to probation.
Let's set a further date.

After the next court date was set, Connor, his aunt, and Sybil convened
in the hallway just outside the courtroom. Sybil quickly explained what
had just happened. She said that Connor needed to go downstairs to the
probation department to begin the diversion process. She explained that
diversion would likely entail ninety days of administrative probation. If he
was not rearrested during that period, his case would be dismissed, and
the judge would likely allow the arraignment to be vacated from his record. Vacating his arraignment would allow him not only to avoid a guilty
conviction but also to have a clean court record. Sybil asked if Connor had
any questions. After a considered pause, he shook his head. His aunt, however, asked two follow-up questions: "Is there anything he needs to do in
the meantime before the next court date?" and "What did the other lawyer
[the ADA] say?" Sybil patiently answered both of his aunt's questions as
Connor stood by, quiet but attentive. He seemed pleased with the likelihood that his case would be diverted, and he would soon be free of the
charge. After the aunt's questions were answered, she told Connor to go
downstairs to probation and fill out the required forms. She would wait for
him outside the courthouse, with his cell phone now in her purse instead
of Sybil's.

Inexperience is followed by engagement—from the defendant and/
or their family—and then, later, deference to their lawyer's advice. Lack
of understanding about the law and the legal process often pushes the
privileged to depend on their lawyers, the only authority they feel they can
confidentially speak to about criminal law.

## Engagement

Engaging with one's lawyer, as Connor's aunt did on his behalf and as
Arnold and Brianna did on their own, is common among privileged defendants who not only trust their lawyers but also have a lot to lose. Once
they recognize their lack of legal expertise, they seek out answers from
their lawyers. They tend to feel comfortable talking with their attorneys,

seeking advice on many things, small and large—from when to arrive in court and what to wear to what legal outcomes are in their best interests and what the best strategies are for achieving those outcomes.

Nearly all the privileged defendants I spoke with either engaged directly with their lawyer or had someone (typically a parent, guardian, or spouse) engage on their behalf as they listened intently. They talked with their lawyer about their legal choices. They asked questions. They solicited the lawyer to get a sense of what they might choose to do if they were in the defendant's situation. That instinct to engage allowed them to share important details with their lawyers. Privileged defendants (or their stand-ins) felt free to be blunt if need be. They could do all the things that you do in a relationship of mutual trust. And in that process, various important details—about their personal lives and their legal preferences—emerged, providing lawyers insight into their clients' concerns about the potential consequences of different strategies. For instance, a routine driver's license suspension following an OUI could be inconsequential to a person who takes public transportation to work but costly to a person who must use their car for work. Just about every defense lawyer I spoke to reported their willingness to advocate for whatever legal outcome is most helpful to their client; yet, lawyers can do so only when clients share these crucial details with them and defer to their strategies for achieving such outcomes. Moreover, such details allow lawyers to identify impor tant information about their client that could serve as fodder for mitigating arguments made during various court hearings. For instance, defense lawyers often like to share details about clients' impressive work history, efforts at maintaining sobriety, or attempts to further their educations. Such bits of information are shared only when a client feels comfortable opening up to their lawyer.

Don, a light-skinned black man in his early fifties with a graying beard, illustrates how engagement emerges from trust and a recognition of a lack of legal experience. When I met Don, he was nearing the end of a more than two-year court case involving several charges related to the possession and distribution of heroin. In our interview, I learned that Don first started selling drugs in his late twenties and early thirties after dropping out of community college—much to the dismay of his college-educated mother, who worked for decades as a secondary school teacher. After a couple run-ins with the law and a three-year prison sentence, he tried to get clean. He stopped selling drugs and went to substance abuse programs to manage his heroin addiction. With the emotional support of his wife, he maintained a stable job as a janitor at a local college. But after a few years, he was laid off and was desperate for money to ensure his daughter could stay enrolled in college—a dream that he was never able to fulfill for himself. He said:

> I was clean for a lot of years. So, I was working at [the college] and I was doing janitorial work there. And so what happened was I was working there, and their enrollment was down, so they started laying people off. Now at the time, my daughter was going to college, and I was helping to pay. At the time, I had a good job, and my wife had a good job. My daughter, she bagged this thing and got an apartment off campus. So, we said, "Yeah." And we got her an apartment off campus, and she got a roommate. I'm paying $600 a month, and her roommate's family is paying $600 a month. I get laid off from my job, and I'm trying to figure out what to do. I get unemployment nowhere near what I was getting on the job, so I got to thinking I need quick cash. So I started selling drugs again, started selling heroin. Then I started using it again.

Without telling his wife, he started selling drugs again so they could make ends meet. Within a year, he was arrested.

Initially, when Don was arraigned on his charges and assigned a court-appointed lawyer, he thought he would pull together the money to hire a private attorney: "We was going to hire a private lawyer." After speaking with his wife, they decided to first ask his wife's mother, a retired detective from a police department in the Boston area, whether she had ever heard of the lawyer he had been assigned. She had, and he was known to be good. So, they decided to keep the court-appointed lawyer. As Don told me, "She called some people and asked about him, and they said he was one of the best, so that's why we stuck with him." With his mother-in-law's recommendation, Don quickly felt able to trust his lawyer: after some initial hesitance, he started sharing his struggles with addiction, his willingness to go into treatment programs, and his fears of going back to prison. They worked collaboratively on several motions to dismiss evidence and specific charges. Don also recalls that his lawyer took seriously his desire to go into treatment, using this information to negotiate with the ADA. But the ADA refused to offer treatment without a sentence of incarceration:

> My lawyer lets them know I'm a prime candidate. I'm a man with kids, always worked. I'm a prime candidate for a drug treatment facility. But it's like that part of it is out of the question. . . . They want time. They just want time. . . . I think it's racism. I really believe that with all my

heart. Because I've seen it over and over and over again where certain people get it. Treatment facilities. They go to drug court.

Despite his frustration, Don's feeling about his lawyer was unchanged: "this guy, right, he works so hard." As Don told it, his lawyer's inability to negotiate a plea deal with drug treatment conditions instead of prison time had to do with the court and the prosecutor's racism against him, not his lawyer's lack of advocacy.

After our interview, Don had his next and final court date, where I would watch him plead guilty to his charges. He was sentenced to two years of prison followed by three years on probation. This sentence was much lighter than the maximum he could have received, according to the state statute; part of the reason for this relatively light sentence was the prosecution's decision to drop some of his charges in exchange for his plea. Don still felt that the ADA's racism prevented him from receiving an even lighter sentence. Rather than share his frustration aloud, however, he shared it with me and his lawyer. He told me, "It's crazy. I mean, there's no doubt in my mind that if you ain't got a lot of money and you ain't white . . . it's just that simple. I believe that with all my heart, and there's nothing to tell me anything different." But that was Don expressing his frustration in private. In his final public words to the court, he was deferential: "I know I'm better than this, but I am also a drug addict. The opioid epidemic is real. I've been going to get help at meetings for years now. And I feel I need that more than anything else—I need help. I apologize to the court for my actions." The judge responded: "Well, you've got the right attitude. You will continue treatment after these two years, and I know you will continue down the right path." The trustworthiness of Don's lawyer allowed him to engage in a productive attorney-client relationship for more than two years. Trust in his lawyer also resulted in his ultimate deference to his lawyer's suggestion that he take the plea offer, despite his frustration that he would have to serve time in prison.

A defendant's engagement with their lawyer can also assist them in learning how to avoid many of the hidden collateral consequences of their sentence. When I observed lawyers meeting with their clients, I noticed that they did a consistent job of sharing the most common potential side effects of various legal outcomes with their clients. Some of these collateral consequences are explicitly spelled out in the tender of plea—a document that lawyers are legally required to go over with their clients before they take a plea deal.[10] Collateral consequences, depending on the charge and ultimate sentence, include anything from being deported and losing your job to losing your license, right to vote, or opportunity to serve on a jury.[11] These and other consequences may not apply to, or at least not be important to, all clients. If their client does not engage with them and ask follow-up questions, many lawyers may discuss only the most obvious and common consequences and fail to mention the others.

One day while shadowing Tom, the same public defender who represented Drew from the introduction, I observed the benefits of engagement with another client of his. That day, Tom's client Gabe was in court to plead guilty to a first-offense OUI charge. A working-class Latino man in his forties dressed in a fitted suit and tie, Gabe seemed reserved. He spoke few words. Although he works as a technician and has only a high school education, he could have easily been mistaken for a lawyer that day in court given his suit. With him that day was his wife, a white woman who was inquisitive and talkative by comparison. It was Gabe's wife (not Gabe) who asked me a couple follow-up questions about the purposes of my study before feeling comfortable that Gabe should participate; she even kept the consent form in her purse rather than handing it back to Gabe. Whereas Gabe was born outside the United States and works in a working-class job, his wife grew up in the North End of Boston, a predominantly white community now teeming with young middle-class professionals.

In a small room in the courthouse, Tom went over the tender of plea form with Gabe and his wife. Tom began by informing them that the state trooper who arrested Gabe while he was driving drunk had just arrived in court to testify, so the prosecutor was ready for trial if they decided to go that route. Tom and Gabe had discussed taking a plea several times before, but Tom checked one final time before going over the plea form with him:

> TOM: So, the trooper arrived. Would you still like to take the plea to a CWOF of one year probation?
>
> GABE: Yes, I would.
>
> TOM: Okay, now I've gone over this with you before, but I want to do it again just to make sure. Probation will usually do a risk assessment of you, overall, after you take the plea. And then they will decide how often you have to report over the year. It could be as often as several times a month. . . . Is this courthouse the closest to where you live?
>
> GABE: No, um—
>
> GABE'S WIFE: No, the closest courthouse is [courthouse name]
>
> TOM: Okay, so they often will be able to transfer the probation reporting to your nearest courthouse, if that's something you want. And

if probation comes with any classes that you are required to take as part of your conditions of probation, they will give you a full explanation of all of that.

Tom's investment in his client was clear in the depth and care of his explanations. Tom noted, early in their conversation, that having to report to probation in a courthouse far from where he and his wife live might be a hassle for them.

For about forty minutes, I observed as Tom, Gabe, and Gabe's wife discussed several other consequences that could arise from taking the plea. Much of the conversation was led by Gabe's wife, who brought up numerous details about Gabe's life and work that she believed might be affected by him taking the deal. She actively sought Tom's legal expertise about whether certain aspects of Gabe's life might be affected by the plea, and if so, how to mitigate those consequences. For instance, she worried that pleading guilty to a CWOF—which results in a dismissal of the case— might nevertheless affect his employment. Even though a CWOF results in a dismissal rather than a guilty conviction, private companies that Gabe contracted with as a technician could still conduct background checks on his arrest record or his court record, which would reveal a dismissed charge even if it did not reveal a conviction:

GABE'S WIFE: And in terms of background checks. What will
   show up?
TOM: It will show up as an open case.
GABE'S WIFE: And after probation is over?
TOM: Nothing shows up [as a conviction]. But, private companies
   can, and sometimes do, go through public records. So, you could
   consider sealing the case after probation is done.
GABE'S WIFE: Okay, what do we need to do to do that?
TOM: You can go down there now [to the clerk's office] to learn how
   to do that. It requires that you come into court right after your
   probation is over. Then, wait thirty days. Then, the case will be
   called, and you come in to court. You would have to say that the
   record poses a risk for your employment or housing—or whatever
   justifications the statute allows. And the judge will seal it. If you
   call me, I can help you with that. I would no longer technically be
   your lawyer, but I'd be happy to help. I've had various, very serious
   cases sealed before.
GABE'S WIFE: And if an employer were ever to find out about this,
   what do we do?

TOM: Well, employers are beyond the reach of the court. They *can* fire you. But honestly, many people do not see OUIs as serious charges.

GABE'S WIFE: But some do! There's a stigma, I think.

Gabe's wife also asked questions about possible ways to deal with Gabe's license revocation (which would hinder his ability to drive for work and drive to the hospital to deal with a recent medical diagnosis); whether there would be restrictions on his ability to travel while he was on probation (which would hinder his ability to visit a family member who lives out of state); and whether they could get his probation fees waived (which could be a burden for them because in the words of Gabe's wife, "we're very low income"). When Tom represented Gabe in front of the judge later that day, Tom used the knowledge he learned from their questions to ask the court for various accommodations. He asked for a reduction of probation fees, which was granted by the judge. Tom also asked whether Gabe could transfer his probation to the courthouse closer to where he and his wife live. This request was not granted, but the clerk nevertheless assured them: "Probation for OUIs is not intensive. You just have to call in once a month, and you don't even have to show up in person."

Later, I asked Tom about his interactions with Gabe and his wife. I wanted to know how typical it was for clients to ask so many questions about their case and how he manages such intense engagement. He told me that their willingness to engage with him is immensely helpful in his advocacy on their behalf—and even on behalf of future clients who may not be as conversant as they are. Early in his career as a public defender, Tom was not aware of all the possible collateral consequences that may be of concern to his clients. But now, after having "these questions come up" time and again from several clients, he has a "general spiel" for his clients about collateral consequences. And he makes "mental notes" to update his spiel every time a client asks a new set of questions he has not thought about before.

Asking these kinds of follow-up questions is a key component of attorney-client relationships of delegation. Ultimately, as the experiences of Don and Gabe reveal, engagement requires trust and emerges from uncertainty and inexperience. Don, Gabe, and Gabe's wife all listened intently to their lawyers. Once they engaged with them, they ultimately deferred to their lawyers' knowledge about which legal strategies were the best for them to take and how they might go about avoiding collateral consequences arising from their legal entanglements. By asking questions and sharing their expectations, privileged defendants often were able to avoid collateral consequences, or at the very least be aware of them, in ways that disadvantaged defendants could not. For instance, Jaylan, from chapter 2, did not ask follow-up questions of Selena because he was resigned to the legal process. Therefore, unlike Gabe, Jaylan neither learned that he could seal his record if he successfully completed his probation nor did he receive the offer of help to seal his record that Tom extended to Gabe.

## Deference

Deferring to a lawyer's expertise—and to judges and other court officials—is the final step for privileged defendants who delegate in the attorney-client relationship. When defendants defer, they often find that they are rewarded with the legal outcomes their lawyers have taught them to expect. Unlike the disadvantaged, privileged defendants are convinced by their lawyers of the practical necessity of certain legal outcomes, even if they were initially hesitant or frustrated by having to plead guilty or serve a longer sentence than they had hoped. Privileged defendants more often felt relieved that they were able to avoid far worse outcomes. Moreover, defendants who defer to their lawyers also report experiencing relative ease as their lawyers guide them through court. They may be nervous and anxious about their cases, but they find their lawyers to be calming rather than aggravating.

Deference, to be clear, is distinct from the resignation characteristic of some of the disadvantaged. The privileged are very much present and engaged in the details of their cases. Thus, even when the privileged defer to their lawyers in determining what legal strategies to employ in court, the privileged still make known their hopes and expectations for legal sentences and other outcomes. Unlike the disadvantaged who are resigned, the privileged who defer still show up to court and to meetings with their lawyers. Moreover, the privileged in these situations are often quite worried about their cases, in ways that the disadvantaged who are resigned are not, given the myriad problems they face outside the court process. For these privileged defendants, their legal problem is a startling public blemish on a life that may otherwise appear quite functional, at least to outsiders who are unaware of any struggles they may have with alienation from family or substance use disorders.

Deference to a lawyer's expertise was so formidable among the privileged that they deferred even in the rare instances when they strongly believed a different legal strategy would result in a better outcome. When conflicted between their own instincts about legal strategy and the advice of their lawyers, the privileged chose their lawyers' recommendation (which they viewed as expert) over their own instincts (which they viewed as wishful and likely ill advised). Take the case of Waine, a working-class white man. Waine was arrested for an OUI in his late thirties. His father helped him find and pay for a private attorney—an older man whom his father had used as a defense attorney decades earlier. A routine first-time OUI, Waine's case was fairly straightforward. Waine's lawyer suggested that he plead to a CWOF. The lawyer had spoken to the ADA and worked out a standard, if not relatively lenient, deal—just one year of administrative probation and a drunk-driving class. Waine recalled that his lawyer wanted him to take the deal rather than go to trial: "Oh, he was definitely pushing me not to go to trial. Definitely. One hundred percent." But Waine and his dad both thought he had a defensible case. When he had been arrested, Waine had almost passed the field sobriety test. He also refused to take the Breathalyzer. So, he felt he had a case to contest the charge that he was under the influence. Waine said:

> I didn't fail the field sobriety test except for one little hiccup—one little stumble when doing one of the walks. The hands out walk or something like that. So then—so it was after they did the field sobriety test, and they asked for me to take a Breathalyzer. And I told them, "No." I wasn't comfortable with that.

After reading the police report, both Waine and his father felt there was little evidence to convict him of an OUI. Waine said, "My dad was pushing to go to trial because he liked the police report. He was like, 'The police report looks good,' and he's like, 'We can beat this.'" Waine felt caught between the advice of his lawyer and that of his father. And his own instincts suggested he could win at trial: "It was a pride thing. . . . Me and my dad together were like, 'No, we can beat this.'" But Waine ultimately deferred to his lawyer's expertise. In part, the process of going to court started to feel "exhausting," whereas following his lawyer's advice provided him an easy way out. "I just wanted to take it [the CWOF] and move on," he reflected. Moreover, his lawyer persuaded him that, given his professional experience handling other OUIs, it would be a mistake to turn down this particular plea deal. Waine recalled that his lawyer said that "what they [the DA] were offering was pretty good."

For many privileged defendants who know little about the law, decision-making conflicts rarely arise between them and their lawyers. Unlike Waine, they do not have gut instincts about choosing one legal option versus another. And unlike many disadvantaged people, they have not cultivated their own legal expertise. Instead, they tend to fully defer to their lawyers throughout the process, sharing their concerns and trusting that their lawyers will be able to accommodate those concerns. Their lawyers guide their case, negotiate with relevant parties on their behalf (prosecutors, probation officers, judges, alleged witnesses, and alleged victims), and report back to them.

How Ryan dealt with his most recent shoplifting case provides a revealing example of such deference. I accompanied Ryan, the middle-class white man mentioned in chapter 1, to court for a possible disposition hearing on his shoplifting charge. During this hearing, Ryan's lawyer would have to tell the judge whether they had decided to take a plea or go to trial, depending on the final offer from the prosecution. When I arrived at the courthouse, I found Ryan sitting alone on a bench in one of the main hallways. He was wearing a loose-fitting polo shirt, khaki pants, and white sneakers. His leg bounced up and down; his eyes wandered warily each time a handful of lawyers walked past carrying manila folders. His cheeks were bright red, and little beads of sweat gathered at the top of his forehead. He wiped his forehead clean as I walked up to him and said good morning. "I'm a little bit worried. I don't know what to expect, and I don't want to have to keep coming back here," he said. I asked if he had spoken to his attorney since our interview a month prior, and he told me he had not. But he still felt that his lawyer was his only chance at a good outcome because he did not know anything about the law around shoplifting or the typical punishment levied on shoplifting cases in the courthouse. As he told me earlier in the interview, his lawyer likely "has three or four of these [cases] a day for shoplifting, so he probably knows what he's talking about, you know?"

Chester, Ryan's lawyer, is a court-appointed bar advocate. I later learned that he regularly practices in this particular courthouse. A white man in his sixties or seventies, Chester is known by other lawyers for being a little spacey. As one lawyer told me, Chester is a nice person who means to do well by his clients, but he is disheveled and often unprepared. He is also often late to court. Ryan and I both witnessed these characteristics during court that day; yet, Ryan maintained his faith in Chester despite his readily discernible eccentricities and faults.

When Ryan's case was called at the start of the session, Chester was absent. Ryan shuffled up to the bar and sheepishly told the court that he did not know where his attorney was. The judge said, "second call," meaning they would hear his case later in the session, when Chester arrived.

Ryan made his way back to his seat in the gallery. This leniency toward lawyers who are habitually late to court is inconsistently afforded to defendants, based on defendants' histories of compliance and their lawyers' advocacy. For example, just after Ryan's case was called, another defendant's case was called, and this defendant was found to be absent from the courtroom. The ADA recommended the court issue a warrant for this person's arrest, arguing that the defendant had defaulted in previous cases. The defendant's lawyer—a bar advocate who was present—said, "Communication with my client has been spotty, Your Honor," suggesting that a warrant would perhaps be the only way to compel his client to court. The judge issued a warrant for the defendant's arrest immediately. This inflexibility toward the late defendant contrasts with the leniency afforded to Connor (described above), who was late to his court session but was likely afforded leniency because he was considered a first-time offender and because Sybil, his public defender, told the judge that she expected he would be in court that day.

While waiting for Chester to arrive, Ryan seemed unbothered by his attorney's tardiness. He simply sat in the session, waiting patiently (albeit nervously), his leg continuing to bounce up and down. Ryan's patience surprised me. Over the years, I had watched numerous instances of the exact same event, often with the exact opposite result. If a disadvantaged defendant's lawyer was late, oftentimes the defendant would grow frustrated, taking their lawyer's absence as evidence of their lawyer's inability to handle their case effectively. Sometimes, a defendant might remark, under their breath but loud enough that the whole gallery could hear, that their lawyer was incompetent, racist, or careless. In the same courtroom during another day of observation, I overheard grumbles from the gallery, including statements like: "Damn. It's about fucking time" when a person's lawyer arrived; and "This is super disrespectful to people. All this waiting around. We've got things to do" when it was almost lunch time and a person's case had yet to be called a second time. I often felt immense sympathy for defendants who sat in court for hours while officials seemed to ignore them; yet, I also understood the pressures faced by their court-appointed lawyers, who were often stretched too thin by the demands of too many clients with matters spanning multiple courtrooms—or even courthouses—on any given day. When Ryan's case was called again, Chester had just stumbled into the room. Chester apologized to the judge: "Hi, Your Honor. I believe I'm on this case. Sorry I'm late. I grabbed the wrong file this morning." Chester turned and shook hands with Ryan, who was standing behind the bar. He whispered something in Ryan's ear and then approached the ADA to chat. Chester then turned to the judge and asked for a further call as he worked to negotiate with the prosecutor to reach an agreed-on sentence. Chester walked Ryan outside the courtroom and into the hallway.

A few minutes later, Chester returned to the courtroom to deal with a pretrial hearing for another client. I watched, with curiosity, as he decided to make a motion for discovery of evidence at the last minute. The judge was willing to hear his motion, but Chester did not have a copy of the official form for the motion. Searching around frantically, he decided to simply scribble the motion on his legal pad. He ripped the yellow paper from his pad and asked to approach the judge's bench. He walked up to the bench and handed the paper—now a legal motion—to the judge. The informality of this motion (written last minute and not on the official court form) underscores how lawyers' professional position in the court enables their own informality. At the same time, it is easy to see how Chester's last-minute decision to make a motion for discovery and his lack of preparation could contribute to unease and mistrust in the eyes of defendants already prone to mistrust lawyers.

After a court recess, during which Ryan told Chester about his background and recent employment for several minutes, Ryan's case was called again. Chester and the ADA had reached an agreement—Ryan's case would be dismissed as long as he completed eight hours of community service:

> ADA: Your Honor, we have a possible resolution. We move to dismiss his charges on eight hours of community service. We base this dismissal on the fact that we have investigated more into this incident. The police report says that the defendant was wielding a knife, but the complaining witness said no knife was present both at arraignment as well as later when we interviewed him. The charge is shoplifting by asportation, but he did not actually leave the premises with the item.

The judge took a few minutes to read the police report. He then looked up:

> JUDGE: It says in the police report that the object was taken outside of the store by the defendant. Counsel [Chester], what do you have to say about this proposal?
>
> CHESTER: Your Honor, my client has a slight record. He is thirty-two years old. Grew up in Quincy.

Ryan whispered to Chester, to clarify his hometown. Chester continued:

> CHESTER: Sorry, he grew up in Springfield. Went to [college name] and received his B.A. The last time he had a drink was the day of this event. He went to detox, then to a halfway house, then, just a month or two ago, he went to a sober house where he is now in Jamaica Plain. He is currently employed.
>
> JUDGE: Based on the report of the Commonwealth and Mr. [Chester's last name], the motion to dismiss is allowed on eight hours of community service.
>
> CHESTER: Okay, my client could probably do the eight hours in a month. Also, Your Honor, he asks if he can do it at a charitable organization rather than court-sponsored—
>
> JUDGE: No, I will not allow that.

After court, I asked Ryan how he felt about his sentence:

> MATT: Do you think your sentence was fair?
>
> RYAN: Eight hours?
>
> MATT: Yeah.
>
> RYAN: Yeah—definitely glad I got it. But I don't know about the other people. They didn't seem to get treated as fairly. She [the judge] was pretty tough. I was so worried as I watched other people's cases.

Despite being pleased with his own sentence, Ryan was not so sure about how other defendants fared that day. He seemed to be telling me, as other privileged defendants shared with me in more explicit ways, that he recognized that his privileges afforded him better treatment in court than others.

## Conclusion

This chapter describes and considers the conditions that account for relationships of delegation between defendants and their lawyers. Privileged defendants often trust in their lawyers and develop relationships of delegation with them. Delegation consists of attorneys and clients who develop mutual trust. Often, middle-class and white working-class people have few, if any, prior experiences with the legal system. And when they do, their experiences are often positive or otherwise unremarkable. They are less likely than their disadvantaged peers to experience police surveillance in their communities or feel the weight of discrimination from legal officials. They are naïve, in many ways, about the legal system and have had less reason to cultivate their own forms of legal expertise. Thus, they

are more likely to believe their lawyers are more knowledgeable and sav-
vier in navigating the court's rules and procedures. As these defendants
begin to recognize their inexperience with the law, they engage with their
lawyers, sharing important information about themselves as well as their
legal hopes and expectations. Even in the face of uncertainty, the typical
privileged client ultimately defers to their lawyer's professional judgment,
confident that their lawyer has understood their legal expectations.

Before I began my research among defendants and lawyers in the Boston courts, I expected the opposite. After all, from decades of research
in sociology, we know quite a lot about how privileged people interact
with professionals in a wide variety of institutional settings. Upper- and
middle-class people are said to be demanding and assertive. Research on
parent-teacher and doctor-patient interactions, for example, has documented how the middle class assert themselves with teachers and demand
attention and constant updates in medical settings.[12] In a wide swath of
institutions—from schools, to workplaces, to doctor's offices—the patterns
appear consistent: the middle class are more assertive with professional
intermediaries than the working class and poor, who defer to professionals
and other authorities.[13]

Yet in the criminal courts, privilege works differently. While the privileged people I spoke with and observed certainly do articulate their hopes
and expectations to their lawyers—and are engaged when telling their
lawyers exactly what they want—they do so in a deferential way. And
they do so behind closed doors—in the privacy of an attorney's office or
a hushed conversation in a courthouse hallway before entering the courtroom. They are more likely than disadvantaged defendants to ultimately
defer to their lawyers' professional expertise and accept the authority both
of their lawyers and of the court. To be sure, delegation in the attorney-
client relationship can occur among people from all backgrounds, even
among some poor people and working-class people of color. When they
were younger and inexperienced with the law or when they happened on
lawyers with whom they could establish trust, the disadvantaged sometimes were able to experience the advantages of a relationship of delegation. But over time, disadvantaged people were far more likely than the
privileged to report withdrawal from their lawyers. Meanwhile, in most
court proceedings, and especially when faced with the threat of severe
criminal punishment, privileged people almost always delegate decision-
making authority to their lawyers (whom they trust to advocate on their
behalf) and perform deference to judges and the legal system in court
proceedings.

Unique features of the criminal courts help to explain why the privileged appear to act differently here compared to how they interact with officials and professionals in other, more mainstream institutions. First, unlike mainstream everyday institutions, criminal courts are less often encountered by the privileged. The privileged spend much of their adolescence and early adulthood attending school, going to doctor's appointments, and spending afternoons and weekends in extracurricular activities, at summer camps, and at sports events. As they enter adulthood, they spend most of their day engaging with workplace colleagues, assistants, and bosses. Going to court as a defendant is far from routine. The privileged people I spoke to have much less knowledge about courts and other criminal legal institutions—such as police, probation, and parole—than the disadvantaged. Ryan, Waine, and Arnold, for instance, readily admitted their lack of knowledge to me.

By contrast, in places where they have routine interactions and track records of success, such as schools and workplaces, the privileged are quite knowledgeable (or at least they believe themselves to be) about how to make institutions work to their benefit, using and directing—rather than relying on and deferring to—institutional authorities. In schools, privileged people (when they are young) ask their teachers for accommodations and (when they grow up) advocate for their children's success.[14] Some upper-middle-class parents may view teachers to be of a lower social standing.[15] Meanwhile, in doctor's offices, the privileged tend to feel entitled and empowered to gather medical knowledge on their own, and they feel as if they are experts of their own bodies, which they routinely monitor.[16] In workplaces, privileged people who work as managers and higher-level professionals feel they have more knowledge about business culture, relying on such knowledge to dominate their employees.[17] They also rely on their cultural tastes to select people like them to join their workplace environments, reproducing their cultural dominance.[18] The privileged feel they have expertise and understanding in these everyday institutions but not so much in criminal justice institutions. In the criminal courts, they feel they must rely on the expertise and authority of others, namely their lawyers.

Second, unlike mainstream institutions, criminal courts are designed to take away rights and resources, rather than grant them. Whereas educational institutions and doctor's offices provide valuable resources to their clients, criminal courts threaten to do the opposite, with no return on investment. A person's most precious resource—their freedom—is threatened in the courts in a way that it is not in other institutions. Being demanding and assertive with a teacher, a doctor, or an employer is often less risky. At best, a person can accumulate more resources; at worst, especially if someone is middle class, a person whose assertiveness backfires can find a new doctor, attend a different school, or apply for a new job. Although middle-class defendants could also (and sometimes do) hire different lawyers, the costs are different. Criminal courts operate on their own time, judges have no interest in slowing down their dockets for people to jump from lawyer to lawyer, and, ultimately, defendants cannot choose which courtroom or judge will determine their legal fates. For the privileged, there is little upside to asserting themselves in court and with their lawyers, as Brianna quickly came to learn in her interactions with Leya and in her willingness to allow Leya to advocate for her without being present in the lobby hearing. For the disadvantaged, however, there is comparatively less to lose by being assertive (given the disadvantages they experience in everyday life). Indeed, for the disadvantaged, there may possibly be more to gain, with respect to dignity, having their voice heard, or taxing the system with their resistance.

# CHAPTER FOUR

# Punishing Withdrawal, Rewarding Delegation

ONE ORDINARY MORNING in court, Sybil and I sat waiting for one of her clients to show up to a pretrial hearing. While she sat in the jury box, crammed next to several other defense attorneys, I sat in the front of the gallery. It was just before 9 a.m., and the judge had yet to arrive, but the courtroom was already abuzz. In the well, where the lawyers work and clients are called one by one from the gallery or from the holding cell to stand before the judge, about fifteen defense attorneys and a few prosecutors moved between the counsel tables and the jury box. Some shuffled papers quietly, while others checked the docket with the clerk, and still others bantered about the morning's news or made last-minute negotiations about a client's case. Behind me, the gallery was packed. A diverse group of people—about a quarter of them white and the rest black, Latino, or both—were finding their seats. Some whispered with family members seated next to them, others sat quietly with worry in their eyes, and still others appeared blank faced, just waiting. Minutes later, one of the court officers shouted: "All rise!" The room fell silent and stood in unison as the judge, a middle-aged black man, appeared from his chambers and sat down at his bench.

The first few cases were called; routine decisions were made—about discovery of evidence deadlines, motion dates, and the like. These first few defendants were silent as their lawyers spoke. Whenever the judge asked a personal question, the defendant would turn and whisper a response to their lawyer. Their lawyer would then share the information aloud on their behalf. It was hard to determine the character of these relationships just from these brief observations. It is possible that these relationships were positive—the kind typical of privileged clients, in which the defendant willingly delegates authority to their lawyer. It is also possible that the opposite was true, and like so many relationships between disadvantaged clients and their lawyers, these defendants may have been mistrustful and withdrawn. Rather than a sign of delegation, their whispering perhaps belied a simmering conflict, one that had yet to burst forth for all to see. Either way, there was a sense of calm and regularity to these interactions. The world of the courtroom was working in apparent harmony; the morning was proceeding just as, I assumed, the judge, the lawyers, the clerk, the probation officer, and the court officers all wanted it to.

But sometimes, attorney-client relationships are so strained that resistance does bubble to the surface in open court; the apparent consensus and order of the court process is revealed as vulnerable to contention and disruption. That is what happened when Frank was called.

Frank was a black man who looked to be in his late twenties or early thirties, lanky, with curly hair. He wore a plaid flannel shirt. As he approached the well and looked around for his lawyer, I could tell something was bothering him—he was eager to say something to the court. His lawyer joined him at the podium, and they stood side by side in the well, just barely on the other side of the gallery. As the judge and his lawyer began to talk about the case, it became clear that Frank was dealing with two charges—disorderly conduct and assault on a police officer—after a fight at a house party. He was in court today to set a date for trial. But the lawyer, a white man whose law firm represented members of a worker's union that Frank was a part of, told the judge that he no longer felt he could represent Frank—that he wanted, in legal terms, to "withdraw."[1] Then Frank jumped in, unable to contain himself: his lawyer was refusing to file motions in his case, he explained to the judge, and this was the true source of their disagreements. All he wanted was for his lawyer to defend him, Frank pleaded. At this remark, the lawyer stepped away from Frank and deeper into the well. He now stood closer to the judge's bench than he did to the podium, leaving Frank standing alone. Visibly trying to restrain his annoyance, the lawyer said, "I want to withdraw because there's a breakdown in the relationship." Frank raised his arms in the air, clearly agitated. He said:

FRANK: But why is he withdrawing?! I need someone from his firm. He is a union lawyer. But he's not doing what I ask him to do.
JUDGE: But he is withdrawing from you because there is a breakdown in the relationship. You have to get another lawyer, sir.

FRANK: But how do I do that? I need help getting a lawyer. See, this is why I have to have him as my lawyer. I can't get another lawyer on my own. I need his representation—or at least representation from someone.

JUDGE: But you're not indigent! You make too much money to get appointed counsel.

FRANK: But I need his representation!

JUDGE: Look, the fact that you all keep going back and forth up here in court suggests to me that there is a breakdown in communication between you all. The motion for withdrawal is allowed.

Frank began pacing back and forth at the podium. Frustrated, his hands were on his hips, wrinkling his untucked shirt. The judge leaned forward, as if to get Frank's attention. The judge continued:

JUDGE: Sir, you need to come back to court on the first [of the next month] for your next court date.

FRANK: Okay, can I get another date? I won't be able to get a lawyer by then.

"Nope. You have a date set for the first," the judge said, rolling his eyes. Frank turned his back to the judge and walked past me and straight to the courtroom exit, all the while muttering to himself. The judge's words suggested that the problem was clear: the bickering between Frank and his lawyer was proof of an attorney-client relationship beyond repair.

Rather than encouraging the lawyer to listen to Frank's desire to file certain motions, the judge allowed the lawyer to withdraw. The result was that Frank was now without professional legal representation. Prior to his lawyer's refusal to represent him that day, Frank had been able to receive free legal representation through his union, which provided legal aid to its members. Now with his union lawyer no longer willing to defend him, Frank was stuck: he was told his income was too high to qualify for indigency (and thus be assigned a court-appointed lawyer), but he knew his income was too low to hire a different private attorney. As the courtroom doors closed behind Frank, the clerk had already called the next case. Order was restored; the day pushed onward. Frank's outburst seemed almost instantly forgotten. And yet as I sat in the gallery, I wondered about the injustice of a court process that not only ignores the procedural requests of defendants but also appears to punish them for asking their lawyers to make such requests.

I did not interview Frank or his lawyer, but their withdrawn relationship was available for all to see. In the privacy of their conversations, I
inferred, Frank and his lawyer could not agree on whether to file motions
in the case. Frank wanted certain motions filed, but his attorney was
unwilling to file them. Another defense lawyer who was in court that day
told me that lawyers do not file motions if they do not think they will be
granted or if they do not think they will matter for the legal outcome of the
case. About Frank's case, the lawyer remarked, "It's unclear what motions
the guy [Frank] was asking to file, but the motions probably wouldn't work
or matter in this kind of case . . . the case will likely be dismissed anyway."
Even though the final legal outcome—in this lawyer's assessment—would
likely be a dismissal, Frank was either unaware of this outcome or unsatis-
fied with its possibility, perhaps feeling that more was at stake in the court
process itself, as so many disadvantaged defendants in this study did.

Frank had been punished, both by his lawyer and then by the judge,
for his withdrawal and resistance. Not only did his lawyer decide he would
no longer represent him, but the judge then ignored his appeals and mandated he come back to court in thirty days, with or without a lawyer. The
judge refused to consider providing him with court-appointed counsel,
despite Frank's insistence that he could not hire a lawyer on his own. And
the judge refused to extend his court date any further, which would have
slightly relieved Frank of the pressure of quickly hiring a new lawyer.

Neither of the judge's decisions were inevitable. Indeed, in small procedural moments like these, judges have broad discretion. The judge could
have asked the probation department to reassess Frank's indigency status,
or at least suggest to Frank that he could go down to the probation department to have it reassessed. I have observed how probation officers in many
courthouses can be lenient with defendants when they fill out their intake
forms, rarely verifying their claims about their income or their receipt of
public benefits. Moreover, in Massachusetts, defendants can qualify as
"marginally indigent," whereby they are deemed too poor to hire a private lawyer for thousands of dollars but financially secure enough to be
able to contribute much more than the typical $150 to be assigned court-
appointed counsel. The judge also could have offered Frank a later court
date, and the prosecutor would likely not have objected. But the judge
appeared too annoyed by Frank to consider any of these lenient options.
He punished Frank for making a scene, and for not deferring to his lawyer.

So far I have focused attention largely on defendants, and the ways
their adolescent experiences, their race/ethnicity, and their economic class

all influence the kind of relationships they are able to create with their lawyers. Those relationships, as we have seen again and again, are central to defendants' unequal experiences of the court system. But the portrait so far painted of inequality and injustice in the courts is not yet complete. We also need to explore in further depth how court officials, especially lawyers and judges, respond when defendants withdraw (into resistance or resignation) or when they delegate authority. Our account so far has viewed lawyers' responses through the eyes of defendants, whose interpretations are central to the feeling of inequality as it is constituted in small and large moments of interaction. But in this chapter, I shift attention to the interpretations and actions of court officials, examining how they view and respond to their clients. Doing so provides a closer look at how inequality is reproduced symbolically and materially through the levying of consequential legal outcomes. This chapter asks: How do officials respond to defendants who withdraw and defendants who delegate authority, and with what consequences?

The answer can be found within the hidden legal rules of the courts and the repeat relationships that defense attorneys have with other court officials. For defense attorneys, the attorney-client relationship is viewed as but one relationship among many they must manage.[2] Unlike defendants, whose main experience of the court is filtered through the relationship they have with their lawyer, defense lawyers have routine and professional relationships with prosecutors, judges, probation officers, court clerks, court officers, and other defense lawyers. They also have experiences with multiple clients at once, and they have memories of relationships with various clients over the course of their careers. In this sense, the attorney-client relationship (from the perspective of defense attorneys) is embedded in a web of other relationships. And these relationships come with expectations and norms.

From my interviews, conversations, and observations with defense attorneys, I came to see how despite their impassioned recognition of the injustices their clients have faced and despite their overarching commitment to effectively representing their clients, they often felt pressured by the expectations, norms, and power of prosecutors and judges. Defense attorneys largely defined effective representation as an effort to use their expertise to mitigate the potential legal consequences that could arise from the charge their client faced. In their efforts to reduce the legal consequences their clients might be subject to, they considered their knowledge of the behaviors of prosecutors and judges as central components of their professional expertise. Defense attorneys regularly warned of harsher sentences pursued by prosecutors if their client did not agree to a plea deal.[3] Such warnings, as we have seen, often feel like coercion to disadvantaged defendants. Defense attorneys also described the importance of maintaining their credibility as reasonable negotiators in front of prosecutors.[4] Maintaining such credibility was important for defense lawyers' future negotiations on behalf of future clients. From judges, defense attorneys felt pressure to maintain decorum in the courtroom, which meant they needed to silence clients who spoke up. Moreover, judges themselves, as in Frank's case, sometimes directly silenced or punished defendants for their violation of the court's norms—unwritten rules that value deference and acceptance of fault over the assertion of constitutional rights. Judges and defense attorneys alike rewarded those who delegated authority to their lawyers and deferred to the court's expectations; these rewards included reduced sentences, the option of drug or mental health treatment as an alternative to more punitive sentences, and even a defense attorney's offer to help agreeable clients in future cases or with respect to the mitigation of collateral consequences that arise from their legal sentences.

These realities can be understood as a covert, and often unintentional, form of racial and class discrimination. The resistance and resignation characteristic of disadvantage is punished, whereas the delegation characteristic of privilege is rewarded. Given such differential sanctions and rewards, these processes likely contribute to race and class disparities in legal outcomes (though I do not statistically test this logical inference).[5] There are, of course, many other causes of disparities between the wealthy and white and the poor and people of color. Direct forms of racism and class prejudice (that is, feelings of antipathy and bias against the disadvantaged, and feelings of warmth and leniency toward the privileged) likely play a considerable role in contributing to inequality at various points of the criminal legal process.[6] Other forms of racism and classism precede— and contribute to the inequalities of—the attorney-client relationship itself.[7] In addition, variation in the quality of lawyers assigned to poor people and that of the lawyers privileged people can hire has been shown to account for a proportion of disparities in certain court outcomes.[8] But even when defense attorneys are committed to representing all their clients, effective legal representation as they define it may not be enough. This chapter shows how attorney-client interactions, and the taken-for-granted responses of court officials, can contribute to unequal outcomes between the privileged and the disadvantaged. As we will see, effective legal representation does not ensure justice.

## Effective Representation

Scholars, appellate courts, and bar association guidelines establish that defendants are entitled to "effective legal representation."[9] But what is effective legal representation? What, exactly, do legal scholars and officials imagine that defense attorneys should be effective at doing for their clients?

Effective representation—and its antithesis: *in*effective representation—is vaguely defined but revolves around whether and how defense attorneys influence the legal outcomes of a case. The Supreme Court has excused various behaviors among defense attorneys that you might imagine would constitute ineffectiveness, such as lawyers using drugs or sleeping through parts of trial. One trial court judge infamously told a journalist, "The constitution doesn't say the lawyer has to be awake."[10] Such behaviors are excused because the Court considers representation to be ineffective only when it can be shown to have had a negative effect on the legal outcome of the case, especially the conviction and sentence that result from trial.[11] Of course, much ineffectiveness can occur prior to trial—in decisions about bail recommendations, pretrial meetings, motion hearings, and negotiations with prosecutors. Claims to ineffectiveness can be raised in relation to these earlier moments of the court process. Yet, most defendants plead guilty, meaning they rarely have the chance to raise ineffectiveness claims on appeal.[12] Meanwhile, trial court judges are instructed to presume that most lawyers are behaving professionally and with an "objective standard of reasonableness" in their decisions.[13] In the everyday practice of law in courtrooms across the country, judges typically have limited awareness of the dynamics of most attorney-client interactions. Attorney-client meetings occur behind closed doors, where disadvantaged defendants in this study often developed feelings of mistrust and frustration that judges may never know about. For all these reasons, various kinds of seemingly ineffective decision making among defense attorneys can go unchecked, including lawyers missing court dates, citing inappropriate case law, and belittling their clients in front of the jury.[14]

I spoke to more than forty defense attorneys and spent a month getting to know three public defenders (Selena, Sybil, and Tom) personally.[15] This group of defense attorneys is diverse in professional experience (in years practicing), race, and gender.[16] For every one of them, effective legal representation was largely defined in relation to whether and how their strategies, advice, and actions influenced their client's formal legal outcomes (such as charge dismissal, bail amount, verdict, sentence type, and sentence length). Defense attorneys viewed their professional role as assisting in the mitigation of these outcomes. Such an understanding of their role as defense attorneys is not too surprising, given what we know about the constitutional standards described above. But defense attorneys' focus on effectiveness at mitigating punitive legal outcomes, more often than not, eclipses a deeper understanding of their clients' broader interests and desires to achieve justice.

Many defendants wanted more than to simply avoid harsher legal outcomes. They also wanted to express their dissatisfaction with the legal system, contest the characterization of their alleged criminal behaviors, litigate the validity of police work, and clear their name. Some even wanted more meaningful reconciliation with their victims. For instance, Glasses, a black man currently on parole, faced a potential parole violation when a woman friend accused him of harassment. Although the court ultimately found that he did not harass her and therefore did not violate parole, he felt that justice was not served. He felt terrible that what he thought were friendly interactions felt like harassment to her. He also regretted that the court did not consider, or try to ameliorate, the woman's struggles with mental illness. "What I think she needed was mental health counseling, you know," he said. He felt that the adversarial nature of criminal law—what he termed an "'us versus them' theory"—meant that neither he nor his alleged victim could heal from their pain. Glasses concluded: "I'm glad I'm not inside of a prison, you know, [but] I don't feel victorious. I don't feel as though justice was served." Such incongruences between a client's vision of justice and a lawyer's legal strategies commonly existed in attorney-client relationships between court-appointed lawyers and disadvantaged defendants—people who often felt there was more at stake in the court process than the reduction of their sentence.

The public defenders I got to know all expressed passion for their clients, frequently recognizing the injustices their disadvantaged clients face in their everyday lives and in relation to the legal system.[17] Tom, the public defender first mentioned in the introduction, is a serious-looking white man. He has nearly a decade of experience as a public defender. Before becoming a defender, however, he had another career. In that line of work, he would go on ride alongs with police officers. That is when he realized the injustices of policing: "I started to get really, really concerned about the classist and the racist nature of our criminal legal system." He told me that racist police practices in the Boston area result in the disproportionate presence of poor people of color in the courts: "You don't find them patrolling in the South End. You don't find them in West Roxbury. You find them in Forest Hills. You find them in Roxbury, Dorchester, Mattapan—that's the criminogenic factor. Police presence; not citizen criminality." Tom described how his realization about unequal policing motivated him to apply to law school. After talking to friends who were lawyers, he believed that there was no way for him to "change the system without going to law school." Immediately following law school, he applied to work as a staff public defender with CPCS.

Selena similarly recounted how concerns about racial injustice motivated her decision to become a public defender. Introduced in detail in chapter 2, Selena is a Latina woman in her twenties. She had wanted to be a lawyer since she was a kid, but it was not until college that she developed an ethical stance toward the importance of public defense work. She told me:

> It was a lot of thinking about stuff in ways that I'd never thought about it before. I had some really great colleagues in college who were really smart, and we would talk about these things like for hours and hours and hours, and so, it just kind of really worked my idea of ethics and what is right and what—how you can achieve the goals of something that's ethical or moral. I think it was kind of like around that when I was like, "I don't think that being a prosecutor and working for the state is the only way to come to do what I think is right." It kind of changed my ideas of justice and equality and all of that kind of stuff. I also took a class in college that was like "Race, Class, and the Law"—I think is what it was called—and it was kind of like an introduction to critical race theory. . . . That I think was one of the first times where I was like, "Oh, how doesn't anyone see that the way things are now, especially for people of color, all comes from history."

Realizing that becoming a prosecutor would not be the best means for her to "do what I think is right," she applied to law school with the intention of becoming a defender.

Sybil also described the racism her clients face in the legal system, noting how her own experience as a black woman influences the way she interacts with defendants. "I love my clients, and I can see myself in so many of them," she said. She continued, describing the injustices faced by her typical clients: "It's just like, ugh. If you weren't black and if you didn't have dreads and if you weren't like 6'4, 250 pounds, this wouldn't have happened to you. If you were a little white boy with the same amount of drugs on you and in the same car, everything would be fine." Sybil, first introduced in detail in chapter 2, is a tall black woman in her twenties. She has personally experienced racism and misogyny in the legal system.[18] She told me, "As a young black woman, especially starting out . . . I'm always like, 'the baby mama' or the probationer. [People ask] 'Are you here to visit somebody at the jail?' 'You're not an attorney!' Like, it always was like they assumed that, even though I was in a suit." Sybil concluded that "the legal system is not fair; I don't think it's ever going to be fair. But, I do think it can be better. So, I'm just doing what I can to be a little bit of help." Like Tom and Selena, Sybil views her role as a public defender as helping to right the system's wrongs.

Compared to bar advocates, public defenders appear more likely to be aware of the disadvantages their clients face and to express passion for their work. Recall that bar advocates—private defense attorneys who take on indigent clients in addition to their private clients—handle most disadvantaged defendants' cases in Boston. Therefore, defendants who are represented by court-appointed lawyers are more likely to work with bar advocates than public defenders. Bar advocates select into legal practice differently than public defenders. According to Tom, public defenders are hired, in part, on the basis of their expressed commitment to caring for disadvantaged clients: "The interview [to be hired] is extremely focused on that component: your dedication, your commitment, your emotional connection, your willingness to give and be available and to go beyond what others do." Public defenders are mandated to participate in about thirty days of training sessions before they begin practicing, whereas bar advocates receive seven days of training.[19] In 2016, I attended part of the public defender training session in Boston. The walls of the rooms where the sessions took place were plastered with newspaper clippings portraying public defenders as "unsung heroes" and "justice's gatekeepers." New defenders received lessons from veteran defenders throughout the state, who covered topics as wide ranging as the immigration consequences of various kinds of convictions to working with social workers. Concepts like "racial justice" and "systemic change" were unpacked and debated. Once newly minted defenders enter their offices, they are provided further resources either unavailable to—or at best, harder to be accessed by—bar advocates. Comparing defenders to bar advocates, Selena said, "We do have [more] benefits." Such benefits and resources include investigators, social workers, and frequent brainstorming sessions. Such sessions, one of which I observed over lunch in the defender's office, help lawyers think through difficult aspects of their current cases and function as teachable moments for future cases.

Public defenders regularly expressed to me their belief that the average bar advocate is not as passionate as the average defender. The verdict on bar advocates was a mixed one—some did their jobs well, but many others made their peers look bad. Tom said, "Bar advocates get a bad reputation. There are a few very good ones." Selena said:

> I think that there are some who are good bar advocates, but I think a lot of them, the older ones—especially the ones that have been doing this for a long time—are like . . . they just kind of stroll in at 10:30 a.m. I've definitely seen bar advocates who like come to court without a file, and then they have to go to trial, and they're like, "Oh, I didn't prep anything because I didn't think it was gonna happen."

Beyond some older bar advocates not being prepared for trial, other bar advocates are described as uncaring toward their clients and racist:

> SYBIL: It seems as though they'll just take anyone to be a bar advo-
> cate. It doesn't seem like they are looking for people who are really
> trying to understand where our clients are coming from and the
> situation they are going through outside of just the criminal com-
> plaint. Whereas with a staff attorney [public defender], I think
> there's a lot more that goes into vetting out who gets chosen as a
> staff attorney for CPCS.
> MATT: Interesting.
> SYBIL: I think a lot of our [bar] advocates—they are annoying as well.
> Like, some of the stuff that they say is ridiculous. It's racist. It's like
> some of them are, like, so clueless about, like, police misconduct
> and stuff that we'll talk about [in the public defender's office] . . .
> I've seen bar advocates find out the cop is lying and be so shocked
> that they want to change their job. They can't believe that a cop
> would lie, and it's just like, "How are you doing this job?" . . . How
> could you be doing this job and this is the first time you realize
> that a cop may possibly be lying?

Beyond public defenders, other court officials similarly suggested that bar advocates were a mixed bag. While waiting for Tom in a courthouse hallway one day, I struck up a conversation with a court interpreter—a person who translates court proceedings for defendants, victims, and other people who do not speak English. After I told her I was working as an intern in the defender's office, she said, "Public defenders here are excellent." I said, "Yeah, they're great. The bar advocates here seem to be as well." She replied: "Um, . . . some of them, yes." After a pause, she said, "But not all." Analysis of my own observations, once I had left the field, confirmed that bar advocates sometimes seemed unprepared, harsh on their clients, or even racist. Not all, but some.

While public defenders commonly described some bar advocates as uncaring, racist, or ineffective, Selena noted that public defenders are not immune to these same problems. She told me:

> I think that public defenders in general, myself included, can feel like we are so, like, progressive and we're doing all this stuff, and, like, we're so helpful that sometimes people forget to check themselves just in their own interpersonal relationships. There has been—just like in every office in all the world, I'm sure—there have been some issues interpersonally. And I've been trying to—and have been successful I think—talk about race more. Talk about, you know, issues very openly.

Selena felt that her colleagues all have the right "intentions" but operate within a "racist society." Such a reality, she said, affects the subtle ways they talk about and engage with clients.

Despite bar advocates' fewer resources and seemingly less passionate approaches to legal representation on average, all defense attorneys I spoke to sought to mitigate the myriad legal consequences that could result from a defendant's charge. Mitigation of legal outcomes was the common way they defined effective representation. Indeed, even for public defenders, their commitment to such a definition of effective representation often meant that their passions for broader forms of justice were secondary to the legal practicalities of achieving less punitive outcomes for their clients.[20]

When asked about prosecutors, defense attorneys often described the necessity of negotiating with them to obtain less costly legal outcomes. Tom described most line prosecutors and other court officials in Boston as reasonable:

> It's remarkable how much capacity there is on both sides, and people don't realize that. Don't get me wrong, I've been here for a long time and the problems—our system of grand juries and prosecutor power. [But] we're really lucky, really lucky. Our judges are compassionate, our ADAs are reasonable, probation officers are professional, clerks are nailed down in tight. We are really lucky.

Tom is friends with some prosecutors and feels that his cultivation of such cordial, professional relationships can facilitate less punitive legal outcomes for his clients. When I asked him about the prosecutors in the courts he regularly practices in, he said:

The line ADAs are fantastic, really good. I told you about the recommendation with my client, the addict, who deserved a two and a half [year] sentence. They offered [him] a very tightly constructed set of conditions for drug treatment. That was remarkable, and it's by no means the only time that's happened. Very, very compassionate people. . . . They treat us as professionals; I treat them as professionals. I regard them as professionals [with] communications open, and they're professionals. As I told you before, we have to create that atmosphere of cordiality—not to be friends, but I have become friends with a couple. I like them very much. They are nice people.

Defense attorneys like Tom strive to maintain agreeable, professional relationships with prosecutors to negotiate less punitive deals for their clients. Tom even felt that negotiation itself could allow for more "fair" outcomes—resolutions of a criminal case that considered "both sides" to "resolve issues in a way that society feels that it should be done."

Not all defense attorneys, however, described their relationships with prosecutors as friendly or felt that negotiations with prosecutors could resolve criminal complaints in a fair way. Selena and Sybil both acknowledged the importance of negotiating with prosecutors but did not describe their professional relationships as anything other than professional necessity. I asked Sybil about the nature of the relationship between the defender's office and prosecutors. She said:

Um, so, everyone's different. Generally, I think people have, I don't know, a level of respect [with prosecutors]. Some people go and have drinks with ADAs. There was an ADA who had left and was going to superior court and had like, um, you know a goodbye party—an after-work type of thing—and a few of the attorneys from this office went there. So, it's like, it depends. Me, personally, it's totally professional. I don't want to be seen with you. I don't want my clients to see me out having a drink with you. Like, I just, "you do you and I do me" type of thing. Because I have a better relationship with some than others. Um, but it's still just court, professional type stuff, never anything more than that.

Selena similarly remarked:

I don't talk to . . . There are some people who will try to get the prosecutors on their side—like, try to convince them that this is the best recommendation. Especially bar advocates. [They] will just sit there and just like shoot the shit with the prosecutors, and I don't like doing

that. I mean, if they talk to me, I'll talk to them. You know, I'm nice; I
like to be professional. I'd like to have a good relationship with them.
But I don't want my clients to think I'm friends with them, and I don't
want to be friends with a lot of them, frankly. The least amount that
I have to talk to them, I will.

Like Tom, both Sybil and Selena recognize the utility of talking to prosecutors to mitigate. But sometimes, they felt negotiations with prosecutors
were unnecessary and costly for their image in the eyes of their clients.

For low-level offenses that do not have mandatory sentences attached
to them, defense attorneys are more focused on understanding and accommodating judges' preferences than on negotiating with prosecutors. When
a conviction on a charge does not trigger a mandatory sentence, a judge
has discretion at sentencing. Therefore, negotiations with prosecutors are
less important. Sybil explained:

> I go disparate all the time [offer a different sentencing recommenda-
> tion], and most of the time I'm successful . . . 'Cause, like, it doesn't
> really matter what they [prosecutors] want, you know. It'd be helpful
> if they agreed with me, but it's up to the judge, and I know my judge,
> and that's one thing you have to know. It's like, the person who makes
> the decision is the judge. You need to know what to say to your judge.
> Because there's certain things I would say to one judge, and certain
> things I'd emphasize to another judge, and certain things I would
> diminish a little in front of other judges. Um, but the DA's going to say
> the same thing no matter what.

Prior to sentencing, such as during arraignment and bail hearings
and during motion hearings, judges also occupy center stage in defense
attorneys' strategizing. Many defense attorneys described the importance
of aligning their arguments to a judge's way of thinking about crime and
legal procedures. Some judges were described as having preferences with
respect to certain crimes, such as a judge who is "soft on drug offenders."
Public defenders often "share information" about judges, developing collective understandings of judges' preferences that are known throughout
the "criminal defense bar in Massachusetts." One lawyer described how
she seeks to gather information in the moment if she finds herself in front
of a new judge: "If a judge walks up who I've never seen before, I will
immediately turn to the lawyers around me and say 'Who is the judge?
Do you [know] who this judge is? Do you know anything about them?'"
Such information can assist lawyers in tailoring their recommendations to

specific judges. But judges were sometimes described as more alike than different. As a group, judges' behaviors could be predictable. For instance, one defense attorney described how more than one judge will typically "split the baby" between a prosecutor's bail recommendation and a defense attorney's bail recommendation. Common ways that most judges are thought to behave pattern defense attorneys' general approaches toward, and feelings about the plausibility of, certain legal strategies. For instance, from the beginning of this book, we saw how Tom warned Drew about the small chance that the judge would rule favorably on the motions he proposed. Tom's decision making about motions was made in reference to his knowledge about judges' preferences, as well as his professional ethical unease about making "frivolous" motions. What constitutes frivolity to court officials and according to everyday legal norms, of course, rarely comports with the cultivated expertise of disadvantaged defendants.

In interactions with prosecutors and judges alike, defense attorneys regularly recounted a need to maintain their credibility as reasonable. Leya, Brianna's defense attorney from chapter 3, described to me how credibility is maintained by knowing when and how to dispute unfair procedures. Her philosophy as a lawyer is that "you don't fight for every small thing or every small battle." She provided an example of how doing so can negatively affect a client's legal outcomes. While Brianna and I were waiting for Leya in the hallway, Leya was working with another client in the arraignments session. When she came back for us, Leya told us about a defense attorney in the session who insisted that the ADA file his client's complaint correctly. The ADA had apparently made a small clerical error in the way the charge was formally listed, and the defense attorney insisted the error be corrected. The judge, reluctantly, agreed. Leya guffawed as she recounted the story to us. She felt the defense attorney's actions were a distraction—and could harm his client more than help. To correct the mistake, the clerk would have to create a new docket number, making the defendant's record appear longer than it actually was. "So now, just visually, it looks like his client has a longer record," she explained. She also said that "you start to lose credibility if you fight for every little thing." Defense attorneys who routinely make procedural motions may come to be taken less seriously by judges and other officials.

Defense attorneys were also aware of judges' general desire for order in their courtroom. And although they did not necessarily agree with judges' seeming unwillingness to hear from their clients or allow certain motions, they felt pressure to abide by such norms to secure less punitive outcomes. Sybil told me:

I'm part of the system. I know that if I act a certain way, or say certain things in front of judges, it's probably going to hurt me and my client more than help. Even though the judge does need to hear this, and the judge needs to understand that this isn't fair and that this happens all the time, you know. But I also know that I need to keep my mouth shut sometimes, and I need to know my judge, and I need to know my audience and really keep my client's best interest at heart.

Sybil described how, given her understanding of judges' expectations, she has had to control her clients' anger when discussing legal strategy behind closed doors. She said:

I've had clients that are like, you know, "this is so unfair, this is what needs to happen, like we need to sue the police department, tell the judge fuck you." And I'm just like, "Okay, but we're not going to do that, because that's not going to help us, and if I do it this way, it's going to take a little longer, and it's not going to be as 'fight the power' as you want it to be, but the end result is going to be exactly what you want it to be."

Sybil's comments illustrate the central logic of effective representation: "the end result"—or the final legal outcome—is more important than the humiliation and frustration of the process of getting to that outcome.

Of course, many disadvantaged defendants, as we have seen, feel that their lawyers are neither effective at mitigating their legal outcomes nor considerate in acknowledging their frustrations and taking their cultivated expertise seriously. Lawyers sometimes recognize that clients are frustrated, but they nonetheless seek to persuade their clients that their professional legal expertise is more accurate and that clients may not really know what is in their own best interests. Although privileged defendants are more willing to defer to lawyers and abide by the norms of effective legal representation (as imagined and explained by their defense attorneys), disadvantaged defendants are more likely to resist or be resigned. Judges and defense attorneys—even when expressing passion for their disadvantaged clients and recognizing the system's injustices—nonetheless ignore, silence, and coerce defendants for their withdrawal in the attorney-client relationship.

## Punishing Withdrawal

Nearly all the lawyers I spoke to had more than one story to tell about "uncooperative" and "difficult" clients—defendants who, in the terminology developed in this book, withdrew from them. In in-depth interviews and in casual conversations, I asked lawyers about the kinds of defendants they prefer and the kinds that frustrate them. I asked them about the different kinds of relationships they find themselves in and the kinds that they strive to cultivate with their clients. And I asked how they react to these different kinds of relationships. Nearly every lawyer I spoke with was aware of the need to gain the trust of their clients. Some recognized defendants' distrust of the legal system and defendants' frustrations of being charged with a crime. Selena, for instance, said, "A lot of clients get worked up, which is totally understandable. And I like giving them space to do that because I don't know if other people give them the space to just feel and, like, let their emotions out."

At the same time, defense attorneys admitted that they were not always able to gain the trust of their clients: many of their most disadvantaged clients did not seem to engage with them or defer to their expertise. Worse, they felt that some of their clients were outwardly hostile. One public defender told me, "Clients are always looking for a reason as to why they shouldn't trust you." Another public defender said, "Clients are quick to trash lawyers." A bar advocate reflected, "Sometimes you and your client don't hit it off or get along. There's sometimes a perception that if you don't pay for attorneys, then they won't represent you well."

Selena recalled a particularly difficult client. The client, charged with A&B on an acquaintance, seemed to mistrust Selena from the beginning. "I felt like he didn't trust me," she said. In their meetings, he was distant and resigned. Over the course of several months, they met to discuss his options. She worked out a possible plea deal: a guilty conviction, no jail time but some time on probation. She also told him she would still prepare for trial, while warning him that he would likely lose because the alleged victim was an acquaintance who was eager to testify against him. Although the client did not seem to like the suggestion that the plea may be his best option, he did not ask Selena for other possible conditions as part of his plea deal or alternative strategies to prepare for trial. Rather than engaging with Selena and voicing his concerns, he "kept trying to go around me and do things behind my back." For instance, he told Selena he wanted to have another lawyer he knew talk to the prosecutor. Selena recalled:

> He was like, "I have this friend who's an attorney, and I was wondering if he could talk to the prosecutor about the case." I was like, "No. I'm not going to let another attorney talk to the prosecutor when it's my case! If

you want to have them represent you, that's totally fine. I'm not going to take offense to that. I'll go withdraw right now, and we can get him appointed." He is like, "Well, he doesn't really do criminal work." And I was like, "No, I'm not going to do that."

On the date of trial, she asked her client whether he would like to go to trial or take the plea. He refused both options:

> We get there, and we go over all of this, and then suddenly he just seemed like, "I'm not taking any guilty. I'm not doing this. Do we have to go to trial today? What if we—can't we get a continuance?" I was like, "No. Today's the trial day. We have to try [to tender the plea], but I need to know if the judge comes back insisting on a guilty, do you want to go to trial or do you want to accept it [the guilty plea]?" . . . He ended up just not wanting to do the plea and not wanting to go to trial either. I was like, "Well, we've gotta do one today." He ended up just leaving. He just left the courthouse and never came back. And so, they put out a default warrant for him. And I had to go up [to the judge's bench] and be like, "I think he went to the store to get a coffee." He just never came back, and I was like, "Well, all right."

After he left court in a panic and a default warrant was issued, Selena was annoyed, to say the least. She called him, telling him he needed to remove his warrant and to let her know if he planned to try to hire a new attorney. "He just gave me some like weird roundabout answer," Selena recalled. "Fine, whatever. Just let me know," she told him, exhausted by his avoidance, his resignation throughout the course of their interactions, and his ultimate resistance to her authority and the court on the day of trial.

Default warrants present problems for future legal outcomes and constitute a punitive outcome themselves. A default warrant is issued when a defendant misses a court date, affording police officers the authority to arrest the person to compel their return to court. An arrest is itself a form of punishment. Moreover, defaults are added to a defendant's criminal record. When a defendant is sentenced, judges look at their criminal record to get a sense for what kind of person they have before them. Moreover, if a defendant is arrested in the future on a new charge, judges consider a defendant's history of defaulting when determining the bail amount.[21] Scholars have shown that bail determinations have important implications for defendants; when bail is set too high, defendants unable to afford their bail amount are incarcerated while awaiting trial, making it more likely that they will plead guilty.[22] Across the country, most of the people sitting in jails are awaiting trial.[23] Pretrial incarceration is far too commonly implemented as a form of punishment for defendants who have yet to be proven guilty beyond a reasonable doubt.

When defendants are unable or unwilling to communicate because of their resignation, much like Selena's client above, defense lawyers may not fully invest their time in preparing for their cases. For instance, Sybil described how, over time, she has come to be able to identify those clients who just might not show up for court. The reasons are numerous, but three scenarios, in Sybil's experience, are the most common: they are managing homelessness, have a drug addiction, or simply do not have a way to stay in contact because they are too poor to have a phone. Sybil waits to prepare motions for these defendants only after they show up a second time to court at their pretrial hearings. She said:

> There are a lot of times when I know I'm never going to see a client again. At arraignment, especially clients with heroin issues, I can always tell. Especially if you don't have a phone. I can always tell that I probably won't see you again. And I have learned—when I first started, I would completely prepare cases like that. But I feel like now, if I have a client and I have any type of concern about whether I might not ever see them again and there's no contact or if there's a drug issue, I don't prepare, like, motions to dismiss or do all that for the pretrial hearing. And stuff like that. I would just wait until after, because I want to make sure that they are actually going to be there rather than—it just ends up being a waste of time.

For Sybil, preparing motions after the pretrial hearing rather than before for certain clients could possibly save her time for other tasks and other clients. Of course, such a practice could contribute to clients feeling that their lawyers are not taking their cases seriously—a common complaint among disadvantaged defendants.

When clients are so resigned that they do not meet with their lawyers or answer their phone calls between court dates, defense attorneys respond by making their own decisions about what legal outcome they believe to be in a client's best interest. Such decision making can become routine: lawyers prepare for the possibility of trial but expect to negotiate a reasonable and standard plea deal that they assume their clients would not mind taking. Even without a client's input, lawyers must make these choices on behalf of their clients because the court process requires that, at some point, a decision be made. Selena described this process to me:

SELENA: I would say 99 percent of the time, you go into a trial date having either never talked to your client about the trial or talked to them on the phone very briefly about it.

MATT: Okay, and so, having never talked to them about the trial, how do you know they even want to go to trial or not?

SELENA: I will usually ask that question by the pretrial hearing. I have an okay idea by then of where they want to go. Either they'll outright tell me, or I'll look at it and be like, "This is not a great case for trial. I need to talk to them about the possibility of a plea." Or we just kind of leave it up in the air, and I prepare the trial anyway. Well, I usually prepare the trial anyway. . . . You can set either for a trial date or a potential disposition date, where you can come in and everybody thinks it's going to be a plea. You try to do the plea. If the judge does something you don't want or the plea doesn't go through, then you can pick the trial date in the future. . . . I try very hard not to pressure them to plea. Like, this is your life; this is your case. If you want to go to trial, and I think it's the most losing-est trial ever, I'm going to do it because that's on you. It's all you.

Selena, like nearly all the other defense lawyers in this study, is adamant that she does not force defendants to take plea deals. This was confirmed in my observations. At the same time, defendants who are resigned—such as Jaylan, described in chapter 2—tend to be lulled into plea deals that have been negotiated by their lawyers with little of their explicit input. Moreover, a lawyer's strong suggestion that it is in a defendant's best interest to take a plea can feel like coercion for defendants who do not want to, such as Drew, Troy, Jeffrey, and others from chapter 2.[24]

Some defendants resist the plea deals their lawyers negotiate, much like Selena's client, who kept avoiding her and then fled the courthouse. For a small number of these defendants, resisting their lawyers can pay off with respect to the final legal sentence, even in the face of the other negative legal consequences that can emerge from frustrating the attorney-client relationship. There are myriad costs to resisting defense attorneys' advice regarding pleas—such as the process of returning to court and abiding by pretrial conditions for that much longer. Troy, the poor white man described in chapter 2, recounted to me how he initially refused his attorney's suggestion that he plead guilty to one year of probation for his first drug possession charge. He felt he should have been able to get a better deal given his clean record:

> Like, he [my lawyer] was coming back to me like, "Yeah, just plead guilty and take a year probation, and do this right now." No, I'm not doing it. You know what I mean? Because at this point, I didn't have a record. And usually the first couple of times, they're easy on you—like, they'll work with you. So I said to him, "This is my first arrest. I'm not taking a year probation. For what?"

While waiting for his lawyer to negotiate a better deal, Troy was fortunate to be out on bail. But he had several pretrial conditions. One condition was that he had to complete a detox program. Such mandated pretrial conditions are, for many defendants, perceived to be a form of leniency, at least as compared to incarceration. But such conditions also serve the purpose of surveilling defendants and monitoring their behaviors, even when they have yet to be convicted of a crime.[25] Several months later, after not showing up to court and being rearrested on default warrants, Troy learned that his attorney had finally negotiated a CWOF with terms of probation. He took this deal. It was a marginally better outcome than immediately pleading guilty with terms of probation because it would not leave a conviction on his record (assuming he abided by his probation terms). Troy's experience reveals the sentencing benefits of waiting out a plea for some defendants, as well as the legal and nonlegal costs of pretrial conditions and the risks of rearrest.

In small and large moments behind closed doors and in court, lawyers respond negatively to other kinds of resistance among their clients beyond the refusal to take a plea. Clients perceived to be resistant are described with even more annoyance and frustration than the resigned. Tom described his least favorite client as an "asshole," given his perceived rudeness as well as his resistance to Tom's expertise. The client was charged with drug distribution and kept insisting that Tom make motions to suppress or dismiss evidence—motions that he felt were inappropriate to make, given the police report and evidence collected in the case. Tom said:

> TOM: Just an ass, just a jerk. He acted like I didn't know what I was doing, like I wasn't doing enough. There's no motion to dismiss because the police report is complete and accurate. There's no motion to suppress because there are no rights that have been violated.
>
> MATT: Was he asking you to do all these things, or something?

TOM: Yeah: "Why aren't you doing any motions? Why aren't you
doing more motions?" And mostly I'm known as sort of a "motions
guy". . . . I file motions like crazy, but this guy was just an asshole.

Ultimately, the client decided he wanted to go to trial. Throughout
trial, the client kept questioning Tom's legal strategy. Right after Tom presented his closing arguments to the jury, his client was upset that Tom had
not brought up various aspects of the case that he thought were important
to share with the jury. Tom remembered: "He said to me, 'You didn't say
this. You didn't say this. And you didn't say that!'" His client wanted the
jury to know the full context surrounding his alleged drug distribution,
but Tom insisted that many of the circumstances about his case would
raise questions in the minds of the jurors that would only end up con-
tradicting his version of events. Tom chose to ignore many of his clients'
protestations. The jury quickly returned a verdict of not guilty. Tom said:

> Jury came back in five minutes: Not guilty. I don't think he even shook
> my hand, which we learned early on is okay. In training, they told us:
> "Don't be surprised if you get some very ungrateful clients. Don't take
> it the wrong way. You are doing your job." You know, not every client
> needs to be grateful. You're just doing your job.

Despite his irritation, Tom insisted that his frustration did not affect his
effectiveness in representation. In general, he tries not to be affected by his
negative feelings about certain clients. He told me, "It didn't diminish my
commitment to the case. . . . It didn't diminish my enthusiasm from my
argument at all. I knew I had a strong case."

Other lawyers, however, more readily acknowledged less investment
in clients who frustrate them or question their authority, underscoring
how relationships of withdrawal are marked by lawyers withdrawing from
their clients as much as they are by clients withdrawing from lawyers. For
instance, a bar advocate I spoke with over lunch told me that she loses
patience with clients like the one Tom described. She recounted a time
when one of her clients similarly pressured her to file motions that she
believed to be inapplicable. She declined to do so. In response, her client
attempted to file a motion without her knowledge while he was detained
in jail. The client submitted the motion directly to the judge, without
informing her or the prosecution. The bar advocate explained to me that
the defendant's motion constituted "*ex-parte* communication"—because
a motion must be submitted to a judge in the presence of the ADA on
the case or another representative from the DA's office. She said, "It really

pisses me off" when defendants seek to file motions on their own because it calls into question her "legal expertise and practice of the law." She also noted that doing so reflects poorly in the eyes of the court: "When that happens to me, it's a disservice to the client. Sure, they feel empowered, but they screw themselves over because they look stupid in court and are aggravating to the court."

In public proceedings, defense attorneys sometimes let their frustrations with their clients become known to other officials. I observed such open frustration among a number of bar advocates. Public defenders, meanwhile, were often quite critical of bar advocates who "threw their clients under the bus" in open court. Whereas public defenders largely kept their annoyances with their clients to themselves or only shared them with colleagues back in the privacy of the defender's office, some of the bar advocates I observed let slip their annoyances in front of judges, prosecutors, and a gallery full of other defendants and onlookers. The open frustrations of some bar advocates no doubt contribute to perceptions among disadvantaged defendants that all court-appointed lawyers cannot be trusted, given that defendants rarely differentiate between public defenders and bar advocates and that about three-fourths of indigent cases are handled by bar advocates.

For instance, one bar advocate, a white woman, shamed her client, a young black man, for being late to a hearing that would ultimately result in the dismissal of his case. The lawyer appeared to shame her client as a way to express her frustration and also display to the judge that she could exert control over his behavior. Their conversation unfolded as such:

> JUDGE: Where were you? You weren't here at 9:15 this morning.
> DEFENDANT: No, but I was parking, uh.
> JUDGE: No, you weren't.

The lawyer turned toward her client but spoke loudly enough for everyone in the courtroom to hear:

> LAWYER: You weren't! I was calling you all morning!
> JUDGE: Okay. I already yelled at him. Don't you yell at him too!

After admonishing the lawyer, the judge looked down at his papers. He shuffled through some files and looked up again. He decided to dismiss the case:

> JUDGE: Dismissing the case. What about the attorney's fee?
> LAWYER: Um, he's unemployed and is unable to work.
> JUDGE: Okay. Community service.

Despite the lawyer's shaming of her client in front of the judge, the judge chose to be lenient. Moreover, he called the lawyer out for attempting to shame her client. The judge ended up dismissing the case, allowing the defendant to work several hours of community service in lieu of payment for his attorney's fee.

In another instance, I watched a white male bar advocate and his black male client openly express their mutual frustrations during a pre-trial hearing. The lawyer asked the judge for a motion to suppress hearing, which would determine whether video footage of his client's arrest would be admissible as evidence at trial. The prosecutor argued that the video footage should be included because it showed the defendant resisting arrest. At this suggestion, the defendant suddenly shouted, "Man, I'm only one person. I can't fight four officers!" His outburst appeared to be an attempt to articulate how his actions did not meet the legal definition of resisting arrest. At this point, the judge was visibly annoyed. Yet to hear full arguments from the ADA, she said, "Please speak through your attorney, sir." His attorney tried to quiet him and insist that now was not the time to make his case, but the client rebuffed his attorney. He turned to him and yelled, "Man, but I didn't resist arrest!" His lawyer yelled back: "Stop talking! Why would you do this? What are you doing? Stop talking!" The judge interrupted their squabble and said, "Okay, okay. Second call." "Thank you, Your Honor," the lawyer muttered, as he and his client brushed through the gallery and out into the hallway. Through the doors, I could hear the muffle of the lawyer's shrill voice as he reprimanded his client.

Oftentimes, as in the above scene, defense attorneys seek to control their clients in court as a way to protect them from accidentally incriminating themselves or damaging their image in the eyes of the court.[26] In the lawyer's eyes, their efforts at control are therefore well intentioned. Lawyers told me, again and again, that even though clients technically have certain due process rights, they rarely advise them to speak out or draw attention to themselves in court proceedings. They realize that a defendant's cultivated legal expertise carries little currency.

Judges are not always indifferent; some shame defendants for their poverty or for behaviors they believe to be associated with poverty and disadvantage—a reality that defense attorneys report they must navigate and predict. In this sense, a lawyer's efforts at controlling their client in court can be understood as a performance for judges known to be harsh or belittling. In moments when judges shame defendants, defense attorneys feel they must subordinate their clients' understandable hurt to their overarching professional goal of mitigating their clients' legal outcomes. Selena, for instance, recounted a story of one judge who shames poor defendants:

> My client had been arrested for trespassing and maybe possession of marijuana with intent to distribute or something like that. This was a probation violation. He had picked up a new offense; he had been on probation and picked up a new offense. And the judge was trying to decide what to do about it, whether or not he violated probation. My client was Latino, and he says, "I was just walking from my apartment to the trash to throw the trash, and there were people outside playing music really loudly. And that's what got the cop's attention." And he was like, "I live here." Like, "I was just going to throw out the trash." The judge ends up not finding [him in] violation [of his probation]. . . . But then, she starts going into this long speech, scolding him about how he's lucky because in some places, people get shot by the police for doing less and this and that, or whatever, and it was . . . Those are the most difficult moments where the judge is doing what you want them to do, and they're letting your client go. . . . They're not threatening their liberty, they're not extending their probation, they don't have any conditions. But then you have to sit there and listen to the scolding and the bullshit that she's talking about.

After enduring the judge's lecture, her client was upset. Selena comforted him: "I agree with you 100 percent—that was racist bullshit. And I'm sorry, you know, that you had to hear all that."

Judges directly silence and coerce defendants for their resistance in court in addition to shaming them for their behaviors outside court. Judges commonly silence defendants who attempt to speak to them absent the mediation of their defense attorneys. Some of the judges I observed were more willing to entertain a defendant's voice than others, but even the most willing judges reacted negatively to defendants speaking out before asking their lawyers for permission. Moreover, when defendants did speak for themselves or attempt to make legal arguments on their own (such as filing motions pro se), they could be penalized for speaking or making legal arguments at inappropriate times or in inappropriate ways. Tonya, from chapter 2, exemplifies this tricky position. Against her lawyer Mollie's warnings, she attempted to share the mitigating circumstances of her drug use during her probation hearing. She was technically correct in her knowledge—judges do often consider mitigating factors, such as histories of substance misuse or a lack of housing, when making their final judgments. Yet, the judge made it clear to her (later in the hearing) that he was unpersuaded by her sharing of mitigating factors at that moment. Instead, as Mollie had insisted to her before they walked into the courtroom, the judge wanted to hear her accept fault and exhibit a willingness to change.

Such silencing happens not just at sentencing but also at the earliest stages of the court process. At a bail hearing on an A&B case one day in court, I observed a black male defendant, standing in handcuffs in the holding cell, attempt to represent himself. When his name was called, he looked around for his lawyer. The judge commented that the lawyer had yet to arrive. Through the small circle in the glass of the holding cell, the defendant tried to speak up in his lawyer's absence, asking the judge if he could represent himself:

> DEFENDANT: If I could continue this matter pro se and request personal recognizance, Your Honor.
> JUDGE: Okay, wait just a minute, sir.

The clerk called the defendant's lawyer over the intercom. His lawyer, a bar advocate who had been running up and down from the lockup area all morning to meet with clients, arrived to the podium, flustered and out of breath.

> CLERK: Attorney [attorney's last name], are you ready?
> DEFENSE ATTORNEY: Yes. The witness is here today, Your Honor.

The defendant waited in the holding cell, his neck craning in the direction of his attorney. Meanwhile, his attorney turned toward the ADA. The defense attorney and the prosecutor whispered quietly back and forth for nearly two minutes, as the judge watched patiently from his bench. The prosecutor then approached the podium, asking for the case to be called again after they had more time to negotiate with the defense attorney:

> ADA: Yes, let's have a second call on this matter.
> CLERK: Second call.

"And please, sit down, sir," the clerk said to the defendant, who was still standing near the glass opening in the holding cell, eager to speak. The defense attorney then seemed to notice his client for the first time. "Just wait," he mouthed in the direction of the holding cell, his finger pointed in the air toward his client. The defense attorney and the ADA took a seat in the well, just across from where I was sitting. I watched as they whispered and shuffled papers back and forth for the next ten minutes, while another case was called. Then, the clerk called their case again:

> DEFENSE ATTORNEY: Your Honor, I represent [client's name] on this [bail] motion.
> JUDGE: What's the Commonwealth's position?
> ADA: We're seeking $500 cash bail. The defendant's girlfriend is here today, and the defendant has the ability to pay. The defendant is charged with an A&B on the girlfriend, so we would ask for conditions on bail including a stay away no contact order.

All of a sudden, a woman's voice came from the gallery behind us. "Your Honor, may I speak?" the woman, who I later learned was the defendant's girlfriend, asked. The judge, clearly startled, looked up and out into the gallery. "No, thank you, ma'am." The court officials in the well returned to their business:

> ADA: Conditions are just that the client abide by the restraining order already in place.
> DEFENSE ATTORNEY: I do represent [client's name] in a pending matter and also on the abuse prevention order. I think you should know the procedural history of these cases. . . . You should also know that the complaining witness [the girlfriend] is in court today, but in support of my client. She wanted the order modified from a stay away order to just an order of no abuse. My client's current charge stems from him being arrested on the erroneous assumption that there was a stay away order in place rather than there just being a no abuse order in place.
> JUDGE: But it seemed that their argument violated the no abuse order.
> DEFENSE ATTORNEY: Your Honor, it's clear statutorily that an argument does not violate a no abuse order.
> JUDGE: Yes, agreed. And the case [the earlier case] was dismissed anyway, so.
> DEFENSE ATTORNEY: I would ask the court to release him on his own recognizance. There's no allegation here that he attacked anyone.

The judge turned toward the ADA. He asked:

> JUDGE: Has your office spoken with the witness [the girlfriend]?
> ADA: Yes. She has said she no longer seeks the restraining order.
> JUDGE: Okay. No bail, given that she has spoken with the government and no longer wants a restraining order.

With the judge's ruling, the clerk turned toward the defendant: "Okay, you are released. Please appear at your next court date." The defendant, standing up again in the holding cell, said, "I understand. Thank you, Your Honor. Thank you, [defense attorney]. Thank you, Madam Clerk."

In this case, the defendant attempted to use his cultivated legal expertise rather than rely on his lawyer. He wanted to explain to the court that his girlfriend (the alleged victim of the A&B) wanted him back at home and that he would not be a threat if he were released while awaiting trial. He was quieted, and his girlfriend, too, was ignored when she requested to speak. Rather than hear from them, the judge preferred the professional statements of the defense attorney and the prosecutor. The judge's decision had to do with concerns over the legitimacy of the court record. The judge formally asked the ADA whether she had asked the girlfriend about her wishes with respect to the restraining order. Doing so allowed the judge to have an official statement from the prosecution on the court record, which afforded him the justification to make his decision to release the defendant. His decision would have less legitimacy and apparent accuracy, with respect to legal norms, if it were based only on the direct statements of the defendant or his girlfriend, since neither of them had been sworn in, and since they were not professional members of the courtroom workgroup. Although the defendant and his girlfriend were not punished for their attempts to insert their voices into the process, they were ignored and made to feel peripheral to a public discussion concerning their own lives. This is one of the many ironies of a legal system that prioritizes formal legal outcomes over the feel of justice and the dignity of the people who are dragged into court.

Some defendants are aware of the formal legal costs of resistance; yet, they may nevertheless be willing to incur them because they care about more than their legal outcomes. This is particularly the case when defendants feel deeply that the system is morally wrong or illegitimate. Such a feeling is most common among those who are marginalized and feel they have been treated unfairly by police. Joe, a white working-class man with long eyelashes, told me about a codefendant of his named Bob who refused to listen to his lawyer's advice. Joe described how they were both arrested for distributing heroin in Cambridge. They were stopped by the police after Joe handed Bob several bags of heroin through his car window. Joe was stopped while in his car, and Bob was stopped while running up the sidewalk. But before the police apprehended Bob, he threw the heroin to the ground and thus was caught without the drug on his person. Joe recounted that the police report, however, said that Bob was caught with heroin in his possession. "They lied and lied and lied and lied," Joe told me.

Joe chose to hire a lawyer he trusted and delegated authority to the lawyer; Bob, according to Joe's telling, resisted his lawyer's expertise. Both of their lawyers suggested that they work to negotiate a plea deal and strive to get the prosecution to drop some of their charges. Joe was hesitant but ultimately decided to work with his lawyer toward a relatively light plea deal because his lawyer "had friends in the court system. Like, he had an amazing record. He was a good fucking lawyer." Ultimately, the strategy worked. Joe's lawyer told him that the ADA offered to "drop five of the six charges, and he's going to leave you on the distribution, and he's going to give you two years' probation. Take it or leave it." Joe pleaded to two years of probation time. Meanwhile, Bob's lawyer extracted an even better plea deal. According to Joe, Bob was offered a year of probation. But Bob refused to take the deal. He wanted to go to trial just so he could watch his lawyer cross-examine the police and see if they would lie to the court. Joe said:

> [Bob] is crazy. I mean they were going to offer him a year probation, and he's like, "No, fuck that." He's like, "I'd rather spend a year in jail just to see the cops on the stand and lie to my face." And he did. He's getting out in 12 weeks. He spent two years in jail just to see the fucking cops lie. He's crazy.

Bob's refusal to take a plea and defer to his lawyer's expertise ultimately resulted in a guilty conviction and a sentence of two years in jail. Yet, according to his friend, it was important for Bob to maintain his innocence and resist the police's authority throughout the process. Similarly, Tom told me about a client of his who also wanted to maintain his dignity by having Tom cross-examine the police on the stand to expose his experiences of police abuse. This particular client was accused of assaulting a police officer, but the client alleged during trial that the officer was the one who assaulted him. About such clients, Tom said, "For some clients, all they want to do is expose what the cop did wrong. And you'll sit down after cross-examining, and they'll say, 'That was great.' That's the mode of victory. That's all they wanted."

## Rewarding Delegation

Defense attorneys also spoke about the kinds of clients they liked. Clients they liked were those who, in this book's terms, delegated authority to lawyers by recognizing their inexperience with the law as defendants,

engaged with their lawyer's expertise, and deferred to their lawyer's decisions. In court, these clients remained quiet, deferring to the court's
expectations of silence. Nearly every middle-class defendant in this study
delegated authority to their lawyers, but a fair number of working-class
and a small minority of poor defendants did so too. Thus, court-appointed
lawyers, not just privately retained lawyers, have had experience with defendants who delegate in the attorney-client relationship. Defense attorneys
and judges reward such defendants by affording them assistance in future
legal cases, drug or mental health treatment alternatives, and reduced sentences through the legal norms surrounding the guilty plea process.

Lawyers offered future legal assistance to defendants who delegated
authority to them. Recall from chapter 3 how Tom offered to help Gabe,
the working-class Latino man who faced an OUI charge, seal his record
after he completed the terms of his CWOF. He said to Gabe and his wife,
"If you call me, I can help you with [sealing your case]. I would no longer
technically be your lawyer, but I'd be happy to help. I've had various very
serious cases sealed before." Tom's offer to help seal Gabe's case is surprising because it goes well beyond his obligations as his court-appointed
lawyer. Typically, it is expected that court-appointed lawyers only offer
legal help to clients during the course of their case. Once the case is
over, they are not obligated to remain in contact, much less assist them
in mitigating the collateral consequences that may arise from their legal
sentence. Yet, several public defenders told me about staying in the lives
of the indigent defendants they got along with or felt especially close to.
Meanwhile, privileged defendants who privately retain lawyers can simply
spend money to hire the same or a different lawyer to reap the rewards of
future legal assistance, such as sealing a case, rather than relying on the
beneficence of a court-appointed lawyer. Just before I saw Frank (from
the opening of this chapter), I watched a white man in his thirties wearing a gray suit at the same podium. He was in court that day asking to
have his criminal record sealed. With his hands clasped in front of him,
he stood silently next to his lawyer, as his lawyer explained his situation
to the judge:

> He is having trouble getting a promotion at his job. He works for a bus
> company, and they won't give him a promotion because of his prior
> arrests. He explained to his company that these arrests ended in dis-
> missals, not convictions, but they said he still has an arrest record. So,
> Your Honor, his record has presented a hardship where he can't further
> advance in his career.

The judge turned to the prosecutor: "Do you have a position on this?" The prosecutor shook her head, "No, we do not." The judge ruled: "Okay, I will take your word that this is presenting a hardship for him and will seal his record."

Some defense attorneys reward engaged and deferential defendants by investing more time and resources in their current cases. Sybil, for instance, described a young black defendant she had gotten to know well, who fully engaged with her throughout the court process and trusted in her expertise. She described him as "just really cool. Like, he was someone who could be my friend. We just got along. I would spend hours in the jail with him." He was facing a gun charge. Ultimately, they agreed that, even though the evidence against him was strong, he could risk taking his case to trial because the prosecutor was unwilling to negotiate a lesser sentence. Sybil was "scared" for him, because there was a high likelihood that he would be convicted and sentenced to jail just before his daughter's birthday. She started strategizing possible ways to delay his trial just long enough for him to celebrate with his daughter. Sybil said:

> I'm just like trying to think of everything I can do. I was like, maybe I could just go to court and answer "not ready," which is something I've never done, and it just looks so horrible on my behalf. It's, like, very unprofessional. I was trying to think of everything, . . . but I didn't end up doing it. [But] I was going through discovery, and I was like, "Oh, there's some information here that I don't have about this fingerprint aspect [of the case]." They [the DA] don't really need or care about it, but they owe [the evidence] to me, so I asked the prosecutor for it. She's like: "It's going to take a couple weeks to get that. I don't think I'll be able to get that in time for trial." I'm like, "Oh no." [chuckles] . . . So, she agreed to move the date. . . . [W]e ended up getting a trial date [months later].

For Sybil, pursuing strategies that might be viewed as "unprofessional" was worth it for her "favorite client." It turned out, perhaps because of her investment in his case, that her client's two-day trial resulted in a not guilty verdict. Such immense investment, however, is reserved for few clients. As Sybil told me, "I felt like it was probably a bad thing that I had gotten so close to him, because I felt this huge burden on me. . . . If I lose this, I'm going to probably cry, just because I thought of him as more than a client. He was like a friend."

Beyond rewards from defense attorneys, court rules and norms (rules that are enacted by prosecutors and judges in tandem) reward defendants who delegate authority. Court norms specifically reward defendants' deference—the last component of delegation in the attorney-client relationship. The customary rewarding of deference in the legal process is most evident in the process of pleading guilty. Many scholars have described what is known as the "trial penalty," or the increase in the punitiveness of the sentence you receive if you are convicted at trial rather than if you voluntarily plead guilty.[27] Social psychologist Mona Lynch has shown how changes to federal drug laws since the 1980s have granted prosecutors growing power to compel defendants to plead guilty through the fear of harsher penalties at trial.[28] Some scholars have suggested that the trial penalty is justified because, by coercing defendants to plead, it saves the court time and resources that would have been expended at trial, and because it provides the community (and victims) some measure of closure when the offender formally admits guilt. In sum, there are organizational incentives to defendants pleading guilty.[29]

Defense attorneys facilitate guilty pleas through delegation in the attorney-client relationship—sharing with clients their expertise about the formal benefits of taking a plea deal. Several of the stories presented in this book so far have shown how this process works. Connor, Gabe, and Ryan's experiences in chapter 3 all revealed, in varying ways, how delegation to your lawyer facilitates deference to the court during the plea process. For these men, the willingness to delegate facilitated their relatively weightless interactions with the court. Don, the working-class black man from chapter 3, accepted his plea without drama; his apparent compliance in court resulted in dropped charges and far less prison time than he otherwise would have received. Numerous stories like these confirm the legal benefits of exhibiting deference through pleading guilty. These stories all also revealed that when defendants plead guilty, they do so almost always because they recognize these benefits not because they truly feel they are guilty or feel the desire to admit fault.

Indeed, although most defendants plead guilty, their final choice to do so does not always emerge from attorney-client relationships of delegation. Pleading guilty results from withdrawn attorney-client relationships too, but only after a period of denial, resistance, and persistent cultivation of lay forms of legal expertise. These are characteristic of withdrawal as resistance. Guilty pleas that come later in the process often bear scars that emerged from earlier efforts at resistance: relatively less-beneficial plea agreements or, more commonly, a longer experience of the processing costs that come along with being involved in a court case.[30] We have seen how Troy, the poor white man from earlier in this chapter, drew out his plea deal and faced numerous processing costs as a result, such as mandatory drug treatment. Defendants who are unable to make bail and therefore are incarcerated while awaiting trial often take pleas because they want to get out rather than because they have engaged with and deferred to their lawyer's expertise. Indeed, Nicholas, the white man from chapter 1 who grew up working class and has spent much of his life in and out of homeless shelters, was in jail for several days while his case was active. He had been charged with verbally assaulting his girlfriend and malicious destruction of property. His lawyer told him that he could wait to take the case to trial or he could take a plea, which in addition to him being found guilty of the charge would require him to take a batterer intervention program and be on probation for eighteen months. He recounted discussing his options with is lawyer:

> And then he [my attorney] came into the, um, the jail a couple of times and said, "You know, this is what your options are: We can wait and take it to trial, but you'll stay here another month; or you can plea out and you're going to have to take probation, a batterer's course, and all this other nonsense. Do you think you can do it?"

Both he and his attorney believed he could win at trial because his girlfriend refused to testify against him; but trial was scheduled to take place in a month. Rather than follow his attorney's suggestion to, in this case, pursue trial, Nicholas took the plea deal because it was the middle of summer and jail was miserable without his medication. He "just wanted to get out."

Beyond the guilty plea, formal court norms and processes related to drug and mental health treatment reward deference. Not all defendants, as we saw in chapter 2, desire alternatives to carceral sentences, especially if such alternatives entail mandatory drug treatment or probation surveillance. Some, however, do desire access to drug and mental health treatment resources, especially if they are provided through alternative court sessions that do not abide by the same punitive rules as the traditional court and probation process. In Boston, mental health sessions and drug sessions provide a means of obtaining treatment resources without the same potential consequences of failing to abide by treatment mandates. According to the lawyers I spoke to, only a small percentage of defendants are afforded the opportunity to take part in these sessions. During one of my lunch breaks at the defender's office, a couple lawyers, a social worker, and I chatted about how the process works. To be assigned to one of these sessions, a defendant's lawyer must first decide whether they are an appropriate candidate. To do so, the lawyer must determine whether the person has a diagnosed mental health condition or substance use disorder, sometimes in consultation with probation. Once that determination is made, the lawyer then decides whether they believe the defendant can "comply with" and "abide by the terms" of such alternative courts. One lawyer said that they have often decided not to refer clients whom they believe "won't want to start taking treatment or would be resistant." Although some lawyers worried that sending certain clients to these sessions would set them up for failure, mental health and drug sessions are designed to provide defendants with second chances, rather than punishment, when they fail to comply. Defense attorneys often mentioned that judges, when they oversee mental health and drug sessions, are more lenient and forgiving. Consequently, defendants adjudicated through the traditional court process not only are less likely to receive services for the very problems that accounted for their court involvement in the first place, but they are also more likely to be punished if they fail in the treatment programs attached to their pretrial release or final sentence.

Remaining silent in court is another form of deference from defendants that is highly valued by court officials, who view themselves as experts in the matters at hand. Participation from defendants is devalued. Ironically, the matters being discussed are about the defendant's life. We might posit a very simple explanation for court officials' silencing of defendants: when defendants do not participate, things move more quickly, and judges simply prefer the efficiency. Attempts by a defendant to use their cultivated legal expertise, work around their lawyers, or simply speak up in open court are sometimes viewed as needlessly slowing down the legal process. Efficiency, however, is not the only explanation. In Boston, many judges spend a considerable amount of time on each case. They think carefully through their decisions, articulating their reasoning aloud for the record and, ostensibly, for the edification of the defendant. For instance, I watched as a judge spent several hours—between other cases and after a lunch break—deciding whether to revoke bail on Camila, a black Latina woman client of Sybil's who was awaiting trial on two violent offenses and had just been arrested on a drug charge. The judge entertained various legal arguments. At one point, he spent fifteen minutes in his chambers to consider how he might factor in the fact that Camila was currently a "compliant" participant in a drug session. He ultimately decided to revoke Camila's bail for sixty days. Given her compliance in the drug session, however, he chose to revoke her bail on only one of the underlying charges: "I'm only revoking on the [courthouse name] case and setting a $1 bail on the new case. . . . Obviously this case has presented great difficulty for me, but I'd be interested to hear what Judge [name] says in the [drug court] session. I'll be willing to hear this matter again." Such lengthy deliberation suggests that judges in Boston have lower caseload pressure compared to judges in other jurisdictions and periods.[31]

What I therefore came to realize from my observations and interviews is that defendants' participation in court is thought to not just slow down the process, but also to make the process less accurate—or at the very least, less justifiable. For instance, judges, prosecutors, and defense attorneys that I spoke with were concerned about how they were perceived—by other officials and the general public. They took pains to ensure that other officials believed that they had set justifiable bail amounts, made justifiable calls about admissible evidence, and ensured that plea deals were voluntary. They were concerned about justifying these decisions for the court record and, to some extent, in the eyes of the public. Consequently, they preferred defendants' silence when court was in session. Defendants' voices were presumed to be biased, inaccurate, or simply noncredible when it came to certain aspects of the court record. By contrast, the voices of defense attorneys or prosecutors—sworn-in professionals—were taken as credible and legitimate even if they articulated the very same statements and perspectives that defendants were attempting to articulate. For lawyers and judges, making justifiable and ostensibly accurate decisions reflects their concerns with procedural regularity, not necessarily their concerns with getting to the real and true facts of the case.[32]

Rewards for those who delegate authority to their lawyers sometimes entail clear material benefits—such as access to drug treatment resources—but more often entail a lack of punishment, such as a lack of coercion and silencing or the reduction of a sentence made possible by the norms of pleading guilty. Effective representation for lawyers therefore entails their clients' avoidance of formal legal punishments more so than their clients' receipt of clear benefits.

## Conclusion

Lawyers' and judges' responses to the dynamics of the attorney-client relationship have implications for defendants' legal outcomes—large and small. Beyond constituting inequalities in the quality of court experiences, different attorney-client relationships can shape the legal outcome: whether a person is found guilty or innocent; whether a person is sentenced to incarceration instead of probation; whether a person is incarcerated for a long or short period. Court officials' preference for delegation and devaluation of withdrawal generally favors the privileged over the disadvantaged. Thus, these practices should be understood as institutionally legitimated forms of race and class discrimination that likely contribute to race and class disparities in legal outcomes.

This chapter shows that the relationship between a defendant and their lawyer matters in court proceedings. The court, as a whole, inserts itself into the dynamics, constraints, and possibilities of the relationship. Judges and lawyers respond negatively when clients exhibit the signs of withdrawal; that negativity is especially pronounced when withdrawal manifests as resistance in open court. When disadvantaged defendants attempt to use their cultivated expertise during proceedings—or simply speak up—they are often ignored, silenced, or even punished. In my many days observing court, rare was the moment when an outspoken defendant was acknowledged for what they were saying. Instead, the consequences of withdrawal were nearly always negative. The flipside was equally true. Delegation was often met with courtesy and resulted in various upsides, some seemingly intangible and some very real. Lawyers preferred when clients delegated in interactions through engagement with them and through the sharing of their legal goals. Once they had a sense of what a client hoped to accomplish (whether to minimize jail time, or to avoid probation, or to gain access to drug treatment services), lawyers preferred that clients let them handle the process of achieving these goals through their own professional expertise. Often, their instincts were right. They could mitigate formal legal outcomes more effectively than the client acting alone. After all, lawyers have legitimacy as court professionals and greater familiarity with, and working knowledge of, the preferences, expectations, and power of judges and prosecutors. Knowledge of these norms allowed lawyers to advise clients about the most likely strategies that would convince a judge or prosecutor to accept a certain kind of legal arrangement.

Deference, one of the central components of delegation, was beneficial with lawyers behind closed doors and in front of judges. Scholars studying other punitive institutions, such as juvenile probation hearings, police interactions on the street, and hearings held by child protective services, have documented how deference is also rewarded in these adjacent spaces.[33] In all these punitive spaces, people find themselves accused, in one way or another, of committing a crime or violating a social norm. By exhibiting deference to an empowered social authority (whether a juvenile judge, a police officer, or a case worker), they can help to display their shame and reveal their willingness to be reintegrated into society.[34]

Resistance, however, signals the opposite. In response to resistance, authorities tend to exert even greater social control; resistance suggests that the individual needs to be further reformed. In the context of child welfare, for instance, sociologist Jennifer Reich shows how social workers, judges, and counselors in child protective services seek to modify the behavior of parents accused of mistreating or neglecting their children. Deferring to the assessments of social workers and judges, and agreeing to their plans for counseling, treatment, and behavioral change, enabled some parents to get their children back; contesting the judgment of these experts, more often than not, meant losing their children for good.[35]

Defense attorneys were not necessarily happy about the unwritten rules of the courts even as they abided by them; indeed, the most passionate defense attorneys I met were well aware of, and frustrated by, their "beleaguered" position among other court officials.[36] Even when they were passionate about righting the injustices in their clients' lives, defense attorneys were aware of the many constraints they faced—from other court officials, and even from their own clients. A defense attorney's passion could not overcome a disadvantaged defendant's deep-seated mistrust, nor could their passion overcome the power of prosecutors and judges. Nearly every lawyer I spoke with described some version of the same frustration: feeling they must persuade a client to understand why certain motions are impermissible, or why certain plea deals may be to their advantage, or why they should keep quiet in court. These forms of coercion were subtle, legally permissible, and often well intentioned, at least in the lawyer's mind. Being an effective lawyer was, in their minds, measured by their ability to mitigate the myriad legal consequences that could result from a defendant's criminal charge. Their focus was on finding ways to negotiate with prosecutors and convince judges to reduce bail amounts or plea sentences. Defense attorneys routinely described how achieving relatively less punitive legal outcomes for their clients depended on negotiations with prosecutors, knowledge of judges' preferences, and knowledge of judges' views about when it is credible to exercise certain procedural rights, such as motions to dismiss or suppress evidence.

But legal outcomes were not all that was at stake for defendants. The common way that defense attorneys define effective representation does not always align with the way disadvantaged defendants desire to be represented. Even among public defenders in this study, who seemed the most attuned to the needs and wishes of disadvantaged clients and the injustices they faced, disagreement with clients could emerge around ultimate legal goals as well as the means of achieving them. Disadvantaged defendants often wanted more than mitigation: some wanted to be heard and believed; others wanted to contest police misconduct and abuse; and still others did not mind a seemingly harsh legal outcome if such an outcome meant they would be free of the legal system's surveillance after a certain period. The desire for their voices to be heard should not be mistaken as a mere desire for procedural justice, defined as perceptions that legal authorities are fair in their decision making and treat people with respect.[37] It is true that defendants did want to be treated with respect and dignity. But more than that, they viewed the inclusion of their voice in the process as a way for their version of events to live on the court record and maybe even take down a police officer who abused them or shed light on an unfair legal practice that affected them and members of their community. Given disadvantaged defendants' experiences in daily life, they had little reason to believe that legal officials could ever really be fair.

Throughout this book, I demonstrate that attorney-client relationships of withdrawal are more common among the poor and working-class people of color, and that middle-class and white working-class people, by contrast, are more likely to experience relationships of delegation. Therefore, court officials' negative responses to withdrawal and positive responses to delegation may contribute to group-level disparities in legal outcomes, not just differences in the quality and experience of court processing. I do not statistically test this claim, but the in-depth qualitative evidence and logical inferences presented in this chapter suggest as much.

For more than a century, sociologists and criminologists have documented race and class disparities in the US criminal legal system.[38] From arrest to incarceration, African Americans, Latinos, and the poor experience disproportionate contact and prolonged entanglement with our country's institutions of criminal punishment.[39] Relying on quantitative analyses of administrative data across various jurisdictions, scholars have shown that a meaningful proportion of these disparities cannot be explained by legal factors that many people believe should matter in determining a person's legal sentence—such as a person's charge or the length of their criminal record. Consequently, scholars assume that unfair discrimination of some kind is to blame. Researchers often assume this discrimination results from explicit or implicit forms of racism or classism operating at the individual level. Some experimental research in psychology, for instance, has documented implicit bias but has resulted in mixed conclusions about whether such bias results in discrimination against the disadvantaged in experimental vignettes.[40] Meanwhile, qualitative research has documented racism and classism among legal officials in certain jurisdictions. [41] Some scholars, however, have found evidence that biased beliefs may not result in biased outcomes; indeed, the opposite could be the case: people who exhibit prejudice may seek to correct for it in their decision making.[42] In Boston, one is hard pressed to find prosecutors, defense attorneys, or judges who make explicitly racist statements in court or behave in explicitly classist ways. To be sure, such individual bias likely exists, but it is artfully concealed in the minds of legal officials. The result is that it is difficult to make a direct link between explicit or implicit racism and classism and disparities in court outcomes, net of existing inequalities that differentially filter disadvantaged people into the courts in the first place.

This book offers an additional way that racial and class discrimination operates—through the enactment of institutional rules and procedures relating to the attorney-client relationship. Unlike explicit or implicit forms of individual-level racism or classism, punishing defendants for relationships of withdrawal, and rewarding them for relationships of delegation, operates as an institutionally legitimated form of discrimination on the basis of relations and interactions, so common in other social institutions.[43] Unlike individual-level bias, such institutional discrimination is perceived to be unproblematic. Indeed, most court officials would likely scoff at my characterization of this punishing and rewarding as "discrimination." After all, many are adamant that discrimination is morally problematic and illegitimate, and that it has no place in the courtroom. They might think of themselves as the last people to consciously, and repeatedly, discriminate. And yet, the discrimination I have uncovered occurs not through personal antipathy against one racial group or class group but rather when "a given set of rules and procedures . . . are constructed in ways that favor members of one group over another."[44] These rules are enacted by individual legal officials' "unconsidered repetition of cognitively familiar routines."[45] Courts and their officials routinely discriminate in ways so taken for granted that we rarely view them as problematic. For instance, judges give longer sentences to people with longer criminal records and are lenient on people who have only committed a minor offense for their first time. This practice is a form of discrimination, albeit one that is justified by legal norms and that, most would argue, appears fair. Courts also discriminate against people facing similar charges, levying harsher punishments on those whose behaviors appear more blameworthy or heinous even if the legal charge is technically the same. Again, many of us might argue that this too, at least in the abstract, is fair. What this book has shown is that the court system also allows its legal officials to discriminate on the basis of withdrawal and delegation—a kind of discrimination that we should understand as unfair given the disadvantages and advantages that make these different kinds of attorney-client relationships possible.

This understanding of discrimination complements recent research and theory on criminal courts, which has documented how inequalities can become normalized and unproblematic in the eyes of court officials.[46] Sociologist Nicole Gonzalez Van Cleve has shown how moral attributes— such as perceived laziness or degeneracy—are used to justify harsher treatment of black and Latino defendants in Cook County, Illinois.[47] Her work reveals how defense attorneys selectively advocate for defendants based on these moral attributes, which draw on racialized and classed tropes of worthiness that exist in broader society. I argue that court officials' decisions are influenced not just by a defendant's moral worth *as a person* but also by a defendant's appropriate interactions *as a criminal defendant*. Court officials reward defendants who engage in ways that suggest they understand the hidden legal rules and expectations of what it means to be and act like a defendant accused of a crime and like a client in an appropriate relationship with their lawyer. Sociologist Issa Kohler-Hausmann finds that officials in New York City misdemeanor courts "observe and judge" the "unfolding performance" of each defendant as a means to assess their moral worth.[48] She argues that the court rewards those "delivering successful performances of self-discipline or personal responsibility."[49] We have seen that, in Boston, to be an appropriate, morally worthy defendant, one must remain silent, delegate authority to one's lawyer, and defer to the court's rulings.

One plausible alternative explanation to my theory of discrimination revolves around the quality of defense attorneys assigned to disadvantaged people. It is possible that defendants mistrust their lawyers, and withdraw from them, because these lawyers are not very good. In this alternative account, ineffective lawyers contribute both to a defendant's likelihood of withdrawing from the attorney-client relationship as well as to (and independently of) the likelihood of a defendant receiving a worse legal outcome. In other words, bad lawyers may make legal choices that affect the case for the worse, regardless of the quality of the attorney-client relationship. Indeed, as chapter 2 showed, some disadvantaged people described mistrusting their lawyers, in part, because they believed them to be ineffective, incompetent, or unwilling to do what their own cultivated legal expertise suggested they must.

It seems safe to assume, as with every profession, that some lawyers are likely more effective at their jobs than others. Some can take on more cases at any one time; some are better able to befriend prosecutors or persuade juries. I do not have access to objective indicators of the quality of the lawyers in this study, such as their dismissal rate, conviction rate, or average sentence length for their clients. What I do know, however, is that the attorneys were all pretty blunt about the range of their cases: they found some clients difficult to work with and other clients far easier to work with. Thus, the same lawyer—no matter their effectiveness—can devote more time and effort to some of their clients and less to others. These decisions, as we have seen, are often made on the basis of whether their clients delegate authority to them or withdraw from them. Moreover, it is not just lawyers' actions that matter; judges also play a role in the equation. An explanation that focuses only on differences in lawyers' abilities cannot account for judges' responses to withdrawal and delegation.

Another alternative account is that defendants are likely to find themselves withdrawing from their lawyers the more they find that their case is unwinnable. It is difficult for many clients to hear that the violent police stop they endured is considered legal or that there are no legal procedures available to exclude certain unflattering forms of evidence. It is also difficult for clients to hear that a plea deal is their best option at achieving a lesser sentence. Thus, withdrawal may be more likely to occur in weaker cases that are going to result in relatively worse legal outcomes anyway; meanwhile, delegation could be more likely to occur in stronger cases that are going to result in more favorable outcomes. There is no doubt that the weakness, or strength, of a case has a direct effect on legal outcomes; indeed, this is an explicit and well-known feature of the legal system. Moreover, there is little doubt that the tempering of a client's expectations when they have a weak case can affect the quality of the attorney-client relationship, as was partly the case with Drew and other disadvantaged defendants described in chapter 2.

Yet, the strength or weakness of the client's case is only one of several factors that influence the attorney-client relationship—and is by no means determinative. Even the weakness of Drew's case, from the very beginning of the book, could have been mitigated by a relationship with Tom that was productive. Other defendants' experiences showed how the weakness of their court case had no effect, or even the opposite effect, on the attorney-client relationship than this alternative explanation might suggest. For instance, Brianna's case, from chapter 3, was weak. Her lawyer warned her that if she could not obtain the prescription, she would likely have to plead guilty. And yet, Brianna was engaged and deferential in her interactions with Leya. And even though her case resulted in a plea to a guilty conviction, she was ultimately able to avoid the surveillance of drug treatment, because she delegated authority. Meanwhile, other defendants may have a fairly strong case, or at least a clear legal avenue for avoiding a harsher sentence, and yet they withdraw and resist by insisting on certain motions, speaking out in court, or taking their case to trial, because they want to maintain their dignity against an oppressive legal system. Moreover, defendants like Mary, Jaylan, and others who experience resignation in their relationships with their lawyers often appear to care little about their formal legal outcome. Instead, their relationships with their lawyers are withdrawn due to factors beyond the criminal courts.

# Conclusion

"I AM EXTREMELY LUCKY," Jane thought aloud. After spending an hour telling me, with a mix of tears and relief, about her childhood and the details of her arrest, Jane reflected on the costs of being involved in the court system. She mentioned the financial cost of hiring a lawyer—a sum of $2,000. But for her, that financial cost was largely inconsequential. "It wasn't like a big deal for me because my dad left me some money when he died," she explained. Recall from chapter 3 that Jane is a college-educated white woman who grew up the daughter of a judge and a schoolteacher. As she spoke about how easy it was to deal with her case, she grew embarrassed:

> But I basically have a mini freaking trust fund, . . . which is even more embarrassing, actually, because the fact I easily got out of the money aspect [of court] kind of makes it like . . . I don't know. It's just, well . . . it's just sickening. I don't know. I feel I should have struggled more with that because a lot of people are completely screwed with the money aspect, and they're in debt more. And it's going to be more debt for them. But I got—or I am really lucky. It wasn't like a huge financial burden.

Like Jane, several privileged people in this study, even as they recounted their own frustrations, are well aware of their relative advantages in relation to the tens of thousands of disadvantaged people who populate our nation's courtrooms on any given day. Waine, a working-class white man also discussed in chapter 3, has struggled with feelings of alienation and various adversities in his life, including his alcoholism, which was abetted by his work as a bartender and musician. Still, Waine feels privileged in many ways, especially as compared to poor people of color. During his case, he relied on his father's social ties and financial resources to hire a lawyer he trusted; and, over his life, he has had few interactions with the police despite his heavy use of illegal drugs. He reflected: "All my friends that aren't white have been a victim of stop and search. Every single one. Every single one. My white friends? None of them. And that's a pretty transparent divide I've seen in person, you know?"

More and more Americans are beginning to recognize, as Jane and Waine have, that something is wrong with our criminal legal system. People from many walks of life and from opposite ends of the political spectrum agree that the United States imprisons its residents too often, and that our legal system is much harsher if you are black, Latino, or poor. Much of this realization has come because we are neck deep in an era of mass criminalization. The late twentieth century saw a massive increase in arrest rates, conviction rates, and jail and prison admissions, though the past few years have brought a hopeful period of stabilization and even modest decline in these various tools of control.[1] Still, more and more facets of our daily lives continue to be criminalized by new laws in the twenty-first century.[2] Around a million residents are arrested at least once in any given year.[3] And each year, hundreds of thousands or more people—the marginalized, like always, but also some socioeconomically and racially privileged Americans as well—will find themselves arraigned in court and in front of a judge.[4] Alongside these statistics, we cannot escape the devastatingly routine images and videos of police violence in communities of color replayed on cable news and our social media newsfeeds. The Movement for Black Lives—a collective of organizations and activists associated with the hashtag Black Lives Matter—has played a vital role, over the last several years, in exposing these injustices and shifting our national conversation.[5]

In Washington, DC, and in states across the country, criminal justice reform has now become a key political issue on both sides of the aisle. At times, political leaders from both parties have come together to pass reforms. For instance, the bipartisan First Step Act of 2018, signed by President Trump, includes modest steps to reduce incarceration and dampen the pains of imprisonment: sentencing reforms for certain federal drug offenses, early release among some people incarcerated in federal prisons, and funds for educational programming. These reforms, however, have been criticized for the likely minimal impact they will have on the incarceration rate, their investments in for-profit forms of surveillance, and their inattention to difficulties faced by the formerly incarcerated as they reenter society.[6] Moreover, the legislation provides precious few solutions to the specific problem of race and class inequality and injustice. Existing political reforms are important—and any such progress is practically miraculous, in our moment of absurd partisanship—and yet these attempts are a tiny Band-Aid stuck atop a vast wound. Any real attempt at healing requires a much deeper acknowledgment and understanding of the profound disparities and injustices that continue to tarnish our criminal legal system—and, importantly, a radical willingness to move from reform to transformation and abolition.

It is my hope that this book has demonstrated how the criminal courts are central to the inequalities and injustices of the criminal legal system, and of American society more broadly. Specifically, this book details the race and class injustices of the attorney-client relationship. Much of our national conversation around reform of the courts revolves around the power of prosecutors to pressure defendants to plead guilty, the injustice of monetary bail systems that detain legally innocent people in jail pretrial, and the underfunding of public defense systems. Reforms around these issues seek to alter the balance of power between defendants and the government, to give defendants a better chance to exercise their rights in an adversarial legal system. The relative power deficit that all defendants— the poor and wealthy alike—face in relation to prosecutors and judges is clear. For the privileged, a competent, trustworthy, and well-resourced defense lawyer can help alter the balance of power to some degree. And the privileged fare far better than the disadvantaged with respect to the resources, trustworthiness, and mutual engagement necessary for effective legal representation, as I have shown.

Yet, a central lesson of this study is that effective legal representation alone is not justice. Access to a lawyer is not itself a form of justice. Even when defendants are afforded lawyers, they can experience mistrust, confusion, disagreement, and frustration. Some withdraw from their lawyers and resist their lawyers' legal expertise, whereas others find themselves resigned to the entire legal process. But even an exceedingly competent and trustworthy lawyer who can achieve their client's legal goals is not necessarily acting as a conduit to justice either. Effective defense attorneys can certainly do a lot for their clients. They can secure an acquittal or mitigate a potentially lengthy sentence. The privileged defendants in this study can attest to such benefits, which can importantly alter the course of individual lives for the better by preventing the collateral consequences of a conviction or a prison sentence. But these remedies rarely constitute social justice. Such legal wins occur within a fundamentally unjust court system that is unequal in its application across race and class groups and that pressures all defendants to remain silent, defer to the state's authority, and accept unjust police and prosecutorial practices. Victims also lose in an adversarial system built on silence and coercion. Defendants who may feel remorse for the crimes they committed have little incentive to express their remorse throughout the court process, save for the guilty plea hearing or sentencing after trial. Even then, victims are rarely afforded meaningful moments of healing or restoration with those who have harmed them. Guilty pleas are typically taken not because a defendant recognizes the harm they may have caused but because a defendant has been coached by their lawyer to recognize the many costs of taking their case to trial. Although this book has focused on defendants' experiences and relationships with lawyers, it is important to recognize that our current court system undercuts justice for victims as well. Justice demands fair treatment of not only defendants, most of whom have experienced alienation from society, but also victims of crime, who deserve not to have their rights or bodies harmed by others.[7]

## Inequality and Injustice

Social scientists today talk a lot about inequality, but not as much about injustice. Where this book has documented inequality (that is, race and class differences in defendants' court experiences), it has also documented social injustice. Sociologist Erik Olin Wright and political scientist Joel Rogers define social injustice as "an inequality which is unfair *and which could be remedied* if our social institutions were different."[8] Determining whether a difference is unfair requires, in their words, "a moral judgment." Philosopher Elizabeth Anderson defines injustice as a feature of unfair social relationships. She writes, "An inequality in the distribution of some good is unjust if it *embodies* unjust social relations, is *caused* by unjust relations (interactions, processes) among people, or *causes* such unjust relations."[9] Anderson's definition of social injustice draws on the work of relational sociologists, especially Charles Tilly, just as this book does. Thus, Anderson's interpretation of injustice emerges from an empirically based sociological understanding of how the social world works, namely that inequalities emerge not from "internal characteristics" of groups but from the unequal relations between individuals and between groups occupying certain social positions.[10] Principles of social justice therefore demand an institutional remedy when inequalities in a material or symbolic resource between groups constitute or are caused by empirically observable relationships that we understand to be unfair.

Drawing on relational theory and contributing to cultural sociology, this book demonstrated not only how the attorney-client relationship embodies inequality but also how differences in attorney-client interactions result in unfair consequences that allow the privileged to maintain certain advantages in their lives over their disadvantaged peers. We can understand these inequalities as unfair because it is evident that they emerge from differences that are largely out of people's control. Beginning with chapter 1, I showed how inequalities in everyday life—in adolescent experiences, neighborhoods, policing, financial resources, and social ties—shape the attorney-client relationship in court. Defendants, when they arrive in court, carry these lifelong racialized and classed advantages and disadvantages with them.

Although the well-resourced often come out on top, privilege does not operate in the criminal courts in quite the same way as it does in more mainstream institutions. In schools, hospitals, or workplaces, where Americans spend much of their lives, the privileged exhibit entitlement and make demands of schoolteachers, doctors, employees, and (to some extent) employers. In the courts, however, privilege manifests through cultural performances of deference in interaction. The privileged arrive in court with little knowledge of criminal law and much uncertainty about how to proceed. They depend on their lawyers, whom they can trust to have their best interests at heart (either because they are paying them or because they share cultural commonalties), to shepherd them through the system. They are rewarded for deferring to their lawyer's expertise and to the court's expectations. Meanwhile, the disadvantaged have had more experience with the law. When they seek to use their legal knowledge (accrued through lives marked by police surveillance and routine encounters with legal officials) and demand their legal rights be exercised, their attempts often backfire and result in negative legal experiences. In some sense, the disadvantaged often put more effort and energy into their criminal cases. They strive to take control of their fates but are punished for doing so. These realities contrast with what cultural sociologists have found in other institutions, such as schools and doctor's offices, where working-class and poor people are described as passive, deferential, and resigned to professionals, such as teachers and physicians.[11] It is often argued that disadvantaged people would gain more resources and help if only they were more assertive and cultivated knowledge of institutional procedures.[12] In the courts, such strategies often backfire, revealing the unfair bind in which working-class and poor defendants find themselves.

This book, therefore, offers a revision to cultural sociological theories of privilege and inequality in institutional interactions.

Because the injustices embedded in the attorney-client relationship are routine and legitimated by the system, they are often hard to see. Their taken-for-granted qualities are also what may make them difficult for some to view as injustices. In our culture and law, it is common to believe that injustice exists only where there is direct evidence of explicit, individual-level forms of unfair discrimination at play. Successful legal challenges against racial bias, for instance, require evidence of "discriminatory intent," or proof that an individual actor, such as a prosecutor or a judge, purposefully discriminated against a person based on their race. Such evidence, of course, is difficult to muster because racists today know how to obscure their racism.[13] It is rare for a prosecutor to explicitly articulate their efforts to remove black people from the jury pool (though it happens) or for a juror to make racist comments about a Latino defendant (though that too has happened).[14] Rather, a prosecutor may provide a "race-neutral" reason for removing a black juror (such as, the juror's residence in a high-crime neighborhood) or an empaneled juror may come up with seemingly-inoffensive reasons to convince their fellow jurors to convict a Latino man they hold prejudices against.[15] There is undoubtedly a lot of injustice that occurs through these colorblind and subtle forms of racism (and classism), as numerous scholars have documented in the courts, policing, and broader society.[16] Even though scholars and even some everyday legal officials may view these subtle forms of racism as unfair, the law does not.[17] In addition, this book documents how racial bias and class bias operate through institutional expectations of appropriateness in interaction as an engaged yet pliant defendant—unwritten norms that put the poor and working-class people of color at a disadvantage with respect to their formal legal outcomes. This kind of discrimination is institutionally legitimated but nonetheless unfair.

Beyond their unequal implications for the likelihood of conviction, incarceration, or sentence length, the frustrations, uncertainties, and miscommunications characteristic of withdrawn interactions between disadvantaged defendants and their lawyers are an injustice, too. When thinking about inequality, we tend to focus on differences in material outcomes between groups. Social scientists, for instance, often measure whether certain groups have more or less income, more or less health care, or, in the criminal legal system, more or less of a chance of being convicted or incarcerated. That focus on material outcomes makes sense because they are important in people's lives, of course, and because they can be more easily measured, given their materiality. But the more subtle, more symbolic dimensions of inequality matter as well, as a decades-long tradition of theory in cultural sociology has insisted. In sociologist Michèle Lamont's recent presidential address to the American Sociological Association, she argued that scholars must pay attention to what she calls "recognition gaps," or disparities in the worth that societies afford to different groups of people.[18] This study has demonstrated that, in the courts, how privileged defendants interact with their lawyers is deemed worthy, but how the disadvantaged interact is deemed unworthy.

I want to suggest that scholars studying the courts consider not just differences in formal legal outcomes (such as one's sentence length) or even differences in procedural justice outcomes (such as a defendant's subjective perceptions that legal officials are fair and respectful in their decision making) but also differences in the worth and dignity afforded to different people who interact with the court in different ways. We should be concerned not just about differences in court outcomes but also differences in the quality of the court experience. Unlike the procedural justice literature, which considers how feelings of fairness and respect influence people's willingness to obey the law or even to participate in democratic institutions, this book pushes scholars to consider how differences in worth and dignity under the criminal law are themselves an injustice.[19] Procedure and the exercise of legal rights are important to disadvantaged defendants not only because they signal that the system is legitimate but also because they are chances to set the record straight about their alleged crimes in front of a judge, the courtroom gallery, and their community. This is a form of substantive justice. For the privileged, setting the record straight may not be as important to them, perhaps because they are more likely to be factually guilty given their lower odds of being arrested in the first place or perhaps because the costs of lost dignity in court are not as grave when dignity is readily afforded to them in their everyday lives outside court.

In today's criminal courts, the hidden rules enforce this gap in dignity and worth. The norms of the court allow judges and lawyers to treat defendants differently depending on whether they delegate authority to their defense attorneys or, by contrast, withdraw from them and engage in forms of resistance or resignation. There are no legal rules against the silencing of defendants who seek to speak in court proceedings. There are no legal rules against the discouragement, whether subtle or explicit, of defendants who seek to exercise their presumed legal rights. There are no policies in place that seek to account for how being a disadvantaged person living in a poor community of color can make purportedly lenient legal choices, such as choosing to take probation over incarceration, unappealing or inaccessible. Indeed, the essence of the problem is not merely that there are no rules in place to account for and counteract these issues; the heart of the matter is that few court officials think that silencing and coercing defendants who are resistant or resigned is a problem at all. Many well-intentioned defense attorneys feel that, given the power of prosecutors in the current system, the best thing they can do for a client is to coerce them into pleading guilty in exchange for a lesser sentence.[20] Moreover, under the current norms of the system, there are no legal remedies that account for how adversity in everyday life and unequal forms of policing and surveillance make court involvement far more likely for the poor and working-class people of color, or how those inequalities shape the quality of attorney-client relationships in the first place.

Indeed, *not* accounting for race and class inequalities that exist in broader society and bleed into courthouse interactions allows the court system to function. Courts maintain their legitimacy as neutral arbiters by striving *not* to account for differences in the privileges and disadvantages in the lives of the defendants before them. Judges strive to base their decisions only on the official documentation they can see with their own eyes—the behaviors alleged to have brought the defendant into court (the charge), the defendant's past interactions with the court (the criminal record), and the defendant's demeanor in court (an indication of the quality of the attorney-client relationship). Courts are better able to come to legitimate decisions about the cases before them, with efficiency and justification, when defendants defer to their lawyers, forgo their legal rights, and do not add their voices to the court record. The personal and community histories of racism and classism experienced by disadvantaged defendants in their lives are rarely taken into account in any affirmative way.[21] Such histories are deemed either irrelevant or unverifiable, save for how such incomplete information may factor into assessments of the risk of future criminal behaviors.[22] It is ironic that a social institution ostensibly meant to ensure justice in our society seeks instead to avoid accounting for the injustices that bring people in contact with it and that influence the way people are able to navigate its halls.

Injustices that occur in court have implications beyond the criminal legal system. Privileged defendants, though they experience their own injustices when occupying the role of the accused, leave the court process far less scathed than the disadvantaged. They are less likely to be detained pretrial, convicted, or sentenced to incarceration. As a result, they are less likely to bear the collateral consequences of certain forms of criminal justice contact—from employment and housing discrimination to losing the right to vote.[23] What happens in the courts does not stand apart from what happens in the rest of society. It reflects, legitimates, and hardens broader race and class injustices. What can be done?

## Possibilities for Change

This book reveals how a racially and socioeconomically diverse group of sixty-three people understand and navigate their relationships with their defense attorneys while being processed in the Boston-area courts. I detail how interactions between lawyers and their clients in courthouse hallways, law offices, and in front of judges can have profound implications for an individual's experiences and dignity, for the formal outcomes of their case, and, in turn, for their status in broader society once their case has been resolved. The privileged (whose advantages enable them to trust their lawyers and delegate authority to them) experience relative ease in comparison to the disadvantaged (whose mistrust and withdrawal from their lawyers sets them up for coercion, silencing, and punishment). We might imagine, then, that one solution to this injustice would be to convince disadvantaged defendants to delegate authority to their lawyers and defer to other court officials, to accept the court's characterization of their alleged crimes, and to remain silent. To be sure, such counseling occurs in public defender's offices across the country every day. Telling defendants to keep quiet and defer certainly has its immediate benefits.

And yet, individual-level solutions of this sort would do little to rectify the overarching injustice of what this book documents. Beyond race and class disparities in legal outcomes that emerge from attorney-client interactions, the hidden rules of deference, coercion, and silencing are injustices all their own—for defendants and victims alike. What is needed is not simply more coercive legal representation for the purposes of achieving a relatively lesser sentence; instead, we need a more capacious social and political praxis that fundamentally transforms the institutional rules of the game. In what follows, I discuss possibilities for change at three levels—first, the level of the attorney-client relationship within the existing court system; second, the level of the courthouse and the courtroom workgroup; and third, the level of broader law and society. The first level of possibilities focuses on reforming the attorney-client relationship to better function for defendants within the existing institutional norms of the courts. The second level considers how we might alter these norms, suggesting reforms of the court's way of responding to the attorney-client relationship. The third level suggests ways to transform or abolish institutional features of the criminal legal system more broadly, making the attorney-client relationship a less necessary component of the way our society deals with criminal wrongdoing. From the first level to the third, possibilities grow more radical.

At the level of the attorney-client relationship within the current system, defense attorneys should focus on instilling trust in every interaction with their clients. From the moment they meet their client at arraignment, in a courthouse hallway, or in lockup, attorneys should be aware that their clients are trying to assess whether they can be trusted. Defendants look for clues—attentiveness, listening to their side of the story (even details that do not matter for the purposes of arraignment), and cultural similarities in taste or style. Defense attorneys could be trained in client-centered approaches to legal representation that teach them to be more attuned to their clients' needs and the unique needs of their communities.[24] Client-centered approaches have been implemented in major jurisdictions across the country and are supported by the Community-Oriented Defender Network, a collection of more than one hundred indigent defense organizations.[25] Such approaches dictate that attorneys focus on what the client wants rather than what the attorney thinks is best. Sometimes, as I have shown, a client desires an approach that has a high risk of failure or a legal outcome that seems harsher than other alternatives. Lawyers taking a client-centered approach would seek to understand these preferences (and inform clients of potential collateral consequences they may be unaware of) rather than alter them.

There is a certain paternalism inherent in any professional-client relationship, and especially the relationship between a lawyer and a poor defendant.[26] Lawyers' professional expertise provides them important insight into the many ways a criminal case can go off the rails and strategies for how to mitigate these negative legal consequences within the courtrooms they work in every day. Many clients, especially privileged ones, lean heavily on their lawyers' expertise. But many disadvantaged clients represented by court-appointed lawyers often resist or are resigned to professional expertise. When lawyers find that their clients are resistant to their expertise, it may be difficult for them to watch their client constantly insist on a path that is almost certainly doomed to (legal) failure. Some lawyers in the study reported that they themselves withdrew from such clients. Instead, lawyers should seek to pull such clients in more, taking care to recognize and validate their unique needs and preferences. There are caveats to such client-centered representation. Some clients may not be competent, due to mental illness or substance use disorders.[27] They may not fully comprehend legal consequences. But these are exceptions that should be dealt with on a case by case basis. Most defendants are competent, and their preferences regarding legal outcomes and procedures should be central to a lawyer's decision making.

The assessment of a defendant's competence could be managed by a broader form of representation called holistic defense, which requires reforms at all three levels. Holistic defense moves defense attorneys from considering the legal hopes of a client and the potential legal consequences of their choices to also considering the problems faced by clients in their everyday lives. Holistic defense, when implemented well, enables lawyers to refer their clients to other professionals, such as social workers, who can assist defendants in managing their everyday lives and, in turn, more effectively abiding by the requirements of the court. Defendants in this study who were resigned and focused on other challenges beyond their court case would likely find support from such a model of legal representation. Some public defender's and legal aid offices, such as the Bronx Defenders, have successfully incorporated immigration lawyers, housing lawyers, social workers, and other advocates in their offices—with positive results for their clients' legal outcomes.[28] In Boston, CPCS provides public defenders and bar advocates access to social workers, investigators, and immigration lawyers. Access varies depending on a lawyer's awareness of, and proximity to, these other professionals. In some offices, social workers work within the same office building as public defenders and join them for lunch. But for court-appointed attorneys working in other offices or in solo practices, engagement with social workers, investigators, and immigration lawyers is hardly routine. Holistic defense is not cheap. It requires an investment of financial resources from state legislatures—to hire social workers and other professionals, as well as to hire more defense attorneys to limit lawyers' caseloads.[29] Thus, implementing this reform requires not just commitment to changing the culture of the attorney-client relationship but also commitments at the level of the courthouse and the level of the broader law and society.

Structural changes to the criminal court, its allocation of resources, and its workgroup culture would help to alter the hidden rules of the game that disadvantage all defendants, but most especially working-class defendants of color and the poor. One common complaint among the disadvantaged in this study was their inability to choose their lawyers.[30] In Boston, as in many jurisdictions, lawyers for the indigent are appointed by the court, and it is difficult to change one's appointed counsel. Allowing defendants to choose their lawyers at arraignment may alleviate the lack of control and frustration that contributes to resistance and resignation. There may be practical limitations to allowing choice in lawyers.[31] Lawyers may grow annoyed, or even feel professionally threatened, if they are rarely chosen. Lawyers who are commonly chosen may grow overburdened by their caseloads. If defendants can choose lawyers more than once (say, when they find that they do not get along with their original choice and want to choose a different lawyer), judges may grow impatient. But these issues with attorney choice rarely concern questions of justice. Indigent defense systems could begin to experiment with ways to introduce lawyer choice into the system, perhaps beginning by allowing defendants to choose their lawyers at arraignment and change lawyers no more than once in any one case. One informal solution that could be implemented in public defender's offices is for defense attorneys to swap clients among themselves. Sometimes, public defenders do just that. If one public defender finds that their relationship with a client is on the skids, they might ask another defender in the office to take on the client. Such swapping of clients, however, appeared to be largely unavailable to bar advocates, many of whom work in small or solo practices. Moreover, among the cases I observed, such swapping centered the lawyer's perspective rather than that of the client. A client might feel withdrawn in the relationship, but their lawyer could be unaware of their client's feelings. Thus, courts—led by judges—are best suited to experiment with structural changes to the assignment of counsel.

So much of the frustration of disadvantaged people in this study revolved around their silencing. Contrary to popular and scholarly accounts of passive criminal defendants, many disadvantaged people are quite active. They actively study the law in jail and in their communities. For them, being ignored can be a demeaning experience. Some scholars and activists have advocated for ways of more fully incorporating ordinary people into the criminal justice process and, in turn, reducing the imprint of the state and legal officials. Legal scholar and federal judge Stephanos Bibas has written about imagining a "participatory criminal legal system," and legal scholar Jocelyn Simonson has argued for the popular participation of "the People" in criminal procedure.[32] Community court models have experimented with how to integrate procedural justice principles—such as communicating directly with defendants and providing them with opportunities to speak—into traditional court procedures.[33] In civil courts, it is far more common for litigants to represent themselves without lawyers than it is in criminal courts. Some rely on nonlawyer advocates, whereas others represent themselves pro se.[34] As scholars studying the legal consciousness of ordinary people who dispute with neighbors over parking spaces, deal with street harassment, and bring family disputes to small claims court have noted, many ordinary people have their own conceptions of the law and legal processes—conceptions that legal officials routinely attempt to shape, contain, or rearticulate in ways that serve the legal system's function as a governing institution.[35] Criminal defendants, especially the disadvantaged, also have their own conceptions of, and expertise in, criminal law. They expect the court to take seriously the inaccuracies of police work or the extenuating circumstances surrounding their alleged wrongdoing.

Judges could help shift norms around criminal procedure to provide more opportunities for defendants to voice their concerns. One procedural tool that defendants regularly described as meaningful to them but underused by their lawyers were motions—a request for the judge to rule on various pretrial questions, such as whether evidence is admissible or whether a charge should be dismissed. A motion requires the judge to adjudicate, or to make decisions about aspects of the case. Often, lawyers in this study told their clients that motions would not work, were a waste of time, or would backfire by making the judge annoyed. These lawyers were, as far as I could tell, never lying to their clients. They were simply aware that judges have a limited interest, at best, in spending their time adjudicating the legitimacy of police work in collecting evidence, or prosecutorial work in determining whether there is probable cause to file a charge. Although defendants are technically presumed innocent until proven guilty, the assumption that a defendant likely did something wrong—regardless of how imperfect the evidence of that wrongdoing is—undergirds our criminal legal system.

Judges who recognize the racial and class injustices of the system must be willing to place their concerns for efficiency and legitimated accuracy behind their broader concerns for social justice.[36] Such judges could signal to defense attorneys and prosecutors that they will entertain questions regarding probable cause and the admissibility of evidence. Legal scholar David Sklansky reminds us that our existing legal system views procedural rights to be "elective."[37] That is, procedural rights—such as the right to a trial, the right to confront witnesses, the right to make motions about evidence, and the right not to testify against yourself—are waivable and only apply if the defendant (specifically, the defendant's lawyer) invokes them.[38] Therefore, judges rarely feel that it is their place to remind lawyers of procedural rights that they do not assert. This hesitancy could change. Social justice–minded judges could more actively begin to engage in what sociologist Alix S. Winter and I describe as "interventionist decision-making," whereby they "contest other actors" in court.[39] Instead of deferring to prosecutors or even public defenders (who refuse to bring motions out of fear), judges could themselves intervene by bringing up certain procedural rights and encouraging defense attorneys to employ them. Doing so would slow down the system, opening space for defendants' voices, and forcing prosecutors—and by extension, state legislatures—to choose what kinds of crimes truly deserve the expenditure of our society's punitive resources. Of course, not all judges are bothered by the race and class inequalities they see in court every day. Some do not recognize them as an injustice. Some make interventionist decisions that entrench, rather than rectify, such injustices. Therefore, trial court judges—many of whom are elected in states across the country—would need to be held accountable by citizens in their jurisdictions and by appellate court decisions that enhance defendants' constitutional rights.[40]

Outside accountability and monitoring are critical complements to any proposed changes to the institutional culture of the courts. In journalist and lawyer Amy Bach's book *Ordinary Injustice*, she argues that monitoring the health of the courts—by, for example, establishing metrics for attorney performance and demanding transparency about prosecutorial decisions—is critical for ensuring that courts are aware of their own errors, inconsistencies, and lack of adversarialism.[41] She proposes that a third-party entity should collect information about local courts and share that information with people living in the courts' jurisdictions. "Court watching," which involves community members themselves taking notes on prosecutors' actions and judges' decisions, could also help to hold courts accountable.[42] In New York City, Court Watch NYC's mission is to "demand transparency and accountability" by "watching court proceedings, reporting what we see, and organizing around the systemic injustices that we witness . . . aim[ing] to shift courtroom policies, practices, and culture towards a more equitable NYC."[43] Court watching therefore involves members of the community observing routine court proceedings as well as the collection of community-generated data that can be used to expose injustice and alter court cultures. Like court watching, "participatory defense" seeks to not only hold courts accountable but also transform the criminal legal system more broadly. Community organizer Raj Jayadev coined the term participatory defense to communicate how the participation of the family, friends, and neighbors of defendants in their legal defense can both assist defendants in their individual court cases and build a broader movement of people invested in transforming the punitive imprint of the criminal legal system in their communities. Participatory defense seeks to center defendants and their communities as "change agents" who engage in "public protest and celebration, through which community members expose systemic flaws, force systemic change, and honor transformational successes."[44]

Community organizers and critical scholars increasingly question whether the criminal legal system, with its current tools of punishment, is even an appropriate place for our society to deal with social problems (such as drug addiction and mental illness) or with social harms (such as assault, domestic violence, and even murder). Activists in the Movement for Black Lives and scholars such as Amna Akbar, Paul Butler, Angela Y. Davis, Ruth Wilson Gilmore, and Dorothy Roberts invite us to imagine and invest in radical ways of dealing with such problems—ways that do not involve the punitive presence of the state.[45] In particular, scholars have considered whether we should abolish police and prisons, the tail ends of the system that have historical connections to slavery (and other forms of racial social control) and that produce much harm in the lives of marginalized individuals and communities today.[46] How should we think about abolition in relation to the courts? Skeptics might argue that the criminal courts are not as punitive as policing or incarceration. Even so, the courts certainly enable incarceration and legitimate policing. Courts facilitate incarceration through bail decisions that keep people in jail while awaiting trial and through conviction and sentencing decisions that rely on incarceration as a sanction. And courts legitimate policing by largely leaving police work uninterrogated.

Alongside efforts to alter the dynamics of the attorney-client relationship and the norms of courtrooms, we should give serious consideration to radical ways of transforming—or even altogether abolishing—existing criminal courts. Problem-solving courts, such as drug courts and mental health courts, have been touted as one way to deal with crimes related to addiction and mental illness through nonpunitive and nonadversarial means. Such courts often require a defendant to consent (and sometimes admit guilt) before being transferred. Such a process reduces the influence of lawyers in the court process and centers defendants' interactions with judges and other professionals, such as social workers, who work with defendants to manage the problems presumed to underlie their criminal behavior. Some of these courts rely on theories of procedural justice, emphasizing how the use of public celebrations, eye contact, giving voice, and meaningful interactions can imbue defendants with feelings of respect for the law.[47] Critics, however, note that selection into and completion of such alternative courts can be racially and socioeconomically biased.[48] Furthermore, as sociologist Rebecca Tiger argues, the rehabilitative and therapeutic logics that undergird these alternative courts can themselves be coercive and punitive, forcing people to view their use of drugs as a medicalized problem that should be fixed so that they can be productive citizens.[49] And, if people do not comply with the rehabilitative mandates of these alternative courts, they may be returned to traditional criminal courts, resulting in further punishment. In Boston courts, drug and mental health sessions operate as an alternative to the traditional court process. Some public defenders and social workers I met expressed reservations about sending certain defendants to these sessions, fearing they would be unwilling or unable to abide by treatment requirements.

Other alternatives could altogether remove the court or any other government authority from the process of managing these social problems. So-called progressive prosecutors recently elected across the country have, to varying degrees, declined to charge certain crimes.[50] Abolishing laws that regulate social problems such as drug use, mental illness, consenting sex work, and homelessness (e.g., trespassing laws and anticamping laws) would remove the power of prosecutors to charge such crimes in the first place. Such laws could be replaced with laws and policies that promote harm reduction. Rebecca Tiger describes how drug consumption rooms and safe injection sites could enable people to safely use drugs.[51] Scholars have also described how police could play a positive role in fostering harm reduction by instituting policies that instruct patrol officers to channel people struggling with drug addiction or mental illness to social services rather than the court system.[52] Some cities, such as Denver, Colorado, have considered adopting a policy whereby 911 call operators direct calls related to mental illness toward medical and mental health professionals rather than police.[53] Crimes that involve harm to others, such as assault, rape, and murder could also be dealt with outside the traditional court system, even if we maintain laws and social norms against such crimes. Such harms could be managed and prevented by communities rather than courts. The philosophy of restorative justice views crime as "fundamentally an offense against another person or the community and secondly an act in violation of the law," and therefore advocates for shifting the management of crime away from courts and toward community stakeholders, including the victim, the accused, and other interested parties.[54]

In the United States and around the world, some communities are beginning to experiment with restorative justice approaches, which include victim-offender mediation, community conferences, and school-based programs.[55] Rather than referring a criminal offense to the police or a criminal court, criminal offenses could be referred to these entities. One of the injustices of the criminal courts, for defendants and victims alike, is that it is rarely to a defendant's advantage to admit fault and attempt to repair the harm they have caused others. Worse, some defendants, even those who may be factually guilty, leave court feeling mischaracterized, unheard, and—at times—adamant that because their rights were violated, they do not owe their victims or the community anything other than the time they serve in jail or prison. Restorative justice could provide a space for repair and truth for both victims and offenders. Many victims report satisfaction with restorative justice processes, though some studies suggest that a minority of victims are less satisfied by such processes than by the traditional court process.[56] Moreover, some scholars argue that restorative justice processes require some form of external accountability if stakeholders are unable to work toward restoration.[57] External accountability may also be necessary if violent or retributive proposals emerge from community-driven conferences and mediation programs. Community forms of "justice" outside the courts—such as lynching—have historically been racist and violent. Still, restorative justice programs today appear promising. In New York, the Center for Court Innovation operates two peacemaking programs that appear to be rooted in restorative justice principles. In these programs, "those affected by a dispute . . . 'talk it out' and reach agreement about restitution and repair."[58] Yet, these peacemaking programs are elective rather than default ways of dealing with crime. In other words, prosecutors and victims—rather than the community as a whole—decide whether they want to pursue this method of resolution on a case-by-case basis. Thus, the power to determine the mechanisms of justice still rests largely with the state. Like any new system or practice, the devil is in the detail with respect to restorative justice.

These alternatives to the existing criminal courts may be imperfect, but they encourage us to imagine how we might deal with social harms in the absence of police, prosecutors, defense attorneys, judges, and prison guards. What is clear is that the problems of crime and injustice cannot be fully remedied within the courtroom. Defendants' and victims' needs are rarely met, and the courts unfairly punish the disadvantaged more harshly than the privileged. In the past and in relation to certain social groups, our society has dealt with criminalized social problems and social harms in ways that do not involve state punishment. In *The Condemnation of Blackness*, historian Khalil Gibran Muhammad describes how reformers and social scientists during the Progressive era responded to high crime rates among poor white immigrants with calls for "less policing and more pro-social interventions."[59] Today, as legal scholar Paul Butler reminds us, many communities and individuals do not call the police when harm occurs. "What this means," he writes, "is that for most people who survive violence, doing nothing is a preferable option to involving the state."[60] A lasting cure to criminalized problems and harms will come not from court punishment but rather from social, political, and personal investments in the well-being and dignity of the most marginalized among us. In our individual lives, we must be willing, in the words of Bryan Stevenson, to extend mercy to those who commit crimes that shock and harm us.[61] Socially and politically, we must be willing to advocate for legislation that provides material resources to the most disadvantaged among us. Shifting resources from courts and prisons to housing and healthcare would constitute what sociologist Bruce Western describes as "thick public safety"—a kind of public safety that focuses on socially integrative prevention of crime rather than retribution for crime once it has already occurred.[62]

Such commitments to bringing about justice will not, and have not, come easy. The history of this country is a history of struggle—and missteps—toward ensuring equality and justice among all its people. Today, race and class injustices in the United States appear most strikingly in the form of unequal mass criminalization in city streets, courthouses, and prisons. Tomorrow, we may be fighting a different battle against social injustice. No matter what we face in the years to come, we must listen to, take seriously, and critically evaluate the experiences of those most marginalized by systems of oppression. This book is one contribution to this enduring endeavor.

# Appendix

## THE STUDY'S METHODS

THIS BOOK FOLLOWS in a long tradition of qualitative research in the social sciences. In sociology, scholars have relied on interviews and ethnographic observations to examine how people understand and navigate their everyday lives and interpersonal interactions. For decades, such scholarship has carefully documented how people make sense of, and engage with, other people and social institutions (such as schools, workplaces, and community organizations) under changing structural conditions (such as welfare reform, immigration reform, and mass incarceration). This book has relied on interviews and ethnographic observations to describe and analyze the way a diverse group of criminal defendants navigates the attorney-client relationship during an era of mass criminalization.

Talking to and observing people for research purposes can be a daunting and meandering task. Some of the dilemmas I encountered in conducting this study are common to many qualitative studies, but others are unique to studying people vulnerable to legal punishment. In general, people can be hesitant to let researchers into their lives, especially when a researcher arrives with a tape recorder, a consent form on university letterhead, and a catalog of warnings about the potential risks of participation. If the person agrees to participate, interviews and observations present different challenges. In interviews, a researcher might spend several hours asking personal questions, listening intently for contradictions, probing for crucial details, and, when the conversation turns to difficult childhood memories or socially stigmatized beliefs, toeing the line between maintaining professional distance and being emotionally supportive. Following people as they go about their lives can be just as arduous and uncertain as interviewing them. Plans to meet can be cancelled, and people get cold feet about the prospect of a stranger hovering in the background of their daily routines. It can also be tricky negotiating access to, and consent from, research participants' family and friends—people who may be tangential to the researcher's interests but central to respondents' lives. Observing attorney-client interactions comes with particular social and legal quandaries, such as the legal privilege of confidentiality between a lawyer and their client. Moreover, negotiating access to legal institutions, such as a courthouse, can require years of investment in relationships with officials who may be skeptical of a researcher's motives or the social scientific enterprise writ large. Upon gaining access, legal practices may restrict the way research can be conducted.

In the following pages, I describe the dilemmas and opportunities I encountered while gathering and analyzing data for this book. I begin by discussing how I gained access to courthouses, defendants, and court officials. I detail the ethical dilemmas of observing privileged attorney-client conversations and how I resolved them. I then discuss how I analyzed this rich amount of data. I describe the process of comparing similar and different defendants, interactions, and court cases to identify the book's main findings regarding race and class inequalities in attorney-client interactions. Finally, I consider how my social position as a middle-class black man without a criminal record may have informed the process of data collection and analysis.

## *Access*

The study took place from October 2015 to January 2019. On and off over this period, I interviewed and observed defendants and officials in the Boston area. Collecting these data required gaining access to institutions (such as courthouses, police stations, probation offices, jails, and various justice-involved and grassroots organizations) in addition to individuals.

Boston courthouses are open to the public. Anyone can enter a courthouse and observe proceedings in adult criminal courts. From October 2015 to July 2017, I spent more than one hundred hours observing court proceedings as an ordinary anonymous person sitting in the gallery. I would typically spend a block of three to six hours at a time observing court on any given day. Sometimes, during breaks in court sessions, court officers would ask me if I was waiting for a case or needed any help, but more often than not, I was unnoticed—free to sit in the gallery and take notes either on a small notepad or on my cell phone (when in a courthouse that allowed phones). I observed the courts intermittently, in between conducting interviews and attending graduate school classes. I spent at least three hours in every state-level courthouse in Boston and Cambridge. The goal was to identify what routines were common across every courthouse. But the bulk of my time was spent observing routines in Suffolk County Superior Court and one of the Boston Municipal Courts (BMC), as described in the introduction.

At first, these observations were meant only to complement and confirm the dynamics I found in the interviews I was conducting over this same period, and to recruit interview respondents. During the day, I observed arraignments, pretrial hearings, bench trials, and jury trials in between meeting people for interviews. In the evenings, I read research on the courts, carefully taking note of how the court sessions I observed during the day compared to what other scholars had observed in other jurisdictions. I also visited five police stations, one jail, and a handful of justice-involved and grassroots organizations (residential sober houses, nonresidential drug abuse programs, needle exchanges, homeless shelters, and advocacy organizations against mass incarceration). I would email or call people in positions of authority in these organizations, explain my research, and set up a time to meet. These meetings would typically last between thirty minutes to an hour. Although I did not record our conversations, I took copious written notes. Meetings served as what social scientists refer to as informant interviews, or interviews about how an organization operates, rather than personal in-depth interviews about people's personal attitudes or experiences.[1] I also used these meetings as an opportunity to recruit defendants to participate in the study. I would leave my business card with the person I spoke to as well as flyers for them to put up in public spaces around the organization.

In summer 2017, I left the field and moved to Philadelphia, where I spent my last year in graduate school as a Quattrone Center Research Fellow at Penn Law. At that point, I had collected forty-nine interviews with defendants, several interviews with legal officials, and hundreds of pages of ethnographic fieldnotes. No longer collecting data, I began analyzing it, writing my dissertation, and applying for academic jobs. My committee told me that my data were rich and compelling, but as I presented my preliminary findings at job talks and conferences, colleagues were often curious to know whether I had observed attorney-client interactions in real time. At that point, my observations were largely secondary to my interview data. I had spent hours in court and even accompanied six of the defendants I interviewed as they attended court dates, but my analyses centered on narratives from interviews. Colleagues found the interview data to be novel and persuasive, but they wondered whether defendants' recollections of their interactions with their lawyers accurately reflected the reality of these moments.

Sociologists have long debated whether, and to what extent, researchers should rely on their respondents' accounts of their own beliefs and behaviors as articulated in interviews or surveys.[2] With respect to articulations of beliefs, values, and sentiments, researchers have questioned whether people will tell the truth, given the pressures of social desirability (that is, a desire to appear morally appropriate in front of the interviewer).[3] With respect to behaviors, researchers have questioned not only desirability bias but also the accuracy of a person's memory or even their behavioral consistency. Even if respondents make a good faith effort to be honest about their behaviors, they may simply forget important details or exhibit behavioral inconsistency across situations.[4] Such problems, of course, exist with large-scale quantitative survey research too.[5] Some argue that ethnographic observational data allow researchers to make more reliable claims about situational behaviors; and yet, observations alone do not provide insight into respondents' interpretations and meaning making.[6]

Presaging these very epistemological debates and criticisms, Bart Bonikowski (a member of my dissertation committee) had suggested I include an observational component to my research design years before I started presenting my early findings. He suggested I follow attorney-client pairs as they worked on a case together. At that time, I had pushed back, telling him that I was worried that the Institutional Review Board (IRB)—and defense attorneys themselves—would be hesitant to give me access to private meetings between attorneys and their clients.[7] But Devah Pager, one of my cochairs and ever the methodological visionary, regularly reminded me that I should not avoid collecting certain data just because it might be difficult. I should at least give it a try. Ultimately, these many comments pushed me back into the field one more time. My goal now was to collect in-depth observational data on attorney-client interactions behind closed doors that would complement, revise, and clarify the existing interview data and the existing observational data I had gathered from public proceedings.

In fall 2018, I returned to Boston to gather additional data on attorney-client interactions. During this period, I was no longer an anonymous citizen observing court, as I had been in 2015–2017. Now, I was an unpaid intern in the defender's office. In this role, I spent about 120 hours over the course of one month observing three public defenders in their offices and in court proceedings in three courthouses, as described in the introduction. I watched them work with twelve clients during the month, following up by phone in winter 2019 to learn about how their clients' cases ultimately ended. The challenges of observing attorney-client interactions through the defender's office were many. Some of these challenges I anticipated as I worked with Penn's IRB and CPCS to get the study approved. Other challenges emerged while I was in the field, requiring me to think carefully about my ethical obligations to all my respondents—defendants and defense attorneys alike.

As you know by now, I followed three defenders: Selena (a Latina woman), Sybil (a black woman), and Tom (a white man). They were intentionally selected, with the help of a CPCS administrator, to occupy a diverse set of race and gender backgrounds as well as to have different levels of experience in the office. Before arriving at the office, I called each of them to introduce myself, share my consent form, and ensure that each of them understood the risks of participation and consented to be a part of the study. Risks to the defense attorneys included the potential loss of their employment if I were to observe them engaged in unethical behavior. Each of them agreed over the phone to participate. When I arrived at the office, I asked for their consent a second time and had them sign a consent form. Sharing these many warnings about participation with defense attorneys may have heightened their awareness of my presence as a researcher, encouraging them to change their behavior. Perhaps, when I was present, they obscured problematic ways they practice law when no one is watching. I will never know for sure. But I did happen to observe Tom in 2016 before he was part of the study and aware of my presence as a researcher. His actions then were similar to his actions when I shadowed him in 2018. In my fieldnotes, I described how he "politely (but boldly)" asked a judge "to waive the probation fee" for his client in court that day, much as he did with Gabe from chapter 3. I also overheard his discussion with his client about taking a plea deal: "Attorney [Tom] asks if she [his client] has any questions about her rights or the rights she's giving up. The attorney says he hopes that he can get her out of here quickly today." Even if the public defenders sought to go above and beyond in their representation while I was present, chapter 4's findings reveal how their representation still fell short of the kind of representation many disadvantaged defendants seek.

Conversations between attorneys and their clients are privileged, presenting obvious challenges given my position as a researcher entering, and taking notes on, the relationship.[8] To maintain privilege, I was hired as an unpaid intern. As a member of the public defender staff, my field-notes would be afforded a layer of legal protection. In addition, I agreed to use pseudonyms for defendants as well as the three defenders. I also took care to train the defenders on how to introduce the study to their clients. I could not be part of this introduction, per IRB protocol. Defendants' consent to participate in the study needed to be voluntarily obtained first through their lawyers. Such a practice reduced the likelihood that defendants would feel pressure from me to participate. At the same time, defendants might still feel pressure from their lawyers. Thus, I trained the lawyers on best practices for sharing the opportunity to participate and for obtaining verbal consent. I emphasized that they should be clear with their clients: their clients' choice to participate (or not) would have no bearing on their legal defense. If the client consented, the defender would then invite me into the conversation. At that time, I would briefly reshare the risks of participating in the study, ask the defendant if they had any questions, and then ask again for their verbal consent. As part of their consent, clients agreed that their attorneys could share information about their records and case outcomes with me. In total, thirteen eligible defendants were asked to participate in the study during the month of observation. Of these, twelve agreed to participate, and one refused.

Once a defendant agreed to participate, another challenge arose: figur-ing out how to comport myself while observing private meetings. Observ-ing attorney-client interactions required a mixture of professional reserve and emotional presence. Not wanting to alter the dynamics, I mostly tried to be as invisible as possible. I often sat in the corner of rooms rather than at the table or desk. I tended to keep my head down except to observe facial and bodily positions. I tried not to make eye contact with either the defender or their client while they were talking. The need to capture details for my fieldnotes helped to keep me invisible in many ways; I sat quietly, jotting their conversations, facial expressions, and bodily positions in my notepad. Of course, complete invisibility was impossible. Sometimes clients would glance over at me if they made a joke or felt emotionally distressed.[9] I would respond by quietly smiling or furrowing my brow with concern. None of the twelve clients asked for my legal advice, and I offered none (but every now and then, other defendants in court would ask me for directions to courtrooms or the probation office, assuming I was a lawyer). Though challenging, direct observation of these interac-tions proved immensely useful in enriching the study. In particular, the observations revealed how some disadvantaged defendants do delegate authority, even though disadvantage makes it far more likely that a person will withdraw. Also, the observations made clear the unique constraints defense attorneys feel given the norms and expectations of prosecutors and judges.

Indeed, my month as an intern afforded me greater access to, and awareness of, the place of other court officials in the attorney-client relationship. When observing court earlier in 2015–2017 as an anonymous person, I would sit in the gallery of each courtroom jotting notes and trying to keep up with the fast pace of proceedings and the legal terminology used by officials. Sometimes, I would miss crucial details. I saw firsthand how defendants' cultivation of legal expertise, when sitting and observing in court, could result in misunderstandings about certain legal procedures. When observing as an intern, however, I was part of the backstage working of the system.[10] At first, I was unprepared for this kind of access. I had assumed that, even though I was part the defender's office, I would sit in the gallery and wait for the public defenders I shadowed to retrieve me when we met with their clients. Instead, shadowing the defenders meant that I could sit on the other side of the bar whenever I liked. There, I would often sit next to other officials. The defenders were eager to introduce me to bar advocates, court officers, clerks, and prosecutors. Within a week, I could walk around the metal detector at the entrance, just like the other officials. When seated on the other side of the bar, I was within earshot of the courtroom workgroup, hearing the side comments of ADAs and bar advocates. I was also able to observe Selena, Sybil, and Tom as they sifted through court documents and mumbled aloud about the prosecutor or their client. One afternoon on my walk from the courthouse back to the place I was staying, it became clear that I had become an almost-regular member of the courthouse workgroup. As I was walking, a middle-aged black woman on the sidewalk asked me for spare change. "Sorry," I told her after rummaging through my briefcase and coming up empty. "Oh! But you look like a lawyer, young man. That's why I asked," she responded cheerily.

The above data collection strategies worked out, but not all my efforts to access institutions and their data unfolded as I had hoped. For instance, near the end of 2015, I had considered adding a quantitative component to the study. I planned to collect administrative data on a representative sample of defendants in one or, possibly, two courthouses—one in a low-income, predominantly black neighborhood and one in a wealthier, whiter neighborhood. I had two goals. First, I wanted to assess whether, within each courthouse, a defendant's race, education, and employment status were associated with legal outcomes, net of various controls. Second, I wanted to assess whether similarly situated defendants received different outcomes between courthouses. After drafting a research proposal, I met with a few court administrators. They told me that the data I sought were not currently available in any database. But they would be willing to allow me to gather the data myself.

One of the court administrators put me in touch with the Massachusetts Probation Services, which, in addition to providing defendants with probation services, also stores complete files on every defendant arraigned in Massachusetts. Tucked away in filing rooms in every courthouse, each defendant's file included a police arrest record, a probation intake form (which includes information about employment, income, and residence asked at the time the person is arraigned), and the Court Activity Record Information (CARI). The CARI includes information about the defendant's court dates and the legal decisions made at each court date. In this way, the CARI provides officials with a comprehensive look at the defendant's adult state criminal record. With the generous help of a couple probation officers, I spent several weeks in spring 2016 pulling 550 defendants' files from one BMC courthouse and inputting their information into a spreadsheet.

Ultimately, I did not use the administrative data I collected. The data were incomplete and imprecise. Far too often, information was either missing or inconsistent. For instance, race/ethnicity—an important variable for my purposes—was inconsistently recorded. The same person might be classified as black on the police report, Cape Verdean on the probation intake form, and Hispanic on the CARI. Often, Hispanic ethnicity was inconsistently classified between police reports and intake forms because the police department did not always fill out the "ethnicity" box— only filling in the "race" box. In addition, information about employment and income—two additionally important variables for my purposes— was routinely missing on the intake form. Observing probation officers, I quickly learned that this information was often not recorded because officers typically would ask defendants only whether they were on social security insurance to determine whether they were indigent; rarely did they inquire into the defendant's employment history or personal finances. In short, the administrative data had too many absences, leaving me with more questions than answers.[11] The study's strength, I realized, was in documenting how race and class inequalities were made in everyday interactions rather than offering a statistical analysis of disparities in legal outcomes.

Access to these various institutions facilitated access to the main people in the book. This study centered the experiences of defendants and their defense attorneys, though I also interviewed and observed police officers, probation officers, judges, prosecutors, and other people affiliated with the courts or other justice-involved organizations, such as sober houses and needle exchanges.

I recruited defendants to participate in interviews through numerous sources. Interview recruitment mostly took place between 2015 and 2017. Given my focus on race and class inequalities, I sought a diverse range of people occupying various race and class positions.[12] I employed four recruitment strategies. First, I identified two arrest logs of all adults arrested by BPD and CPD in 2014. Arrest logs included arrestees' names and addresses. I mailed letters to all people with complete addresses arrested for a drug/alcohol-related crime by CPD. I also mailed letters to a purposive sample of people arrested by BPD for similar offenses, seeking to send more letters to addresses in high-income neighborhoods. In total, I sent letters to 167 homes. Forty-seven (or 28 percent) of the letters were formally returned to me by the post office as undeliverable. Of the letters not returned, 14 people responded and were interviewed, resulting in a response rate of 11 percent. Second, to recruit individuals similar to those who may not have received letters as a result of living in institutionalized spaces or having their mail returned as undeliverable because they moved or for other reasons, I shared flyers with sober houses, shelters, organizations for the formerly incarcerated, and a defender's office. Nineteen people responded to this recruitment strategy. Third, to increase the chances of recruiting individuals who may be wary of talking about their criminal history (and perhaps generally less trusting), I snowball sampled by asking those I had already interviewed and people in my personal network to share my study with an acquaintance. Eighteen people responded to this recruitment strategy. Fourth, one of the twelve defendants I got to know during my time in the defender's office sat for an in-depth interview, and the other eleven were informally interviewed during breaks in court proceedings and conversations in the defender's office.

Fifty-two people sat for an in-depth semistructured interview about their experiences as criminal defendants. Table 1 displays the characteristics of this sample. Forty-five of the defendants interviewed are men, and seven are women. Thirty-one identify as white, nineteen as black, three as Latino/a, and one as Native American.[13] When I met them, eleven were middle class, twenty-four were working class, and seventeen were poor, as defined by their level of education and most recent occupation

**Table 1.** Summary characteristics of interview sample of defendants ($N=52$)

| | |
|---|---|
| Race/ethnicity* | |
| White | 31 |
| Black | 19 |
| Latino/a | 3 |
| Native American | 1 |
| Gender | |
| Male | 45 |
| Female | 7 |
| Educational attainment at interview | |
| Four-year college degree or above | 11 |
| Some college or associate's degree | 18 |
| High school degree or GED | 18 |
| Less than high school degree | 5 |
| SES in adolescence | |
| Middle class | 19 |
| Working class | 25 |
| Poor | 8 |
| SES at interview | |
| Middle class | 11 |
| Working class | 24 |
| Poor | 17 |
| SES at interview, by race/ethnicity* | |
| Middle class | |
| White | 6 |
| All nonwhite | 5 |
| Working class | |
| White | 13 |
| All nonwhite | 11 |
| Poor | |
| White | 12 |
| All nonwhite | 6 |

*Total is more than $N$ because of respondents who identify as more than one race/ethnicity.

at the time of our meeting.[14] Nineteen were raised in middle-class homes, twenty-five in working class homes, and eight in poor homes. Although I group respondents into these three discrete class groupings, I generally referred to people in the study as privileged or disadvantaged—a relative indication of their access to situational resources and experiences associated with race and class and influential in shaping their relationships with lawyers. As described throughout the book, these resource and experiential differences between the privileged and the disadvantaged include the nature of policing in their neighborhoods, their access to empowered social ties, and their access to financial resources. Attention to these specific resources and experiences, rather than to their general class grouping, was of greater explanatory value in this study.[15] One limitation of this study is its inability to make claims about gender, as well as the potentially unique way race/ethnicity matters for Asians and Latinos. There were too few women in the study to make cross-class or cross-race comparisons among them, and the study included relatively few Latinos and Native Americans, and no Asian Americans. Issues regarding English-language proficiency and the legal considerations of the United States' complex immigration system could complicate how courthouse interactions are experienced among Asian and Latino immigrants. Future research could incorporate a larger number of people from these groups into the analysis of the attorney-client relationship.

The median interview lasted seventy-five minutes and focused on defendants' everyday lives and their experiences in court. A short survey assessed defendants' income, employment status, education, parents' education, attitudes about the law and legal authorities, and depressive symptomatology. I administered the survey at the start of the interview to ensure that people's responses were not influenced by the topics discussed in the more open-ended part. The interview guide followed a semi-structured format, asking respondents details about their experiences with parents, school, and friends in adolescence; their present-day experiences with friends and family; their experiences with police; and their perspectives on crime and inequality. One part of the interview asked respondents to think about at least one court case in depth, probing them to share details about their case—from the moment of arrest/summons to final adjudication. Questions included:

> First, let's start from the very beginning. Where were you when you
>     were caught?
> How did you get caught?
>     Were you arrested, or were you issued a summons to appear?

Where were you picked up/summonsed?
What was the experience like?
How did you feel when you were summonsed/arrested?
What was going through your mind?

After you were brought in/summonsed, what happened next?
Were you in jail? If so, how long were you detained?
When did you get a lawyer / first meet your lawyer?

Let's talk about your experiences in court.
Do you recall the very first time you were in court?

What was that first time like?
Did anything worry you?

How many times did you go to court?
Were those times any different? How so?
How far apart were your court dates?
What were you doing between your court dates?
How did you feel during this time?
What was going through your mind?

How did your case end up?
Did you go to trial or did you take a plea deal?
Why did you decide to go to trial / take a plea deal?
If you were convicted, what was your sentence?

Did you have any strategies for winning your case?
Tell me more about your thought process / why you thought certain
strategies might work.
Did they work?
Did anyone other than your lawyer help you out?
Family?
Friends?
How so?
During the court process, did you think you were treated fairly?
Did you think the outcome of your case was fair?
Overall, how did you feel your lawyer did?[16]
What would you have changed?

After they detailed their experiences with one court case, I invited
respondents to answer the same questions regarding another case that

they found meaningful or important in their lives. Respondents often took the opportunity to discuss one additional case, but some discussed more. The median respondent discussed two court cases. In all, defendants discussed or were observed in relation to 150 court cases, as I describe below.

To guard against social desirability bias and other limitations of interviews, I asked multiple follow-up questions about incidents that people recalled. I asked not just about their interpretations of events but also about the specific steps they remembered taking as they navigated the court process and everyday life. By asking questions about specific steps in a sequential manner, I was able to elicit rich details in a way that likely made it difficult for respondents to either obfuscate the truth or forget important events. Furthermore, to do my best to protect against social desirability bias in defendants' answers to more subjective questions regarding beliefs about fairness and inequality, I strove to invest them in the interview experience by being affirming and empathetic.[17] Many times, I was surprised by how effective my nonjudgmental affect was in eliciting racist or homophobic statements from respondents, as I discuss below.

In addition to the fifty-two interviews, eighteen defendants agreed to be observed interacting with their lawyers in court and in closed-door meetings, either in addition to, or in place of, being formally interviewed. Seven of them were part of the formal in-depth interview sample, and the other eleven were interviewed informally, in courthouse hallways or during other down time. Table 2 summarizes the characteristics of this sample. Eleven of the defendants observed are men, and seven are women. Five identify as white, ten as black, five as Latino/a, and one as Native American. When I met them, two were middle class, eleven were working class, and five were poor. I do not have detailed information about the adolescent SES of the people who were only observed; therefore, I do not summarize adolescent SES for this sample.

Table 3 lists all sixty-three defendants interviewed and/or observed in the study. The table shows their birth decade, race, gender, SES, age of first arrest, and the data sources from which I collected information about their lives and court experiences.

In addition to the perspectives of defendants, I drew on the perspective of more than 150 legal officials. Thirty-nine legal officials were interviewed as informants. These thirty-nine officials included one judge, three prosecutors, two public defenders, nine bar advocates, nine probation officers, eight police officers, and seven people from other organizations. Of these thirty-nine people, six were black, four were Latino/a, one was Asian, and twenty-eight were white; fourteen were women, and twenty-five were

**Table 2.** Summary characteristics of observational sample
of defendants ($N = 50$)

| | |
|---|---|
| Race/ethnicity* | |
| White | 5 |
| Black | 10 |
| Latino/a | 5 |
| Native American | 1 |
| Gender | |
| Male | 11 |
| Female | 7 |
| Educational attainment at observation | |
| Four-year college degree or above | 2 |
| Some college or associate's degree | 4 |
| High school degree or GED | 9 |
| Less than high school degree | 3 |
| SES at observation | |
| Middle class | 2 |
| Working class | 11 |
| Poor | 5 |

*Total is more than $N$ because of respondents who identify as
more than one race/ethnicity.

men. In addition to informant interviews, I conducted in-depth interviews
with Selena, Sybil, and Tom. They were each interviewed twice—at the
beginning and end of my month-long observation. Their interviews were
recorded and followed a semistructured interview protocol. In the first
interview, I asked them about their personal backgrounds, their beliefs
about the criminal legal system in Boston, their experiences as public
defenders, and their experiences with clients they had a positive working
relationship with and those they had difficulty working with. In the second
interview, I asked them numerous clarifying questions about the specific
clients I observed during the month and about their own career goals.
Finally, in earlier research conducted with Alix S. Winter when we were
graduate students, we gathered in-depth, semistructured interviews with
court officials practicing in a statewide trial court system in the Northeast.[18] Because this court system was similar in many ways to the Boston
courts, I relied on these interviews to provide further context to court procedures and routines documented in this study. In all, we interviewed 111
officials, including 59 judges, 25 prosecutors, and 27 public defenders. We

**Table 3.** Names and details of total defendants interviewed and observed (*N* = 63)

| Name | Birth | Race | Gender | SES in adolescence | SES during study | Age of first arrest | Data sources |
|------|-------|------|--------|--------------------|------------------|---------------------|--------------|
| Alejandro | 1980s | L | M | Unknown | P | 14 | Court observation; interview with lawyer; administrative records |
| Amanda | 1980s | W | F | MC | WC | 19 | In-depth interview |
| Arnold | 1980s | B | M | WC | MC | 20 | In-depth interview; court observation; conversations with lawyer |
| Brianna | 1970s | W | F | MC | WC | 24 | In-depth interview; court observation; conversations with lawyer |
| Caleb | 1980s | B | M | MC | MC | 27 | In-depth interview |
| Camila | 1990s | B/L | F | Unknown | WC | 15 | Court observation; interview with lawyer; administrative records |
| Carlos | 1990s | B/L | M | Unknown | WC | 28 | Court observation; interview with lawyer; administrative records |
| Charlie | 1950s | W | M | WC | MC | 18 | In-depth interview |
| Christopher | 1970s | W | M | MC | P | 16 | In-depth interview |
| Connor | 1990s | W | M | Unknown | WC | Unknown | Court observation; interview with lawyer; administrative records |
| Devin | 1980s | W | M | MC | WC | 21 | In-depth interview (with father) |
| Diego | 1990s | L | M | WC | MC | 21 | In-depth interview |
| Don | 1960s | B | M | MC | WC | 20 | In-depth interview; court observation |
| Donna | 1970s | W | F | P | P | 14 | In-depth interview |
| Drew | 1980s | B | M | Unknown | WC | Unknown | Court observation; interview with lawyer; administrative records |
| Esther | 1980s | B | F | Unknown | WC | Unknown | Court observation; interview with lawyer; administrative records |
| Frederick M. | 1970s | W | M | WC | P | 12 | In-depth interview |
| Gabe | 1970s | L | M | Unknown | WC | 45 | Court observation; interview with lawyer; administrative records |
| Glasses | 1950s | B | M | WC | MC | 13 | In-depth interview |

*Continued on next page*

**Table 3.** (*continued*)

| Name | Birth | Race | Gender | SES in adolescence | SES during study | Age of first arrest | Data sources |
|---|---|---|---|---|---|---|---|
| Gregory | 1960s | B/L | M | P | P | 17 | In-depth interview |
| Ivan | 1970s | B | M | Unknown | P | Unknown | Court observation; interview with lawyer; administrative records |
| J. M. | 1960s | W | M | MC | MC | 12 | In-depth interview |
| Jackson | 1990s | B | M | WC | WC | 16 | In-depth interview |
| Jade | 1990s | B | F | Unknown | WC | 16 | Court observation; interview with lawyer; administrative records |
| James P. | 1980s | W | M | WC | P | 22 | In-depth interview |
| Jane | 1990s | W | F | MC | MC | 24 | In-depth interview |
| Jason | 1980s | W | M | MC | MC | 19 | In-depth interview |
| Jaylan | 1990s | B | M | Unknown | P | 16 | Court observation; interview with lawyer; administrative records |
| Jeffrey | 1960s | B | M | WC | P | 15 | In-depth interview |
| Jimmy | 1990s | B | M | MC | WC | 16 | In-depth interview |
| Joe | 1990s | W | M | MC | WC | 15 | In-depth interview |
| John Blaze | 1980s | W | M | WC | WC | 18 | In-depth interview |
| Joseph | 1960s | B | M | MC | WC | 16 | In-depth interview |
| Josh | 1970s | B | M | WC | P | 16 | In-depth interview |
| Justice | 1950s | B | M | WC | WC | 14 | In-depth interview |
| Justin | 1960s | W | M | WC | P | 18 | In-depth interview |
| Kareem | 1970s | B | M | WC | WC | 16 | In-depth interview |
| Keith | 1950s | B | M | MC | P | 14 | In-depth interview |
| Kema | 1960s | W | F | MC | MC | 19 | In-depth interview |
| Ken | 1960s | W | M | WC | WC | 12 | In-depth interview |
| Kevin | 1970s | W | M | WC | WC | 15 | In-depth interview |

| Name | Decade | Race | Gender | Class | Class | Age | Method |
|---|---|---|---|---|---|---|---|
| Lisa | 1980s | B | F | Unknown | WC | 20 | Court observation; interview with lawyer; administrative records |
| Mary | 1990s | L | F | WC | WC | 19 | In-depth interview; court observation |
| Michael | 1970s | W | M | P | P | 15 | In-depth interview |
| Mitchell | 1980s | W | M | MC | WC | 18 | In-depth interview |
| Nicholas | 1980s | W | M | WC | P | 24 | In-depth interview |
| Owen | 1970s | W | M | P | P | 12 | In-depth interview; court observation; interview with lawyer; administrative records |
| Paul | 1960s | W | M | MC | WC | 16 | In-depth interview |
| Red | 1980s | W | M | P | WC | 11 | In-depth interview |
| Richard | 1970s | B | M | WC | WC | 15 | In-depth interview |
| Robert | 1970s | W | M | WC | WC | 17 | In-depth interview |
| Royale | 1980s | B | M | WC | WC | 14 | In-depth interview |
| Ryan | 1980s | W | M | MC | MC | 19 | In-depth interview; court observation |
| Scott | 1960s | W | M | WC | P | 18 | In-depth interview |
| Slicer | 1970s | B | M | MC | WC | 37 | In-depth interview |
| Stephen Douglas | 1970s | W | M | MC | P | 17 | In-depth interview |
| Tim | 1970s | B | M | P | P | 19 | In-depth interview |
| Tonya | 1960s | W/N | F | P | P | 32 | In-depth interview; court observation |
| Troy | 1980s | W | M | P | P | 25 | In-depth interview |
| Tweedy Bird | 1950s | B | M | WC | WC | 20 | In-depth interview |
| Waine | 1970s | W | M | WC | WC | 15 | In-depth interview |
| William | 1960s | B | M | WC | MC | 29 | In-depth interview |
| Wolf | 1970s | W | M | WC | WC | 14 | In-depth interview |

For race, B = black, W = white, L = Latino, N = Native American. For gender, M = male, F = female. For class, MC = middle class, WC = working class, P = poor.

asked them about their professional decision making at various stages of court processing as well as their beliefs about defendants.

## Analysis

Analysis of these data was iterative but proceeded in two general ways. First, I wrote memos summarizing the narratives and perspectives of each defendant, paying close attention to their everyday life experiences and how those experiences constituted, and were shaped by, race and class inequalities. This analysis drew heavily on the interviews, as well as survey responses. Second, I analyzed each court case that the defendants shared with me and the nature of the attorney-client relationships in each of these court cases. Recall that defendants often shared more than one court case experience in interviews, and I captured additional court cases in my ethnographic fieldnotes. In analyzing these cases and their attorney-client relationships, I examined defendants' narratives about their lawyers in each case and compared these narratives to my observations of attorney-client interactions behind closed doors and in public proceedings, as well as my in-depth and informant interviews with officials. This process of triangulation—or using multiple data sources and perspectives to analyze the same phenomenon—afforded me the chance to provide a fuller account of attorney-client interactions.[19]

Coding categories emerged gradually over the study period and followed a case-based logic of analysis. Case-based analysis seeks to develop logical theories about social processes and mechanisms by comparing similar cases of social phenomena to one another.[20] For instance, in this study, I considered one defendant and one attorney-client relationship at a time, developing theories about how the defendant's resources influenced the way they interacted with their lawyer. Each new case refined my theories. By systematically comparing a set of prior defendants and attorney-client relationships to subsequent defendants and attorney-client relationships, I refined my theories about how and why trust, resources, and other social entities influenced defendants and their relationships with their lawyers. Over time, I identified two main ways attorney-client relationships operate: relationships of withdrawal (which manifested as either resistance or resignation) and relationships of delegation (which manifested in one common way, involving recognition of inexperience, engagement, and deference). These categories emerged through both inductive reading of my data as well as deductive reasoning from existing literature.[21] In final rounds of coding, I systematically coded my interviews and fieldnotes for

**Table 4.** Median age of first arrest, by SES (in adolescence) and race ($N=52$)

| | |
|---|---|
| Race | |
| White | 18 years old |
| Black | 16 years old |
| All nonwhite | 16.5 years old |
| SES in adolescence | |
| Middle class | 19 years old |
| Working class | 16 years old |
| Poor | 17 years old |

several themes, including delegation and withdrawal, adolescent experiences of delinquency and drug use, adolescent alienation in the home and school, police avoidance and negotiation, trust and mistrust of court officials, the cultivation of legal expertise, the development of legal preferences, and court officials' responses to delegation and withdrawal.

In response to the surveys provided at the beginning of each interview, defendants reported prior experiences with and perceptions of police and their lawyers in addition to the basic demographic characteristics reported above. Tables 4–7 summarize people's responses to survey items about arrest, policing, and lawyers. These summary statistics give an overview of perceptions about police and lawyers that complement, but do not fully capture, the complexities and nuances captured in the interview and observational data. The total number of people in each table varies slightly, as not all fifty-two interviewed defendants responded to every question on the survey.

Table 4 shows median age of first arrest in the interview sample, by race and adolescent SES. As we can see, the age of first arrest for white people was older, on average, than it was for black people and other nonwhite groups. With respect to class in adolescence, people who were middle class were first arrested later in life than people who were working class or poor. Working-class people, though, were first arrested at a younger age than poor people.

Table 5 shows the median number of reported lifetime arrests, by race, adolescent SES, and current SES. Perhaps surprisingly, white people in the study reported a higher average number of arrests in their lifetime. This may be because white people who are involved in the criminal legal system are more disadvantaged, on average, than minorities, given that minorities are pulled into the system to a disproportionately high degree.

**Table 5.** Median number of lifetime arrests, by SES and race (*N* = 50)

| | |
|---|---|
| Race | |
| White | 10.5 arrests |
| Black | 8 arrests |
| All nonwhite | 8 arrests |
| SES in adolescence | |
| Middle class | 5 arrests |
| Working class | 10 arrests |
| Poor | 12 arrests |
| SES at interview | |
| Middle class | 5 arrests |
| Working class | 7 arrests |
| Poor | 15 arrests |

In relation to table 4, this might further suggest that once white people are caught by police (later in life), they are more routinely involved for the rest of their lives. These are speculations. Another reason for this racial pattern may be because a disproportionate number of people of color in the sample are socioeconomically advantaged. Table 5 shows that class structures lifetime number of arrests in ways we might expect.

Table 6 reports the extent to which defendants agreed with the statement "The police treated me fairly [in my most recent arrest]," by race and current SES. Working-class people were less likely to agree than both poor people and middle-class people. About equal percentages of people across all classes disagreed. White people were more likely to agree than black people and other people of color.

Table 7 reports the extent to which defendants agreed with the statement "My lawyer did his/her best to defend me [in my most recent court case]," by race, current SES, and type of attorney. As described in detail throughout the book, disadvantaged people (along both race and class) were more likely to disagree, and privileged people were more likely to agree. None of the people who privately retained their lawyers disagreed.

From interviews and observations, I captured data on the sixty-three defendants' experiences with 150 unique court cases. The following tables summarize the characteristics of these cases. These summary statistics give an overview of the types of cases people experienced, the types of attorney-client relationships they experienced, and the connection between attorney-client relationship types and demographic characteristics. Much like the tables summarizing defendants' perceptions, the

**Table 6.** Perceptions of fair treatment by the police, by SES (at interview) and race ($N=51$)

|  | Strongly agree/ agree (%) | Neutral (%) | Disagree/strongly disagree (%) |
|---|---|---|---|
| White ($n=30$) | 50 | 23 | 27 |
| Black ($n=19$) | 32 | 16 | 53 |
| All nonwhite ($n=22$) | 27 | 18 | 55 |
| Middle class ($n=11$) | 55 | 9 | 36 |
| Working class ($n=23$) | 30 | 35 | 35 |
| Poor ($n=17$) | 47 | 12 | 41 |

Respondents were asked the extent to which they agree with the following statement: "The police treated me fairly [in my most recent arrest]." Percentages for each subgroup may total slightly more or less than 100 percent due to rounding.

summary statistics in these tables do not capture the full complexity and nuance of the qualitative data. The main chapters of the book, of course, serve that purpose.

Table 8 shows the number of cases in relation to the type of criminal charge, the race/ethnicity of the defendant, and the SES of the defendant at the time they were dealing with the case (for example, if a person described one case occurring in their adolescence when they were middle class and another case occurring in their adulthood when they were working class, their first case would be coded as middle class, and their second case would be coded as working class). About half of the court cases in this

**Table 7.** Perceptions that lawyers did their best to defend them, by SES (at interview), race, and lawyer type ($N=50$)

|  | Strongly agree/ agree (%) | Neutral (%) | Disagree/strongly disagree (%) |
|---|---|---|---|
| Middle class ($n=11$) | 82 | 18 | 0 |
| Working class ($n=22$) | 59 | 23 | 18 |
| Poor ($n=17$) | 35 | 12 | 53 |
| White ($n=29$) | 62 | 21 | 17 |
| Black ($n=19$) | 42 | 16 | 42 |
| All nonwhite ($n=22$) | 45 | 18 | 36 |
| Private ($n=10$) | 90 | 10 | 0 |
| Court appointed ($n=40$) | 48 | 20 | 33 |

Respondents were asked the extent to which they agree with the following statement: "My lawyer did his/her best to defend me [in my most recent court case]." Percentages for each subgroup may total slightly more or less than 100 percent due to rounding.

**Table 8.** Characteristics of court cases discussed in interviews and/or observed in court ($N = 150$)

|  | No. of court cases |
|---|---|
| Case type* | |
| Drug possession or distribution | 58 |
| OUI | 23 |
| Other nonviolent offenses | 48 |
| Other violent offenses | 21 |
| SES of defendant during case | |
| Middle class | 28 |
| Working class | 82 |
| Poor | 40 |
| Race/ethnicity of defendant† | |
| White | 88 |
| Black | 57 |
| Latino/a | 9 |
| Native American | 2 |

*Categorized by most serious offense.
†Total more than $N$ because of those who identify as more than one race/ethnicity.

study dealt with drug- or alcohol-related crimes. Most court cases involved defendants when they were working class. Future research could benefit from capturing people engaged with court cases when they are poor or middle class, to get a better sense of these extremes. Most of the court cases involved white defendants. Future research could benefit from capturing a larger number of cases among people of color, especially Latinos, Native Americans, and Asians.

Tables 9–14 report the number of cases that were coded as involving attorney-client relationships of withdrawal versus attorney-client relationships of delegation. Not all cases discussed in interviews provided enough information for me to be able to confidently code the nature of the defendant's relationship with their lawyer. Thirty-six cases were therefore coded as missing. About 60 percent of court cases in the study involved attorney-client relationships of delegation, whereas about 40 percent involved relationships of withdrawal. This greater incidence of delegation is likely because of the greater number of middle- and working-class white people in the study, who are typically privileged. Among the disadvantaged—working-class people of color and the poor—withdrawal was relatively more common.

Among poor people of color, about 90 percent of their attorney-client relationships were withdrawn. Because poor people and working-class people of color are disproportionately represented in the court system, we might expect that withdrawal would be more common in a representative sample of criminal defendants than it appeared to be in this study.

**Table 9.** Attorney-client relationship types in individual court cases ($N = 150$)

| | |
|---|---|
| Delegation | 61%<br>(69 of 114 cases) |
| Withdrawal | 39%<br>(45 of 114 cases) |
| Resignation | 55%<br>(25 of 45 cases) |
| Resistance | 45%<br>(20 of 45 cases) |
| Missing* | 36 cases |

*The number of court cases where there is not enough information to code the kind of attorney-client relationship.

**Table 10.** Attorney-client relationship types in individual court cases, by SES

| | Middle class<br>($n = 28$) | Working class<br>($n = 82$) | Poor<br>($n = 40$) |
|---|---|---|---|
| Delegation | 92%<br>(22 of 24 cases) | 66%<br>(40 of 61 cases) | 24%<br>(7 of 29 cases) |
| Withdrawal | 8%<br>(2 of 24 cases) | 34%<br>(21 of 61 cases) | 76%<br>(22 of 29 cases) |
| Missing* | 4 cases | 21 cases | 11 cases |

*The number of court cases where there is not enough information to code kinds of attorney-client relationships.

**Table 11.** Attorney-client relationships in individual court cases, by race

| | White<br>($n = 88$) | Black<br>($n = 57$) | All nonwhite<br>($n = 64$) |
|---|---|---|---|
| Delegation | 63%<br>(41 of 65) | 57%<br>(25 of 44) | 55%<br>(28 of 51) |
| Withdrawal | 37%<br>(24 of 65) | 43%<br>(19 of 44) | 45%<br>(23 of 51) |
| Missing* | 23 | 13 | 13 |

*The number of court cases where there is not enough information to code the kind of attorney-client relationship.

**Table 12.** Attorney-client relationships of the middle class, by race in individual court cases

|  | White middle class (n=16) | Black middle class (n=11) | All nonwhite middle class (n=12) |
|---|---|---|---|
| Delegation | 93% (14 of 15) | 88% (7 of 8) | 89% (8 of 9) |
| Withdrawal | 7% (1 of 15) | 12% (1 of 8) | 11% (1 of 9) |
| Missing* | 1 | 3 | 3 |

*The number of court cases where there is not enough information to code the kind of attorney-client relationship.

**Table 13.** Attorney-client relationships of the working class, by race in individual court cases

|  | White working class (n=42) | Black working class (n=37) | All nonwhite working class (n=40) |
|---|---|---|---|
| Delegation | 70% (21 of 30) | 61% (17 of 28) | 61% (19 of 31) |
| Withdrawal | 30% (9 of 30) | 39% (11 of 28) | 39% (12 of 31) |
| Missing* | 12 | 9 | 9 |

*The number of court cases where there is not enough information to code the kind of attorney-client relationship.

**Table 14.** Attorney-client relationships of the poor, by race in individual court cases

|  | White poor (n=30) | Black poor (n=9) | All nonwhite poor (n=12) |
|---|---|---|---|
| Delegation | 30% (6 of 20) | 12% (1 of 8) | 9% (1 of 11) |
| Withdrawal | 70% (14 of 20) | 88% (7 of 8) | 91% (10 of 11) |
| Missing* | 10 | 1 | 1 |

*The number of court cases where there is not enough information to code the kind of attorney-client relationship.

## Positionality

Just as race and class mattered in the lives of the participants in this study, my own social positions undoubtedly influenced my research. Social scientists increasingly consider how their social identities may influence their scholarship. Entire fields are devoted to such inquiry. A social scientist's identities can shape the kind of data they gather, the patterns they see (or find surprising) in their data, and the power they have over their research participants (both in the field and in the act of writing). I have touched on many of these issues, in various ways, throughout the book and in this appendix. But let me share some closing reflections.

I am the son of two black physicians, who raised me in a predominantly white suburb of Nashville, Tennessee. My brother and I attended private schools, where we were one of a handful of black kids. On weekends, we would spend hours doing community service or attending sleepovers with other kids in our local chapter of Jack and Jill, a social organization for affluent black children. Over winter breaks, we would go skiing in Canada or Park City, Utah. On evenings when my parents were on call at the hospital, au pairs and babysitters would make sure we did our homework and brushed our teeth before bed. My family's economic and cultural privileges, however, did not protect us from racism. I will never forget when a high school teacher, impersonating a Jim Crow–era southern senator, thought it would be a good idea to refer to me as "the Negro" in front of my history class. Jack and Jill, for me, was as much a refuge from the racism I experienced at school as it was a curiously exclusive enclave of upper-middle-class privilege. And so, I grew up keenly aware of the privileges and perils of race and class in this country.[22]

My awareness of social inequality drew me to study government and African American studies as an undergraduate at Harvard College. I wrote my senior thesis on black elites' political beliefs about racial inequality. Even though I was a political science student at the time, my thesis was motivated by the work of a sociologist. In E. Franklin Frazier's 1957 book *Black Bourgeoisie*, he critiqued the black middle class as superficial, aspiring to whiteness, and unconcerned with the struggles of the black poor.[23] He pilloried their social organizations as frivolous distractions rather than as spaces of social uplift. My childhood had afforded me a different perspective, and I wanted to know if Frazier's critique still applied. The summer I conducted my thesis research was the summer before Barack Obama's election as the nation's first black president. Just after Obama had secured the Democratic nomination, I returned home to Nashville to interview and survey members of Nashville's black middle class. I found that middle-class black people who were involved in the very same elite black social organizations that Frazier had criticized—organizations like the Boulé and the Links—appeared to be more committed to fighting racial (and sometimes class) inequality through both traditional political routes (such as voting and writing letters to congresspeople) and nontraditional political routes (such as protest and rallies) than their middle-class peers not involved in these organizations.

Later, in graduate school at Harvard, my questions about racial inequality in the political process morphed into questions about racial and class inequality in the criminal legal system. I was deeply affected by the killing of Trayvon Martin and watched the trial of George Zimmerman with much anxiety. Just after Zimmerman's acquittal, I marched alongside hundreds of concerned people just like me in a rally in Dudley Station in Boston. That rally and other protests that summer and fall sparked a need for me to better understand our contemporary court system—how our legal system could allow a man to kill a boy out of nothing more than antiblack fear, while at the same time sending young black men to prison every day for far less. I started researching the criminal courts, inspired largely by a new generation of young black activists taking to the streets. Later, when I would happen on my cousin in court in Chicago, my thinking would be pushed further. Seeing my own extended family deal with arrest, court processing, and jail suggested to me that the problems were not just racialized but also profoundly classed.

Beyond motivating my work and informing my analysis, my experiences and identities likely influenced the data collection process. Being a Harvard graduate student certainly opened some doors and may have closed others. When accessing institutions such as the administrative offices of the court, my Harvard affiliation likely encouraged responses to my many and persistent cold calls and emails. When I mailed letters to people for interviews, I mailed them on Harvard letterhead. My flyers also mentioned my university affiliation, per IRB guidelines. Perhaps my affiliation signaled the legitimacy of the study and encouraged some to respond. Perhaps others had negative perceptions of the university and therefore decided not to respond. I cannot be sure.

Of course, I was not just a Harvard student, but, importantly, I was a black student studying inequality. I was concerned that potential respondents may search for me online before deciding to participate in the study. I worried that if they were to do so, they may form opinions about me, influencing their decision to respond to my letters—and perhaps influencing the interview itself. During most of the study period, I chose to keep social media accounts like Twitter and Instagram private. I deleted Facebook. I also removed much of the "Biography" section of my professional website, concealing my research interests in race and class inequality. I hoped these efforts would lessen the chance that respondents would arrive at the interview ready to tell me what they thought I wanted to hear, rather than what they truly believed, about their experiences. Anyway, it appeared that most of the people I met had not searched for me online. When meeting people for the interview, they often had no idea what I looked like; I could tell that a few white respondents were quite surprised that the Harvard graduate student conducting the study was a skinny black guy.

In the interview setting, I strove to mitigate everyday racial and class dynamics when speaking to nonblack respondents and those who did not share my class background. In general, I strove to allow all respondents to speak freely and without fear of judgment. I was open, attentive, and friendly. Even when a person said something offensive, I remained affable, often laughing off respondents' remarks about "ghetto baby mamas,"[24] "Spanish" drug dealers,[25] and "faggots."[26] A childhood spent navigating the racism of my teachers and peers proved useful. Still, letting these comments go and maintaining a smile required emotional labor on my part. In my everyday life, such comments would not go unchallenged; but in the interview setting, I had to bite my tongue. My efforts seemed to pay off.

I would be lying if I said that I hit it off with every respondent. A handful of interviews with defendants were brief. The shortest two interviews were twenty-five and thirty-one minutes each. These were my first and third interviews. Their brevity probably says more about me—about my uncertainty in the earliest stages of the research—than about the willingness of my respondents to share their stories. Some of my conversations with bar advocates and other court officials were hurried. When I was shadowing the defenders, I was worried how I might handle a situation in which the three defenders I had selected did not like me or want me around. Luckily, Selena, Sybil, and Tom were enthusiastic, thoughtful, and helpful participants. I shared with them an early draft of parts of the book where they appeared. Selena did not respond to my email, but Tom and Sybil seemed to agree that I had captured them faithfully. Tom wrote, "I enjoyed that, Matt! You have a very readable style. Can't wait to read the book." Sybil wrote, "This was awesome to read! It brought back memories and was also kind of funny. It's really well written. I didn't see any inaccuracies. Thanks again for allowing me to be a part of your book!!" They might disagree with some of my conclusions, but I am reassured that they see this work as an accurate description of what took place.

Ultimately, defendants and court officials alike opened up to me in ways I could not have imagined. Defendants shared stories not just about their court experiences but also about their struggles with addiction, their infidelity with their partners, and other sensitive topics. The longest defendant interview was with Wolf, the white working-class man from chapters 1 and 3, and lasted a staggering 282 minutes (nearly five hours). "I like having conversations," Wolf told me at one point. At the end of each interview, I asked defendants to share why they decided to participate in the study. Sometimes they mentioned the twenty-dollar compensation, an amount of money that I hoped would be just enough to compensate people for their time but not too high that they felt undue influence to share their stories. More common than mentioning the money, defendants shared that they participated to help me shed light on problems they have faced in the criminal legal system. Richard, the working-class black man from chapter 2, said, "I decided to do this interview because, you know, I see a young brother trying to do the right thing and trying to help out. Twenty dollars definitely doesn't hurt. . . . I feel it was a win-win situation."

# NOTES

## Preface

1. For estimates, see Enns et al. (2019).

2. C. Wright Mills (1959, 7) famously described the "sociological imagination" as "the capacity to shift from one perspective to another—from the political to the psychological; from examination of a single family to comparative assessment of the national budgets of the world; from the theological school to the military establishment; from considerations of an oil industry to studies of contemporary poetry. It is the capacity to range from the most impersonal and remote transformations to the most intimate features of the human self—and to see the relations between the two."

## Introduction

1. Most names in this book are pseudonyms, sometimes chosen by the respondents. Details about people's experiences in court were collected from my personal observations, my interviews with them, and my interviews with their lawyers. Some details about their lives, such as their specific occupation or neighborhood, were changed just enough to obscure their identities while staying true to the character of their lives. For more details on the study's research design, analysis, and how I sought to confirm the veracity of my respondent's recollections, see the appendix.

2. Forman (2017).

3. See, for example, Lareau (2011, 2015); Stephens, Markus, and Phillips (2013).

4. See Calarco (2018); Gage-Bouchard (2017); Lareau (2011); Shim (2010).

5. This is a descriptive claim about what makes the courts unequal. I focus on interactions, revealing how they are very different for the privileged and the disadvantaged. This kind of claim can be understood as a constitutive explanation about the microlevel realities that define inequality. In other words, I am asking what realities give the court system the "causal capacity" (Ylikoski 2013) to be understood as unequal. The key realities that I focus on are the agreements and disagreements between lawyers and their clients. For more on constitutive explanations, see Salmon (1984); I. Kohler-Hausmann (2019).

6. This is an explanatory claim about how the court system reproduces unequal outcomes such as differences in dismissal rates, dignity, sympathetic judging, conviction rates, and sentence lengths between groups of people. Whereas the constitutive claim above defines inequality as differences in the realities of interactions among privileged people and disadvantaged people, the explanatory claim considers inequality as differences in the system's formal and informal legal outcomes between privileged and disadvantaged groups. The data in this book do not statistically test whether differences in attorney-client relationships independently cause one outcome or another net of other factors, but the data provide evidence to support the logical inference that such processes contribute to group differences in legal outcomes. See

Gerring (2009) and M. L. Small (2009) on how qualitative data can provide evidence for such claims.

7. The term "privilege" is often used in popular culture. I refer to "privilege" and "disadvantage" to denote the resources and experiences that people have access to (or do not have access to) given their social position (especially their race or social class) in everyday life (see Black and Stone 2005; McIntosh 1992; Lucal 1996). Specifically, I focus on resources and experiences that matter in establishing a relationship of delegation with one's lawyer (or by contrast, the resources/experiences that result in a relationship of withdrawal). These resources and experiences include racism and classism in neighborhood policing, histories of legal system involvement, social ties, and access to financial resources.

8. See, for example, Fiske and Markus (2012); Lareau (2011).

9. On intersectionality, see Crenshaw (1991); McCall (2005). See also Collins (2002) on the interpersonal domain of the matrix of domination.

10. For a lengthier theoretical discussion of this distinction, see Clair (2018, 45–55).

11. For instance, the race-gender group least subject to mass criminalization in the United States is white women. White women in the United States nevertheless have a higher incarceration rate than the average incarceration rates of Germany, Sweden, Norway, Japan, and India (Gottschalk 2016, 5).

12. A systematic study of the court experiences of women from different race and class backgrounds—in comparison to one another and to men and gender nonconforming people—would likely uncover important realities about gendered oppression in American society. Sexism and gendered cultural differences have been shown to be an important aspect of interactions with legal officials (see, e.g., Chesney-Lind and Pasko 2013; Daly 1994; Levine and Mellema 2001; Steffensmeier 1980) and engagement in delinquent behaviors (see, e.g., Jones 2009; Peterson and Panfil 2017) among women and girls. Examining the experiences of marginalized women, especially black, Latina, and queer women, could provide nuanced insight into the machinations of legal control in attorney-client relationships (see Jones 2009; Leverentz 2014). Yet, a detailed analysis of gender is beyond the scope of this study. Only eleven of the defendants interviewed and observed for this book identified as women, and the interviews and observations focused more on race and class than on gender. Moreover, analyzing gender would require engagement with an additional set of literature—requiring careful consideration of scholarship on gender inequalities.

13. Garland (2001).

14. From the Bureau of Justice Statistics' Corrections Statistical Analysis Tool, accessed October 9, 2018, http://www.bjs.gov/index.cfm?ty=nps. These rates include only individuals sentenced to a year or more of incarceration.

15. Kaeble and Glaze (2016).

16. Phelps (2016); DeMichele (2014); I. Kohler-Hausmann (2018); Stuart (2016); Harris (2016).

17. K. D. Martin et al. (2018).

18. Kaeble and Glaze (2016).

19. See the Bureau of Justice Statistics' special report *Contacts between Police and the Public, 2015* (Davis, Whyde, and Langton 2018). In 2011, 1.6 million US residents over the age of sixteen were estimated to have been arrested by the police in the past

twelve months. In 2015, the BJS estimated that 814,000 US residents of the same age were estimated to have been arrested by the police in the past twelve months. The 2015 estimate, however, importantly "only includes residents who reported an arrest as the sole type of contact with police, occurring outside of the context of a traffic stop, street stop, or traffic accident. In 2011, the context of arrest was not specified" (Davis, Whyde, and Langton 2018, 6). Thus, the 2015 estimate is likely an underestimate of the number of people arrested. Moreover, the Police-Public Contact Survey from which these estimates were drawn does not survey transient and institutionalized populations, such as the homeless—a population that is probably more likely, on average, to be arrested in any given year.

20. D. Small (2014) contrasts policy reforms around "mass incarceration" with policy reforms that could be imagined around a term like "mass criminalization." Small's interpretation of mass criminalization centers particularly on the criminalization of communities of color. Pushing further, my use of the term additionally speaks to the way such criminalization has punitive, though unequal, effects across multiple communities—marginalized and privileged. Mass criminalization, as I use the term, captures the fact that, over the last four decades, Americans from nearly all demographic groups have witnessed an increased likelihood of punitive contact with the police, courts, probation, incarceration, and other techniques of punitive control. Unlike terms such as "mass incarceration" or "mass probation," the term "mass criminalization" speaks to all forms of legal control along the continuum from arrest to court processing to incarceration and reentry. Thus, the term better captures the full scope of punishment by federal, state, and local authorities as well as by everyday citizens and nongovernmental organizations, such as employers who discriminate against former felons (see Pager 2008) and people who make residential choices based on publicly available databases of convicted sex offenders (see Pickett, Mancini, and Mears 2013; Wacquant 2009). And unlike macrolevel concepts like the "carceral state," mass criminalization captures the lived reality of the use of penal techniques in people's everyday lives.

21. Hinton (2016); Miller and Alexander (2015); Murakawa (2014).

22. Wacquant (2010a, 80); see also Beckett and Western (2001); J. Kohler-Hausmann (2017); Schoenfeld (2018).

23. Alexander (2012); Hinton (2016).

24. Wacquant (2010b, 214).

25. See Travis, Western, and Redburn (2014) on the relationships between changes in crime rates, policy changes, and mass incarceration.

26. Critical perspectives suggest that racial disparities are intentional outcomes of a racist, even if legal, form of social control. For example, Alexander (2012) argues that mass incarceration constitutes a form of racialized social control analogous to Jim Crow in its treatment, segregation, and stigmatization of African Americans. Mass incarceration affects not just black people who are currently trapped in prisons, but also whole communities of marginalized black people—family members, neighbors, and friends of policed and incarcerated people who witness the criminalization of their communities. Formerly incarcerated individuals also face legal exclusions in voting, housing, and employment—exclusions that can have implications for their social networks (Asad and Clair 2018).

27. Black people and Latino people are disproportionately arrested at higher rates than white people (Barnes et al. 2015; Brame et al. 2014; Travis, Western, and Redburn 2014). At incarceration, race and class disparities are more extreme. For instance, Western and Pettit (2010) estimate that 68 percent of black men without a high school education born in the mid-1970s had been incarcerated in prison by the age of 30–34, compared to 28 percent of white men without a high school education and 1.2 percent of white men with at least some college education. In this same cohort, about 27 percent of all black men, 12 percent of all Latino men, and 5 percent of all white men had experienced incarceration. In another study, Shannon et al. (2017) estimate that in 2010, over 33 percent of all black men had at least one felony conviction, compared to nearly 13 percent of all men.

28. Western and Pettit (2010).

29. Recent research suggests that incarceration may be shifting its geographic location—from mostly urban areas to suburban and rural areas. A recent study of prison admissions in Massachusetts in 2009–2014 found that suburbs and small cities like Lynn, Brockton, and Pittsfield had surprisingly high prison admissions rates over the period—some even higher than Boston (Simes 2018). Several of these smaller cities have experienced economic decline and increased rates of drug use. Some scholarship suggests that the geographic expansion of incarceration may help explain increased incarceration rates among whites. A recent report by the Vera Institute of Justice found that whereas black incarceration rates in jails nationwide have been declining since 2005, white incarceration rates have been increasing since 1990 (Subramanian, Riley, and Mai 2018). The report found that white incarceration rates have increased most notably in smaller city and rural jurisdictions.

30. Blumstein (1982); Beck and Blumstein (2018).

31. Relatively little research on disparities has examined Asian American or American Indian defendants' outcomes. Some work has suggested that Asian Americans tend to fare similarly to whites (e.g., Johnson and Betsinger 2009). American Indians, on the other hand, face correlated disadvantages similar to blacks and Latinos. These disadvantages likely translate into their legal processing. For example, American Indians have a relatively high lifetime risk of death by police (Edwards, Lee, and Esposito 2019). In addition, little research has been able to consider SES differences other than employed/nonemployed because courts rarely collect data on income, education, or specific occupation of defendants.

32. "Unwarranted" race and class disparities (that is, disparities that cannot be explained by legal factors) have been documented along all stages of the court process—from charging, bail/pretrial detainment, charge dismissal and reduction, conviction, and sentencing. Numerous peer-reviewed studies, relying on administrative records, estimate the extent to which disparities can be considered warranted or unwarranted. Studies control for ostensibly race- or class-neutral causes (e.g., legal factors such as one's criminal charge or prior criminal record) to assess the extent to which disparities are unwarranted. This line of research continues to find evidence for unwarranted race and class differences (for reviews, see Mitchell 2005; Spohn 2000, 2013; Zatz 2000). For instance, direct race or class effects have been observed at bail/pretrial release (Chiricos and Bales 1991; Demuth 2003; Kutateladze et al. 2014; Schlesinger 2005), at the decision to dismiss or reduce charges (Spohn, Gruhl, and

Welch 1981; Shermer and Johnson 2010), and at sentencing (Chiricos and Bales 1991; D'Alessio and Stolzenberg 1993; Johnson and DiPietro 2012; Kutateladze et al. 2014; MacDonald et al. 2014; Nobiling, Spohn, and DeLone 1998; Petersilia 1985; Shermer and Johnson 2010). While such evidence varies by jurisdiction (see Baldus, Pulaski, and Woodworth 1986; Johnson 2006) and crime type (Mitchell 2005), these studies provide cumulative evidence of the unequal treatment of similarly situated defendants along race and class lines. Scholars continue to debate the specific forms of these race and class biases (Baumer 2013; Spohn 2000; Ulmer 2012).

33. But for a critique, see I. Kohler-Hausmann (2018).

34. An important literature on "legal consciousness" considers how ordinary people view and engage with the law amid various constraints and opportunities. See DeLand (2013); Merry (1990); Nielsen (2000); and Sarat (1990). See also Young (2014); Young and Billings (2020). Patricia Ewick and Susan Silbey define legal consciousness as the cultural practices that individuals engage in with respect to the law in everyday life (Ewick and Silbey 1998, 38–39; Silbey 2005, 334). They argue that studying how people engage with the law can help to explain the law's hegemony, or its durability as a "legitimate and governing institution" (Silbey 2005, 337) despite the "concrete inequalities" (359) it reproduces. This literature is important, but it does not afford much insight into criminal legal contexts or how relational interactions constitute and reproduce inequality—two central concerns of this book. Therefore, I have chosen to engage with fundamental tools in relational theory and cultural sociology and apply them to my empirical examination of the attorney-client relationship in criminal court. Doing so draws clearer connections between criminal law and core sociological questions of race and class inequality in broader society.

35. Other scholars of this period also began to refer to criminal courts, especially lower courts where low-level crimes such as misdemeanors are handled, using the "assembly line" justice metaphor. For a summary, see I. Kohler-Hausmann (2018, chapter 2).

36. Blumberg (1967, 41).

37. *Gideon v. Wainwright* 372 US 335 (1963) interpreted the right to counsel to mean that all states must provide defense attorneys to those who cannot afford them. *Miranda v. Arizona* 384 US 436 (1966) required that police inform arrestees of their rights to remain silent and have an attorney present, if their statements are to be able to be used at trial. *Brady v. Maryland* 373 US 83 (1963) required prosecutors to share any evidence that might suggest that the defendant did not commit the crime.

38. *Gideon v. Wainwright.*

39. See, for example, *Escobedo v. Illinois* 378 US 478 (1964), which provided for the right to counsel during police interrogations. *Argersinger v. Hamilton* 407 US 25 (1972) expanded the right to counsel to defendants facing a charge that could incur jail time. In Massachusetts, the right has additionally been extended to probation revocation hearings (*Williams v. Commonwealth* 350 Mass. 732 [1966]), as well as to juvenile defendants (*Marsden v. Commonwealth* 352 Mass. 564 [1967]).

40. Eisenstein and Jacob (1977); on this point, see also Flemming (1986); Schulhofer and Friedman (1993).

41. Feeley ([1979] 1992, 13–29).

42. Feeley ([1979] 1992, 152); see also Mather (1979, 10).

43. Casper (1972); O'Brien et al. (1977); Wilkerson (1972).

44. Casper (1971).

45. Wilkerson (1972).

46. Casper (1972); O'Brien et al. (1977).

47. Boccaccini, Boothby, and Brodsky (2004).

48. Travis, Western, and Redburn (2014).

49. On the definition of broken windows policing, see Wilson and Kelling (1982). In New York City, I. Kohler-Hausmann (2018, 51) shows that the Hispanic-white disparity and the black-white disparity in misdemeanor arrests both peaked in 2007.

50. American Civil Liberties Union (2013).

51. Van Cleve (2016).

52. I. Kohler-Hausmann (2018).

53. Feeley ([1979] 1992) suggested that defendants might influence their formal legal outcomes. He called for research on defendants that would draw on "interviews with large numbers of defendants, which is much more difficult than interviewing a handful of officials" (152). Van Cleve (2016) refers to defendants' legal consciousness, which she defines as "the perceptions of law that are gained through daily experience, images, and encounters with legal systems" (163). While she argues that court officials often disparage defendants' "street law," she does not systematically examine whether and how defendants use their street law. I. Kohler-Hausmann (2018) sometimes refers to the "structure of incentives" that defendants face as they are marked, tested, and monitored by court officials. She also incorporates defendants' perspectives about various legal sanctions throughout the second part of the book. But she does not systematically consider how defendants' perspectives influence their ways of engaging with court officials and the court—and to what effect. See also Mather (1979, 10).

54. Most notably, political scientist Jonathan D. Casper's 1972 book *American Criminal Justice: The Defendant's Perspective* draws on interviews among mostly white, poor, and incarcerated men in Connecticut. Most men in the study reported feeling resigned to the law and the court process (Casper 1971, 1972). Casper argued that their resignation stemmed from their lack of knowledge about certain legal defenses, their distrust of lawyers, their sense that fighting their case may backfire, and their acknowledgment of their factual guilt. Yet, his study and other research on defendants' attitudes often focuses only on disadvantaged defendants' perspectives, without comparison to the privileged. Moreover, this literature does not examine how defendants interact with their lawyers in real time or report doing so in retrospect. As such, these studies often reinforce the dominant assumption that defendants are passive. Defendants may complain about their lawyers, but, these studies assume, they do not make much of an effort to shape their own trajectories through the system (for an exception, see Moore et al. [2019], which finds, among a sample of twenty-two public defense clients, that some exhibit agency in communications with their lawyers). For more interview-based studies of defendants' attitudes, see Boccaccini, Boothby, and Brodsky (2004); O'Brien et al. (1977); Tyler (1984); Wilkerson (1972).

55. Bertenthal (2017); Feierman (2006).

56. See Schulhofer and Friedman (1993); Spiegel (1979); Uphoff (2000); Uphoff and Wood (1998). For theoretical considerations of defendants' ways of engaging with criminal court processing, see Black (1989) and Mather (2003). For legal scholarship

debating the proper role of defendants' decision making within the attorney-client relationship, see Natapoff (2005); Spiegel (1979); and Uphoff (2000).

57. See Kritzer (1990); Rosenthal (1974); and Sarat and Felstiner (1997) on power dynamics in attorney-client relationships in civil litigation.

58. See Ulmer (2019). On the need to understand individual social action in institutions, Max Weber (1978, 13) classically wrote that it may "be convenient or even indispensable to treat social collectivities, such as states, associations, business corporations, foundations, as if they were individual persons. . . . But for the subjective interpretation of action in sociological work these collectivities must be treated as *solely* the resultants and modes of organization of the particular acts of individual persons, since these alone can be treated as agents in a course of subjectively understandable action."

59. These officials, who are often repeat players in the courtroom and who must work together to dispose of cases, are often referred to collectively as a "courtroom workgroup" (Eisenstein and Jacob 1977). See also Klepper, Nagin, and Tierney (1983); Ulmer (1997).

60. Clair and Winter (2016); Eisenstein, Flemming, and Nardulli (1988); Feeley ([1979] 1992); Johnson (2006); I. Kohler-Hausmann (2018); Lynch (2017); Peterson and Hagan (1984). See also Seim (2020) on the vertical and horizontal relations of production endemic to other street-level bureaucracies (Lipsky 1980).

61. Though I have not seen these letters, I learned of this practice from conversations with a Boston-area public defender in March 2019.

62. Bishop and Frazier (1996); Bridges, Crutchfield, and Simpson (1987); Clair and Winter (2016); Van Cleve (2016).

63. Evidence of blatant racial and class discrimination exists in many court jurisdictions in the United States, as documented in appellate litigation (e.g., in *Peña-Rodriguez v. Colorado* 580 US ___ [2017], a juror was revealed to have made explicitly racist comments against a Latino defendant, and in *Foster v. Chatman* 578 US ___ [2016], a prosecutor's office highlighted and struck all the black jurors in a jury pool while explicitly articulating bias against black jurors), journalistic accounts (e.g., racist text messages uncovered among police officers in San Francisco [Serna 2016]), and government investigations (e.g., the racial and class exploitation uncovered in the Department of Justice's 2014 investigation into the City of Ferguson).

64. On "code of the street" attitudes, see Mears et al. (2017). On defendants' resources, see Holmes et al. (1996).

65. See Tilly (1998, chapter 1).

66. E. Goffman (1959); Blumer (1986).

67. On attorney-client interactions in divorce law, employment law, and other civil settings, see Berrey, Nelson, and Nielsen (2017, chapters 5 and 6); Kritzer (1990); Sarat and Felstiner (1997). See Bertenthal (2017) on the role of lawyers in self-help legal services. See Lipsky (1980) for a theorization of the constraints attendant to being "nonvoluntary clients" of street-level bureaucrats—constraints that exist in criminal courts.

68. See Desmond (2014, 568).

69. I use the term "distrust" when referring to defendants' prior negative experiences with legal officials over their lives. I use the term "mistrust" when referring

to defendants' uncertainty toward a lawyer they are currently working with. Both distrust and mistrust suggest a lack of trust, but they are slightly different. Distrust suggests that there are clear and identifiable reasons for the lack of trust that the person can articulate, and often these reasons are systemic and have been experienced throughout their lives and in their communities (see Hardin 2002, which refers to this type of distrust as "well-learned distrust"). On the other hand, mistrust, as I use it here, suggests a general uncertainty with respect to a person or a situation absent clear evidence for the lack of trust. Mistrust is more amenable to change from situation to situation but still has profound implications. Mistrust of a certain person or situation can arise from distrust of similar types of people and situations that one has had untrustworthy experiences with in the past. On these points, see Lenard (2008).

70. Tilly (1998).

71. See Seamster and Ray (2018, 25).

72. Bourdieu (1984). See also Lamont and Lareau (1988); Sewell (1992).

73. See Desmond (2014); Emirbayer (1997); Lamont, Beljean, and Clair (2014); Ridgeway (2014); Tilly (1998); Vallas and Cummins (2014); Schwalbe et al. (2000).

74. Tomaskovic-Devey (2014, 52).

75. Emirbayer (1997, 293).

76. For instance, Lareau (2011) speaks of middle-class versus working-class/poor logics of childrearing; Jack (2019) speaks of the cultural and social attributes of the "doubly disadvantaged" versus the "privileged poor"; and Lamont (1992, 2000) speaks of upper-middle-class versus working-class men's self-definitions of their class group and the boundaries they draw against other groups. Each of these scholars argue that the cultural attributes of groups matter insofar as they are valued or devalued by powerful gatekeepers; yet, the unit of analysis is the social group rather than the social interaction. On this point, see Vallas and Cummins (2014, 237).

77. Lareau (2015).

78. Lareau (2011).

79. Calarco (2018); Carter (2003); Jack (2019); Lareau (2015); Rivera (2016); Shim (2010).

80. Stephens, Markus, and Phillips (2014); Calarco (2014); Gage-Bouchard (2017); Lareau (2011, 2015); Streib (2011); Lamont (1992, 2000).

81. Lareau (2015). See also Calarco (2018), which shows how middle-class children have a "negotiated advantage" in school whereby their demands for teacher attention result in resource acquisition not because teachers find their cultural styles appropriate but more so because teachers are overwhelmed and do not want to risk dealing with assertive middle-class parents if their children's needs are not met.

82. Young and Billings (2020, 36).

83. Reich (2005). Other research has also revealed the importance of deference when people engage with punitive institutions. For example, Harris (2009) shows how judges and other court officials in juvenile probation hearings demand deference from juvenile offenders. My findings regarding delegation and deference in the attorney-client relationship are perhaps even more drastic, given that lawyers are professionally designated to protect defendants' rights, whereas case workers in child protective services and probation officers in juvenile hearings are more analogous to investigators in criminal law, such as police or prosecutors.

84. Clair (2018, 45–55).

85. Bourdieu recognized how one's habitus accumulated through one's life course. At the same time, Bourdieu emphasized childhood socialization as largely determinative and long lasting ([1980] 1990). And most research on class habitus focuses on how class dispositions in childhood are durable and have profound implications in adulthood. See, for example, Streib (2015). For a notable exception, see Jack (2019), which documents how adolescents from similarly disadvantaged childhoods can accrue different forms of embodied cultural capital given differences in their high school environments.

86. See tables 1–3 in the appendix.

87. Defendants in the study faced a range of charges—from low-level misdemeanors, such as disorderly conduct, to felonies, such as cocaine distribution and felony murder. Misdemeanors are defined as charges that do not carry a possible state prison sentence (but may carry a sentence of up to 2.5 years in county jail). These are typically handled in district courts. Felonies are charges that carry a possible state prison sentence. More-serious felonies are typically indicted by a grand jury and adjudicated in countywide superior courts, though some felonies are adjudicated in district court. My analysis focuses on moments between attorneys and clients that are common across charges and courthouses. In either the district court or superior court, defendants must make decisions at arraignment, bail, pretrial hearings, plea hearings, and trial.

88. See table 8 in the appendix.

89. Some respondents experienced and told me about court cases in other states. I was careful to consider how state-level differences might influence their experiences with their lawyers. Every respondent experienced at least one court case in the Boston area. One respondent, Diego, experienced his only criminal charge initially in another state but completed aspects of his court-mandated probation requirements in the Boston area. Moreover, much of the fallout from his criminal charge was experienced while living in the Boston area.

90. Nine district courthouses (eight of which are also known collectively as the Boston Municipal Courts [BMC]) and two superior courthouses have jurisdiction in the cities of Boston and Cambridge. The district courts are BMC–Central (downtown), BMC–Brighton, BMC–Charlestown, BMC–Dorchester, BMC–East Boston, BMC–Roxbury, BMC–South Boston, BMC–West Roxbury, and Cambridge District Court. The superior courts are Suffolk County Superior Court (jurisdiction is Boston) and Middlesex County Superior Court (jurisdiction includes Cambridge and numerous other cities in Middlesex County).

91. To protect the confidentiality of the public defender's office, I do not reveal the name of these three district courthouses. I spent my time alongside public defenders as an intern in two of the courthouses and alone as a researcher in one of them.

92. In Massachusetts, a continuance without a finding (CWOF) is a plea deal that results in a finding of no guilt (dismissal) if the defendant abides by the court's conditions (e.g., stays out of trouble by not getting arrested again) for a mandated period pretrial. Sometimes a CWOF involves pretrial administrative probation during this period. A CWOF is technically an admission of guilt, or an admission to "sufficient facts," but results in a dismissal of the case if pretrial conditions are abided by.

If the conditions are not abided by, the judge can revoke the continuance, find the defendant guilty, and impose the typical sentence. This is similar to what I. Kohler-Hausmann (2018) describes in New York City courts as adjournment in contemplation of dismissal (ACD), though ACDs do not require an admission of guilt (see also Worden, McLean, and Kennedy 2012).

93. This is a commonly recognized point in the court ethnography literature, largely the result of the influence of Eisenstein and Jacob's (1977) concept of the "courtroom workgroup." They posited that differences in defendants' outcomes could best be explained by differences in courtroom workgroups (interactions between officials working the same courtroom) than by differences in defendants' characteristics. Thus, it is important to compare courtrooms and courthouses to one another. But, unlike comparative ethnographies that seek to examine differences between court systems, courthouses, or even courtrooms within the same courthouse (e.g., Eisenstein, Flemming, and Nardulli 1988; Eisenstein and Jacob 1977; Lynch 2016; Ulmer 1997), my research question bears on differential experiences of court processing within similar court system contexts and between defendants with varying levels of resources.

94. During the study period, the Middlesex DA's office appeared to be more punitive—with respect to bail amounts, the likelihood of charge reductions, and the length and type (incarceration or not) of sentencing recommendations—than the Suffolk DA's office. I came to this understanding through interviews with prosecutors, judges, and defense attorneys, as well as my own observations. I do not have administrative data to compare differences between courthouses. Future research could seek to confirm whether my observations and information from court officials is accurate. For the purposes of this study, however, I was careful to consider the potential effect of the local DA's office when comparing people in my sample facing similar charges in different courthouses. But prosecutorial policies are varied and change over time; for example, just as I was leaving the field, the Middlesex DA announced that line ADAs will no longer request bail in low-level cases (Cramer 2018).

95. According to 2012 arraignment data provided to me by the Massachusetts Probation Services (see Clair 2018, 63), whites tend to be underrepresented in arraignments across Boston-area courthouses and across charge types. Blacks and Hispanics, on the other hand, tend to be overrepresented. This pattern does not hold for certain charges, however, such as OUI charges, where whites—and blacks, to a lesser degree—are often overrepresented, and Hispanics are underrepresented. But blacks and Hispanics are more likely to be arraigned for more-serious crimes if we take arraignments in superior courts as indicators of case seriousness. This likely contributes, in part, to disparities at the tail end of the system, where blacks and Hispanics are convicted and imprisoned at disproportionately high rates.

96. In 2012, racial minorities constituted 22 percent of the adult population but 33 percent of adults convicted for any crime and 38 percent of adults sentenced to incarceration for any crime. With respect to state-level incarceration rates, Massachusetts has a higher than average black-white and Hispanic-white disparity compared to other states: in 2015, black people in the state were incarcerated at almost eight times the rate of white people, and Hispanic people were incarcerated at almost five times the rate of white people. Statistics retrieved from the Massachusetts Sentencing

Commission, "Selected Race Statistics," Mass.gov, September 27, 2016, https://www
.mass.gov/files/documents/2016/09/tu/selected-race-statistics.pdf.

97. In the 1980s, BPD initiated a "search on sight" policy that justified police
officers' searching anyone who was "allegedly 'associated with a gang' in Boston's
predominantly-black Roxbury neighborhood" (American Civil Liberties Union 2014,
3). Although this policy ended in the 1990s, BPD—following cities like New York—
engaged in stop-and-frisk practices.

98. An analysis by Fagan et al. (2015) of a sample of police-civilian encounters
from 2007 to 2010 found that more than 63 percent of these encounters were initiated
with black residents in Boston, far greater than their proportion of the city's population. Moreover, the report found that, when stopped, black and Hispanic alleged
offenders were more likely than similarly situated whites to be frisked or searched and
were more likely to be repeatedly targeted for police encounters. Similar racial/ethnic
disparities exist in other police departments in Massachusetts (Farrell et al. 2004).

99. A study by Crutchfield, Bridges, and Pitchford (1994) suggests that only
30–40 percent of the black-white disparity in imprisonment in Massachusetts is
explained by arrest differences (175, 178). Following Blumstein's (1982) approach to
measuring racial disproportionality, these findings suggest that, in the 1980s, a substantial proportion of disparities in imprisonment (60–70 percent) was likely due to
some form of unwarranted discrimination during court processing.

100. See "Eligibility Requirements for Indigency (Waiver of Fees)" on the Mass
.gov website, accessed December 24, 2018, https://www.mass.gov/service-details
/eligibility-requirements-for-indigency-waiver-of-fees. For more details, see chapter 2. Defendants who are deemed indigent typically pay a $150 fee to the court for
their court-appointed lawyers. But some defendants' fees are waived at arraignment
if they are deemed too poor to afford the $150 fee. For many others who have a job
or other financial resources but cannot afford to hire a privately retained lawyer (e.g.,
those deemed "marginally indigent"), the $150 fee must be paid at adjudication. At
this time, a judge can waive or reduce the fee if a lawyer argues that their client cannot afford the fee or is willing to do community service instead. A judge can also ask
a defendant to pay more than the $150 if their ability to contribute is deemed to be
higher.

101. In Boston, several CPCS offices serve the district and superior courthouses,
including an immigration impact office and youth advocacy office. Overall, the per
capita expenditure on indigent defense in Massachusetts is higher than the average
expenditure of other states (Strong 2016; see also Worden, Davies, and Brown 2010).
In addition, the operation of the system encourages defense attorneys to engage in
"client-centered" advocacy, whereby public defenders are explicitly trained, and provided the resources, to build client trust, listen to clients' interests, and be aware of
the civil collateral consequences of various criminal sentences. In fall 2016, I attended
several sessions of a new lawyer training for CPCS public defenders. I also reviewed
materials provided to public defenders who took part in the 2016 and 2018 trainings.

102. Throughout the book, I sometimes contrast bar advocates and public
defenders. But both groups of lawyers serve the same client population of indigent
defendants, and defendants can rarely tell the difference between them. When referencing both public defenders and bar advocates, I refer to them collectively as

court-appointed defense attorneys. Public defenders handle about 25 percent of the state's indigent cases (Gurley 2014). In 2013, the median annual caseload for public defenders in Massachusetts was 165 cases (Cruz, Borakove, and Wickman 2014). This caseload is much lower than caseloads in other states. Moreover, public defenders in the state have access to investigators and social workers in their offices. In addition, public defenders are salaried, affording them a fair amount of flexibility in how they spread their time between their clients. In contrast to public defenders, bar advocates handle about 75 percent of the state's indigent caseload. Bar advocates are managed by CPCS administrators, technically affording them access to many of the same resources as public defenders. It is unclear to what extent they actually use these resources. Bar advocates are compensated by the state for each hour they work, rather than for each client they serve. This payment scheme does not encourage flipping cases quickly, unlike payment schemes in other states (see Eisenstein and Jacob 1977). At the same time, if a bar advocate also represents paying clients, they may devote more time to their paying clients than to their indigent clients. The effectiveness of private lawyers (e.g., bar advocates) versus public defenders in representing indigent defendants has been debated. Anderson and Heaton's (2012) study comparing private lawyers to public defenders in Philadelphia finds that public defenders achieve considerably better case outcomes for indigent clients charged with murder than private lawyers who represent the same population of indigent clients. (See also T. H. Cohen 2014.) But the bar advocates I spoke to told me that because they are audited by CPCS, they are careful to bill appropriately and regularly discuss appropriate caseloads and time spent on clients with their supervisors.

## Chapter 1. Different Paths to the Same Courts

1. During most of their adolescence (defined as being between the ages thirteen and nineteen), 37 percent (19 of 52) of the defendants interviewed in the study lived in middle-class homes, 48 percent (25 of 52) lived in working-class homes, and 15 percent (8 of 52) lived in poor homes or experienced homelessness.

2. As noted in the introduction, pleading to a CWOF in Massachusetts means that a person admits that there are sufficient facts to find them guilty but is not formally convicted of the crime. Thus, the person's record does not show a criminal conviction.

3. Concerned with understanding the transition to modern society, the earliest sociologists theorized how individuals could feel separate from society and how such feelings reflected larger social problems. In the "Economic and Philosophic Manuscripts of 1844," Karl Marx (1978) described how industrial capitalism alienated workers in several ways. In *Suicide* and other writings, Émile Durkheim examined how the division of labor in society, when still in transition, could threaten social solidarity and how political and economic crises could weaken moral regulation (Durkheim [1951] 1979).

4. See Agnew (1992); Merton (1938).

5. See Elijah Anderson (1999); Cloward and Ohlin (1960).

6. Kirk and Papachristos (2011); Sampson and Bartusch (1998).

7. As Monica Bell (2017, 2085) writes about attitudes toward policing in poor communities, "the word 'cynicism' suggests that the attitudinal perspective of

communities is the issue rather than the process that led to a cultural orientation toward distrusting police. . . . However, anomie refers not only to the subjective feeling of concern; it is also meant to implicate a particular set of structural conditions that produced that subjective feeling."

8. Of those who sat for an in-depth interview, forty-four of fifty-two reported substance use disorders.

9. In response to a two-item question used by physicians to screen for depression, thirty-four of fifty respondents (68 percent) answered yes to at least one of the questions, indicating potential depression. I relied on the two-item screen for depression described by Whooley et al. (1997). This screen has been shown to capture nearly everyone who would be diagnosed as depressed in a detailed examination by a medical professional. Nonetheless, the screen has a high false-positive rate. In response to the question "Has a doctor or other health professional ever told you that you have depression?," thirty-one of fifty-one respondents (61 percent) answered yes. And in response to the question "In the last year, have you talked to a mental health professional such as a psychologist, psychiatrist, psychiatric nurse or clinical social worker about your health?," thirty-five of fifty-one respondents (69 percent) answered yes. These responses do not vary by current class status or childhood class background, but they do vary by race. Blacks are less likely than both whites and Latinos to report having ever been told by a doctor that they have depression (only five of eighteen, or 28 percent, reported in the affirmative), and black respondents are slightly less likely to respond yes to the questions regarding depressive symptomatology (nine of eighteen, or 50 percent, respond yes to each question).

10. See Fong (2017); Reich (2005).

11. In general, crime rates at the city or even the neighborhood level may obscure the microspatial way crime exists on street corners and city blocks (smaller geographic units than cities or even neighborhoods). Still, Roxbury, on average, has been shown to have more incidents of violent crime since the 1980s than other parts of Boston. For example, on gun violence in Boston, see Braga, Papachristos, and Hureau (2010).

12. Of the people interviewed, forty-seven of fifty-two completed high school, and eleven of fifty-two (or 21 percent) received at least a bachelor's degree. See the appendix for more details on the study sample.

13. According to the Census Bureau's 2015 Current Population Survey, about 33 percent of Americans over the age of twenty-five reported having a four-year college degree.

14. See Singer (2014) on the importance of meaningful relationships with authority figures in adolescence, even among suburban middle-class children.

15. See Rios (2011); Shedd (2015).

16. See Harding (2010).

17. See Contreras (2013) on constraints among poor youth of color and Loughran et al. (2016) on offending and rational decision making among low-income adolescents. See also Websdale (2001, chapter 5) on the necessity of dealing crack cocaine and engaging in prostitution among some poor black people in Nashville's urban core. See also Jacobs (1999).

18. Interviews provide insight into people's interpretations of their and others' lives and behaviors, especially their justifications for their behaviors (Lamont and

Swidler 2014). The earliest work in sociology, such as that of Max Weber and W. E. B. Du Bois, was concerned with people's interpretations. Today, cultural sociologists variously refer to such interpretations as "accounts," "stories," "justifications," or "narratives." Such interpretations may contain inconsistencies, but they are understood to guide future action by making social action intelligible (Presser 2009; Somers 1994).

19. Scholars have examined how people justify continued engagement in illicit acts. Often the cause of the first engagement in an illegal act can be accidental or arise from peer pressure. Continued engagement, however, likely requires a rationalization or justification. For instance, Becker ([1963] 1991) describes the process of becoming a marijuana user. He argues that this process transpires in a group setting, among peers who provide access to drugs, the methods for experimenting with drugs, and ultimately, justifications for drug use. Scholars have suggested that such justifications can motivate future delinquent behaviors (Sykes and Matza 1957).

20. Formisano (2004).

21. See Stuart (2016) on police officer suspicion of white people in poor communities of color.

22. Jacques and Wright's (2015) study of a group of white middle-class adolescent drug dealers in suburban Atlanta also finds that drug dealing and using was done "in the pursuit of coolness." Although the individuals in their study rarely recounted the trouble at home and school that the privileged people in my study recounted, similar themes of partying and increased status among peers was reported in their sample.

23. This was similar to the process of the "ghetto trance" among middle-class black kids living in a black Chicago neighborhood described by Pattillo (2013), or the "thrills" described by J. Katz (1988).

24. Criminologists, sociologists, and psychologists have long studied the relationship between peer groups and delinquent behaviors. See, for example, Becker ([1963] 1991); Dishion and Tipsord (2011); Matsueda and Anderson (1998).

25. I asked the fifty-two defendants I interviewed to estimate how many times they had been arrested in their lives. With respect to class, those who grew up in middle-class homes reported many fewer arrests over the life course (5 median arrests) than those from working-class (10 median arrests) or poor (12 median arrests) family backgrounds. Current socioeconomic status presents a similar pattern. Currently middle-class people experienced fewer arrests (5 median arrests) than working-class people (7 median arrests) and poor people (15 median arrests). Race presents a different pattern than expected, likely because there is a higher proportion of socioeconomically advantaged people of color in the study as compared to white people (see table 5 in the appendix). With respect to race, median number of arrests is higher among whites (10.5 median arrests in life) than among blacks (8 median arrests) and all nonwhites (8 median arrests).

26. See Alward and Baker (2019) on how procedural justice perceptions of police spill over to perceptions of the fairness of courts.

27. Fagan et al. (2015).

28. Beginning in 2009, Massachusetts decriminalized marijuana. If an adult was caught with less than an ounce, they faced only a civil fine of up to $100. In December 2016, recreational use of the drug was fully legalized.

29. Once an individual becomes known to the criminal legal system through a prior citation, arrest, or conviction, avoidance becomes ever more difficult (see Goffman 2014; Stuart 2016). Many people in this study recognized their heightened vulnerability to detection, seeking to avoid certain areas or interaction with certain individuals and institutions (see Brayne 2014). In Asad's (2020) research on undocumented and documented immigrants in Dallas, Texas, he shows how legibility to the immigration system—either through prior experiences with deportation or simply by being formally included in the bureaucratic records of the system by acquiring legal papers—shapes the risk perceptions of all immigrants. Immigrants who have documented status also fear immigration enforcement and control, some even wishing they had not opted into the legal process altogether. Thus, Asad's findings reveal how what he defines as "system embeddedness"—or perceived legibility to inclusion in institutions that maintain records—leads to uncertainty among all immigrants, including those who have followed the law to the letter and are only included because they are on a pathway to citizenship. Similarly, Michael's quotation here reveals that it is not just those who have active warrants out for their arrest who seek to avoid the police; in addition, individuals who have served their time and paid their debt to society as mandated by the court continue to fear, and seek to avoid, police contact. Even when Michael does not have a warrant out, the hassle of being stopped and having his name run by police is an annoyance to him.

30. See Brunson (2007); Fox-Williams (2019).

31. Bell (2017); Jones (2014).

32. See the analysis of Fagan et al. (2015) of a sample of police-civilian encounters and observations conducted by BPD over the period 2007 to 2010.

33. I interviewed eight police officers in the Boston area, as described in the appendix.

34. See Piliavan and Briar (1964); Westley (1953).

35. Voigt et al. (2017).

36. Existing research on police-civilian interactions commonly shows how perceived disrespect matters in the escalation of police encounters. See Alpert, Dunham, and MacDonald (2004); Black and Reiss (1970); Duck (2017); Reisig et al. (2004).

37. Fox-Williams (2019) describes how some black youth in New York "practice deference" in response to police encounters. See also Duck (2017).

38. Police officers in the United States are, by and large, working-class (and mostly white) men. For example, in BPD, 66 percent of police officers are white (higher than their proportion in the city's population). The percentage of BPD officers who are black is roughly proportionate to the share of black residents, whereas the percentage of Hispanic officers and Asian officers is less than their relative proportions of the population. The racial demographics of CPD are similar, except with respect to Hispanic officers, who are represented in equal proportion to their share of the population. These statistics are taken from Governing.com, which analyzed the Bureau of Justice Statistics' 2013 Law Enforcement Management and Administrative Statistics (LEMAS) survey. *Diversity on the Force: Where Police Don't Mirror Communities: A Governing Special Report*, September 2015, http://media.navigatored.com/documents/policediversityreport.pdf.

39. See Natapoff (2009).

40. The median age of first arrest for people in the study who grew up middle class is nineteen years old; for people who grew up working class, it is sixteen years old; and for people who grew up poor, it is seventeen years old. The median age of first arrest for white people is eighteen years old; for black people, it is sixteen years old. See table 4 in the appendix.

41. Bourdieu (1984); Bourdieu and Passeron (1977); Coleman (1968); Jencks (1972).

42. Peterson and Krivo (2010); Sharkey and Faber (2014); Winter and Sampson (2017); Wilson (1987).

43. Massey and Denton (1993); Peterson and Krivo (2010); Squires and Kubrin (2006).

44. Boston is one of the most racially and economically segregated cities in the country. A city of about 620,000 residents in 2010, Boston is about 54 percent white, 24 percent black, 17 percent Hispanic, and 9 percent Asian (2010 census, Massachusetts). Cambridge is about a sixth the size of Boston, with a greater share of white and Asian residents. The Metropolitan Statistical Area, which includes Boston, Cambridge, and smaller cities like Framingham, has a total population of more than 4.5 million. The state of Massachusetts, in 2010, had a population of more than 6.5 million. In the 2010 census, 80 percent of Massachusetts residents were white, 7 percent were black, 10 percent were Hispanic, and 5 percent were Asian. Throughout the twentieth century, Boston has grappled with racism, racial inequality, and class inequality in schools, housing, and employment (see Formisano 2004). These inequalities persist today. Recent research has found that Boston is one of the most economically and racially segregated cities in the United States, as measured by the number of census tracts in the city that are considered "Racially Concentrated Areas of Affluence," or where "90 percent or more of population is white and the median income is at least four times the federal poverty level" (Semuels 2015; see Goetz, Damiano, and Hicks 2017). Higher rates of lead toxicity, lower levels of social capital and trust, higher rates of violence, and lower levels of voter participation all cluster in the same geographic areas of the city, where disproportionate numbers of poor residents and residents of color live (Zimmerman et al. 2012). Neighborhoods like Roxbury, North Dorchester, and East Boston often experience these forms of disadvantage, whereas neighborhoods like Beacon Hill and the South End are relatively privileged. At the same time, some research has shown that people who live in black neighborhoods in Boston are more likely to make demands for basic public services, net of indicators of objective need for these services, likely because they expect government discrimination (Levine and Gershenson 2014).

45. For more on this point, see Singer (2014).

46. Crime statistics, such as data from the FBI Uniform Crime Report, are often assumed to be objective indicators of the prevalence of crime in certain areas, but scholars—as early as W. E. B. Du Bois—have debated whether official arrest statistics are valid measures of crime rates versus the unequal enforcement of laws across groups (see Thornberry and Krohn 2000). These debates are far from settled (see Shoemaker 2009, chapter 6). On the one hand, some analyses of self-report data suggest that various kinds of delinquency are common across all class groups—and

perhaps even more common among the middle and upper classes (Tittle and Meier 1990; but see Elliott and Ageton 1980). Scholars have also documented parity in both drug use and drug distribution across racial groups (Tonry and Melewski 2008). On the other hand, more-serious forms of delinquency appear to exist at higher rates among the poor and members of marginalized racial/ethnic groups (Elliott and Ageton 1980; Hawkins, Laub, and Lauritsen 1998; Morenoff 2005). On the racial implications of crime statistics, see Muhammad (2019).

47. On the life course pathways of criminalized behaviors studied in criminology and psychology, see, for example, Lacourse et al. (2003); Elliott, Huizinga, and Menard (1989); Farrington (1995); Sampson and Laub (1995). On the relationship between economic inequality and crime, see Neckerman and Torche (2007).

48. For instance, strain theory (A. Cohen 1955; Cloward and Ohlin 1960; Merton 1957) and social disorganization theory (Shaw and McKay 1942)—two classic criminological theories of violence and delinquency—generally argue that sources of strain in one's life or disorganization in one's environment cause criminal behavior. Where strain theory might suggest that abusive parents or unmet economic desires contribute to greater involvement in crime among the poor and the racially marginalized (Agnew 1992), social disorganization theory would suggest that breakdowns in community cohesion, residential stability, mainstream cultural norms, or traditional two-parent family structures contribute to higher rates of crime in marginalized communities (Sampson and Wilson 1995; Sharkey, Torrats-Espinosa, Takyar 2017). For critiques of this literature, see Martinez (2016); Vargas (2016).

49. Sharkey (2018).

50. Jacques and Wright (2015); Mohamed and Fritsvold (2010); Salinas (2017).

51. See also Chambliss (1973), which compared the delinquent behaviors of, and community reactions to, two groups of boys living in the same community and attending the same high school but of different class backgrounds.

## Chapter 2. Disadvantage and Withdrawal

1. Forty-five percent of the time, defendants' withdrawal in this study is exhibited as a form of resistance. Fifty-five percent of the time, defendants' withdrawal is exhibited as resignation. See table 9 in the appendix.

2. In Massachusetts state courts, defendants are assigned court-appointed lawyers at probation revocation hearings. Tonya's experience with this probation revocation hearing, however, is the only case in the study that took place in a federal criminal court rather than a state court. There are important differences between federal and state courts, but Tonya's experience with probation in federal court is quite similar to the probation experiences in Massachusetts state courts that I observed. Her story is thus a representative illustration of the average disadvantaged person's experiences with probation revocation hearings in the study.

3. See table 7 in the appendix. Sixty-two percent (18 of 29) of white people agreed their lawyer did their best to defend them, whereas 42 percent (8 of 19) of black people and 45 percent (10 of 22) of all racial minorities agreed. The same percentage of black people who agreed that their lawyer did their best disagreed with the statement. The pattern is even more striking with respect to class. Whereas 82 percent (9 of 11) of

middle-class people agree, only 35 percent (6 of 17) of poor people do. No middle-class person disagreed, but a majority of poor people did (53 percent, or 9 of 17). Furthermore, trust is patterned with respect to representation by a court-appointed lawyer, as prior research would predict. (The majority of people [80 percent, or 40 of 50] in the interview sample were represented by a court-appointed lawyer in their most recent case.) No person who had a private lawyer felt that their lawyer did not do their best to defend them. By contrast, 33 percent (13 of 40) of those with court-appointed lawyers felt their lawyers did not do their best. Still, nearly half of defendants with court-appointed attorneys trusted them, suggesting that other elements related to disadvantage in everyday life—beyond the courts—may influence defendants' trust in their lawyers.

4. Scholars measure trust in various ways, and there is no universally accepted definition. Although the question I used in the survey did not ask whether a person trusted their lawyer, it was a good proxy for whether the person felt that their lawyer worked hard to defend them. This sentiment is important in understanding the key differences between attorney-client relationships of delegation and those of withdrawal.

5. See Jenness and Calavita (2018) on the importance of outcomes in prisoners' evaluations of fairness in prisoner grievance hearings.

6. Social psychological research shows that individuals differentiate between distributive justice (i.e., fair outcomes), the favorability of a justice outcome, and procedural justice (i.e., fair and trustworthy institutional processes; see Tyler and Huo 2002). Indeed, several people in this study recount trusting their lawyers but being dissatisfied with their outcomes, and vice versa.

7. With respect to lawyers' incentives and the structural constraints of the system, a handful of existing studies on mistrust of lawyers among disadvantaged clients focuses on defendants' awareness of the structural features of the indigent defense system that they believe do not work in their favor. Poor defendants perceive that attorneys pressure them to take plea deals against their best interests (e.g., Wilkerson 1972). Scholars have also suggested that court-appointed lawyers, who are often courtroom "regulars" (meaning they tend to practice in the same courthouses and become recognized members of the courtroom workgroup), may feel pressure to maintain collegial relationships with prosecutors and judges they see weekly, if not daily (see Van Cleve 2016). Such pressure may result in them attempting to control their clients by coercing them to take plea deals and keep the system running efficiently (see Eisenstein and Jacob 1977; Feeley [1979] 1992; Heumann 1981; Sudnow 1965; but for contrary evidence, see Emmelman 2003). Heavy caseloads may make it difficult for court-appointed lawyers to exercise due process procedures that force adjudicative decision making (see Blumberg 1967; Uphoff 1992; Van Cleve 2016). Many of these scholarly criticisms of indigent defense are recognized among the people in this study.

8. See Tyler (1988); Tyler and Huo (2002).

9. Scholars have long observed relatively higher levels of distrust of legal authorities and legal institutions among the poor and racial/ethnic minorities. Racial minorities have higher levels of distrust of legal institutions (e.g., the police and the courts; Bobo and Thompson 2006; Hagan and Albonetti 1982; MacDonald and Stokes

2006; Muller and Schrage 2014)—and, to a lesser degree, so do working-class and poor people of all racial groups (Hagan and Albonetti 1982; but see Brooks and Jeon-Slaughter [2001] on higher levels of distrust of certain legal institutions among high-income blacks as compared to low-income blacks). Much of this distrust has to do with perceptions of unfair treatment (Hagan and Albonetti 1982). Social psychologists have shown that among individuals who have interacted with various facets of the court system, perceptions of fairness are associated with their satisfaction of their treatment by legal authorities—or their sense of procedural justice (Tyler 1988; Tyler and Huo 2002). One study has shown that satisfaction can be influenced by whether people share their racial identity with individual officials (Baker et al. 2015). Simply having more contact with legal authorities has been shown to be associated with procedural injustice (Hagan, Shedd, and Payne 2005; Weitzer and Tuch 2005). And sociologists have shown how living in overpoliced poor communities of color alienated from a functioning legal system is associated with legal cynicism, or a cultural frame that interprets legal authorities to be ill equipped to fairly ensure public safety (see Elijah Anderson 1999; Bell 2017; Kirk and Papachristos 2011; Sampson and Bartusch 1998).

10. Gurley (2014).

11. See Eisenstein and Jacob (1977); Feeley ([1979] 1992); Heumann (1981); Sudnow (1965), but for contrary evidence, see Emmelman (2003). Levine (2013) makes a similar argument among low-income women in their interactions with welfare office case workers. Welfare case workers have structural incentives to reduce the size of their caseload directly counter to the interests of welfare recipients.

12. Alesina and Ferrara (2002); Kramer and Cook (2004); S. S. Smith (2010).

13. On power differences and trust, see Cook (2005, 11–12); Levine (2013).

14. Just under 25 percent of staff public defenders serving in Boston-area courthouses in 2016 were racial minorities, whereas nearly 67 percent of defendants in 2012 were racial minorities. These calculations are my own and are based on data provided to me by CPCS (data on staff public defenders) and data provided to me by the Massachusetts Probation Services (data on arraigned criminal defendants). For this comparison, I included only counts on staff public defender trial attorneys who are classified as being assigned to practice in the Boston and Roxbury district/municipal courts and the Suffolk County Superior Court; counts on criminal defendants similarly included only those arraigned in BMC–Central, BMC–Roxbury, and the Suffolk County Superior Court. In addition, poor defendants often hold occupations far less prestigious than that of their lawyers. Given these gaps, poor defendants and those from marginalized racial groups in Boston appear more likely to experience cultural mismatching than their middle-class or white peers.

15. In Lauren Rivera's (2012) research on hiring in investment banks, law firms, and consulting firms, she describes how employers prefer to hire job seekers who share tastes and experiences—such as scuba diving or an interest in a sports team—with them. She refers to the sharing of these cultural attributes as "cultural matching," arguing that job seekers who have expansive cultural repertoires of experiences and tastes are more likely to find commonality with potential employers.

16. Overwhelmingly, the defense attorneys I observed—public defenders, bar advocates, and prosecutors—did not use racist language. Nonetheless, I coded four

instances of explicit or subtle racism in my fieldnotes. I observed them among court officials who were speaking freely in open court as I sat in the gallery or in the well next to the public defenders I was shadowing. The remarks I heard would likely have been overheard by many of the defendants sitting in the courtroom in those moments as well. Therefore, even if such instances were rare, their occurrences likely mattered for the defendants who witnessed them. Specifically, three of the racist comments I observed were antiblack, and one was biased in favor of white people. For instance, during a lull in a court session, a Latino bar advocate turned to me and whispered, "Oh my god, I have a funny story." I smiled and leaned in to hear his story. He said, "Just now back there in lockup, my client said to me: 'Why y'all have me back here with all these Niggers?!'" I gave a closed-lipped smile, waiting to hear if there was a punchline somewhere in this story. The bar advocate then laughed and said, "My client is black! Isn't that so crazy?" I retreated back to my notepad, unclear as to why this story was so humorous, why the bar advocate felt he needed to share it with me, and why he felt so comfortable saying "Nigger." Another bar advocate on another day made a racist joke about gentrification when chatting with a court clerk before the start of a court session. An Asian man, the bar advocate was asking the clerk about the number of cases they could expect to be arraigned that day. The clerk said there would not be many cases that day. The bar advocate responded, chuckling: "You know, ever since there was gentrification in this neighborhood, I haven't had as many cases as I used to." On subtle racism and racist talk generally, see Bonilla-Silva (2010); Clair and Denis (2015). On racism among court officials, see Bridges, Crutchfield, and Simpson (1987); Clair and Winter (2016); Van Cleve (2016).

17. The term "the New Jim Crow" refers to the idea, popularized by legal scholar Michelle Alexander (2012), that mass incarceration is a tool of racial social control that developed in response to the dismantling of Jim Crow racism in the middle of the twentieth century. See also Roberts (2007).

18. On everyday forms of resistance, see C. J. Cohen (2004); Kelley (1996); Scott (1990). Scott (1990) argues that oppressed people can feign consent to their oppression all the while engaging in subversive and subtle forms of "hidden" resistance. Kelley (1996) describes "everyday forms of resistance" among the black working class.

19. Scholars generally define expertise as the knowledge, skills, and relationships that people employ to solve problems or complete tasks (Collins and Evans 2007). Just like other kinds of expertise in other fields, such as medicine or science (See Haug and Sussman 1969; Hodson and Sullivan 1990), expertise in the law is professionalized and guarded by professional associations (e.g., bar associations) and professional schools (e.g., law schools).

20. "Every Inmate shall have access to legal materials. As suggested by federal and state court rulings and national standards, legal materials should include at a minimum: state and federal constitutions, state statutes, state decisions, procedural rules and decisions and related commentaries, federal case law, court rules, practice treatises, citators, and legal periodicals." This statement was retrieved on February 5, 2018, under file number 103 CMR 478: Library services and regulatory authority MGL c. 124, § 1(c) and (q), Mass.gov, https://www.mass.gov/files/documents/2017/09/04/103cmr478.pdf.

21. Ken's reference to "Ramos" likely refers to a 2015 case, *Ramos v. International Fidelity Insurance Company* 87 Mass. App. Ct. 604 (2015).

22. An organization in San Jose, California, called Silicon Valley De-Bug was one of the first to formally establish "participatory defense" (Moore, Sandys, and Jayadev 2015).

23. See Abu-Jamal (2009); Milovanovic (1988).

24. Morris and Tonry (1991, 4).

25. See Phelps (2016).

26. See Petersilia (1990); Wood and May (2003). Among samples of convicted offenders and/or incarcerated individuals, scholars have found that certain intermediate punishments were perceived as harsher than certain periods of incarceration (see Martin, Hanrahan, and Bowers 2009; Petersilia and Deschenes 1994; Spelman 1995). Some scholars have considered whether preferences vary by race/ethnicity. For example, Wood and May (2003) find that, on average, about a quarter of black probationers in their sample reported that they would rather serve time in prison than various alternatives. I am unaware of research that has considered class differences, however, or considered how such preferences constrain defendants' legal decision making.

27. Bell (2017).

28. See Sandefur (2015) on lay versus professional expertise in civil courts. Professional expertise is typically understood to contain at least two components: substantive expertise (i.e., knowledge of law and procedure) and relational/process expertise (i.e., the skills and relationships necessary to put substantive expertise into action, such as relationships between court officials) (see Barley 1996; Kritzer 1998; Sandefur 2015). A colleague once suggested to me that it is inapt to characterize the legal knowledge and skills of criminal defendants as "expertise." Yet, I have pushed back against this criticism because I believe that naming their knowledge and skills as a form of expertise (albeit lay expertise) recognizes how often their knowledge of legal rights is technically accurate even if their knowledge is ultimately disregarded by legal professionals. In chapter 4, I show how judges and lawyers respond negatively to defendants' attempts to use their expertise. On the devaluation and complexities of lay legal expertise in civil legal settings, see Bertenthal (2017); Galanter (1974); Kritzer (1998); Sandefur (2015).

29. Kirk and Papachristos (2011); Sampson and Bartusch (1998).

30. See Lerman and Weaver (2014).

31. Scholars studying legal cynicism have noted other paradoxes, including the existence of legal cynicism alongside a willingness to rely on certain authorities in certain situations (see Bell 2016; Carr, Napolitano, and Keating 2007) as well as legal cynicism alongside a faith in the "substance of the law," or the legitimacy of laws that penalize certain crimes (see Kirk and Papachristos 2011, 1191). The paradox I identify is different—it suggests legal cynicism alongside faith in the ideal *procedures and rights* of the law.

32. Calavita and Jenness (2015, 18).

33. See Clair (2020); Rios, Carney, and Kelekay (2017); Stuart, Armenta, and Osborne (2015).

34. See Young (1999) on the cultural capital of low-income African American men—cultural habitus that allows them to navigate their lives in disadvantaged

communities while at the same time hindering their mobility in dominant society. See also Carter (2003).

35. Some research argues that defendants do not appear to exercise their formal due process rights, such as taking their case to trial (see, e.g., Blumberg 1967), and other research more generally suggests that defendants are passive "consumers" of legal sanctions. On this latter point, Jonathan Casper, for instance, noted that most of the defendants he interviewed in the early 1970s exhibited resignation and simply wanted to get the process over with (Casper 1971, 1972). According to Casper, their resignation stemmed from their lack of knowledge about certain legal defenses, their distrust of lawyers, their sense that fighting their case may backfire, and their acknowledgment of their factual guilt. Malcolm Feeley similarly noted that defendants represented by public defenders "have much less intensity and interest than the clients of private lawyers" (Feeley [1979] 1992, 89).

36. For one exception, see Moore et al. (2019). In civil contexts, see, for example, Sarat (1990) on resistance among the "welfare poor" in their relationships with lawyers and welfare institutions.

37. Emmelman (2003); Flemming (1986).

38. Freidson (1986); Haug and Sussman (1969); Lipsky (1980); Saks (2012).

39. Haug and Sussman (1969); Kritzer (1990); Lipsky (1980); Rosenthal (1974); Seim (2020).

40. Haug and Sussman (1969).

41. Haug (1972).

42. For example, Collins and Evans (2007).

43. See MacFarlane (2017); Mather, McEwen, and Maiman (2001); Rosenthal (1974); Sarat and Felstiner (1997).

44. See Rios (2011) on black and Latino youths' disrespect toward probation officers as attempts to maintain dignity. See Werth (2012) on autonomy and efforts at redemption among people on parole who abide by some rules and resist others, ever aware of the threat of reimprisonment. On resistance among marginalized black people generally, see C. J. Cohen (2004); Kelley (1996).

45. Ewick and Silbey (1998, 249).

## Chapter 3. Privilege and Delegation

1. See tables 10–14 in the appendix. Whereas 92 percent of the time, people delegate authority when they are middle class, only 24 percent of the time do people do so when they are poor. When white people are working class, they delegate 70 percent of the time, whereas nonwhite people delegate 61 percent of the time when they are working class.

2. In other studies, defendants who retain private attorneys have been shown to exhibit higher levels of trust in their lawyers (Casper 1972) and a greater belief in their lawyers' legal competence (O'Brien et al. 1977)

3. Yet, privately retained defense attorneys may have their own perverse incentives. For example, they may encourage defendants to go to trial to exact a higher fee, even if trial may not be in the client's best interest (Schulhofer and Friedman 1993).

4. Boccaccini et al. (2004) find that higher levels of trust in lawyers are associated with defendants' perceptions that their lawyers (whether they be court appointed or privately retained) allowed them to participate in their own legal defense.

5. See "Eligibility Requirements for Indigency (Waiver of Fees)" on the Mass .gov website, accessed December 24, 2018, https://www.mass.gov/service-details /eligibility-requirements-for-indigency-waiver-of-fees.

6. See Casper (1972, 112) on defendants' "sense of leverage" when paying for attorneys.

7. See Khan (2010) on the socialization of the upper middle class into ease across social spaces and cultural referents.

8. See table 4 in the appendix.

9. Lareau (2011, 2015).

10. For instance, section two of a tender of plea form is titled "Defendant's Waiver of Rights and Alien Rights Notice." It states, in part, "I understand that if I am not a citizen of the United States, the acceptance by this court of my plea of guilty, plea of nolo contendere, or admission to sufficient facts may have consequences of deportation, exclusion from admission to the United States, or denial of naturalization, pursuant to the laws of the United States."

11. On the collateral consequences of involvement in the criminal legal system in general, see Clair and Winter (2020); Kirk and Wakefield (2018); Lageson and Maruna (2018); Pager (2008). On the intersection between criminal law and immigration law, see Asad (2019); Stumpf (2013).

12. Calarco (2018); Gage-Bouchard (2017); Lareau (2011); Shim (2010).

13. Lareau (2015); Stephens, Markus, and Phillips (2014).

14. Calarco (2018); Lareau (2011).

15. Reay (1998), as cited in Stephens, Markus, and Phillips (2014).

16. Shim (2010).

17. Erickson (1996).

18. Rivera (2016).

## Chapter 4. Punishing Withdrawal, Rewarding Delegation

1. When lawyers say to judges that they want to "withdraw" from a client, they are saying that they no longer wish to serve as the client's lawyer for one reason or another. Sometimes declining to remain as a client's lawyer reflects a relationship characterized by withdrawal as I have been using the term throughout the book. Other times declining to remain as a client's lawyer is simply something that lawyers have to do if they have a conflict of interest or if the defendant has decided to hire a private lawyer.

2. Blumberg (1966); Eisenstein and Jacob (1977).

3. See Lynch (2016).

4. Other scholars have similarly documented defense attorneys' need to maintain credibility with prosecutors and judges (see, e.g., Skolnick 1967; Van Cleve 2012).

5. See Gerring (2009) and M. L. Small (2009) on the use of qualitative data to identify processes and develop logical inferences about causal relationships.

6. Baumer (2013); Clair and Winter (2016); Emmelman (2003); Spohn (2000); Van Cleve (2016).

7. Beyond the previous chapters of this book, see also Murakawa and Beckett (2010).

8. T. H. Cohen (2014).

9. See American Bar Association (2003); *McMann v. Richardson* 397 US 759 (1970); *Powell v. Alabama* 287 US 45 (1932); *Strickland v. Washington* 466 US 668 (1984).

10. I. Katz (1995), as cited in Kirchmeier (1996, 426–27).

11. *Strickland v. Washington.* A recent fourth circuit appellate case, however, did find that a lawyer's excessive sleeping during trial constituted ineffective assistance of counsel (*United States v. Ragin*, no. 14-7245 [4th Cir. 2016]).

12. See Zeidman (1998).

13. *Strickland v. Washington*; see also Kirchmeier (1996); Troccoli (2002).

14. See D. L. Bazelon (1973).

15. I interviewed five public defenders and nine bar advocates in Boston at least once. Additionally, in a study conducted with Alix S. Winter, we interviewed twenty-seven public defenders in a northeastern state trial court system similar to the Boston-area courts (Clair and Winter 2020; Winter and Clair 2020). See the appendix for more details.

16. See the introduction and appendix for more details.

17. See Gould and Barak (2019) on similar findings among capital defense lawyers.

18. On the gendered racism experienced by black women lawyers, see Melaku (2019).

19. This information on training comes from an interview I conducted with a managing public defender in 2016. I noticed that one training schedule appeared to show that public defenders participate in only nineteen full days of training, but there may have been other training days not included in that schedule.

20. But see Farbman (2019) on the possibilities of "resistance lawyering," whereby lawyers can work to mitigate outcomes for individual clients on a case by case basis alongside working toward broader political reforms inside and outside the courtroom.

21. Winter and Clair (2020).

22. Dobbie, Goldin, and Yang (2018); Heaton, Mayson, and Stevenson (2017); M. T. Stevenson (2018).

23. Wagner and Sawyer (2018).

24. Some lawyers even use the term "coercion" to describe their efforts to convince defendants to take guilty pleas they believe are in their best interests (A. Smith 2007).

25. I. Kohler-Hausmann (2018) refers to this as a "performance-conditioned" form of leniency that allows the court to monitor defendants' behaviors. See also Winter and Clair (2020).

26. See Natapoff (2005).

27. Bibas (2004); Blumberg (1967); Bushway, Redlich, and Norris (2014); Mnookin and Kornhauser (1979); Sklansky (2017); but see Abrams (2011).

28. Lynch (2016); see also E. Bazelon (2019).

29. Blumberg (1967, 32).

30. See Lynch (2016).

31. For example, Blumberg (1967).

32. Thank you to Issa Kohler-Hausmann for this helpful point.

33. For example, Harris (2009); Reich (2005).

34. Braithwaite (1989).

35. Framing CPS as part of the "therapeutic state," Reich (2005) argues that it seeks to coerce parents into accepting the state's definitions of what it means to properly raise one's children. She shows how one middle-class black woman who contests a case worker is unable to get her child back even after hiring a lawyer and writing a letter to her state representative. There are striking similarities between the experience of CPS proceedings and that of criminal court proceedings. In Tonya's case, for instance, the judge overseeing her probation used therapeutic language similar to that used by CPS in Reich's study. He told Tonya in open court that the purpose of probation is "to make you comport to the rules that we choose to help you find growth in your life." What is distinct in my findings, however, is that deference is beneficial not just in interactions with a punishment authority (i.e., a court, judge, or social worker who can take your kids away) but also in interactions with one's own lawyer. Unlike social workers or judges in CPS, defense lawyers in the criminal courts are not invested with the authority to punish an individual presumed guilty. Rather, they are institutional mediators whose legal role is protection of an individual's due process rights. Yet, I find that lawyers who sense their client's unwillingness to delegate authority to them may abrogate this role to the detriment of their clients.

36. Uphoff (1992).

37. See Tyler (1984, 1988); Tyler and Huo (2002).

38. For the earliest statements, see Du Bois ([1899] 1996); Sellin (1928); Von Hentig (1939).

39. See chapter 1. See also Travis, Western, and Redburn (2014).

40. Rachlinski et al. (2008).

41. Bridges, Crutchfield, and Simpson (1987); Van Cleve (2016).

42. Rachlinski et al. (2008); see also Clair and Denis (2015) on the distinction between racism (as ideology) and racial discrimination (as behavior).

43. Institutional discrimination on the basis of perceived cultural differences has been documented by scholars studying various institutions, such as schools, workplaces, and other front-line public service bureaucracies. Drawing on relational theory, I argue that these cultural differences emerge in interaction rather than being stable characteristics of groups. See, for instance, Maynard-Moody and Musheno (2003) on "cultural abidance," or the common way street-level public servants, such as police officers and schoolteachers, make decisions based on the perceived moral character of the people before them. See also Lipsky (1980, chapter 8). Lamont, Beljean, and Clair (2014) argue that such bias operates as a key driver of social inequality in many organizations: certain cultural standards are valued, and others are devalued. Lamont and colleagues argue that discriminating on the basis of cultural differences can come to be taken for granted by the institutions themselves—and even by the people those institutions are supposed to be serving—as everyone involved comes to believe that the standards of an institution, no matter how arbitrary or biased, are legitimate. Ray (2019) theorizes how organizations can function as racial structures that unequally distribute resources along racial lines based on ostensibly neutral organizational templates.

44. Pager and Shepherd (2008, 182).

45. López (2000, 1723).

46. See Clair and Denis (2015); Lynch and Omori (2018); Murakawa and Beckett (2010); Olivier, Clair, and Denis (2019); Van Cleve and Mayes (2015).

47. Van Cleve (2016). See also Mears et al. (2017), which shows that defendants who adhere to a "code of the street" culture are more likely to be arrested and convicted than their same-race peers. The authors suggest that such differences may be due to legal officials discriminating against code of the street behaviors in their decision making.

48. I. Kohler-Hausmann (2018, 230).

49. I. Kohler-Hausmann (2018, 231).

## Conclusion

1. The number of arrests for most crimes fell between 1990 and 2010. Arrests for drug crimes increased from 1990 to 2000 but then declined in the following decade. See Snyder (2012). The number of people incarcerated in jail or prison peaked in 2008 and has declined modestly since. Likewise, the number of people under probation and other forms of community supervision peaked in 2007 and has also modestly declined since. See Kaeble and Cowhig (2018).

2. Husak (2008); Stuntz (2001).

3. See Davis, Whyde, and Langton (2018).

4. It is unknown how many people deal with a criminal court case in any given year. We do know, however, that state courts across the country reported a total of 17.8 million incoming criminal cases in 2016 (See "Total Incoming Criminal Caseloads Reported by State Courts, All States, 2007–2016," National Center for State Courts' Court Statistics Project, accessed January 8, 2020, http://www.courtstatistics.org /~/media/Microsites/Files/CSP/Criminal/PDFs/EWSC-2016-CRIM-Page-1-Trend .ashx). We can assume that among those millions of criminal cases are numerous alleged repeat offenders. The number of incoming criminal cases in state courts has followed the broader recent trend of slightly declining over the last decade.

5. Akbar (2018); Terry (2015); The Movement for Black Lives website, accessed February 18, 2020, https://m4bl.org/. See also the website of the organization Black Lives Matter, which was started by Alicia Garza, Patrisse Cullors, and Opal Tometi, accessed February 18, 2020, https://blacklivesmatter.com/herstory/.

6. Gottschalk (2019); see also Pfaff (2017).

7. See Shelby (2016) on principles of corrective justice.

8. Wright and Rogers (2010, chapter 10). Emphasis in the original.

9. Elizabeth Anderson (2010, 18). Emphasis in the original.

10. Elizabeth Anderson (2010, 16).

11. Calarco (2018); Gage-Bouchard (2017); Lareau (2011, 2015); Shim (2010); Stephens, Markus, Phillips (2014).

12. Bourdieu (1984); Lamont and Lareau (1988).

13. Olivier, Clair, and Denis (2019).

14. In the Supreme Court case *Foster v. Chatman* 578 US _ (2016), a prosecutor's office was found to have highlighted and removed all the black jurors in a jury pool while explicitly articulating a preference to remove these potential jurors. In

the Supreme Court case *Peña-Rodriguez v. Colorado* 580 US __ (2017), a seated juror made an explicitly racist comment about a Latino defendant during jury deliberations.

15. Clair and Winter (2020).

16. Alexander (2012); Bobo, Kluegel, and Smith (1997); Bonilla-Silva (2010); Butler (2015, 2017); Clair and Winter (2016); López (2000); Murakawa and Beckett (2010); Van Cleve (2016); Van Cleve and Mayes (2015).

17. Alexander (2012); Butler (2015).

18. Lamont (2018).

19. On the procedural justice literature, see Meares (2016); Thibaut and Walker (1975); Tyler (1984, 1988); Tyler and Huo (2002). For critiques of the procedural justice literature, see Bell (2017); Bottoms and Tankebe (2012).

20. See, for example, A. Smith (2007), which suggests that lawyers should coerce their clients to plead guilty when "there is no question that going to trial will be to a client's serious detriment" (480).

21. Clair and Winter (2016). See also Delgado (1985) on the "rotten social background" defense.

22. Spohn (2009); Steffensmeier, Ulmer, and Kramer (1998).

23. Asad and Clair (2018); Kirk and Wakefield (2018).

24. Cochran (1990); Uphoff (2000); Uphoff and Wood (1998).

25. See Community-Oriented Defender Network's statement of principles here: "Community-Oriented Defender Network," National Legal Aid and Defender Association, accessed January 14, 2020, http://www.nlada.org/community-oriented-defender-network.

26. Luban (1981).

27. Luban (1981, 493).

28. Anderson, Buenaventura, and Heaton (2019).

29. See Richardson and Goff (2013) on public defender triage.

30. See Tague (1975); Troccoli (2002).

31. See Schulhofer and Friedman (1993).

32. Bibas (2012); Simonson (2019).

33. Connor (2019); Lee (2000).

34. See Abel (2006); Sandefur (2015).

35. Bertenthal (2017); DeLand (2013); Ewick and Silbey (1998); Merry (1990); Nielsen (2000); Silbey (2005); Yngvesson (1988).

36. See Cole (1999).

37. Sklansky (2018).

38. See Sklansky (2018, 42) on how defendants are constrained by the decisions of their lawyers, even when lawyers waive procedural protections that defendants wanted to invoke.

39. Clair and Winter (2016).

40. See Barkow (2019) on the important role of appellate judges and trial court judges in reforming the criminal legal system.

41. Bach (2009). See the work of Measures for Justice, accessed February 27, 2020, https://measuresforjustice.org/.

42. See Van Cleve (2016, conclusion).

43. See Court Watch NYC's mission statement here: "About Court Watch NYC," Court Watch NYC, accessed January 15, 2020, https://www.courtwatchnyc.org/about.

44. Moore, Sandys, and Jayadev (2015, 1282–83).

45. Akbar (2018); Butler (2015, 2017); Davis (2011); Gilmore (2007); Roberts (2007, 2019). See also "End the War on Black People," in *A Vision for Black Lives*, the Movement for Black Lives, accessed January 15, 2020, https://neweconomy.net/sites/default/files/resources/20160726-m4bl-Vision-Booklet-V3.pdf.

46. Roberts (2019).

47. Connor (2019).

48. Dobson (2019); McKean and Warren-Gordon (2011).

49. Tiger (2013). See also Hannah-Moffat and Maurutto (2012); Moore (2011); Paik (2006).

50. E. Bazelon (2019).

51. Tiger (2013, 144).

52. Herbert, Beckett, and Stuart (2018).

53. See L. J. Dawson, "Denver Looks to Take Cops out of Mental Health–Related 911 Rescues," *Denver Post*, October 11, 2019, https://www.denverpost.com/2019/10/11/denver-police-cahoots-mental-health/.

54. Miller (2008, ix).

55. Braithwaite (1999); Sered (2019).

56. Braithwaite (1999, 20–23).

57. Roche (2004).

58. See "Peacemaking Program," Center for Court Innovation, accessed January 21, 2020, https://www.courtinnovation.org/programs/peacemaking-program.

59. Muhammad (2019, xxii). See also Ward (2012).

60. Butler (2017, 232).

61. B. Stevenson (2014).

62. Western (2018, 182–88). See also Braithwaite (1989); Cole (1999).

## Appendix. The Study's Methods

1. Informant interviews are distinct from traditional interviews with research participants because they do not ask about the specific person and their personal experiences or attitudes. Instead, they are interviews meant to understand the way an organization works. Thus, they inform researchers about organizational rules, processes, and policies. Often, informant interviews provide details about other sources of archival data that contain written information about organizational rules and policies. Generally, see Weiss (1994).

2. See, for example, Jerolmack and Khan (2014); Pager and Quillian (2005).

3. Bradburn (1983).

4. Jerolmack and Khan (2014).

5. Pager and Quillian (2005).

6. Lamont and Swidler (2014); Pugh (2013).

7. University IRBs are organizations within universities that work with researchers to determine how best to protect the rights and well-being of research participants—and reduce the liability of the university.

8. See Moore, Yaroshefsky, and Davies (2017).

9. For instance, when I was following Sybil during an arraignments session, Camila, one of her newly assigned clients, was worried she might be jailed for violating probation. The three of us—Sybil, Camila, and me—were huddled on a bench in the hallway as Camila recounted her version of events before she was arrested. At one point, Camila started to cry. Seated between me and Sybil, she looked in both of our directions as tears streamed down her face. Sybil whispered to her: "Oh no, it's going to be okay. Woosah. Woosah." Camila looked over to me, and I tried to comfort her as best I could with a closed-lip smile. I whispered: "You're all right." In my fieldnotes, I reflected: "I'm kind of taking part in this because Camila looks to me every now and then. And I try my hardest to stay quiet and be unobtrusive while at the same time nodding and being as affirming and comforting as I can. It's as if I'm part of the legal team."

10. On the benefits of backstage access, see Emmelman (2003); Van Cleve (2016).

11. For additional points about the limitations of administrative court data, see Feeley ([1979] 1992, 147–53).

12. See Weiss (1994) on sampling for range.

13. Race/ethnicity adds up to more than fifty-two because a few respondents identified as more than one race/ethnicity.

14. I define respondents by both their socioeconomic status (SES) at the time of the interview and their adolescent SES (i.e., parent/guardian with highest SES during their adolescent years), given that many faced charges in middle and late adolescence. For facility in comparison to existing research in sociology on culture and institutional navigation, I grouped respondents into three SES categories—middle class (at least a four-year college degree), working class (less than a four-year college degree but maintains a fairly stable job or occupation), and poor (less than a four-year college degree and no stable job or occupation).

15. Class is a "messy" category (see Armstrong and Hamilton 2013, appendix B), and my analysis is most interested in the class- and race-based experiences and resources that influence the attorney-client relationship. Sometimes, important class-based resources that matter to this relationship and that are typically associated with middle-class status are available to people who are working class or poor (e.g., a sudden windfall of lottery money or a happenstance friendship with a high-powered attorney), and vice versa. Thus, it is more useful to think of people as relatively privileged or relatively disadvantaged with respect to specific dimensions of inequality (Clair 2018).

16. In later interviews, I modified the interview protocol to ask additional questions about lawyers, including "Did he/she help you during these court experiences? How so? Did you trust him/her? Why did you or did you not trust him/her? Can you give me an example of something your lawyer did that was helpful? Can you give me an example of something your lawyer did that was not helpful? Did your lawyer listen to your ideas about case strategy? Did you take your lawyer's advice? Can you give me examples of when you took your lawyer's advice and when you did not?"

17. See Jiménez and Orozco (2020).

18. For details on these interviews and the broader study, see Winter and Clair (2020). As part of this study, we agreed not to reveal the name of the trial court or the state in which we conducted interviews.

19. Mathison (1988).

20. M. L. Small (2009); Weiss (1994).

21. On inductive research design logic, see Glaser and Strauss (1967). On partly deductive qualitative analysis based on engaging with existing literature and theory, see Tavory and Timmermans (2013).

22. See Pattillo (2013) on the "perils" of growing up in a black middle-class neighborhood. Although our neighborhood was mostly white and middle class, many of the perils of black middle-class status existed in my childhood. See also Lacy (2004) on how many black middle-class families, much like mine, enjoy and seek out proximity to other black people in their everyday lives through social activities and residential selection.

23. Frazier (1957).

24. When describing the substance abuse class Jane, a middle-class white woman, was taking as part of her probation, she commented to me about the "cross-section" of people attending the class. She said, "There's a guy from [professional ballet organization] who's from [European country]. An engineer. There's a nurse. There is, like, a construction worker. There's, um, a really ghetto baby momma. I don't know! It's, like, a good cross-section."

25. Joe, a working-class white man who grew up middle class, told me that he would discriminate against and rob "Spanish" (Hispanic) dealers when he would buy drugs from them. He told me, "We'd only rob Spanish dealers. The guys I dealt with are like from here. They're like black guys that I deal with. I don't rob them. I rob, you know, Spanish guys that are coming from Brighton or something like that, you know what I mean?"

26. Paul, who grew up middle class, described to me his experience in high school. He told me, "Yeah, pretty much ran the school, but I wasn't the bully to the nerds because the nerds, you know, I'd take care of them so they'd do my homework. They would tutor me. I just . . . basically, I was a bully towards like the jocks and stuff because they'd pick on the nerds, and the nerds would be like 'I'll do your algebra homework if you get this guy to stop smacking me around.' . . . And of course I had a group of pot heads I used to hang out with, and we were the pot heads, and there were the jocks, the pot heads, the popular yuppies, faggots."

Abel, Laura K. 2006. "A Right to Counsel in Civil Cases: Lessons from Gideon v. Wainwright." *Temple Political and Civil Rights Law Review* 15 (3):527–56.

Abrams, David S. 2011. "Is Pleading Really a Bargain?" *Journal of Empirical Legal Studies* 8:200–221.

Abu-Jamal, Mumia. 2009. *Jailhouse Lawyers: Prisoners Defending Prisoners v. the USA*. San Francisco, CA: City Lights Books.

Agnew, Robert. 1992. "Foundation for a General Strain Theory of Crime and Delinquency." *Criminology* 30 (1): 47–88.

Akbar, Amna A. 2018. "Toward a Radical Imagination of Law." *New York University Law Review* 93:405.

Alesina, Alberto, and Eliana La Ferrara. 2002. "Who Trusts Others?" *Journal of Public Economics* 85 (2): 207–34.

Alexander, Michelle. 2012. *The New Jim Crow: Mass Incarceration in the Age of Colorblindness*. New York: New Press.

Alpert, Geoffrey P., Roger G. Dunham, and John M. MacDonald. 2004. "Interactive Police-Citizen Encounters that Result in Force." *Police Quarterly* 7 (4): 475–88.

Alward, Lucas M., and Thomas Baker. 2019. "Justice-Involved Males' Procedural Justice Perceptions of the Police and Courts: Examining the Spill-Over Effect." *Criminal Justice Studies*, December 26, 2019. https://doi.org/10.1080/1478601X .2019.1706876.

American Bar Association. 2003. "ABA Guidelines for the Appointment and Performance of Defense Counsel in Death Penalty Cases." *Hofstra Law Review* 31 (4): 2.

American Civil Liberties Union. 2013. *The War on Marijuana in Black and White*. New York: ACLU. https://www.aclu.org/sites/default/files/field_document/1114413-mj -report-rfs-rel1.pdf.

American Civil Liberties Union. 2014. *Black, Brown and Targeted: A Report on Boston Police Department Street Encounters from 2007–2010*. New York: ACLU. https:// www.aclum.org/sites/default/files/wp-content/uploads/2015/06/reports-black -brown-and-targeted.pdf.

Anderson, Elijah. 1999. *Code of the Street: Decency, Violence, and the Moral Life of the Inner City*. New York: Norton.

Anderson, Elizabeth. 2010. *The Imperative of Integration*. Princeton, NJ: Princeton University Press.

Anderson, James M., Maya Buenaventura, and Paul Heaton. 2019. "The Effects of Holistic Defense on Criminal Justice Outcomes." *Harvard Law Review* 132:819.

Anderson, James M., and Paul Heaton. 2012. "How Much Difference Does the Lawyer Make: The Effect of Defense Counsel on Murder Case Outcomes." *Yale Law Journal* 122:154–217.

Armstrong, Elizabeth A., and Laura T. Hamilton. 2013. *Paying for the Party*. Cambridge, MA: Harvard University Press.

Asad, Asad L. 2019. "Deportation Decisions: Judicial Decision-Making in an American Immigration Court." *American Behavioral Scientist* 63 (9): 1221–49.

Asad, Asad L. 2020. "On the Radar: System Embeddedness and Latin American Immigrants' Perceived Risk of Deportation." *Law and Society Review* 54 (1): 133–67.

Asad, Asad L., and Matthew Clair. 2018. "Racialized Legal Status as a Social Determinant of Health." *Social Science and Medicine* 199:19–28.

Bach, Amy. 2009. *Ordinary Injustice: How America Holds Court*. New York: Metropolitan Books.

Baker, Thomas, Justin T. Pickett, Dhara M. Amin, Kristin Golden, Karla Dhungana, Marc Gertz, and Laura Bedard. 2015. "Shared Race/Ethnicity, Court Procedural Justice, and Self-Regulating Beliefs: A Study of Female Offenders." *Law and Society Review* 49 (2): 433–66.

Baldus, David C., Charles A. Pulaski Jr., and George Woodworth. 1986. "Arbitrariness and Discrimination in the Administration of the Death Penalty: A Challenge to State Supreme Courts." *Stetson Law Review* 15:133–261.

Barkow, Rachel Elise. 2019. *Prisoners of Politics: Breaking the Cycle of Mass Incarceration*. Cambridge, MA: Harvard University Press.

Barley, Stephen R. 1996. "Technicians in the Workplace: Ethnographic Evidence for Bringing Work into Organizational Studies." *Administrative Science Quarterly* 41 (3): 404–41.

Barnes, J. C., Cody Jorgensen, Kevin M. Beaver, Brian B. Boutwell, and John P. Wright. 2015. "Arrest Prevalence in a National Sample of Adults: The Role of Sex and Race/Ethnicity." *American Journal of Criminal Justice* 40 (3): 457–65.

Baumer, Eric P. 2013. "Reassessing and Redirecting Research on Race and Sentencing." *Justice Quarterly* 30 (2): 231–61.

Bazelon, David L. 1973. "The Defective Assistance of Counsel." *University of Cincinnati Law Review* 42 (1): 1–46.

Bazelon, Emily. 2019. *Charged: The New Movement to Transform American Prosecution and End Mass Incarceration*. New York: Random House.

Beck, Allen J., and Alfred Blumstein. 2018. "Racial Disproportionality in US State Prisons: Accounting for the Effects of Racial and Ethnic Differences in Criminal Involvement, Arrests, Sentencing, and Time Served." *Journal of Quantitative Criminology* 34 (3): 853–83.

Becker, Howard. [1963] 1991. *Outsiders: Studies in the Sociology of Deviance*. New York: Free Press.

Beckett, Katherine, and Bruce Western. 2001. "Governing Social Marginality: Welfare, Incarceration, and the Transformation of State Policy." *Punishment and Society* 3 (1): 43–59.

Bell, Monica C. 2016. "Situational Trust: How Disadvantaged Mothers Reconceive Legal Cynicism." *Law and Society Review* 50 (2): 314–47.

Bell, Monica C. 2017. "Police Reform and the Dismantling of Legal Estrangement." *Yale Law Journal* 126:2054–2150.

Berrey, Ellen, Robert L. Nelson, and Laura Beth Nielsen. 2017. *Rights on Trial: How Workplace Discrimination Law Perpetuates Inequality*. Chicago: University of Chicago Press.

Bertenthal, Alyse. 2017. "The 'Right Paper': Developing Legal Literacy in a Legal Self-Help Clinic." *Law and Social Inquiry* 42 (4): 963–89.

Bibas, Stephanos. 2004. "Plea Bargaining Outside the Shadow of Trial." *Harvard Law Review* 117 (8): 2463–2547.

Bibas, Stephanos. 2012. *The Machinery of Criminal Justice*. New York: Oxford University Press.

Black, Donald. 1989. *Sociological Justice*. New York: Oxford University Press.

Black, Donald J., and Albert J. Reiss Jr. 1970. "Police Control of Juveniles." *American Sociological Review* 35 (1): 63–77.

Black, Linda L., and David Stone. 2005. "Expanding the Definition of Privilege: The Concept of Social Privilege." *Journal of Multicultural Counseling and Development* 33 (4): 243–55.

Blumberg, Abraham S. 1966. "The Practice of Law as Confidence Game: Organizational Cooptation of a Profession." *Law and Society Review* 1:15.

Blumberg, Abraham S. 1967. *Criminal Justice*. Chicago: Quadrangle.

Blumer, Herbert. 1986. *Symbolic Interactionism: Perspective and Method*. Berkeley: University of California Press.

Blumstein, Alfred. 1982. "On the Racial Disproportionality of United States' Prison Populations." *Journal of Criminal Law and Criminology* 73:1259–81.

Bobo, Lawrence D., James R. Kluegel, and Ryan A. Smith. 1997. "Laissez-faire Racism: The Crystallization of a Kinder, Gentler, AntiBlack Ideology." In *Racial Attitudes in the 1990s: Continuity and Change*, edited by J. K. Martin and S. A. Tuch, 15–42. Westport, CT: Greenwood.

Bobo, Lawrence D., and Victor Thompson. 2006. "Unfair by Design: The War on Drugs, Race, and the Legitimacy of the Criminal Legal System." *Social Research* 73:445–72.

Boccaccini, Marcus T., Jennifer L. Boothby, and Stanley L. Brodsky. 2004. "Development and Effects of Client Trust in Criminal Defense Attorneys: Preliminary Examination of the Congruence Model of Trust Development." *Behavioral Sciences and the Law* 22 (2): 197–214.

Bonilla-Silva, Eduardo. 2010. *Racism without Racists: Color-blind Racism and Racial Inequality in Contemporary America*. 3rd ed. New York: Rowman and Littlefield.

Bottoms, Anthony, and Justice Tankebe. 2012. "Beyond Procedural Justice: A Dialogic Approach to Legitimacy in Criminal Justice Criminology." *Journal of Criminal Law and Criminology* 102 (1): 119–70.

Bourdieu, Pierre. [1980] 1990. *The Logic of Practice*. Palo Alto, CA: Stanford University Press.

Bourdieu, Pierre. 1984. *Distinction: A Social Critique of the Judgement of Taste*. Cambridge, MA: Harvard University Press.

Bourdieu, Pierre, and Jean-Claude Passeron. 1977. *Reproduction in Education, Society and Culture*. Beverly Hills, CA: Sage.

Bradburn, Norman M. 1983. "Response Effects." In *Handbook of Survey Research*, edited by Peter H. Rossi, James D Wright, and Andy B. Anderson, 289–328. Academic Press.

Braga, Anthony A., Andrew V. Papachristos, and David M. Hureau. 2010. "The Concentration and Stability of Gun Violence at Micro Places in Boston, 1980–2008." *Journal of Quantitative Criminology* 26 (1): 33–53.

Braithwaite, John. 1989. *Crime, Shame and Reintegration*. Cambridge: Cambridge University Press.

Braithwaite, John. 1999. "Restorative Justice: Assessing Optimistic and Pessimistic Accounts." *Crime and Justice* 25:1–127.

Brame, Robert, Shawn D. Bushway, Ray Paternoster, and Michael G. Turner. 2014. "Demographic Patterns of Cumulative Arrest Prevalence by Ages 18 and 23." *Crime and Delinquency* 60 (3): 471–86.

Brayne, Sarah. 2014. "Surveillance and System Avoidance: Criminal Justice Contact and Institutional Attachment." *American Sociological Review* 79 (3): 367–91.

Bridges, George S., Robert D. Crutchfield, and Edith E. Simpson. 1987. "Crime, Social Structure and Criminal Punishment: White and Non-White Rates of Imprisonment." *Social Problems* 34:345–61.

Brooks, Richard R. W., and Haekyung Jeon-Slaughter. 2001. "Race, Income, and Perceptions of the US Court System." *Behavioral Sciences and the Law* 19 (2): 249–64.

Brunson, Rod K. 2007. "'Police Don't Like Black People': African-American Young Men's Accumulated Police Experiences." *Criminology and Public Policy* 6 (1): 71–101.

Bushway, Shawn D., Allison D. Redlich, and Robert J. Norris. 2014. "An Explicit Test of Plea Bargaining in the 'Shadow of the Trial.'" *Criminology* 52 (4): 723–54.

Butler, Paul. 2015. "The System Is Working the Way It Is Supposed To: The Limits of Criminal Justice Reform." *Georgetown Law Journal* 104:1419.

Butler, Paul. 2017. *Chokehold: A Renegade Prosecutor's Radical Thoughts on How to Disrupt the System*. New York: New Press.

Calarco, Jessica McCrory. 2014. "Coached for the Classroom Parents' Cultural Transmission and Children's Reproduction of Educational Inequalities." *American Sociological Review* 79 (5): 1015–37.

Calarco, Jessica McCrory. 2018. *Negotiating Opportunities: How the Middle Class Secures Advantages in School*. New York: Oxford University Press.

Calavita, Kitty, and Valerie Jenness. 2015. *Appealing to Justice: Prisoner Grievances, Rights, and Carceral Logic*. Oakland: University of California Press.

Carr, Patrick J., Laura Napolitano, and Jessica Keating. 2007. "We Never Call the Cops and Here Is Why: A Qualitative Examination of Legal Cynicism in Three Philadelphia Neighborhoods." *Criminology* 4 (2): 445–80.

Carter, Prudence L. 2003. "'Black' Cultural Capital, Status Positioning, and Schooling Conflicts for Low-Income African American Youth." *Social Problems* 50 (1): 136–55.

Casper, Jonathan D. 1971. "Did You Have a Lawyer When You Went to Court? No, I Had a Public Defender." *Yale Review of Law and Social Action* 1 (4): 4–9.

Casper, Jonathan D. 1972. *American Criminal Justice: The Defendant's Perspective*. Englewood Cliffs, NJ: Prentice Hall

Chambliss, William J. 1973. "The Saints and the Roughnecks." *Society* 11 (1): 24–31.

Chesney-Lind, Meda, and Lisa Pasko. 2013. *The Female Offender: Girls, Women, and Crime*. 3rd ed. Thousand Oaks, CA: Sage.

Chiricos, Theodore G., and William D. Bales. 1991. "Unemployment and Punishment: An Empirical Assessment." *Criminology* 29 (4): 701–24.

Clair, Matthew. 2018. "Privilege and Punishment: Unequal Experiences of Criminal Justice." Ph.D. diss., Department of Sociology, Harvard University, Cambridge, Massachusetts.

Clair, Matthew. 2020. "Criminalized Subjectivity: Du Boisian Sociology and Visions for Change among Criminal Defendants." Working paper. Stanford University.

Clair, Matthew, and Jeffrey S. Denis. 2015. "Sociology of Racism." In *International Encyclopedia of the Social and Behavioral Sciences*, 857–63. 2nd ed. New York: Elsevier.

Clair, Matthew, and Alix S. Winter. 2016. "How Judges Think about Racial Disparities: Situational Decision-Making in the Criminal Legal System." *Criminology* 54 (2): 332–59.

Clair, Matthew, and Alix S. Winter. 2020. "The Administrative Consequences of Mass Criminalization: The Case of Jury Selection." Working paper. Stanford University.

Cloward, Richard A., and Lloyd E. Ohlin. 1960. *Delinquency and Opportunity: A Study of Delinquent Gangs*. New York: Routledge.

Cochran, Robert F., Jr. 1990. "Legal Representation and the Next Steps toward Client Control: Attorney Malpractice for the Failure to Allow the Client to Control Negotiation and Pursue Alternatives to Litigation." *Washington and Lee Law Review* 47 (4): 819–78.

Cohen, Albert. 1955. *Delinquent Boys*. New York: Free Press.

Cohen, Cathy J. 2004. "Deviance as Resistance: A New Research Agenda for the Study of Black Politics." *Du Bois Review: Social Science Research on Race* 1 (1): 27–45.

Cohen, Thomas H. 2014. "Who Is Better at Defending Criminals? Does Type of Defense Attorney Matter in Terms of Producing Favorable Case Outcomes?" *Criminal Justice Policy Review* 25 (1): 29–58.

Cole, David. 1999. *No Equal Justice: Race and Class in the American Criminal Legal System*. New York: New Press.

Coleman, James S. 1968. *Equality of Educational Opportunity*. Washington, DC: US Department of Health, Education, and Welfare.

Collins, Harry, and Robert Evans. 2007. *Rethinking Expertise*. Chicago. University of Chicago Press.

Collins, Patricia Hill. 2002. *Black Feminist Thought: Knowledge, Consciousness, and the Politics of Empowerment*. New York: Routledge.

Connor, Tyrell A. 2019. "Legitimation in Action: An Examination of Community Courts and Procedural Justice." *Journal of Crime and Justice* 42 (2): 161–83.

Contreras, Randol. 2013. *The Stickup Kids: Race, Drugs, Violence, and the American Dream*. Berkeley: University of California Press.

Cook, Karen S. 2005. "Networks, Norms, and Trust: The Social Psychology of Social Capital." *Social Psychology Quarterly* 68 (1): 4–14.

Cramer, Maria. 2018. "Middlesex Prosecutors Told to Stop Asking for Bail in Minor Cases." *Boston Globe*, January 11, 2018. https://www.bostonglobe.com/metro/2018/01/11/middlesex-prosecutors-told-stop-asking-for-bail-minor-cases/ibcFXmvXR1xVO1gWpFdgoM/story.html.

Crenshaw, Kimberlé. 1991. "Women of Color at the Center: Selections from the Third National Conference on Women of Color and the Law: Mapping the Margins: Intersectionality, Identity Politics, and Violence against Women of Color." *Stanford Law Review* 43:1241.

Crutchfield, Robert D., George S. Bridges, and Susan R. Pitchford. 1994. "Analytical and Aggregation Biases in Analyses of Imprisonment: Reconciling Discrepancies in Studies of Racial Disparity." *Journal of Research in Crime and Delinquency* 31 (2): 166–82.

Cruz, Franklin, M. Elaine Borakove, and Aimee Wickman. 2014. *A Study of the Expansion of the Committee for Public Counsel Services' Representation of the Indigent.* Arlington, VA: Justice Management Institute. http://www.jmijustice.org/wp-content/uploads/2014/07/A-Study-of-the-Expansion-of-CPCS-Representation-of-the-Indigent-JMI-Final.pdf.

D'Alessio, Stewart J., and Lisa Stolzenberg. 1993. "Socioeconomic Status and the Sentencing of the Traditional Offender." *Journal of Criminal Justice* 21 (1): 61–77.

Daly, Kathleen. 1994. *Gender, Crime, and Punishment.* New Haven, CT: Yale University Press.

Davis, Angela Y. 2011. *Are Prisons Obsolete?* New York: Seven Stories Press.

Davis, Elizabeth, Anthony Whyde, and Lynn Langton. 2018. *Contacts between Police and the Public, 2015.* Washington, DC: Department of Justice, Bureau of Justice Statistics. https://www.bjs.gov/index.cfm?ty=pbdetail&iid=6406.

DeLand, Michael. 2013. "Basketball in the Key of Law: The Significance of Disputing in Pick-Up Basketball." *Law and Society Review* 47 (3): 653–85.

Delgado, Richard. 1985. "Rotten Social Background: Should the Criminal Law Recognize a Defense of Severe Environmental Deprivation." *Law and Inequality* 3:9–90.

DeMichele, Matthew. 2014. "Studying the Community Corrections Field: Applying Neo-institutional Theories to a Hidden Element of Mass Social Control." *Theoretical Criminology* 18 (4): 546–64.

Demuth, Stephen. 2003. "Racial and Ethnic Differences in Pretrial Release Decisions and Outcomes: A Comparison of Hispanic, Black, and White Felony Arrestees." *Criminology* 41:873.

Desmond, Matthew. 2014. "Relational Ethnography." *Theory and Society* 43 (5): 547–79.

Dishion, Thomas J., and Jessica M. Tipsord. 2011. "Peer Contagion in Child and Adolescent Social and Emotional Development." *Annual Review of Psychology* 62:189–214.

Dobbie, Will, Jacob Goldin, and Crystal S. Yang. 2018. "The Effects of Pretrial Detention on Conviction, Future Crime, and Employment: Evidence from Randomly Assigned Judges." *American Economic Review* 108 (2): 201–40.

Dobson, Cheyney. 2019. "Merging Criminal Justice and Social Welfare in Mental Health Court: The Disparate Impacts and Outcomes of Coercive Aid in the Era of Mass Incarceration." PhD diss., University of Michigan.

Du Bois, W. E. B. [1899] 1996. *The Philadelphia Negro: A Social Study.* Philadelphia: University of Pennsylvania Press.

Duck, Waverly. 2017. "The Complex Dynamics of Trust and Legitimacy: Understanding Interactions between the Police and Poor Black Neighborhood Residents." *Annals of the American Academy of Political and Social Science* 673 (1): 132–49.

Durkheim, Émile. [1951] 1979. *Suicide: A Study in Sociology.* New York: Free Press.

Edwards, Frank, Hedwig Lee, and Michael Esposito. 2019. "Risk of Being Killed by Police Use of Force in the United States by Age, Race-Ethnicity, and Sex." *Proceedings of the National Academy of Sciences* 116 (34): 16793–798.

Eisenstein, James, Roy B. Flemming, and Peter F. Nardulli. 1988. *The Contours of Justice: Communities and Their Courts.* Boston: Little, Brown.

Eisenstein, James, and Herbert Jacob. 1977. *Felony Justice: An Organizational Analysis of Criminal Courts.* Boston: Little, Brown.

Elliott, Delbert S., and Suzanne S. Ageton. 1980. "Reconciling Race and Class Differences in Self-Reported and Official Estimates of Delinquency." *American Sociological Review* 45 (1): 95–110.

Elliott, Delbert S., David Huizinga, and Scott Menard. 1989. *Multiple Problem Youth: Delinquency, Substance Use, and Mental Health Problems.* New York: Springer-Verlag.

Emirbayer, Mustafa. 1997. "Manifesto for a Relational Sociology." *American Journal of Sociology* 103 (2): 281–317.

Emmelman, Debra S. 2003. *Justice for the Poor: A Study of Criminal Defense Work.* Burlington, VT: Ashgate.

Enns, Peter K., Youngmin Yi, Megan Comfort, Alyssa W. Goldman, Hedwig Lee, Christopher Muller, Sara Wakefield, Emily A. Wang, and Christopher Wildeman. 2019. "What Percentage of Americans Have Ever Had a Family Member Incarcerated?: Evidence from the Family History of Incarceration Survey (FamHIS)." *Socius* 5. https://doi.org/10.1177/2378023119829332.

Erickson, Bonnie H. 1996. "Culture, Class, and Connections." *American Journal of Sociology* 102 (1): 217–51.

Ewick, Patricia, and Susan S. Silbey. 1998. *The Common Place of Law: Stories from Everyday Life.* Chicago: University of Chicago Press.

Fagan, Jeffrey, Anthony A. Braga, Rod K. Brunson, and April Pattavina. 2015. *An Analysis of Race and Ethnicity Patterns in Boston Police Department Field Interrogation, Observation, Frisk, and/or Search Reports.* Boston: ACLU of Massachusetts and Boston Police Department. http://raceandpolicing.issuelab.org/resources/25203/25203.pdf.

Farbman, Daniel. 2019. "Resistance Lawyering." *California Law Review* 107 (6): 1877–1954.

Farrell, Amy, Jack McDevitt, Lisa Bailey, Carsten Andresen, and Erica Pierce. 2004. "Massachusetts Racial and Gender Profiling Final Report: Executive Summary." May 4, 2004. Center for Criminal Justice Policy Research, Northeastern University. https://repository.library.northeastern.edu/files/neu:344624.

Farrington, David P. 1995. "The Development of Offending and Antisocial Behaviour from Childhood: Key Findings from the Cambridge Study in Delinquent Development." *Journal of Child Psychology and Psychiatry* 6 (36): 929–64.

Feeley, Malcolm M. [1979] 1992. *The Process Is the Punishment.* New York: Russell Sage Foundation.

Feierman, Jessica. 2006. "The Power of the Pen: Jailhouse Lawyers, Literacy, and Civic Engagement." *Harvard Civil Rights–Civil Liberties Law Review* 41 (2): 369.

Fiske, Susan T., and Hazel Rose Markus, eds. 2012. *Facing Social Class: How Societal Rank Influences Interaction.* New York: Russell Sage Foundation.

Flemming, Roy B. 1986. "Client Games: Defense Attorney Perspectives on Their Relations with Criminal Clients." *Law and Social Inquiry* 11 (2): 253–77.

Fong, Kelley. 2017. "Child Welfare Involvement and Contexts of Poverty: The Role of Parental Adversities, Social Networks, and Social Services." *Children and Youth Services Review* 72:5–13.

Forman, James, Jr. 2017. *Locking up Our Own: Crime and Punishment in Black America.* New York: Farrar, Straus and Giroux.

Formisano, Ronald P. 2004. *Boston against Busing: Race, Class, and Ethnicity in the 1960s and 1970s*. Chapel Hill: University of North Carolina Press.

Fox-Williams, Brittany N. 2019. "The Rules of (Dis)Engagement: Black Youth and Their Strategies for Navigating Police Contact." *Sociological Forum* 34 (1): 115–37.

Frazier, E. Franklin. 1957. *Black Bourgeoisie: The Rise of a New Middle Class in the United States*. Glencoe, IL: Free Press.

Freidson, Eliot. 1986. *Professional Powers: A Study of the Institutionalization of Formal Knowledge*. Chicago: Chicago University Press.

Gage-Bouchard, Elizabeth A. 2017. "Culture, Styles of Institutional Interactions, and Inequalities in Healthcare Experiences." *Journal of Health and Social Behavior* 58 (2): 147–65.

Galanter, Marc. 1974. "Why the 'Haves' Come out Ahead: Speculations on the Limits of Legal Change." *Law and Society Review* 9 (1): 95–160.

Garland, David. 2001. *Mass Imprisonment: Social Causes and Consequences*. London: Sage.

Gerring, John. 2009. "What Standards Are (or Might Be) Dhared." In *Workshop on Interdisciplinary Standards for Systematic Qualitative Research*, edited by Michele Lamont and Patricia White, 107–23. Arlington, VA: National Science Foundation.

Gilmore, Ruth Wilson. 2007. *Golden Gulag: Prisons, Surplus, Crisis, and Opposition in Globalizing California*. Berkeley: University of California Press.

Glaser, Barney G., and Anselm L. Strauss. 1967. *The Discovery of Grounded Theory: Strategies for Qualitative Research*. New York: Aldine.

Goetz, Edward G., Tony Damiano, and Jason Hicks. 2017. "Racially Concentrated Areas of Affluence: A Preliminary Investigation." Draft report. University of Minnesota Humphrey School of Public Affairs, Minneapolis.

Goffman, Alice. 2014. *On the Run: Fugitive Life in an American City*. Chicago: University of Chicago Press.

Goffman, Erving. 1959. *The Presentation of Self in Everyday Life*. New York: Doubleday.

Gottschalk, Marie. 2016. *Caught: The Prison State and the Lockdown of American Politics*. Princeton, NJ: Princeton University Press.

Gottschalk, Marie. 2019. "Did You Really Think Trump Was Going to Help End the Carceral State?" *Jacobin Magazine*, March 9, 2019. https://www.jacobinmag.com /2019/03/first-step-act-criminal-justice-reform.

Gould, Jon B., and Maya Pagni Barak. 2019. *Capital Defense: Inside the Lives of America's Death Penalty Lawyers*. New York: NYU Press.

Gurley, Gabrielle. 2014. "Public Defender Blues." *CommonWealth*, January 15, 2014. http://commonwealthmagazine.org/uncategorized/004-public-defender-blues/.

Hagan, John, and Celesta Albonetti. 1982. "Race, Class, and the Perception of Criminal Injustice in America." *American Journal of Sociology* 88:329–355.

Hagan, John, Carla Shedd, and Monique R. Payne. 2005. "Race, Ethnicity, and Youth Perceptions of Criminal Injustice." *American Sociological Review* 70 (3): 381–407.

Hannah-Moffat, Kelly, and Paula Maurutto. 2012. "Shifting and Targeted Forms of Penal Governance: Bail, Punishment and Specialized Vourts." *Theoretical Criminology* 16 (2): 201–19.

Hardin, Russell. 2002. *Trust and Trustworthiness*. New York: Russell Sage Foundation.

Harding, David J. 2010. *Living the Drama: Community, Conflict, and Culture among Inner-City Boys*. Chicago: University of Chicago Press.

Harris, Alexes. 2009. "Attributions and Institutional Processing: How Focal Concerns Guide Decision-Making in the Juvenile Court." *Race and Social Problems* 1 (4): 243–56.

Harris, Alexes. 2016. *A Pound of Flesh: Monetary Sanctions as Punishment for the Poor*. New York: Russell Sage Foundation.

Haug, Marie R. 1972. "Deprofessionalization: An Alternate Hypothesis for the Future." *Sociological Review* 20 (1): 195–211.

Haug, Marie R., and Marvin B. Sussman. 1969. "Professional Autonomy and the Revolt of the Client." *Social Problems* 17 (2): 153–61.

Hawkins, Darnell F., John H. Laub, and Janet L. Lauritsen. 1998. "Race, Ethnicity, and Serious Juvenile Offending." In *Serious and Violent Juvenile Offenders: Risk Factors and Successful Interventions*, edited by R. Loeber and D. P. Farrington, 30–46. Thousand Oaks, CA: Sage.

Heaton, Paul, Sandra G. Mayson, and Megan T. Stevenson. 2017. "The Downstream Consequences of Misdemeanor Pretrial Detention." *Stanford Law Review* 69:711–94.

Herbert, Steve, Katherine Beckett, and Forrest Stuart. 2018. "Policing Social Marginality: Contrasting Approaches." *Law and Social Inquiry* 43 (4): 1491–1513.

Heumann, Milton. 1981. *Plea Bargaining: The Experiences of Prosecutors, Judges, and Defense Attorneys*. Chicago. University of Chicago Press.

Hinton, Elizabeth. 2016. *From the War on Poverty to the War on Crime*. Cambridge, MA: Harvard University Press.

Hodson, Randy, and Teresa A. Sullivan. 1990. "Professions and Professionals." In *The Social Organization of Work*, edited by Randy Hodson and Teresa A. Sullivan, 257–85. Belmont, CA: Wadsworth.

Holmes, Malcolm D., Harmon M. Hosch, Howard C. Daudistel, Dolores A. Perez, and Joseph B. Graves. 1996. "Ethnicity, Legal Resources, and Felony Dispositions in Two Southwestern jurisdictions." *Justice Quarterly* 13 (1): 11–30.

Husak, Douglas. 2008. *Overcriminalization: The Limits of the Criminal Law*. New York: Oxford University Press.

Jack, Anthony Abraham. 2019. *The Privileged Poor: How Elite Colleges Are Failing Disadvantaged Students*. Cambridge, MA: Harvard University Press.

Jacobs, Bruce A. 1999. *Dealing Crack: The Social World of Streetcorner Selling*. Boston: Northeastern University Press.

Jacques, Scott, and Richard Wright. 2015. *Code of the Suburb: Inside the World of Young Middle-Class Drug Dealers*. Chicago: University of Chicago Press.

Jencks, Christopher. 1972. *Inequality: A Reassessment of the Effect of Family and Schooling in America*. New York: Basic Books.

Jenness, Valerie, and Kitty Calavita. 2018. "'It Depends on the Outcome': Prisoners, Grievances, and Perceptions of Justice." *Law and Society Review* 52 (1): 41–72.

Jerolmack, Colin, and Shamus Khan. 2014. "Talk Is Cheap: Ethnography and the Attitudinal Fallacy." *Sociological Methods and Research* 43 (2): 178–209.

Jiménez, Tomás, and Marlene Orozco. 2020. "Constructing a Better Interview Protocol." Working paper. Stanford University.

Johnson, Brian D. 2006. "The Multilevel Context of Criminal Sentencing: Integrating Judge- and County-Level Influences." *Criminology* 44 (2): 259–98.

Johnson, Brian D., and Sara Betsinger. 2009. "Punishing the 'Model Minority': Asian-American Criminal Sentencing Outcomes in Federal District Courts." *Criminology* 47 (4): 1045–90.

Johnson, Brian D., and Stephanie M. DiPietro. 2012. "The Power of Diversion: Intermediate Sanctions and Sentencing Disparity under Presumptive Guidelines." *Criminology* 50 (3): 811–50.

Jones, Nikki. 2009. *Between Good and Ghetto: African American Girls and Inner-City Violence.* Piscataway, NJ: Rutgers University Press.

Jones, Nikki. 2014. "'The Regular Routine': Proactive Policing and Adolescent Development among Young, Poor Black Men." *New Directions for Child and Adolescent Development* 143:33–54.

Kaeble, Danielle, and Mary Cowhig. 2018. *Correctional Populations in the United States, 2016.* Washington, DC: Department of Justice, Bureau of Justice Statistics. https://www.bjs.gov/content/pub/pdf/cpus16.pdf.

Kaeble, Danielle, and Lauren Glaze. 2016. *Correctional Populations in the United States, 2015.* Washington, DC: U.S. Department of Justice, Bureau of Justice Statistics.

Katz, Ian. 1995. "Reprieve for Man Whose Lawyer Slept." *Guardian*, April 11, 1995.

Katz, Jack. 1988. *Seductions of Crime: Moral and Sensual Attractions in Doing Evil.* New York: Basic Books.

Kelley, Robin. 1996. *Race Rebels: Culture, Politics, and the Black Working Class.* New York: Simon and Schuster.

Khan, Shamus Rahman. 2010. *Privilege: The Making of an Adolescent Elite at St. Paul's School.* Princeton, NJ: Princeton University Press.

Kirchmeier, Jeffrey L. 1996. "Drink, Drugs, and Drowsiness: The Constitutional Right to Effective Assistance of Counsel and the Strickland Prejudice Requirement." *Nebraska Law Review* 75 (3): 425–60.

Kirk, David S., and Andrew V. Papachristos. 2011. "Cultural Mechanisms and the Persistence of Neighborhood Violence." *American Journal of Sociology* 116 (4): 1190–1233.

Kirk, David S., and Sara Wakefield. 2018. "Collateral Consequences of Punishment: A Critical Review and Path Forward." *Annual Review of Criminology* 1:171–94.

Klepper, Steven, Daniel Nagin, and Luke-Jon Tierney. 1983. "Discrimination in the Criminal Justice System: A Critical Appraisal of the Literature." *Research on Sentencing: The Search for Reform* 2:55–128.

Kohler-Hausmann, Issa. 2018. *Misdemeanorland: Criminal Courts and Social Control in an Age of Broken Windows Policing.* Princeton, NJ: Princeton University Press.

Kohler-Hausmann, Issa. 2019. "Eddie Murphy and the Dangers of Counterfactual Causal Thinking about Detecting Racial Discrimination." *Northwestern University Law Review* 113 (5): 1163–1228.

Kohler-Hausmann, Julilly. 2017. *Getting Tough: Welfare and Imprisonment in 1970s America.* Princeton, NJ: Princeton University Press.

Kramer, Roderick M., and Karen S. Cook. 2004. *Trust and Distrust in Organizations: Dilemmas and Approaches.* New York: Russell Sage Foundation.

Kritzer, Herbert Morris. 1990. *The Justice Broker: Lawyers and Ordinary Litigation*. New York: Oxford University Press.

Kritzer, Herbert Morris. 1998. *Legal Advocacy: Lawyers and Nonlawyers at Work*. Ann Arbor: University of Michigan Press.

Kutateladze, Besiki L., Nancy R. Andiloro, Brian D. Johnson, and Cassia C. Spohn. 2014. "Cumulative Disadvantage: Examining Racial and Ethnic Disparity in Prosecution and Sentencing." *Criminology* 52 (3): 514–51.

Lacourse, Eric, Daniel Nagin, Richard E. Tremblay, Frank Vitaro, and Michel Claes. 2003. "Developmental Trajectories of Boys' Delinquent Group Membership and Facilitation of Violent Behaviors during Adolescence." *Development and Psychopathology* 15 (1): 183–97.

Lacy, Karyn R. 2004. "Black Spaces, Black Places: Strategic Assimilation and Identity Construction in Middle-Class Suburbia." *Ethnic and Racial Studies* 27 (6): 908–930.

Lageson, Sarah E., and Shadd Maruna. 2018. "Digital Degradation: Stigma Management in the Internet Age." *Punishment and Society* 20 (1): 113–33.

Lamont, Michèle. 1992. *Money, Morals, and Manners: The Culture of the French and the American Upper-Middle Class*. Chicago: University of Chicago Press.

Lamont, Michèle. 2000. *The Dignity of Working Men: Morality and the Boundaries of Race, Class, and Immigration*. Cambridge, MA: Harvard University Press.

Lamont, Michèle. 2018. "Addressing Recognition Gaps: Destigmatization and the Reduction of Inequality." *American Sociological Review* 83 (3): 419–44.

Lamont, Michèle, Stefan Beljean, and Matthew Clair. 2014. "What Is Missing? Cultural Processes and Causal Pathways to Inequality." *Socio-Economic Review* 12 (3): 573–608.

Lamont, Michèle, and Annette Lareau. 1988. "Cultural Capital: Allusions, Gaps and Glissandos in Recent Theoretical Developments." *Sociological Theory* 6 (2): 153.

Lamont, Michèle, and Ann Swidler. 2014. "Methodological Pluralism and the Possibilities and Limits of Interviewing." *Qualitative Sociology* 37 (2): 153–71.

Lareau, Annette. 2011. *Unequal Childhoods: Class, Race, and Family Life*. 2nd ed. Oakland: University of California Press.

Lareau, Annette. 2015. "Cultural Knowledge and Social Inequality." *American Sociological Review* 80 (1): 1–27.

Lee, Eric. 2000. *Community Courts: An Evolving Model*. Washington, DC: Department of Justice, Center for Court Innovation.

Lenard, Patti Tamara. 2008. "Trust Your Compatriots, but Count Your Change: The Roles of Trust, Mistrust and Distrust in Democracy." *Political Studies* 56 (2): 312–32.

Lerman, Amy E., and Vesla M. Weaver. 2014. *Arresting Citizenship: The Democratic Consequences of American Crime Control*. Chicago: University of Chicago Press.

Leverentz, Andrea M. 2014. *The Ex-prisoner's Dilemma: How Women Negotiate Competing Narratives of Reentry and Desistance*. Piscataway, NJ: Rutgers University Press.

Levine, Jeremy R., and Carl Gershenson. 2014. "From Political to Material Inequality: Race, Immigration, and Requests for Public Goods." *Sociological Forum* 29 (3): 607–27.

Levine, Judith. 2013. *Ain't No Trust: How Bosses, Boyfriends, and Bureaucrats Fail Low-Income Mothers and Why It Matters*. Oakland: University of California Press.

Levine, Kay L., and Virginia Mellema. 2001. "Strategizing the Street: How Law Matters in the Lives of Women in the Street-Level Drug Economy." *Law and Social Inquiry* 26 (1): 169–207.

Lipsky, Michael. 1980. *Street-Level Bureaucracy: Dilemmas of the Individual in Public Services*. New York: Russell Sage Foundation.

López, Ian F. Haney. 2000. "Institutional Racism: Judicial Conduct and a New Theory of Racial Discrimination." *Yale Law Journal* 109 (8): 1717–1884.

Loughran, Thomas A., Ray Paternoster, Aaron Chalfin, and Theodore Wilson. 2016. "Can Rational Choice Be Considered a General Theory of Crime? Evidence from Individual-Level Panel Data." *Criminology* 54 (1): 86–112.

Luban, David. 1981. "Paternalism and the Legal Profession." *Wisconsin Law Review* 3:454–93.

Lucal, Betsy. 1996. "Oppression and Privilege: Toward a Relational Conceptualization of Race." *Teaching Sociology* 24 (3): 245–55.

Lynch, Mona. 2016. *Hard Bargains: The Coercive Power of Drug Laws in Federal Court*. New York: Russell Sage Foundation.

Lynch, Mona. 2017. "The Situated Actor and the Production of Punishment." In *The New Criminal Justice Thinking*, edited by S. Dolovich and A. Natapoff, 199–225. New York: NYU Press.

Lynch, Mona, and Marisa Omori. 2018. "Crack as Proxy: Aggressive Federal Drug Prosecutions and the Production of Black-White Racial Inequality." *Law and Society Review* 52 (3): 773–809.

MacDonald, John, Jeremy Arkes, Nancy Nicosia, and Rosalie Liccardo Pacula. 2014. "Decomposing Racial Disparities in Prison and Drug Treatment Commitments for Criminal Offenders in California." *Journal of Legal Studies* 43 (1): 155–87.

MacDonald, John, and Robert J. Stokes. 2006. "Race, Social Capital, and Trust in the Police." *Urban Affairs Review* 41 (3): 358–75.

MacFarlane, Julie. 2017. *The New Lawyer: How Clients Are Transforming the Practice of Law*. 2nd ed. Vancouver: UBC Press.

Martin, Jamie S., Kate Hanrahan, and James H. Bowers Jr. 2009. "Offenders' Perceptions of House Arrest and Electronic Monitoring." *Journal of Offender Rehabilitation* 48 (6): 547–70.

Martin, Karin D., Bryan L. Sykes, Sarah Shannon, Frank Edwards, and Alexes Harris. 2018. "Monetary Sanctions: Legal Financial Obligations in US Systems of Justice." *Annual Review of Criminology* 1:497–515.

Martinez, Cid. 2016. *The Neighborhood Has Its Own Rules: Latinos and African Americans in South Los Angeles*. New York: NYU Press.

Marx, Karl. 1978. "Economic and Philosophic Manuscripts of 1844." In *The Marx-Engels Reader*, 2nd ed., edited by Robert C. Tucker, 66–125. New York: Norton.

Massey, Douglas S., and Nancy A. Denton. 1993. *American Apartheid: Segregation and the Making of the Underclass*. Cambridge, MA: Harvard University Press.

Mather, Lynn. 1979. *Plea Bargaining or Trial? The Process of Criminal-Case Disposition*. Lexington, MA: Lexington Books.

Mather, Lynn. 2003. "What Do Clients Want? What Do Lawyers Do?" *Emory LJ* 52:1065–86.

Mather, Lynn, Craig A. McEwen, and Richard J. Maiman. 2001. *Divorce Lawyers at Work: Varieties of Professionalism in Practice*. New York: Oxford University Press.

Mathison, Sandra. 1988. "Why Triangulate?" *Educational Researcher* 17 (2): 13–17.

Matsueda, Ross L., and Kathleen Anderson. 1998. "Dynamics of Delinquent Peers and Delinquent Behavior." *Criminology* 36:269–308.

Maynard-Moody, Steven Williams, and Michael Craig Musheno. 2003. *Cops, Teachers, Counselors: Stories from the Front Lines of Public Service*. Ann Arbor: University of Michigan Press.

McCall, Leslie. 2005. "The Complexity of Intersectionality." *Signs: Journal of Women in Culture and Society* 30 (3): 1771–1800.

McIntosh, Peggy. 1992. "White Privilege and Male Privilege: A Personal Account of Coming to See Correspondences through Work in Women's Studies." In *Race, Class and Gender: An Anthology*, edited by Margaret A. Anderson and Patricia Hill Collins, 70–81. Belmont, CA: Wadsworth.

McKean, Jerome, and Kiesha Warren-Gordon. 2011. "Racial Differences in Graduation Rates from Adult Drug Treatment Courts." *Journal of Ethnicity in Criminal Justice* 9 (1): 41–55.

Meares, Tracey. 2016. "Policing and Procedural Justice: Shaping Citizens' Identities to Increase Democratic Participation." *Northwestern University Law Review* 111:1525.

Mears, Daniel P., Eric A. Stewart, Patricia Y. Warren, and Ronald L. Simons. 2017. "Culture and Formal Social Control: The Effect of the Code of the Street on Police and Court Decision-Making." *Justice Quarterly* 34 (2): 217–47.

Melaku, Tsedale M. 2019. *You Don't Look Like a Lawyer: Black Women and Systemic Gendered Racism*. Lanham, MD: Rowman and Littlefield.

Merry, Sally Engle. 1990. *Getting Justice and Getting Even: Legal Consciousness among Working-Class Americans*. Chicago: University of Chicago Press.

Merton, Robert K. 1938. "Social Structure and Anomie." *American Sociological Review* 3 (5): 672–82.

Merton, Robert K. 1957. *Social Theory and Social Structure*. New York: Free Press.

Miller, Holly Ventura, ed. 2008. *Restorative Justice: From Theory to Practice*. Bingley, UK: Emerald Group.

Miller, Reuben J., and Amanda Alexander. 2015. "The Price of Carceral Citizenship: Punishment, Surveillance, and Social Welfare Policy in an Age of Carceral Expansion." *Michigan Journal og Race and Law* 21:291.

Mills, C. Wright. 1959. *The Sociological Imagination*. New York: Oxford University Press.

Milovanovic, Dragan. 1988. "Jailhouse Lawyers and Jailhouse Lawyering." *International Journal of the Sociology of Law* 16 (4): 455–75.

Mitchell, Ojmarrh. 2005. "A Meta-analysis of Race and Sentencing Research: Explaining the Inconsistencies." *Journal of Quantitative Criminology* 21:439–66.

Mnookin, Robert H., and Lewis Kornhauser. 1979. "Bargaining in the Shadow of the Law: The Case of Divorce." *Yale Law Journal* 88 (5): 950–97.

Mohamed, A. Rafik, and Erik D. Fritsvold. 2010. *Dorm Room Dealers: Drugs and the Privileges of Race and Class*. Boulder, CO: Lynne Rienner.

Moore, Dawn. 2011. "The Benevolent Watch: Therapeutic Surveillance in Drug Treatment Court." *Theoretical Criminology* 15 (3): 255–68.

Moore, Janet, Vicki L. Plano Clark, Lori A. Foote, and Jacinda K. Dariotis. 2019. "Attorney-Client Communication in Public Defense: A Qualitative Examination." *Criminal Justice Policy Review*. https://doi.org/10.1177/0887403419861672.

Moore, Janet, Marla Sandys, and Raj Jayadev. 2015. "Make Them Hear You: Participatory Defense and the Struggle for Criminal Justice Reform." In "Special Issue on Research in Indigent Defense," *Albany Law Review* 78:1281–1316.

Moore, Janet, Ellen Yaroshefsky, and Andrew L. B. Davies. 2017. "Privileging Public Defense Research." *Mercer Law Review* 69 (3): 771–804.

Morenoff, Jeffrey D. 2005. "Racial and Ethnic Disparities in Crime and Delinquency in the United States." In *Ethnicity and Causal Mechanisms*, edited by Michael Rutter and Marta Tienda, 139–73. New York: Cambridge University Press.

Morris, Norval, and Michael Tonry. 1991. *Between Prison and Probation: Intermediate Punishments in a Rational Sentencing System*. New York: Oxford University Press.

Muhammad, Khalil Gibran. 2019. *The Condemnation of Blackness: Race, Crime, and the Making of Modern Urban America*. Cambridge, MA: Harvard University Press.

Muller, Christopher, and Daniel Schrage. 2014. "Mass Imprisonment and Trust in the Law." *Annals of the American Academy of Political and Social Science* 651 (1): 139–58.

Murakawa, Naomi. 2014. *The First Civil Right: How Liberals Built Prison America*. New York: Oxford University Press.

Murakawa, Naomi, and Katherine Beckett. 2010. "The Penology of Racial Innocence: The Erasure of Racism in the Study and Practice of Punishment." *Law and Society Review* 44:695–730.

Natapoff, Alexandra. 2005. "Speechless: The Silencing of Criminal Defendants." *New York University Law Review* 80:1449.

Natapoff, Alexandra. 2009. *Snitching: Criminal Informants and the Erosion of American Justice*. New York: NYU Press.

Neckerman, Kathryn M., and Florencia Torche. 2007. "Inequality: Causes and Consequences." *Annual Review of Sociology* 33:335–57.

Nielsen, Laura Beth. 2000. "Situating Legal Consciousness: Experiences and Attitudes of Ordinary Citizens about Law and Street Harassment." *Law and Society Review* 34 (4): 1055–90.

Nobiling, Tracy, Cassia Spohn, and Miriam DeLone. 1998. "A Tale of Two Counties: Unemployment and Sentence Severity." *Justice Quarterly* 15 (3): 459–85.

O'Brien, Stewart, Steven Pheterson, Michael Wright, and Carl Hostica. 1977. "The Criminal Lawyer: The Defendant's Perspective." *American Journal of Criminal Law* 5:283.

Olivier, Jasmine, Matthew Clair, and Jeffrey S. Denis. 2019. "Racism." In *The Blackwell Encyclopedia of Sociology*, vol. 8, edited by George Ritzer and Chris Rojek. John Wiley and Sons.

Pager, Devah. 2008. *Marked: Race, Crime, and Finding Work in an Era of Mass Incarceration*. Chicago: University of Chicago Press.

Pager, Devah, and Lincoln Quillian. 2005. "Walking the Talk? What Employers Say versus What They Do." *American Sociological Review* 70:355–80.

Pager, Devah, and Hana Shepherd. 2008. "The Sociology of Discrimination: Racial Discrimination in Employment, Housing, Credit, and Consumer Markets." *Annual Review of Sociology* 34:181–209.

Paik, Leslie. 2006. "Are You Truly a Recovering Dope Fiend? Local Interpretive Practices at a Therapeutic Community Drug Treatment Program." *Symbolic Interaction* 29 (2): 213–34.

Pattillo, Mary. 2013. *Black Picket Fences: Privilege and Peril among the Black Middle Class*. Chicago: University of Chicago Press.

Petersilia, Joan. 1985. "Racial Disparities in the Criminal Legal System: A Summary." *NPPA Journal* 31 (1): 15–34.

Petersilia, Joan. 1990. "When Probation Becomes More Dreaded than Prison." *Federal Probation Journal* 54:23.

Petersilia, Joan, and Elizabeth Piper Deschenes. 1994. "Perceptions of Punishment: Inmates and Staff Rank the Severity of Prison versus Intermediate Sanctions." *Prison Journal* 74 (3): 306–28.

Peterson, Dana, and Vanessa R. Panfil. 2017. "Toward a Multiracial Feminist Framework for Understanding Females' Gang Involvement." *Journal of Crime and Justice* 40 (3): 337–57.

Peterson, Ruth D., and John Hagan. 1984. "Changing Conceptions of Race: Towards an Account of Anomalous Findings of Sentencing Research." *American Sociological Review* 49 (1): 56–70.

Peterson, Ruth D., and Lauren J. Krivo. 2010. *Divergent Social Worlds: Neighborhood Crime and the Racial-Spatial Divide*. New York: Russell Sage Foundation.

Pfaff, John. 2017. *Locked In: The True Causes of Mass Incarceration—and How to Achieve Real Reform*. New York: Basic Books.

Phelps, Michelle S. 2016. "Mass Probation: Toward a More Robust Theory of State Variation in Punishment." *Punishment and Society* 19 (1): 53–73.

Pickett, Justin T., Christina Mancini, and Daniel P. Mears. 2013. "Vulnerable Victims, Monstrous Offenders, and Unmanageable Risk: Explaining Public Opinion on the Social Control of Sex Crime." *Criminology* 51 (3): 729–59.

Piliavin, Irving, and Scott Briar. 1964. "Police Encounters with Juveniles." *American Journal of Sociology* 70 (2): 206–14.

Presser, Lois. 2009. "The Narratives of Offenders." *Theoretical Criminology* 13 (2): 177–200.

Pugh, Allison J. 2013. "What Good Are Interviews for Thinking about Culture? Demystifying Interpretive Analysis." *American Journal of Cultural Sociology* 1 (1): 42–68.

Rachlinski, Jeffrey J., Sheri Lynn Johnson, Andrew J. Wistrich, and Chris Guthrie. 2008. "Does Unconscious Racial Bias Affect Trial Judges?" *Notre Dame Law Review* 84:1195.

Ray, Victor. 2019. "A Theory of Racialized Organizations." *American Sociological Review* 84 (1): 26–53.

Reay, Diane. 1998. *Class Work: Mothers' Involvement in Their Children's Primary Schooling*. London: UCL Press.

Reich, Jennifer A. 2005. *Fixing Families: Parents, Power, and the Child Welfare System*. New York: Routledge.

Reisig, Michael D., John D. McCluskey, Stephen D. Mastrofski, and William Terrill. 2004. "Suspect Disrespect toward the Police." *Justice Quarterly* 21 (2): 241–68.

Richardson, L. Song, and Phillip Atiba Goff. 2013. "Implicit Racial Bias in Public Defender Triage." *Yale Law Journal* 122 (8): 2626–49.

Ridgeway, Cecilia L. 2014. "Why Status Matters for Inequality." *American Sociological Review* 79 (1): 1–16.

Rios, Victor M. 2011. *Punished: Policing the Lives of Black and Latino Boys*. New York: NYU Press.

Rios, Victor M., Nikita Carney, and Jasmine Kelekay. 2017. "Ethnographies of Race, Crime, and Justice: Toward a Sociological Double-Consciousness." *Annual Review of Sociology* 43 (1): 491–513.

Rivera, Lauren A. 2012. "Hiring as Cultural Matching: The Case of Elite Professional Service Firms." *American Sociological Review* 77 (6): 999–1022.

Rivera, Lauren A. 2016. *Pedigree: How Elite Students Get Elite Jobs*. Princeton, NJ: Princeton University Press.

Roberts, Dorothy E. 2007. "Constructing a Criminal Legal System Free of Racial Bias: An Abolitionist Framework." *Columbia Human Rights Law Review* 39:261.

Roberts, Dorothy E. 2019. "Abolition Constitutionalism." *Harvard Law Review* 133:3.

Roche, Declan. 2004. *Accountability in Restorative Justice*. Oxford: Oxford University Press.

Rosenthal, Douglas E. 1974. *Lawyer and Client: Who's in Charge?* New York: Russell Sage Foundation.

Saks, Mike. 2012. "Defining a Profession: The Role of Knowledge and Expertise." *Professions and Professionalism* 2, no. 1. https://doi.org/10.7577/pp.v2i1.151.

Salinas, Mike. 2017. "The Unusual Suspects: An Educated, Legitimately Employed Drug Dealing Network." *International Criminal Justice Review* 28 (3): 226–42.

Salmon, W. 1984. *Scientific Explanation and the Causal Structure of the World*. Princeton, NJ: Princeton University Press.

Sampson, Robert J., and Dawn Jeglum Bartusch. 1998. "Legal Cynicism and (Subcultural?) Tolerance of Deviance: The Neighborhood Context of Racial Differences." *Law and Society Review* 32 (4): 777–804.

Sampson, Robert J., and John H. Laub. 1995. *Crime in the Making: Pathways and Turning Points through Life*. Cambridge, MA: Harvard University Press.

Sampson, Robert J., and William J. Wilson. 1995. "Toward a Theory of Race, Crime, and Urban Inequality." In *Race, Crime, and Justice: A Reader*, edited by Shaun L. Gabbidon and Helen Taylor Greene, 177–90. New York: Routledge.

Sandefur, Rebecca L. 2015. "Elements of Professional Expertise: Understanding Relational and Substantive Expertise through Lawyers' Impact." *American Sociological Review* 80 (5): 909–33.

Sarat, Austin. 1990. "The Law Is All Over: Power, Resistance and the Legal Consciousness of the Welfare Poor." *Yale Journal of Law and the Humanities* 2:343.

Sarat, Austin, and William L. F. Felstiner. 1997. *Divorce Lawyers and Their Clients: Power and Meaning in the Legal Process*. New York: Oxford University Press.

Schlesinger, Traci. 2005. "Racial and Ethnic Disparity in Pretrial Criminal Processing." *Justice Quarterly* 22 (2): 170–92.

Schoenfeld, Heather. 2018. *Building the Prison State: Race and the Politics of Mass Incarceration*. Chicago: University of Chicago Press.

Schulhofer, Stephen J., and David D. Friedman. 1993. "Rethinking Indigent Defense: Promoting Effective Representation through Consumer Sovereignty and Freedom of Choice for All Criminal Defendants." *American Criminal Law Review* 31:73.

Schwalbe, Michael, Daphne Holden, Douglas Schrock, Sandra Godwin, Shealy Thompson, and Michele Wolkomir. 2000. "Generic Processes in the Reproduction of Inequality: An Interactionist Analysis." *Social Forces* 79 (2): 419–52.

Scott, James C. 1990. *Domination and the Arts of Resistance: Hidden Transcripts.* New Haven, CT: Yale University Press.

Seamster, Louise, and Victor Ray. 2018. "Against Teleology in the Study of Race: Toward the Abolition of the Progress Paradigm." *Sociological Theory* 36 (4): 315–42.

Seim, Josh. 2020. *Bandage, Sort, and Hustle: Ambulance Crews on the Front Lines of Urban Suffering.* Oakland: University of California Press.

Sellin, Thorsten. 1928. "The Negro Criminal. A Statistical Note." *Annals of the American Academy of Political and Social Science* 140:52–64.

Semuels, Alana. 2015. "Where the White People Live: How Self-Segregation and Concentrated Affluence Became Normal in America." *Atlantic*, April 10, 2015. https://www.theatlantic.com/business/archive/2015/04/where-the-White-people-live/390153/.

Sered, Danielle. 2019. *Until We Reckon: Violence, Mass Incarceration, and a Road to Repair.* New York: New Press.

Serna, Joseph. 2016. "More Racist Text Messages Uncovered among San Francisco Police Officers." *Los Angeles Times*, April 27, 2016. http://www.latimes.com/local/lanow/la-me-ln-sfpd-racist-text-messages-20160426-story.html.

Sewell, William H., Jr. 1992. "A Theory of Structure: Duality, Agency, and Transformation." *American Journal of Sociology* 98 (1): 1–29.

Shannon, Sarah K. S., Christopher Uggen, Jason Schnittker, Melissa Thompson, Sara Wakefield, and Michael Massoglia. 2017. "The Growth, Scope, and Spatial Distribution of People with Felony Records in the United States, 1948–2010." *Demography* 54 (5): 1795–1818.

Sharkey, Patrick. 2018. *Uneasy Peace: The Great Crime Decline, the Revival of City Life, and the Next War on Violence.* New York: Norton.

Sharkey, Patrick, and Jacob W. Faber. 2014. "Where, When, Why, and for Whom Do Residential Contexts Matter? Moving Away from the Dichotomous Understanding of Neighborhood Effects." *Annual Review of Sociology* 40:559–79.

Sharkey, Patrick, Gerard Torrats-Espinosa, and Delaram Takyar. 2017. "Community and the Crime Decline: The Causal Effect of Local Nonprofits on Violent Crime." *American Sociological Review* 82 (6): 1214–40.

Shaw, Clifford R., and Henry D. McKay. 1942. *Juvenile Delinquency and Urban Areas.* Chicago: University of Chicago Press.

Shedd, Carla. 2015. *Unequal City: Race, Schools, and Perceptions of Injustice.* New York: Russell Sage Foundation.

Shelby, Tommie. 2016. *Dark Ghettos.* Cambridge, MA: Harvard University Press.

Shermer, Lauren O'Neill, and Brian D. Johnson. 2010. "Criminal Prosecutions: Examining Prosecutorial Discretion and Charge Reductions in U.S. Federal District Courts." *Justice Quarterly* 27 (3): 394–430.

Shim, Janet K. 2010. "Cultural Health Capital: A Theoretical Approach to Understanding Health Care Interactions and the Dynamics of Unequal Treatment." *Journal of Health and Social Behavior* 51 (1): 1–15.

Shoemaker, Donald. 2009. *Theories of Delinquency: An Examination of Explanations of Delinquent Behavior*. New York: Oxford University Press.

Silbey, Susan S. 2005. "After Legal Consciousness." *Annual Review of Law and Social Science* 1 (1): 323–68.

Simes, Jessica T. 2018. "Place and Punishment: The Spatial Context of Mass Incarceration." *Journal of Quantitative Criminology* 34 (2): 513–33.

Simonson, Jocelyn. 2019. "The Place of 'the People' in Criminal Procedure." *Columbia Law Review* 119 (1): 249–308.

Singer, Simon I. 2014. *America's Safest City: Delinquency and Modernity in Suburbia*. New York: NYU Press.

Sklansky, David A. 2017. "The Problems with Prosecutors." *Annual Review of Criminology* 1:471–95.

Sklansky, David A. 2018. "Autonomy and Agency in American Criminal Process." In *Obstacles to Fairness in Criminal Proceedings: Institutional Rights and Institutional Forms*, edited by John D. Jackson and Sarah J. Summers, 37–56. Portland, OR: Hart.

Skolnick, Jerome H. 1967. "Social Control in the Adversary System." *Journal of Conflict Resolution* 11 (1): 52–70.

Small, Deborah. 2014. "Cause for Trepidation: Libertarians' Newfound Concern for Prison Reform." *Salon*, March 22, 2014. https://www.salon.com/2014/03/22/cause_for_trepidation_libertarians_newfound_concern_for_prison_reform/.

Small, Mario Luis. 2009. "'How Many Cases Do I Need?' On Science and the Logic of Case Selection in Field-Based Research." *Ethnography* 10 (1): 5–38.

Smith, Abbe. 2007. "The Lawyer's Conscience and the Limits of Persuasion Lawyering at the Edge: Unpopular Clients, Difficult Cases, Zealous Advocates." *Hofstra Law Review* 36 (2): 479–96.

Smith, Sandra Susan. 2010. "Race and Trust." *Annual Review of Sociology* 36:453–75.

Snyder, Howard N. 2012. *Arrest in the United States, 1990–2010*. Washington, DC: Department of Justice, Bureau of Justice Statistics. https://www.bjs.gov/content/pub/pdf/aus9010.pdf.

Somers, Margaret R. 1994. "The Narrative Constitution of Identity: A Relational and Network Approach." *Theory and Society* 23 (5): 605–49.

Spelman, William. 1995. "The Severity of Intermediate Sanctions." *Journal of Research in Crime and Delinquency* 32 (2): 107–35.

Spiegel, Mark. 1979. "Lawyering and Client Decisionmaking: Informed Consent and the Legal Profession." *University of Pennsylvania Law Review* 128 (1): 41–140.

Spohn, Cassia C. 2000. "Thirty Years of Sentencing Reform: The Quest for a Racially Neutral Sentencing Process." In *Policies, Processes, and Decisions of the Criminal Legal System*, vol. 3, edited by J. Horney, 427–501. Washington, DC: National Institute of Justice.

Spohn, Cassia. 2009. *How Do Judges Decide?: The Search for Fairness and Justice in Punishment*. London: Sage.

Spohn, Cassia C. 2013. "Racial Disparities in Prosecution, Sentencing, and Punishment." In *The Oxford Handbook of Ethnicity, Crime, and Immigration*, edited by S. M. Bucerius and M. Tonry, 166–93. Oxford: Oxford University Press.

Spohn, Cassia, John Gruhl, and Susan Welch. 1981. "The Effect of Race on Sentencing: A Re-Examination of an Unsettled Question." *Law and Society Review* 16 (1): 71–88.

Squires, Gregory D., and Charis Elizabeth Kubrin. 2006. *Privileged Places: Race, Residence, and the Structure of Opportunity.* Boulder, CO: Lynne Rienner.

Steffensmeier, Darrell J. 1980. "Assessing the Impact of the Women's Movement on Sex-Based Differences in the Handling of Adult Criminal Defendants." *Crime and Delinquency* 26 (3): 344–57.

Steffensmeier, Darrell, Jeffery Ulmer, and John Kramer. 1998. "The Interaction of Race, Gender, and Age in Criminal Sentencing: The Punishment Cost of Being Young, Black, and Male." *Criminology* 36 (4): 763–798.

Stephens, Nicole M., Hazel Rose Markus, and L. Taylor Phillips. 2014. "Social Class Culture Cycles: How Three Gateway Contexts Shape Selves and Fuel Inequality." *Annual Review of Psychology* 65 (1): 611–34.

Stevenson, Bryan. 2014. *Just Mercy: A Story of Justice and Redemption.* New York: Spiegel and Grau.

Stevenson, Megan T. 2018. "Distortion of Justice: How the Inability to Pay Bail Affects Case Outcomes." *The Journal of Law, Economics, and Organization* 34(4): 511–42.

Streib, Jessi. 2011. "Class Reproduction by Four Year Olds." *Qualitative Sociology* 34 (2): 337–52.

Streib, Jessi. 2015. *The Power of the Past: Understanding Cross-Class Marriages.* New York: Oxford University Press.

Strong, Suzanne M. 2016. *State-Administered Indigent Defense Systems, 2013.* Washington, DC: US DOJ Office of Justice Programs, Bureau of Justice Statistics.

Stuart, Forrest. 2016. *Down, Out, and Under Arrest: Policing and Everyday Life in Skid Row.* Chicago: University of Chicago Press.

Stuart, Forrest, Amada Armenta, and Melissa Osborne. 2015. "Legal Control of Marginal Groups." *Annual Review of Law and Social Science* 11:235–54

Stumpf, Juliet. 2013. "The Process Is the Punishment in Crimmigration Law." In *The Borders of Punishment: Migration, Citizenship, and Social Exclusion,* edited by Katja Franko Aas and Mary Bosworth, 58–75. Oxford: Oxford University Press.

Stuntz, William J. 2001. "The Pathological Politics of Criminal Law." *Michigan Law Review* 100 (3): 505–600.

Subramanian, Ram, Kristine Riley, and Chris Mai. 2018. "Divided Justice: Trends in Black and White Jail Incarceration, 1990–2013." New York: Vera Institute of Justice.

Sudnow, David. 1965. "Normal Crimes: Sociological Features of the Penal Code in a Public Defender Office." *Social Problems* 12 (3): 255–76.

Sykes, Gresham M., and David Matza. 1957. "Techniques of Neutralization: A Theory of Delinquency." *American Sociological Review* 22(6): 664–70.

Tague, Peter W. 1975. "An Indigent's Right to the Attorney of His Choice." *Stanford Law Review* 27 (1): 73–100.

Tavory, Iddo, and Stefan Timmermans. 2013. "A Pragmatist Approach to Causality in Ethnography." *American Journal of Sociology* 119 (3): 682–714.

Terry, Brandon M. 2015. "After Ferguson." *Point Magazine,* no. 10, June 16, 2015.

Thibaut, John, and Laurens Walker. 1975. *Procedural Justice: A Psychological Analysis.* Hillsdale, NJ: Erlbaum.

Thornberry, Terence P., and Marvin D. Krohn. 2000. "The Self-Report Method for Measuring Delinquency and Crime." *Criminal Justice* 4 (1): 33–83.

Tiger, Rebecca. 2013. *Judging Addicts: Drug Courts and Coercion in the Justice System.* New York: NYU Press.

Tilly, Charles. 1998. *Durable Inequality.* Berkeley: University of California Press.

Tittle, Charles R., and Robert F. Meier. 1990. "Specifying the SES/Delinquency Relationship." *Criminology* 28 (2): 271–300.

Tomaskovic-Devey, Donald. 2014. "The Relational Generation of Workplace Inequalities." *Social Currents* 1 (1): 51–73.

Tonry, Michael, and Matthew Melewski. 2008. "The Malign Effects of Drug and Crime Control Policies on Black Americans." *Crime and Justice* 37 (1): 1–44.

Travis, Jeremy, Bruce Western, and F. Stevens Redburn. 2014. *The Growth of Incarceration in the United States: Exploring Causes and Consequences.* Washington, DC: National Academies Press.

Troccoli, Kenneth P. 2002. "I Want a Black Lawyer to Represent Me: Addressing a Black Defendant's Concerns with Being Assigned a White Court-Appointed Lawyer." *Law and Inequality: A Journal of Theory and Practice* 20 (1): 1–52.

Tyler, Tom R. 1984. "The Role of Perceived Injustice in Defendant's Evaulations of Their Courtroom Experience." *Law and Society Review* 18:51.

Tyler, Tom R. 1988. "What Is Procedural Justice?: Criteria Used by Citizens to Assess the Fairness of Legal Procedures." *Law and Society Review* 22 (1): 103–35.

Tyler, Tom R., and Yuen J. Huo. 2002. *Trust in the Law.* New York: Russell Sage Foundation.

Ulmer, Jeffery T. 1997. *Social Worlds of Sentencing: Court Communities under Sentencing Guidelines.* Albany, NY: SUNY Press.

Ulmer, Jeffery T. 2012. "Recent Developments and New Directions in Sentencing Research." *Justice Quarterly* 29 (1): 1–40.

Ulmer, Jeffery T. 2019. "Criminal Courts as Inhabited Institutions: Making Sense of Difference and Similarity in Sentencing." *Crime and Justice* 48 (1): 483–522.

Uphoff, Rodney J. 1992. "The Criminal Defense Lawyer: Zealous Advocate, Double Agent, or Beleaguered Dealer?" *Criminal Law Bulletin* 28 (5): 419–56.

Uphoff, Rodney J. 2000. "Who Should Control the Decision to Call a Witness: Respecting a Criminal Defendant's Tactical Choices." *University of Cincinnati Law Review* 68:763.

Uphoff, Rodney J., and Peter B. Wood. 1998. "The Allocation of Decisionmaking between Defense Counsel and Criminal Defendant: An Empirical Study of Attorney-Client Decisionmaking." *University of Kansas Law Review* 47:1.

Vallas, Steven, and Emily Cummins. 2014. "Relational Models of Organizational Inequalities: Emerging Approaches and Conceptual Dilemmas." *American Behavioral Scientist* 58 (2): 228–55.

Van Cleve, Nicole Martorano. 2012. "Reinterpreting the Zealous Advocate: Multiple Intermediary Roles of the Criminal Defense Attorney." In *Lawyers in Practice: Ethical Decision Making in Context,* edited by Leslie C. Levin and Lynn Mather, 293–316. Chicago: University of Chicago Press.

Van Cleve, Nicole Gonzalez. 2016. *Crook County: Racism and Injustice in America's Largest Criminal Court.* Stanford, CA: Stanford University Press.

Van Cleve, Nicole Gonzalez, and Lauren Mayes. 2015. "Criminal Justice through 'Colorblind' Lenses: A Call to Examine the Mutual Constitution of Race and Criminal Justice." *Law and Social Inquiry* 40 (2): 406–32.

Vargas, Robert. 2016. *Wounded City: Violent Turf Wars in a Chicago Barrio*. New York: Oxford University Press.

Voigt, Rob, Nicholas P. Camp, Vinodkumar Prabhakaran, William L. Hamilton, Rebecca C. Hetey, Camilla M. Griffiths, David Jurgens, Dan Jurafsky, and Jennifer L. Eberhardt. 2017. "Language from Police Body Camera Footage Shows Racial Disparities in Officer Respect." *Proceedings of the National Academy of Sciences* 114 (25): 6521–26.

Von Hentig, Hans. 1939. "Criminality of the Negro." *Journal of the American Institute of Criminal Law and Criminology* 30:662.

Wacquant, Loïc. 2009. *Punishing the Poor: The Neoliberal Government of Social Insecurity*. Durham, NC: Duke University Press.

Wacquant, Loïc. 2010a. "Class, Race and Hyperincarceration in Revanchist America." *Daedalus* 139 (3): 74–90.

Wacquant, Loïc. 2010b. "Crafting the Neoliberal State: Workfare, Prisonfare, and Social Insecurity." *Sociological Forum* 25 (2): 197–220.

Wagner, Peter, and Wendy Sawyer. 2018. *Mass Incarceration: The Whole Pie 2018*. Northampton, MA: Prison Policy Initiative.

Ward, Geoff K. 2012. *The Black Child-Savers: Racial Democracy and Juvenile Justice*. Chicago: University of Chicago Press.

Weber, Max. 1978. *Economy and Society: An Outline of Interpretive Sociology*. Berkeley: University of California Press.

Websdale, Neil. 2001. *Policing the Poor: From Slave Plantation to Public Housing*. Boston: Northeastern University Press.

Weiss, Robert S. 1994. *Learning from Strangers: The Art and Method of Qualitative Interview Studies*. New York: Free Press.

Weitzer, Ronald, and Steven A. Tuch. 2005. "Racially Biased Policing: Determinants of Citizen Perceptions." *Social Forces* 83 (3): 1009–30.

Werth, Robert. 2012. "I Do What I'm Told, Sort of: Reformed Subjects, Unruly Citizens, and Parole." *Theoretical Criminology* 16 (3): 329–46.

Western, Bruce. 2018. *Homeward: Life in the Year after Prison*. New York: Russell Sage Foundation.

Western, Bruce, and Becky Pettit. 2010. "Incarceration and Social Inequality." *Daedalus* 139 (3): 8–19.

Westley, William A. 1953. "Violence and the Police." *American Journal of Sociology* 59 (1): 34–41.

Whooley, Mary A., Andrew L. Avins, Jeanne Miranda, and Warren S. Browner. 1997. "Case-Finding Instruments for Depression." *Journal of General Internal Medicine* 12 (7): 439–45.

Wilkerson, Glen. 1972. "Public Defenders as Their Clients See Them." *American Journal of Criminal Law* 1:141.

Wilson, James Q., and George L. Kelling. 1982. "Broken Windows." *Atlantic Monthly* 249 (3): 29–38.

Wilson, William Julius. 1987. *The Truly Disadvantaged*. Chicago: University of Chicago Press.

Winter, Alix S., and Matthew Clair. 2020. "Between Punishment and Welfare: How Court Officials Justify Pretrial Control at Bail." Working paper. Columbia University.

Winter, Alix S., and Robert J. Sampson. 2017. "From Lead Exposure in Early childhood to Adolescent Health: A Chicago Birth Cohort." *American Journal of Public Health* 107 (9): 1496–1501.

Wood, Peter B., and David C. May. 2003. "Racial Differences in Perceptions of the Severity of Sanctions: A Comparison of Prison with Alternatives." *Justice Quarterly* 20 (3): 605–31.

Worden, Alissa Pollitz, Andrew Lucas Blaize Davies, and Elizabeth K. Brown. 2010. "A Patchwork of Policies: Justice, Due Process, and Public Defense across American States." *Albany Law Review* 74:1423.

Worden, Alissa Pollitz, Sarah J. McLean, and Megan Kennedy. 2012. "Sidestepping Justice: Adjournments in Contemplation of Dismissal in Misdemeanor Court." *Albany Law Review* 76:1713.

Wright, Erik Olin, and Joel Rogers. 2010. *American Society: How It Really Works.* W. W. Norton and Company.

Yngvesson, Barbara. 1988. "Making Law at the Doorway: The Clerk, the Court, and the Construction of Community in a New England Town." *Law and Society Review* 22 (3): 409–48.

Young, Alford A., Jr. 1999. "The (Non)accumulation of Capital: Explicating the Relationship of Structure and Agency in the Lives of Poor Black Men." *Sociological Theory* 17 (2): 201–27.

Young, Kathryne M. 2014. "Everyone Knows the Game: Legal Consciousness in the Hawaiian Cockfight." *Law and Society Review* 48 (3): 499–530.

Young, Kathryne M., and Katie R. Billings. 2020. "Legal Consciousness and Cultural Capital." *Law and Society Review* 54 (1): 33–65.

Zatz, Marjorie S. 2000. "The Convergence of Race, Ethnicity, Gender, and Class on Court Decisionmaking: Looking Toward the 21st Century." *Criminal Justice* 3 (1): 503–52.

Zeidman, Steven. 1998. "To Plead or Not to Plead: Effective Assistance and Client-Centered Counseling." *Boston College Law Review* 39 (4): 841–910.

Zimmerman, Emily, Benjamin F. Evans, Steven H. Woolf, and Amber D. Haley. 2012. *Social Capital and Health Outcomes in Boston.* Richmond: Virginia Commonwealth University Center on Human Needs. https://societyhealth.vcu.edu/media/society-health/pdf/PMReport_Boston.pdf.

# ACKNOWLEDGMENTS

I AM SITTING in my office at Stanford writing these closing words. Many people have helped me, and my work, get here. Social science research depends on research participants willing to take the risk of sharing their individual experiences for the benefit of broader society. My deepest appreciation is to the people who participated in the study: the defendants and court officials who were generous in sharing their time, as well as the court administrators and staff who assisted me along the way.

This book emerged from my doctoral dissertation, which was chaired by Michèle Lamont and Devah Pager. Michèle invested in me from the very first day of graduate school at Harvard, sharing her unparalleled knowledge of the social sciences and providing me with a seemingly endless number of articles to read. I read them all, and I am better for it. Our conversations taught me to think like an intellectual, and our writing together has been foundational to my understanding of culture and inequality. I am so grateful for our continued friendship. Devah saw the potential of my study from the outset. Our conversations about research design often sent me back to the drawing board, pushing me not only to be more precise empirically but also to think beyond the conventional. Our conversations sparked a central insight about how my findings challenged existing theory in cultural sociology. I am grateful for the time she gave me, and I miss her dearly.

The rest of my committee provided support at critical junctures. Larry Bobo introduced me to sociology in college, laying the foundation for the way I think about racism, politics, and inequality. Throughout graduate school and still today, Larry has been a steadfast mentor. Bart Bonikowski always kept me smiling and optimistic, even when I was facing challenges collecting data. Bart encouraged me to consider observing defendants in court rather than simply interviewing them about their experiences, a suggestion that yielded some of the most compelling evidence in the book. Conversations with Bruce Western pushed me to think deeply about the struggles and harms experienced in defendants' everyday lives, not just in court. Bruce encouraged me to draw connections between complex life histories and social injustice within and beyond court.

Graduate school and beyond have afforded me opportunities to engage with many other faculty and scholars, whose conversations have been supportive and insightful. At Harvard, I thank Paul Chang, Phillipa Chong, Andrew Crespo, Maggie Frye, Filiz Garip, Adriaan Lanni, Ron Sullivan, Brandon Terry, Jocelyn Viterna, Bill Wilson, and Chris Winship. A special thank you to Claudine Gay, who advised my college thesis and was always a pleasure to see on a jog along the Charles River or on a walk near William James Hall. Over the years, I have met many colleagues at conferences or on visits to departments. Many of these meetings were particularly clarifying in sharpening my approach to this book. For their conversations in conference hotels, coffee shops, restaurants, and the backseats of taxi cabs, I thank Walter Allen, Sarah Brayne, Jess Cooper, Andrew Davies, Frank Edwards, Alexes Harris, Kimberly Kay Hoang, David Hureau, Mona Lynch, Devon Magliozzi, Michael Perlin, Michelle Phelps, Justin Pickett, Victor Ray, Jennifer Reich, Mark Suchman, Nicole Gonzalez Van Cleve, Robert Vargas, Teddy Wilson, and Katie Young.

Peter Blair Henry at the New York University Stern School of Business was integral to my decision to become an academic in the first place. I worked as his research assistant many years ago when he was writing his first book. Watching him was inspiring and instructive. Just about every summer since, Peter and other members of the PhD Excellence Initiative at NYU—especially Sandile Hlatshwayo, Conrad Miller, Damon Jones, Curtis James, Mbalou Camara, Brandon Enriquez, and Brandy Edmonson—have provided a nurturing environment to share my work. Their perspectives, as economists, have encouraged me to consider how my work matters beyond sociology.

The first draft of the book manuscript was written while on fellowship at the Quattrone Center at the University of Pennsylvania Law School. In my first year at Penn, I shared an office with Amanda Woog, whose legal background sharpened the book's claims and whose passion for righting injustice expanded my vision for the impact the book could have. Other fellows during my time at Quattrone included Asli Bashir, Amanda Bergold, Rachel Greenspan, and Brian Murray. I learned much from each of them. John Hollway and Paul Heaton, the directors of the center, provided me unwavering intellectual and financial support, including funding to collect more data in Boston and to organize a book workshop. Thank you to Anna Gavin for helping to organize the workshop, and for generally making the center run so well. I am deeply appreciative of the time and feedback provided by the workshop's main attendees: Paul Heaton, Issa Kohler-Hausmann, Judith Levine, John MacDonald, Ryan Sakoda, and Pat Sharkey. Their comments helped me sharpen my analysis in so many ways, showing me how to make a dissertation into something like a book. In addition, Asli Bashir, Dylan Farrell-Bryan, Blair Sackett, and Tom Wooten attended all or part of the workshop; their feedback was smart and encouraging. During my time at Penn, I also got to know Camille Zubrinsky Charles, Charles Loeffler, Ross Miller, and Dorothy Roberts. I am grateful for their check-ins, conversations, and laughs.

I am especially grateful to Annette Lareau, who invited me to lunch during my first month in Philadelphia. Annette read multiple parts of the manuscript, offering feedback that was always constructive and exhaustive. She never told me something was good if she did not actually think it was good. I cannot thank her enough for her honesty and genuine engagement with my ideas. She and the members of her writing group—Sherelle Ferguson, Peter Francis Harvey, Hyejeong Jo, and Blair Sackett—made me a more precise thinker and writer.

I began the second draft of the book when I arrived at Stanford, the summer before my first fall quarter as a professor. My colleagues in the Department of Sociology welcomed me to Palo Alto with open arms; many took me to lunch, coffee, and dinner that summer. I am also grateful to the many graduate students, undergraduates, and staff who stopped by my office and shared tips about life on campus. I cannot name everyone who made my transition here a true pleasure, but I want to extend a special thanks to Forrest Stuart, who provided valuable feedback on the book's introduction and has been a trusted mentor, and David Pedulla, who provided valuable insight into the book publishing process and has been a fantastic tennis partner. I also thank Mariette Conway, Sihla Koop, and Randy Michaud for all their help getting my office set up and helping me access various resources as I revised the book a second and third time. Michael Rosenfeld, our department chair, has made sure that I and the other junior faculty in the department have the time and resources to focus on our work; I am thankful for his leadership. At the law school, Debbie Mukamal, David Sklansky, and Bob Weisberg helped to organize a second book workshop at David's house in fall 2019. In addition to Bob and David, workshop attendees included Rabia Belt, Jeff Fisher, and Amalia Kessler. They provided important reflections about my study from their vantage point as legal scholars.

I have been fortunate to work with Meagan Levinson at Princeton University Press, who recognized the importance of this work from the moment I pitched it to her. She has been an enthusiastic and caring editor, offering advice about various stages of revision and guiding me through the review and production processes. Thank you to the two anonymous reviewers of the full manuscript, as well as the two anonymous reviewers of the proposal. I appreciated their excitement about the manuscript and their encouragement to push it even further. I would also like to thank the authors of the more than fifteen anonymous reviews I have so far received on the paper version of some of the analyses contained mostly in chapter 2. Some of these reviews were constructive and insightful. All of them pushed me to clarify, revise, and strengthen my arguments, leaving an indelible mark on the book. In the last stretch of writing, I was fortunate to work with David Lobenstine. His many edits and comments on the manuscript were thoughtful, nuanced, and comprehensive. They made my writing sparkle.

Financial support to carry out the study's data collection and analysis was generously provided by the National Science Foundation Graduate Research Fellowship, the Harvard Kennedy School's Criminal Justice Policy and Management Grant, the Center for American Political Studies Graduate Seed Grant, the Harvard University Department of African and African American Studies Grant, the Harvard University Department of Sociology Grant, the Law and Society Association Graduate Student Travel Subsidy, the Ruth D. Peterson Fellowship for Racial and Ethnic Diversity, the University of Pennsylvania Pre-Doctoral Fellowship for Excellence through Diversity, the Quattrone Center Research Fellowship, the American Sociological Association Student Forum Travel Award, and the School of Humanities and Sciences at Stanford University.

This life would be dull without my friends from college and graduate school—the ones who generously provided thoughts on my work; the ones who unapologetically provided distractions from my work; and the ones who provided a little bit of both. All of you kept me grounded. I am deeply thankful for all the friends in my life, but I want to especially thank a handful. Lumumba Seegars, where do I begin? We have been best friends since college, and I am on the verge of tears thinking about all the amazing times we have had together—from Dunster House, to Atlanta, to New York, to graduate school. Thank you for your humor, your empathy, and your optimism. Alix Winter, I cherish our friendship in so many ways. Thank you for being my travel buddy, my confidant, and the best research collaborator anyone could imagine. Countless conversations with you left their mark on these pages. Tony Jack, you have been my academic big brother. Thank you for all your advice at every stage of my early career. This book simply would not be what it is without your mentorship and friendship. Thank you to Monica Bell, Clint Smith, and Alba Villamil for providing invaluable comments on ideas central to the book at various stages of the process, often over a meal or drinks. And thank you to other friends who always check in and who have expanded the way I understand the world: Sarah Anoke, Stefan Beljean, Portia Botchway, Ralph Bouquet, Kyrah Daniels, Andy Dominitz, Scott Dzialo, Gabe Fotsing, Nina Gheihman, Brandon Gray, Briahna Gray, Jasmine Hughley, Nene Igietseme, Yennice Linares, Abena Mackall, Amulya Mandava, Meaghan Mingo, Katie Morris, Brittany Northcross, Felix Owusu, Archie Page, Kelsey Palder, Luke Palder, Tyler Payne, Hayling Price, Tripp Rebrovick, Jasmin Sandelson, Michael Sierra-Arévalo, Saron Tesfalul, Tim Turner, Jeff Ugbah, and Nate Wilmers.

To my family, I owe everything. Asad, years ago we chose to make a life together. And every morning, I look over, delighted to choose you again and again. Thank you for teaching me what it means to fight for the world you want, and for becoming the center of mine. Amjad, thank you for your humor and wit. You constantly remind me to never take myself too seriously and to bask, every now and then, in the wonders of everyday life. Brian, thank you for being my lookout, my friend, and my biggest supporter since birth. For as long as I can remember, you have always been my model for how to be in this world. Charity, thank you for being a caring and thoughtful sister since the moment I met you that winter day in Cambridge. Our conversations about partnership and work-life balance remind me of the important things in life. Over the years, you and Brian have brought so much joy and adventure into our family, most notably everyone's favorite little boy, David. David, I love you very much. When you are old enough to read this book, I can only hope the injustices I have documented are a thing of the past.

To my extended family, thank you for the love and support you always show me. Grandma, Aunt Mel, Uncle Wayne, Uncle John, Aunt Michelle, and Aunt Darlene all taught me valuable life lessons that I carry with me every day. Mellie, Nicole, and Jordan, thank you for the laughter growing up and the moments we continue to share as we have grown older. And thank you to the family friends who also had a hand in raising me: Aunt Claudia, Aunt Cynthia and Uncle Mike, Dawn and Steve Sabin, and Leslie Fair-Page.

This book is dedicated to my parents, Drs. Walter Clair and Deborah Webster-Clair. Mom and Dad, I could not imagine a happier or more meaningful childhood than the one you provided me. Writing this book, and collecting all the data that went into it, underscored, time and again, how fortunate I am to be your son. You bathed me, held me, taught me, and protected me. I simply would not be without your unwavering love. Thank you, forever and ever.

# A NOTE ON THE TYPE

{~~~~~}

THIS BOOK has been composed in Miller, a Scotch Roman typeface designed by Matthew Carter and first released by Font Bureau in 1997. It resembles Monticello, the typeface developed for The Papers of Thomas Jefferson in the 1940s by C. H. Griffith and P. J. Conkwright and reinterpreted in digital form by Carter in 2003.

Pleasant Jefferson ("P. J.") Conkwright (1905–1986) was Typographer at Princeton University Press from 1939 to 1970. He was an acclaimed book designer and AIGA Medalist.

The ornament used throughout this book was designed by Pierre Simon Fournier (1712–1768) and was a favorite of Conkwright's, used in his design of the *Princeton University Library Chronicle*.